Roraima – the Robert Schomburgk 1840 print of 'a remarkable range of sandstone mountains in Guiana' – now the tri-junction point on Guyana's boundary with Venezuela and Brazil

"What matters in life is not what happens to you but what you remember and how you remember it."

GABRIEL GARCIA MARQUEZ

"Old men should write; not the young in their prime:
their past's too shallow to enfranchise them.
Just so they write of lasting things, not whine
about love's fleeting, red-nosed-bordered hem."

MICHAEL GILKES

GLIMPSES *of a* GLOBAL LIFE

SHRIDATH RAMPHAL

DUNDURN
TORONTO

Published simultaneously in the U.K. by
Hansib Publications Limited.
P.O. Box 226,
Hertfordshire, SG14 3WY
United Kingdom

Text Design: Hansib Publications Limited, UK
Cover Image: Courtesy of the Commonwealth Secretariat, London
Printer: Marquis

Library and Archives Canada Cataloguing in Publication

Ramphal, S. S., author
Glimpses of a global life / Sir Shridath Ramphal.

ISBN 978-1-4597-3075-5 (bound)

1. Ramphal, S. S. 2. Commonwealth Secretariat—Biography.
3. Diplomats—Guyana—Biography. 4. World politics—1945-1989.
5. World politics—1989-. 6. Commonwealth countries—Biography.
I. Title.

D839.7.R36A3 2014 320.9171'241 C2014-906616-3

1 2 3 4 5 18 17 16 15 14

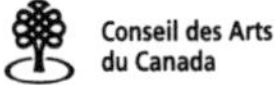

We acknowledge the support of the Canada Council for the Arts and the Ontario Arts Council for our publishing program. We also acknowledge the financial support of the Government of Canada through the Canada Book Fund and Livres Canada Books, and the Government of Ontario through the Ontario Book Publishing Tax Credit and the Ontario Media Development Corporation.

Care has been taken to trace the ownership of copyright material used in this book. The author and the publisher welcome any information enabling them to rectify any references or credits in subsequent editions.

J. Kirk Howard, President

The publisher is not responsible for websites or their content unless they are owned by the publisher.

Printed and bound in Canada.

Visit us at
Dundurn.com | @dundurnpress | Facebook.com/dundurnpress | Pinterest.com/dundurnpress

Dundurn
3 Church Street, Suite 500
Toronto, Ontario, Canada
M5E 1M2

To a brave widow, my great grandmother, whose journeys across the 'kala pani' shaped my global life.

CONTENTS

ILLUSTRATION CREDITS

CHAPTER 1

Portrait of Sir John Gladstone by Thomas Gladstone (oil on canvas, circa 1830) copyright the National Portrait Gallery, London

CHAPTER 4

CF Andrews. University of Boston, Massachusetts, USA. http://www.bu.edu/missiology/missionary-biography/a-c/andrews-charles-freer-1871-1940/

CHAPTER 5

With granddaughter, India, at King's College Mural in the Strand, London. Photograph by Amanda Hennessy

Norman Washington Manley portrait by Barrington Watson by kind permission of Jesus College, Oxford.

CHAPTER 8

Map of the Caribbean. Heritage Foundation, Washington DC. http://www.heritage.org/multimedia/infographic/2012/10/caricom-map

Federal Flag copyright Barbados Museum and Historical Society

Federal Flag Raising Ceremony. Courtesy of the Garnet Ifill Collection, The Alma Jordan Library, University of the West Indies, St Augustine, Trinidad and Tobago

CHAPTER 9

Demas/McIntyre/Carrington courtesy of Lady (Marjorie) McIntyre

CHAPTER 10

P.J. Patterson courtesy of the Office of the Most Honourable P.J. Patterson, Kingston, Jamaica

CHAPTER 11

Signing Treaty of Chaguaramas courtesy of the CARICOM Secretariat, Guyana

CHAPTER 13

HM Queen Elizabeth II with Commonwealth Secretaries-General in 2009 courtesy of the Commonwealth Secretariat, London

King George VI with Commonwealth Premiers in 1949 courtesy of the Commonwealth Secretariat, London

CHAPTER 19

Margaret Thatcher and Kenneth Kaunda copyright the Press Association

CHAPTER 21

Mandela Plaque, Hull. Photo by Jerome Whittingham

CHAPTER 24

Mandela/Tambo reunion in Sweden. Independent Television Services, San Francisco, California; http://www.itvs.org

CHAPTER 26

Grenadians at US gunpoint. http://www.latinamericanstudies.org/grenada-4.htm

All other pictures are from the collection of Shridath Ramphal

ACKNOWLEDGEMENTS

For at least twenty years relatives and friends, among them, scholars, have been asking me, then insistently urging, about 'memoirs'. My answer invariably was that I had not lived my life for a diary and had no plans for memoirs. I could have added that I had not truly retired; that my story was not ended; it was not time to look back. But then at Christmas 2011, as the time for 'resolutions' approached, I decided that they were right. It was time; indeed, it was a duty. It is to them, first of all, that I owe thanks for the book that has emerged, and for the unexpected pleasure of two years of reflection, research and writing that it entailed. To my wife and close family, special gratitude is due for their tolerance of my life of seclusion that followed.

For each of those elements of reflection, research and writing I owe thanks to many. I was surprised how much I recalled once I began the process of remembering; but recall involved roles for others to whom I turned for corroboration or filling in gaps – like Sir Alister McIntyre, or Moni Malhoutra or Brynmoor Pollard or Patsy Robertson, or Janet Singh among others. I wished there were more of their vintage around; but I had deferred writing so long, that many contemporaries had passed on. My Personal Assistants who managed my life at the Commonwealth Secretariat and beyond, Greta Cummings and Elsa Mansell, who have both passed on, were incomparable in their care of me; and would have been invaluable in times of recall.

Research, of course, was paramount. Fortunately, I had many years earlier given my papers to the archives of the Cave Hill Campus of

The University of the West Indies in Barbados. As Barbados was now my regional home that material was at hand; and I received great help and understanding from the Archivist, Cheri Ann Beckles, and her colleagues, in facilitating access to it. So too from the Librarian, Hilary McEwan, of the Commonwealth Secretariat in London. My daughter, Susan (Lady Sanders) did a great deal of archival leg work, including 'family tree' research, in collaboration with my sister, Sita Kawall, in Toronto, and helped me greatly with the photographs which are an integral part of the glimpses I offer.

Part I *(Beginning)* has drawn substantially on an address I gave in Guyana in 1988 called *A Heritage of Oneness* – marking the 150th anniversary of the end of slavery and the beginning of Indian indenture. The original, fully referenced, is available from the Library of the Commonwealth Secretariat.

In recapitulating some episodes of my global life I was a substantial beneficiary of the new rules and culture of the 'freedom of information' age and the particular facility of the Internet. I am specially indebted to the Margaret Thatcher Foundation's archives on the Internet; most of my references to 'declassified' material in Part VI (*The Thatcher Years)* are to material organised with great professionalism and made available in these archives.

The writing has benefited from the many 'readers' I enlisted to the task; but none more so than my son-in-law, Sir Ronald Sanders, who reviewed each Chapter as it was drafted and brought to its improvement his considerable writing skills and judgement, and on occasion his own recall. It was the resulting draft that the other 'readers' read and I am grateful for their further refinement of the text. Rudolph Collins (Georgetown), Vibert Lampkin (Toronto), Clive Jordan (London), Moni Malhoutra (New Delhi), Ian McDonald (Georgetown), and my brother, Raj Ramphal (Toronto), all read the text and made valuable suggestions for its improvement from their unique perspectives. For all that, the *glimpses* are my own. I acknowledge with gratitude all the help of every nature that I have received from every quarter, but for shortcomings of any kind, I alone am responsible.

The bibliography pertaining to the many subjects that these *glimpses* cover is vast, and while I owe much to many sources I am including, (in Appendix I), a select bibliography of source material to which I have specially turned and for which I am specially grateful. I have sought to identify in the text all quotations from these sources. Additionally, every effort has been made to trace and secure all necessary permissions of copyright holders in relation to material in the book both text and photographs. If there has been failure in any respect, the publishers will be glad to rectify in future editions any errors or omissions brought to their notice.

The same applies to the more than 100 illustrations, mainly photographs, with which the text is supplemented. They are rather special glimpses of my global life. I owe thanks to those from whom I needed and received permission in most cases on a complimentary basis. To my daughter, Susan, goes my particular gratitude for managing this major task. I have included a 'List of Illustrations' which sources those beyond my personal domain.

A word about my UK Publishers, Hansib and its guiding spirit, Arif Ali who have been publishers to many developing country writers. My choice of them was recognition of their important contribution to literature which deserved publication. Hansib's Managing Editor, Kash Ali, has been a model of patience with my many exactions and the book owes much to his professionalism. Dundurn Press of Canada unhesitatingly undertook to publish the North American edition of this book and I am grateful to Kirk Howard and his entire team for their confidence in it.

'Acknowledgements' in books is a place to recognise the help the author has received in relation to it; but where the book is in the nature of memoirs its must allow for a wider outreach. I owe an unpayable debt to a multitude of people world-wide who have helped me on life's journey. Some will be apparent from the book itself; but many are unseen benefactors among relatives, friends, colleagues, associates in public life, including national and international leaders. Their companionship on life's journey and their encouragement, and often their inspiration, made journeying possible. The debt may be unpayable; but it is not beyond acknowledgement. This account of my global life is testimony of my gratitude.

PRELUDE

At 86, an autobiography would be too ambitious. But having had the good fortune of a long life and opportunities of living it in satisfying ways, I accept a duty to offer a glimpse of those times and roles, of the people world-wide that shaped them, and of the events that unfolded, in the hope that others may find my account of interest and of help. To that end, I have structured the narrative more in thematic than in strictly chronological ways. Inevitably, much is left out: such as 'growing up in British Guiana' and my early domestic roles; those matters would require a book all their own. But, I hope the glimpses I offer of the 'global' times through which I lived and, initially, of strongly connected times past, provide both useful insights in themselves and guidance to any who seek to fill the gaps.

There is another explanation I must make. Over the last fifty years I have done much public speaking on the issues that informed my life's work. Those contemporary reflections have an authenticity no reminiscence can claim, and I have drawn on them in offering these glimpses of times past – particularly where they were not mere reflections on events but elements of events themselves. I have included in Appendix 2 a guide to those many platforms worldwide from which I spoke, where what I said was published. All in all, what follows are glimpses of a Caribbean life lived to the beat of global drums.

Despite renouncing a chronological structure to these *glimpses*, I must, however, begin at the beginning, and tell of past times that cast their shadow on the present and serve to explain it in ways that only true history can. But first, a flavour of the time and place of the beginning in British Guiana ('BG'), later Guyana. 'Where is that?' a non-Caribbean reader might ask. Without a map, I answer thus:

Gabriel Garcia Marquez is among my favourite writers. I claim no acquaintance with this Nobel Laureate beyond his writing; but we do share some beginnings. Marquez was born on 6 March 1927 in the small town of Aracataca on the coast of Colombia, not far from Cartagena where South American colonial history had so much of its Caribbean origins. Just over a thousand miles from Aracataca to the east, on that same coast bordering the Caribbean Sea, past Venezuela and the mouth of the Orinoco I was born later the next year - on 3rd October 1928, in the small town of New Amsterdam, in the County of Berbice in still colonial British Guiana. Neither of us was born into destitution; but for both, our origins were humble, and the world beyond was beyond contemplation. We were both born in backwaters of even our own countries. It is a commentary on the blundering history of Latin America, of which in *One Hundred Years of Solitude* Marquez wrote so poignantly, that he spoke and wrote in Spanish, and I do so in English – a legacy of the European colonisation that so shaped our lives; mine more proximately than his. For most of our lives, we might have been a continent apart. But one thing we shared: Marquez, gone from us now as this book goes to press, called his memoir published in 2003 *Living to Tell the Tale*. It would be an apt title to the pages that follow.

The Guianas, for long avoided even by adventurous colonisers as the 'wild coast' of South America, were eventually to become colonial enclaves of England, Holland and France – the colonies of British Guiana (an amalgamation of Essequibo, Demerara and Berbice), Dutch Guiana (now Suriname) and French Guiana. Not surprisingly, they had as little in common between them in those early times as had the metropoles that fought over them. Much has changed and is changing now; but the British Guiana into which I was born looked northward - to the British island-colonies of the West Indies with which it shared substantial kinship and, beyond them, to Britain from which it, and they, were ruled. Kinship with the West Indies and the evolution from British colonialism were the central elements that held sway in British Guiana in the days of my birth; and as it transpired, they were in substantial measure factors that were to shape my life.

But the story of my life began long, long before my birth, and was to unfold far beyond Guyana's shores – first in the Caribbean and then, via the Commonwealth, in the wider world. Regionalism and internationalism were not for me intellectual abstractions; they were the practical realities of my life. I became a West Indian and a world citizen by life's commands. This book is about that global life – glimpses of it close enough to offer insights of the times and of the people who made them worthy of recall.

It is not about my life in Guyana save as it bore on that global life, as many aspects did, or about Guyana itself. That must be other writing. The need to which this book responds is to tell the story of my interaction with the world beyond Guyana; to show by that story the integral nature of that world, and the role that every citizen of it can play in its evolution and betterment. It is the story of a world flawed in many ways and everywhere in need of healing. It is an account of my efforts to contribute to that process in the often unplanned and surprising ways that fell to me on the journey of life.

It is inevitably also an account of the people I encountered on that travel – many of them notable people in our civilisation – who helped my own efforts, or allowed me to help theirs; a very few who sought to thwart them; and a multitude of good people everywhere whose needs were palpable and whose support for change was energising. I was never alone in my journeying; and that company made all the difference.

That I offer this account is not fulfilment of a long nourished wish; it is discharge of a duty of which I have been much reminded by friends – to tell the story of that global life that many of them shared, at least in part. I hope I may have come close to doing so. As I said earlier, these are 'glimpses'. I apologise for events overlooked or simply left out; and I thank the many who helped me in developing the narrative, some of whom I specifically mention elsewhere in these pages. Without their help, there would still be no answer to the insistent question: 'When are you going to write?' Well, I have now!

PART 1

BEGINNINGS

CHAPTER 1

Slavery's End in Guiana

Like most of Britain's West Indian 'possessions' from the 17th century onward, now independent countries loosely linked as members of the Caribbean Community, British Guiana ('BG' as it was known in colonial parlance) was in the 20th century an amalgam of early slave plantations that had helped to enrich Britain in the days when sugar flourished as a prized industrial crop. It was on the back of slavery that sugar became 'king' and much was to change with its abolition in the 19th Century: first with the abolition of the gruesome slave trade by Britain (though not slavery itself) in 1807, and the abolition of the whole inhuman system between 1834 and 1838 when slavery's alter ego, the 'apprenticeship' system, collapsed. It is symbolic of slavery's inherent contrarieties that at its end it was not the African slaves, its victims, but the sugar planters, its beneficiaries, who collectively – and in many cases individually – received from Britain massive compensation. That compensation was to resonate in my life in devious ways.

Many factors contributed to slavery's end: the anti-slavery movement in Britain symbolised by Wilberforce, but, truly, by the efforts of many others at Westminster and throughout Britain; the changing economic realities of the system itself, nowhere more forcibly argued than by the West Indian scholar Eric Williams – later a distinguished Prime Minister of Trinidad and Tobago – in his treatise *Capitalism and Slavery*; but, as important as any factor, the scattered yet harmonised rebellion of the slaves themselves throughout the West Indies – in the final push for freedom in the early 19th century. It is in slavery's ending in British Guiana that lies the roots of my beginnings there. The 'Guiana' slave revolts over a hundred years before my birth are germane to the story of my life; and reminders of their relevance have been insistent throughout it.

In April 1953 I was not quite 25. Recently qualified as a lawyer, I was starting my first job as the most junior member of the Chambers of British Guiana's Attorney-General. 'BG' was still a British colony; so the title I carried was that of 'Crown Counsel'. The Attorney-General, Sir Frank Holder Q.C., was a senior Barbadian lawyer, and a kindly man. In those days, the Attorney-General had supervision of the Magistrates' Department as well, and on my first day in the 'Public Buildings', which was the seat of Government (including the then Legislative Council), he put me under the wing of Guy Sharples – a Senior Magistrate – to take me on the rounds of the Law Courts to meet the Chief Justice and Judges and, eventually, the Magistrates. Sharples was a man whose interests and aptitudes went well beyond the law. To this day, his watercolour landscapes – some of them reproduced in Webber's 'Centenary History of British Guiana' in 1931 – are much admired. And he was a man of history. As we did the rounds, Sharples made the point to me that it was on the site of the present Magistrates Courts that the Reverend John Smith had been incarcerated in 1823 pending a trial condemned by all save the West Indian plantocracy as a tragic parody of justice – a trial which led to his conviction and, eventually, to his death in prison.

There is a place for argument about the overall role of Christian missionaries in British colonies; but Smith's Church in Georgetown today is a permanent memorial to this man of God who saw in the slave only his fellow man. That moment of remembrance has always remained with me; for I have come to realise what I think Guy Sharples understood well and hoped I would realise one day: that recalling the events that brought Smith to his end in the cells of a Demerara prison was not just a leap over centuries but a backward glance along a continuous line as well.

The decade or so before the Abolition of Slavery Act was passed in 1834 was a particularly turbulent time throughout the West Indies:

a slave rebellion had taken place in Barbados in 1816, a revolt in Demerara in 1823, an uprising in Jamaica in 1824, an insurrection in Antigua in 1831 and the much larger Jamaica revolt at Christmas of that year. In *Capitalism and Slavery,* Eric Williams sums up well the situation that had been reached on the eve of emancipation:

> *In 1833, therefore, the alternatives were clear: emancipation from above, or emancipation from below. But EMANCIPATION. Economic change, the decline of the monopolists, the development of capitalism, the humanitarian agitation in the British churches, contending perorations in the halls of Parliament, had now reached their completion in the determination of the slaves themselves to be free.*

The Demerara Revolt of 1823 really sounded the death-knell of slavery in Guiana. It was a mighty thunderclap in the gathering storm of slave rebellion. Its reverberations were felt far beyond Guiana's shores – not least because of the indescribable cruelty with which it was eventually put down.

The story of that Revolt has been told many times but some of it bears retelling, especially in the context of my own beginnings. On the evening of 18 August, an uprising started on two estates on the East Coast of Demerara: Plantations *Le Resouvenir* and *Success*. The Revolt centred on the demand for immediate emancipation, which the slaves genuinely believed the Crown had approved but was being denied them locally – a belief substantially, if not yet technically, true. A contemporary account was set down by the artist, Joshua Bryant, in meticulous, if undifferentiated detail, in his *'Account of an Insurrection of the Negro slaves in the Colony of Demerara'*. A more recent version which highlights the manoeuvrings at Westminster is in Robin Furneaux's 1974 publication: *'William Wilberforce'*.

These varying presentations reflect some of the disparate factors influencing the tortuous course of bondage in Guiana – factors that were to remain at work over the transition from slavery. The suffering of those crushed down by the system was of course the bedrock factor.

The ruthless efficiency of their oppression held in check the will to rebel; it never induced acquiescence across the board. Sugar was ever a bitter crop for those who toiled at producing it in Guiana's inhospitable conditions. But at least three other groups of actors would influence the outcome: the planters, the imperial government and the humanitarian movement led by men like Wilberforce and Thomas Buxton.

Too often, and certainly for too long, despite the efforts of the Anti-Slavery Movement in Britain and individual voices of conscience at Westminster and in Whitehall, the British Government remained the protectors of the oppressors rather than the oppressed. British economic interests, the claims of kinship, imperial considerations – all these stood in the way of the Government at Westminster tipping the scales in favour of justice and freedom. When occasionally it did, it was often so half-hearted and reluctant an effort that the planters could continue to oppose, to stall and, sometimes, to prevail. The circumstances leading to the Demerara Revolt of 1823 provide a classic example of this.

On 15 May of that year, Thomas Buxton moved the following motion in the House of Commons:

> *That the state of slavery is repugnant to the British Constitution and to the Christian religion, and that it ought to be abolished gradually throughout the British colonies with as much expedition as may be found consistent with a due regard to the well-being of the parties concerned.*

The Government's response was amelioration not abolition; but, through a series of resolutions, it directed that reforms (like an end to the flogging of female slaves and the carrying of the whip into the field) be put into effect. The planters and the Court of Policy (Guyana's legislature) procrastinated and prevaricated. The slaves knew change was at hand and sensed that the planters were resisting what were their rights. They felt that they had to strengthen the hand of the Governor against the planters. They were only half right; but they moved, naively, to compel 'without bloodshed' but by a show of force the freedom which they believed the King had decreed to be theirs. The Revolt was crushed with frenzied brutality followed by savage vengeance. Thirteen thousand slaves from 37 plantations had joined the rebels; it was a colossal show of strength; but they were poorly armed and easily subdued.

The clemency and overall restraint the slaves showed while briefly in charge of the plantations was not reciprocated. Quamina, their leader, was killed in the revolt. Nearly 50 were hanged, three given the dreadful sentence of 1,000 lashes and condemned to be worked in chains, two for the remainder of their lives. Quamina's son, Jack, was among those hanged; his head, like those of the others executed, was stuck on a pole for public viewing, in the words of the local Gazette, as 'a monument of personal guilt' and 'a caution against like criminality'.

The images taken from Joshua Bryant's 1824 'Account' bore the caption:

> *Five of the culprits in chains, as they appeared on the 20th September 1823: 1), upper right "Quamina, on plantation Success"; 2), upper left, "Lindor, on La Bonne Intention,"; 3), lower left, "Paul on the Friendship and two heads at the middle-walk of Plantation New Orange Nassau"; 4), lower right, "Telemachus and Jemmy on Batchelor's Adventure".*

One hundred and sixty-two years after these developments in British Guiana, and especially in Demerara, I found myself in England's far north as the honoured guest of the ancient University of Durham founded in 1832 just before slavery's abolition. The occasion was the conferment on me of an Honorary Doctorate of Civil Law, and Durham's Public Orator chose Charles Dickens' Mr Pickwick, with a nice appropriateness, to illustrate the *'oddity'*, as he described it, of *'how easily we may leave in obscurity the background to what we take for granted'*. He made the point (in the style of public orators) that, while there can be no character in English fiction better known and better loved than Mr Pickwick, a close reading leads to the awkward conclusion that the accumulation of Mr Pickwick's fortune has been connected with the slave trade: through an acquaintance whose office is in Liverpool, that *'metropolis of the Middle Passage'*, and whose sugar plantations – slave plantations – are in Demerara.

The Pickwick Papers, which first appeared in 1836, were set in the England of the 1820s: the years of the Demerara Revolt. It was a serialised work which fused a journalistic style with the format of fiction and, like so much of Dickens' writing, was a biting social commentary on contemporary evils. We know from the *Argosy* newspaper of that time that one of the characters in *The Pickwick Papers*, Alfred Jingle, was actually believed in Demerara to be based on the real Dr Dodson of Plantation Vive La Force. Could Mr Pickwick's influential friend, his 'Liverpool acquaintance with slave plantations in Demerara', have been Sir John Gladstone?

By 1821, John Gladstone (shown above) was already a Liverpool merchant of substantial means with something like a half of his fortune deriving from slave plantations in Demerara, among them, prominently, *Vreed-en-Hoop* – a sugar plantation that was to touch my life in uncanny ways. That proportion was to rise substantially, as we know from British-Canadian economic historian S.G. Checkland's 1971 'family biography' of the Gladstones. Frustrated in his own desire to represent the Corporation of Liverpool in Parliament, John Gladstone was to have two of his sons go to Westminster – and one of them, William, rise to be one of Britain's great Prime Ministers. William Gladstone came to Westminster in 1832 when the abolition of slavery was an inescapable political issue and one which, as events turned out, he had to face immediately. On 14 May that same year, Lord Howick, a former Under-Secretary of State for the Colonies, laid specific complaints in Parliament against the management of John Gladstone's sugar estate at *Vreed-en-Hoop* alleging 'that the increase in sugar cultivation was in direct ratio with overworking and loss of life on the part of the slave population'. William made the best of a bad job in his father's defence – a vindication of slavery that Eric Williams was later to attribute 'more to filial feelings than Liberal principles'. But for the owner of *Vreed-en-Hoop* this was not the first complaint to reach Westminster, nor was it to be the last.

The Rev John Smith, as already noted, was duly convicted by court martial of complicity in the Demerara Revolt. He was sentenced to death and died in the Georgetown Prison awaiting the outcome of a petition for clemency which the Governor had cautiously referred to the authorities in London. The planters believed they had won again. But had they?

John Gladstone's principal sugar estate in Demerara was *Vreed-en-Hoop*; but it was on another of his estates – *'Success'* – that the revolt had been planned on the 'middle walk dam' on Sunday, 17 August 1823. Quamina, its leader, was from *Success*, and it was there too that his son, Jack, was also enslaved: a son who bore not his father's name but that of his master, 'Gladstone'. It was on the adjoining estate of *Le Resouvenir* that the Rev. John Smith had his

Bethel Chapel, in which Quamina was active. Quamina was killed in the Revolt and his son Jack Gladstone executed, but in the halls of Westminster it was John Smith's 'martyrdom' that most spurred the anti-slavery cause. Despite the initial victory of the planters, the Demerara Revolt, in all its implications, dealt slavery a blow from which it never recovered.

But that, of course, was not how the sugar barons would have seen those events. Wilberforce's pamphlets calling for emancipation had been circulating on the estates. The local Gazette did not conceal the planters' wrath:

> *Perhaps the intriguing saints at home had a hand in it – if so, they will hear with disappointment and pain that a superintending and just providence has frustrated their diabolical intentions.*

The abolitionist cause was 'diabolical': the vengeance on the slaves was part of the interposition of 'a superintending and just providence'. How cosy an inversion of right and wrong! Slavery was at its height when, in 1758, Voltaire wrote *Candide*, his satirical commentary on a philosophy of complacency and acquiescence – the supremacy of hypocrisy over truth, the pretence that however evil and abhorrent the state of individual things, 'this world of ours is the best of all possible worlds'. Its continuing relevance could hardly be more pointed.

In one unforgettable incident, Voltaire pictured the innocent Candide entering Suriname and encountering a Negro slave lying on the ground. The slave, who had lost both a hand and a leg, tells Candide that this is *'the price paid for the sugar you eat in Europe'*. *'Oh Pangloss!'*, cries Candide, *"This is an abomination you had not guessed; this is too much. In the end I shall have to renounce optimism"*. *"What is this optimism"?* asks Candide's footman. *"Alas"*, says Candide, *"it is the mania of maintaining that all is good when all is bad"*. And Candide weeps as he enters Suriname – which neighbours Berbice. By 1838, as Indian indenture to Demerara started, some things had changed; but not such basic attitudes as the supremacy of hypocrisy over truth, the mania of maintaining that all was good when all was bad.

Clinging to illusion as a prop for the status quo, emancipation to the planters was just an interlude in the story of sugar; an imposition they fiercely resented, but one which they had to overcome and continue in business. First, however, they would collect what was on offer; twenty million pounds sterling in compensation for emancipation – the equivalent today of close to one billion (US) dollars. Alan Adamson's 1972 treatise *'Sugar Without Slaves'* confirms that the Guiana planters' share of this was almost £5 million (£4,924,989) for 82,824 slaves. That was almost a quarter of the total compensation paid by the British Government on the abolition of slavery. Vreed-en-Hoop's owner, John Gladstone, alone received almost 85,000 pounds for his five plantations in British Guiana – as the quite remarkable archive below, in the hand of his son William attests.

Class.	Number.	Rate.	Amount of Comp.:
1. Head People	63	£87. 3. 0¾	£5506. 7. 11¼
2. Tradesmen	42	£68. 8. 0½	£2872. 17. 9.
3. Inf. Tradesmen	12	£38. 0. ¼	£456. 0. 3.
4. Field Labourers	756	£64. 8. 4¾	£48701. 7. 3.
5. Inf. ditto	250	£36. 0. 5.	£9005. 4. 2.
Children	139	£19. 0. 0.	£2641. 0. 0.
Invalids &c.	47	£11. 8. 0	535. 16. 0.
	1309.		£69718. 13. 4¼

Per caput £53. 5. 2⅞ nearly.

This handwritten calculation of his father's slave compensation (reproduced in S.G. Checkland's *The Gladstones: a family biography)* by England's future Prime Minister, William Gladstone, in 1835 conjures up images of that time (some 175 years ago as I write) even more evocative than the sums it records.

Through the UK's 'Independent on Sunday' newspaper of 24 February 2013 all this has now received wide publicity. The *'Legacies of British Slavery Ownership Project'* at University College London has released its first data. Commenting on big payments, Dr Nick Draper, a research associate on the Project wrote:

> *But this amount was dwarfed by the amount paid to John Gladstone... He received £106,769 (modern equivalent £83m) for the 2,508 slaves he owned across nine plantations. His son, who served as Prime Minister four times during his 60 year career, was heavily involved in his father's claim.*

Of the nine plantations, five were in British Guiana; the other four in Jamaica.

As Alan Adamson says, *"it occurred to no one to compensate the slaves for their previous bondage"*. Of course it occurred to no one. Remember Candide and 'the mania of maintaining that all is good when all is bad'. In the 1832 debate in the House of Commons on the management of Vreed-en-Hoop, William Gladstone was recorded in Hansard as follows:

> *He deprecated cruelty – he deprecated slavery: it was abhorrent to the nature of Englishmen; but conceding all these things, were not Englishmen to retain a right to their own honestly and legally acquired property?*

So, on slavery's abolition, John Gladstone got the modern day equivalent of 83 million pounds sterling; while his slaves got apprenticeship. In Guiana, the apprenticeship code appears to have been the harshest of all, but that deferral of freedom was to last only four of the six appointed years. By 1838, slavery as an institution had ended in British Guiana; but the shadow it cast was long – and for me immediate.

CHAPTER 2

Another Ferry of Infamy

John Gladstone did not loiter. Supply and demand should have dictated a new economy of the sugar industry – increased wages for freed slaves who chose to remain on the sugar plantations. But that would have meant higher costs, lower profits – perhaps, closure. Instead, the planters pocketed the compensation for their unpaid slave capital and set out to invent what Lord John Russell was later to describe as 'a new system of slavery' – with Vreed-en-Hoop's John Gladstone leading the effort. In the beginning, as John Gladstone would acknowledge to his agent in India, it was not so much a strategy of replacing the entire labour force as a tactic of reducing the bargaining power of the freed slaves by having a reserve labour pool 'to use as a set-off' – and the promise of enlargement if need be.

The English expatriate firm of Gillanders, Arbuthnot & Co. worked from Calcutta. As is known from Checkland – one of its members – F.M. Gillanders, was a cousin of John Gladstone's wife. They had already supplied Indian labour to the sugar plantations of Mauritius. Through the family connection they offered their services to do likewise for Gladstone's Guiana estates at a cost of 'not one-half that of a slave'. John Gladstone jumped at the offer; there might be problems in London where anti-slavery sentiment was still strong, but he had by now powerful political friends. There might be problems in India, but it was not lost on him that another Guiana proprietor, Andrew Colville – who owned *Bell Vue* estate – was a 'near relative' of Lord Auckland, India's Governor General. *"Mr Colville is a near connection of Lord Auckland, your Governor General, to whom he will write on the subject",* wrote John Gladstone to Gillanders, Arbuthnot and Co on 10 March 1837. He duly involved Colville in the enterprise.

The entire correspondence is lengthy, and Gladstone kept the British Government aware of all of it. His opening letter was written to Messrs Gillanders, Arbuthnot & Co from Liverpool on 4 January 1836. Let an extract from it suffice:

> *It is of great Importance to us to endeavour to provide a Portion of other Labourers whom we might use as a Set-off, and, when the Time for it comes, makes us, as far as it is possible, independent of our Negro Population; and it has occurred to us that a moderate Number of Bengalees, such as you were sending to the isle of France, might be very suitable for our Purpose; and on this Subject I am now desirous to obtain all the Information you can possibly give me. The Number I should think of taking and sending by One Vessel direct from Calcutta to Demerara would be about 100; they ought to be young, active, able-bodied People. It would be desirable that a Portion of them, at least One-Half, should be married, and their Wives disposed to work in the Field as well as they themselves. We should require to bind them for a Period not less than Five Years or more than Seven Years....*
>
> *You will particularly oblige me by giving me, on Receipt, all the Information you possibly can on this interesting Subject, for should it be of an encouraging Character, I should immediately engage for one of our Ships to go to Calcutta, and take a limited Number to Demerara, and from thence return here.*
>
> *Yours truly,*
> *JOHN GLADSTONE*

The reply from Gillanders to Gladstone was dated 6 June 1836 from Calcutta. Written in what Tinker was later to describe as a *"curiously proto-Darwinian tone",* is the following extract:

We beg to acknowledge your Letter of the 4th January, referring to your Desire to procure Natives from this Part of the World to work upon your Estates in the West Indies, and in some Degree render you Independent of the Negro Population at the Termination of the present System....

Within the last two years, upwards of two thousand Natives have been sent from here to the Mauritius by several Parties under Contracts of Engagement for Five Years. The Contracts, we believe, are all of a similar Nature; and we enclose Copy of one, under which we have sent 700 or 800 Men to the Mauritius; and we are not aware than any greater Difficulty would present itself in sending Men to the West Indies, the Natives being perfectly ignorant of the Place they agree to go to, or the Length of the Voyage they are undertaking.

The Tribe that is found to suit best in the Mauritius is from the Hills to the North of Calcutta, and the Men of which are all well-limbed and active, without Prejudices of any kind, and hardly any Ideas beyond those of supplying the Want of Nature, arising it would appear, however, more from Want of Opportunity than from any natural Deficiency, of which there is no Indication in their Countenance, which is often one of Intelligence. They are also very docile and easily managed, and appear to have no local Ties, nor any Objection to leave their Country....

We are not aware that we can say any more on this Subject, unless we add, that in inducing these Men to leave their Country, we firmly believe we are breaking no Ties of Kindred, or in any way acting a cruel Part.

The Hill Tribes, known by the Name of Dhangurs, are looked down by the more cunning Natives of the Plains, and they are always spoken of as more akin to the Monkey than the Man. They have no Religion, no Education, and in their present State, no Wants beyond Eating, Drinking, and Sleeping; and to procure which they are willing to labour. In sending Men to such a Distance, it would of course be necessary to be more particular in selecting them, and some little Expense would be incurred, as also some Trouble; but to aid any Object of Interest to you, we would willingly give our best Exertions in any Manner likely to be of service.

Yours very faithfully
GILLANDERS, ARBUTHNOT, AND CO.

This momentous correspondence encourages reflection on the way history permeates lives, guiding destinies in mysterious and unseen ways, revealing the past through unseen links to the present. The lives of all the people of Guyana have been touched thus by the course of history. All Guyanese are what we are because of history's turnings centuries ago. John Gladstone's letter of 28 February 1838 to the Secretary of State forwarding his correspondence with Gillanders, was written from Carlton Gardens, London. In June 1833, John Gladstone, abandoning his nomadic existence, though not yet his sugar interests in Demerara, bought as his London residence 6 Carlton Gardens – the address from which so much of those early negotiations, crucial to Guyana's future, was conducted. One hundred and forty-two years later to the month, in July 1975, I took up my appointment in London as Commonwealth Secretary-General and moved into the Secretary-General's residence – at 5 Carlton Gardens. Numbers 5 and 6 Carlton Gardens by then were in fact one, both incorporated into Wool House – sugar was no longer 'king'.

How full a circle the wheel of history thus described! John Gladstone's letter of 1836 had started a system that would eventually bring my main ancestors from India to Guyana – to the same estate of Vreed-en-Hoop he once owned. Three generations later, those very events would combine with others to take me to London in the service of a Commonwealth of which Gladstone could never have dreamt – to dwell at the address in London he had chosen for his own retirement. The moving finger of history, having written, does move on. But conjectures of this kind help to remind us that every piece of history our actions inscribe today helps to determine the nature of tomorrow's entry and, in so doing, to bind the present to the future and the future to the past.

But let me return to those letters. What they show with starkness is the continuum of which I wrote earlier; the continuance beyond emancipation of that state of mind Candide had encountered in Suriname which accepted massive human suffering as a valid low-cost factor in the price of sugar. But it is, perhaps, the letter from Calcutta (6 June 1836) in response to John Gladstone's enquiry that most clearly reveals the underlying perception of 'otherness' which linked slavery and indenture and gave human bondage under both systems a common root.

The original Gladstone letter was written on 4 January 1836; the reply from Gillanders, Arbuthnot, & Co. on 6 June that same year. The correspondence that followed in 1837 was to deal essentially with the details of that initial voyage of the 'Hesperus' and the 'Whitby': the first ships bringing Indian indentured labourers to Demerara. The 'Hesperus' belonged to Gladstone's firm: 'John Gladstone and Co'. It was a mere 329 registered tons. It was the 'Hesperus' that brought the Gladstone labourers, most of them bound for *Vreed-en-Hoop* – the first real movement of the people from the East Indies to the Western Hemisphere and, in particular, to the West Indies – the region that Columbus had mis-named in 1492 convincing himself that he had reached Asia from the West. That was why he called the first people of the Caribbean – 'Indians'. But, between the voyages of the 'Santa Maria' and the 'Hesperus' were to pass nearly 350 years; and when the 'Whitby' actually anchored in the Demerara River in the early morning of 5 May 1838 its Captain, James Swinton, would be singularly unaware of the historic significance of the moment. It would be lost on him because the newcomers he had brought to the 'new world' were essentially 'cargo', not people. Yet they were the very people of India whom Columbus thought he had reached three and a half centuries earlier.

'S.S. Whitby' and the 'S.S. Hesperus' arriving at port Georgetown, British Guiana, on 5th May 1838

However, there was more for Gladstone to do than merely arrange the transportation of these first immigrants from India to the 'New World'. By 1836, the planters were getting distinctly anxious about the situation that would arise after the apprenticeship system ended and slave labour was finally withdrawn from the plantations. In a letter of 23 February 1837 that he wrote from Carlton Gardens to Sir John Hobhouse, then President of the Board of Control (a copy of which he subsequently sent to Lord Glenelg, then Secretary of State for the Colonies), Gladstone set out the situation and the thinking of the planters with a frankness normally reserved for private correspondence.

> *A considerable Degree of Uncertainty prevails in all our West India Colonies whether the Apprentices, when the Period of their Services expires, on the 1st August 1840, will be disposed to hire themselves to work on reasonable Terms, and on a System of Continuance such as will ensure the regular Cultivation and Manufacture of the Produce, which it is considered can only be ascertained when that Period arrives. It is also thought that by obtaining the Services of other Classes of Labourers in the Interval, and for a Period beyond the Termination of the Apprenticeship, it may materially influence the Conduct of the Apprentices, and induce them more readily to meet the Wishes of their Employers; with this View Labourers have been sent from Germany, Madeira, Ireland, and elsewhere, but these*

> *Experiments have not succeeded, from the Influence of the Climate generally producing reluctance to labour, and increasing the Desire for Spirituous Liquors, which the low Price and Abundance of new Rum enables them to gratify.*

The desire of which the letter spoke was regarded as perfectly legitimate and readily gratified among the planters themselves. They invented that most potent of spirituous liquors, the 'Demerara rum swizzle', and made it virtually a legend. In 1879, for example, in *'Roraima and British Guiana',* J. W. Boddam-Whetham wrote:

> *Demerara and swizzles are inseparably connected in my mind.... The exact time for indulging in a swizzle has not been clearly defined but as a general rule in Demerara it is accepted whenever offered. It is taken in the morning to ward off the effect of chill, before breakfast to give a tone to the system, in the middle of the day to fortify against the heat, in the afternoon as a suitable finale to luncheon, and again as a stimulant to euchre, and a solace for your losses. Before dinner it acts as an appetiser, and it is said that when taken before going to bed it assists slumber.*

That letter to the President of the Board of Control represented the other half of Gladstone's preparation for the voyage of the 'Hesperus' and the 'Whitby'. He needed an indication from the British Government whether an Order-in-Council or any other authorisation was necessary for the purpose of 'carrying this experimental measure into execution, in order to secure us against interfering or prevention by the authorities at Calcutta'. He had good reason to seek that assurance.

Already, on 27 June 1836, the Court of Policy in Guiana had passed *'an Ordinance for the Better Regulation and Enforcement of the Relevant Duties of Masters and Employers, and Articled Servants and Tradesmen in British Guiana'.* It had been transmitted by the Governor, Sir James Carmichael Smyth, to the Secretary of State with a statement that he had *'very little Doubt but that the several Enactments of this Ordinance (prepared as they are in the Spirit of perfect Equality and Reciprocity in compelling the Performance of the Engagements by which the Parties in question may severally be bound) will meet with His Majesty's most gracious Approbation'.*

Such approbation was not forthcoming. The same perception that all was good when all was bad prevailed. Under pressure of the Anti-Slavery Movement, the political situation in Britain had become highly sensitised and the British Government was obliged to proceed with caution. In his reply to the Governor of 31 October 1836, it fell to the Secretary of State, no less, to draw the Governor's attention to the reality that this legislation – which was to be the underpinning for the indenture system – really was ushering in a new system of slavery:

> *The general Effect of this Ordinance (wrote Lord Glenelg) may, with little inaccuracy, be said to be to continue, in respect of all Persons who shall enter into Indentures of Apprenticeship, the existing Relations between the Employer and the apprenticed Labourer, although without the Intervention of a special Magistracy. The most material Exception is, that the Apprenticeship to be constituted under this Ordinance would not render the Apprentice liable to personal Chastisement in case of Misconduct.*

At least initially, that latter exception was to prove hollow – especially at *Vreed-en-Hoop*. In any event, this 'Indenture Law' was allowed to stand with a reduction in the period of indenture from seven years to three and the exclusion of any person recruited 'on the Continent of Africa or in any of the adjacent islands inhabited wholly or in part by the Negro race'. So obvious was it to the authorities in London that what was about to begin was a new system of slavery that Africans simply had to be excluded from it if the Government was to have any chance of rebutting what Lord Glenelg described to Governor Carmichael Smyth (31st October 1836), as *"a plausible, if not a just, Reproach against this Country of Insincerity in our Professions on that Subject"* (of slavery). The system of bondage would continue; but with different bondsmen.

Yet, even this did not suffice for the requirements of *Vreed-en-Hoop* and the plantocracy in general. John Gladstone returned to the charge arguing forcefully for extended periods of indenture. The Secretary of State yielded. On 19 August 1837, he instructed Governor Carmichael Smyth that as a result of the arguments produced:

> *Her Majesty's Government have agreed to Mr Gladstone's Proposal that the Term of Apprenticeship of Natives of any Place within the Charter of the East India Company imported as Labourers into Guiana should be extended to Five Years.*

An order in Council of 12 July 1837 duly gave effect to this further amendment of the British Guiana 'Indenture Law'; but the Order-in-Council was not published and did not come to light until 3 January 1838 when it was denounced in the 'British Emancipator' (the official organ of the British and Foreign Anti-Slavery Society) as *'giving birth to a new slave-trade'*. John Scoble of the Society, who was later to visit Guiana and write his celebrated exposure of *'The Deplorable Conditions of the Hill Coolies'*, and of *'the Nefarious Means by which they were Induced to Resort to British Guiana and Mauritius'*, was later to claim that this Order-in-Council:

> *Gave a carte blanche to every villain in British Guiana and every scoundrel in India to kidnap and inveigle into contracts for labour for five years, in a distant part of the world, the ignorant and inoffensive Hindoo.*

On the fly-leaf to that pamphlet Scoble quoted from the newspaper *'The Friend of India'*, published in Calcutta, of 3 August 1839:

> *Under the colour of a Bill for protecting the Indian labourers, it is proposed to legalise the importation of them into the colonies. ... It was in this manner that the Slave-trade crept in,*

> *under the shadow of Parliamentary regulation; a race was then begun between abusers and legislation, in which legislation was always found to be in the rear. AND SO IT WILL BE WITH THE COOLEY TRADE. We must treat the same circle; and, after years of the most poignant misery, come to the same result, that in the case of the new, as of the old, trade, the only PATH OF SAFETY LIES IN ABSOLUTE PROHIBITION.*

Indenture was indeed to tread the same circle; but 'absolute prohibition' was not to come for some eighty years.

Altogether, keeping sugar on the economic throne involved a continuous process of bondage which began with the induction of the first African slaves into the Guiana colonies and ended with the prohibition of Indian indenture in 1917. It was one experience with differing shades of brutality, differing methods of coercion, but a common experience of human bondage. The condition of slavery in the days of the 1763 Rebellion at Magdalenenberg, for example, was very different from that of indenture in the end years of the system. As Dr Basdeo Mangru reminded in *'Benevolent Neutrality'*, the fact that the slave was private property and that slavery implied permanence were basic differences – however, much they tended to be overshadowed by the similarities. Yet, at the moment of transition in the 1830s, apprenticeship so shaded into indenture that Brougham could speak in the House of Commons of 'indentured apprenticeship' when referring to slavery between 1834 and 1838 and Lord John Russell could himself describe (and reject) indenture in 1840 as 'a new system of slavery'. Apprenticeship was indenture; indenture was slavery; in an important sense, they were all one.

But the truest testimony to that bondage in continuum was not that given by words in the British Parliament but the experience of those who were to labour on the sugar plantations. Like the slaves before them, Indian indentured labourers had first to endure their own passage across the *Kala Pani* – the Black Waters – not so unlike that earlier pernicious traffic in human cargo. The Guyanese poet Arthur Seymour described the Middle Passage in these terms:

A ferry of infamy from the heart of Africa
Roots torn and bleeding from their native soil
A stain of race spreading across the ocean.

And so, indeed, it was. It remains an apt description of the ferry that was to succeed it, beginning with the *Hesperus* and the *Whitby*, crossing from the heart of India, spreading another stain of race across the ocean.

CHAPTER 3

Arrival

On 1 January 1881, (in the wake of Gladstone's first letter to the Calcutta firm) the sailing ship *Ellora* arrived in Georgetown from Calcutta after a voyage of nearly three months. Its human cargo was indentured labourers for the sugar plantations of British Guiana. Among them was a widowed mother, *Doolnie,* and her son of nine, *Ramphul,* bound for that same estate of Vreed-en-Hoop. Her story was already remarkable, though not unique, for this journey across the *kala pani* was for her a third crossing.

In the early 1870s bubonic plague, which was to reach epidemic proportions at the turn of the century in India's United Provinces, had left this woman widowed. She and her husband were high caste Brahmins, but poor. And as so often happened in their circumstances, all but one of their children had succumbed leaving only one son alive. 'Suttee' (immolation on the husband's funeral pyre) had been abolished by law, but remained a sacrifice expected of the orthodox. It was a sacrifice the widow was unwilling to make. She took the only other option – return to her maternal home. But it was not a real option. She was treated as an outcast. The approaches to her home swept before her not in welcome but rejection, for having committed the terrible wrong of losing her husband. To purify herself, she took her infant son to the sacred city of Benares for both to wash in the holy waters of the Ganges. Benares then, as Varanasi now, was a city to which the forlorn and despairing came and there lurked the Arkathis – the touts employed by the agents recruiting labour for the sugar plantations. The lack of women among indentured labourers was always a major problem and it had by then become the law that 40 women had to be recruited for every 100 men indentured. Places of pilgrimage like Benares offered the Arkathis a prime perch to prey on unattached women.

To the rejected widow the promise of a new life must have seemed an answer to her prayers. But who knows with what stories she was lured or how long she believed the journey or the labouring to be, or even where she was going? But to Calcutta with her son she duly went and was recruited for the West Indies arriving eventually in Suriname – Dutch Guiana. Shades of Candide! Did she, too, weep on entering Suriname, sensing the abomination of her indenture? We will not know. Almost certainly she would not have known that the right to recruit her had been traded by Britain to Holland in return for a cluster of old Dutch forts built for the slave trade in what is today Ghana. That traffic to Suriname in 1873 was disastrous; 18 per cent of the immigrants died in the first twelve months. But the widow and her son survived. Eventually, she worked out the five-year contract and, no longer bound, they took the long journey back to India.

'Lalla Rookh': Suriname Memorial to Indian indenture

But the rules of caste were strict and she found no welcome despite her absence of six years. In fact, in her penance she had sinned still further by having crossed the 'Black Waters' and lived among unclean meat-eaters. Once again she went with her son to Benares to wash seven times in the Ganges in the hope of being favoured with better fortune. Her late husband's family was of the priestly class – the Pandas – who it is thought administered the sacred Vishnupad Temple at Gaya in Bihar. For a while, as they lingered by the holy river, the boy was apprenticed to a priest, one of the Pandas of Benares, and began his training in the Hindu scriptures. But, once again they encountered the silver-tongued Arkathis, perhaps this time with a tale of a better life than Suriname had offered. The British sugar planters were said to be less cruel than the Dutch.

A second time they journeyed to Calcutta and a second contract of indenture. This time, however, the widow had no thought of returning to the village and family that had cast her out so cruelly, not once but twice. Harsh and uncertain as were the fortunes of indenture, she was leaving now for good: to give her young son, in particular, a better chance than he might ever have in a village and a family that did not want them. So it was that, in due season, on the ship *Ellora*, the widow and her son reached Georgetown committed to labour on that same estate at *Vreed-en-Hoop* that the abolitionists had singled out for attack almost fifty years earlier and with which, under the then ownership of Sir John Gladstone, the whole system of Indian indenture to the West Indies had begun. The widow fulfilled her contract of labour on the sugar plantations, her son, about whom I will say more later, sharing her burden.

Depôt No. 1710 WOMAN'S
EMIGRATION CERTIFICATE.
No. 277 Ship Ellora
8, GARDEN REACH, CALCUTTA, the 9 Oct 1890
Name .... Doolnie Rfd.
Father's name .... Makkhum Sing
Age 30
Caste .... Chuttry
Height .... 5 Feet 1½ Inches.
Name of next-of-kin ....
If married, to whom .... Moorli Sing
Zillah .... Unao
Pergunnah .... Suffipore
Village .... Makhie
Bodily marks .... Wart near right side nose

We certify that we have examined and passed the above-named woman as a fit subject for emigration as an agricultural labourer; that she is free from all bodily and mental disease, and has been vaccinated.

Surgeon-Superintendent. Depôt Surgeon.

I hereby certify that the woman above described (whom I have engaged as a labourer on the part of the Government of British Guiana, where she has expressed her willingness to proceed to work for hire) has appeared before me, and that I have explained to her all matters concerning her duties as an Emigrant, according to Section 38 of Indian Emigration Act VII of 1871.

COUNTERSIGNED.

Protector of Emigrants at Calcutta. Emigration Agent for British Guiana.

Depôt No. 1711 BOY'S
EMIGRATION CERTIFICATE.
No. 278 Ship Ellora
8, GARDEN REACH, CALCUTTA, the 9 octr 1890
Name .... Ramphul Rfd.
Father's name .... Moorli Sing
Age 9
Caste .... Chuttry
Name of next-of-kin .... parents accompany
Zillah .... Unao
Pergunnah .... Suffipore
Village .... Makhie
Bodily marks .... Scar right ribs

We certify that we have examined and passed the above-named boy as a fit subject for emigration; that he is free from all bodily and mental disease and has been vaccinated.

Surgeon-Superintendent. Depôt Surgeon.

COUNTERSIGNED.

Protector of Emigrants at Calcutta. Emigration Agent for British Guiana.

Ship's papers of 'Doolnie' and 'Ramphul'

So much for the system of indenture of which I am a product. It is my ancestors that carried the burden of its gross inhumanities – starting with my widowed great-grandmother. In 2002, Verene Shepherd, then Professor of Social History at The University of the West Indies, wrote a marvellously compassionate 'fictional' account of the horrifying journey of a lone woman across the *kala pani* under the indenture system. She called it *'Maharani's Misery'*. It was, of course, steeped in history; but it had for me a special poignancy. Maharani's story could have been my great grandmother's too. Indeed, there are in *'Maharani's Misery'* shades of the inhuman and degrading treatment that was the fate of every indentured woman transported to the 'New World' – suffering to which inevitably some succumbed on the journey.

Late in 1983, at the end of the Commonwealth Heads of Government Meeting in New Delhi – the first ever held in India, and held just in time for us to have the privilege of Indira Gandhi's chairmanship – I travelled to Varanasi and the surrounding countryside from where that brave woman and her son had crossed the 'seven seas' three times just over one hundred years before. I took with me my mother; herself sprung from another transplantation that indenture had procured. My own 'widowed mother' went with me to Gaya – as did my cousin Stella Jeffers, shown with her below in the Gaya countryside. It was a return journey of a kind: not one conceived as an intensive search for 'roots', but from which came insistent reminders that they were not far away.

As we sat in the garden of the official Guest House in Gaya, my mother talked with the young wife of the District Magistrate and Collector about the names of vegetables we thought peculiar to Guyana, like 'baigan' and 'bora', only to find that they were similar in this district of Bihar, when even in neighbouring Trinidad they were quite different. We talked too of my friend Guya Persaud, then a distinguished judge in the West Indies, whose parents, we decided, commemorated his roots in the most permanent of ways, in his name. There was a spirit of belonging in that languid Gaya countryside.

The highlight of my pilgrimage was being received by the Pandas of Gaya as a son of the region and admitted to the inner sanctum of the Vishnupad Temple – still one of India's most sacred places. At its centre, encased in solid silver, is a large rock with an indentation worshipped as being the footprint of Lord Vishnu himself. The climax of the visit was being invited to perform a puja at the shrine, which I did with all the awkwardness of a novice, but the humility which the occasion imposed. So ineffable a spirit pervaded the occasion that my wife was in tears at its end.

My ancestral link with Gaya and the Vishnupad Temple is still a matter of inference and surmise. But there were other links even in that place. At the entrance to the Temple is a bell bearing the following inscription: "A gift to the Bishnupad by Mr Francis Gillanders, Gaya, 15th January 1790". Francis Gillanders was a Collector in Gaya in the late years of the eighteenth century. What links were there between this man, who so closely identified with the pilgrims from whom he would have collected the old 'pilgrim tax' as they visited the Vishnupad Temple from all over India, with Gillanders, Arbuthnot & Company of Calcutta, to whom Sir John Gladstone had written that first letter in January 1836: the letter that, in a sense, 'brought' me from Gaya to Guyana?

As I sought out beginnings across the shifting line that divided Bihar from India's United Provinces, flashes of these strange conjunctures came before me, hints of continuity, glimpses of patterns traced over time as if there was a story still unfolding – but only faintly discernible amid the bustle of the time. And some words of Franz Fanon came back to me, words that might stand for the whole story of servitude illumined by the light of the individual human will to overcome: *It Is a story that takes place in darkness, and the sun that is carried within me must shine into the smallest crannies.*

The visit to Gaya was inevitably one of many reflections, not least on the strange pathways that led my forebears to Guyana and now led me back to India through a modern Commonwealth that India made possible. Those pathways, in due course, took me from Guyana to London, to occupancy in 1975, as I said earlier, of the then official residence of the Commonwealth Secretary-General at 5 Carlton Gardens, St James's. July 1833 was just one month before the Emancipation Bill was passed and before Wilberforce himself passed away. In that same month John Gladstone and William Wilberforce breakfasted together in London: two old men at the end of their very different lives which, because of their incongruences, had come together to influence the lives of generations to come – and, rather specially, my own. The records do not reveal whether they breakfasted at Carlton Gardens; I like to think that Gladstone went to Wilberforce.

I have thought much of my great-grandmother in later, more reflective, years. We know from the very comprehensive Registers of Indian indentured immigrants, meticulously inscribed at the time, and now kept in Guyana's Archives, that her name was 'Doolnie'. There is no photograph of her, and with youthful abandon I never questioned my grandfather about his mother. She is lost, save to our family tree and my father's scant memoirs. But not all is lost. When I was at the Commonwealth Secretariat in London in the 1980s there was a young law student from Barbados, Nicholas Forde – son of one of the most distinguished West Indian lawyers of my time and a close friend, Sir Henry Forde – whose antiquarian interests turned up for me a rare find. It was an engraving from a photograph taken in Demerara of Indian indentured arrivals on the *SS Ellora,* the ship my forbears had come on to British Guiana and which, according to the Register of arrivals, came three times to Demerara – twice in 1881 and again in 1882. It was on the first of those journeys that Doolnie had come.

Nicholas knew nothing of the *Ellora,* but thought the archive might be of general interest to me. It was of very specific interest. There were two photographs: one showing the women on board the anchored vessel sitting clustered on the deck, women who had just crossed the 'black waters'. My first thought was: 'could Doolnie be among them'?

The other was of the men and boys; similarly, could among them be my grandfather then 9 years old. The caption, under INDIAN IMMIGRANTS AT DEMERARA reads:

> *Since the abolition of negro servitude the difficulty of obtaining labour for the tropical plantations in the West Indies and the adjacent countries constitutes a problem which is by no means easy of solution. The negro who while he was a slave was compelled to work against his will, now for the most part, except where, as in Barbados, the population is very thick, takes life easily. He prefers to loaf about, doing just work enough to procure the bare necessaries of life, and no more. Hence his place in the labour market is now to some extent filled by the patient, hardworking, but physically less vigorous natives of the East Indies. Our engravings, which are from photographs by Norton Brothers of Demerara, represent the arrival of a large body of Indian immigrants in the colony of British Guiana. The passage from Calcutta was made in 82 days by the Ellora and the immigrants consisted of 320 men, 123 women, 18 boys, 19 girls and 8 babies.*

The engraving, alas, is not a depiction of the journey of the *Ellora* on which Doolnie and her son had come; it is one of the Ellora's two following trips. We know this from the tally of 'souls' aboard, which the Registers recorded. Still, it was the ship that brought them and those faces on the deck were replicas of all who travelled on her. And because the engraving was from a photograph, its authenticity is enhanced. All in all, it remains an iconic possession – a marker of not only when, but how, my ancestors came across the seas, the black waters, to the land that would nurture them within a new system of bondage – often unkindly, but through the generations, to the future whose promise brought them in the first place.

The experience of captivity continued beyond the journey into labouring – an experience in its totality well described by Hugh Tinker as an 'exile into bondage'. Perhaps the truest symbol of the unbroken chain between slavery and indenture was the tenement range or 'logie' of the inherited 'nigger yard': the squalid, foul, degenerate, huddled pens that passed for housing for slave and indentured labourer alike. 'Nigger Yard', 'coolie yard', 'bound yard' were all one, only the labels changed to match the changing style of servitude. Like the African slave, the Indian immigrant was subjected to the coercion of the whip and to the new coercion of criminal law applied for labour offences such as absenteeism and lack of identity documents which were not crimes under the general law. No wonder the Royal Commission in 1870 described the indentured Indian as trapped by the law, *'in the hands of a system which elaborately twists and turns him about, but always leaves him face to face with an impossibility'*.

In his Foreword to Walter Rodney's 'A History of the Guyanese Working People, 1881-1905' – a history whose central thesis was that shared common experience between indenture and slavery – George Lamming sums up the cruel realities of indenture as follows:

> *Indentured labour was bound labour. It was deprived of all mobility and was therefore condemned to provide that reliability of the service a crop like sugar demanded. The planter class, with the full permission of the metropolitan power, had given itself the legal right to deploy this labour as it pleased. As Rodney emphasises, here, with great relevance to many a contemporary situation, what the ruling class could not acquire by the normal play of the market forces had now been appropriated through legal sanctions. Indentured Indian labour was enslaved by the tyranny of the law that decided their relations to the land where they walked, and worked and slept.*

Rodney himself emphasised the link with characteristic penetration:

> *... indentured labour had as its ultimate function the guaranteeing of planter control over the entire labour process ... this alone justified the continuation of indentureship, irrespective of the cost to the individual proprietor and to the*

> *general taxpayer ... More than anything else, it was the regimented social and industrial control which caused indenture to approximate so closely to slavery.*

Not much had changed in the *Vreed-en-Hoop* stable from the days of Jack Gladstone and the 1823 revolt. By now, however, its squalid realities were becoming a problem for its owners' son – the future Prime Minister of England. In 1840, John Gladstone sold up: *Vreed-en-Hoop* went for £35,000, (equivalent today to £27.2 million) with *'an addition of £4,000* (now £810,857) *for the services of the coolies'*. As Checkland recorded, *'The Coolies'*, wrote John Gladstone, *'are excellent bait for effecting the sales'*. They *were* pieces, not people. With the proceeds, Gladstone set up a trust for his children, including William. As Richard Shannon reflected in the first of his Volumes on *Gladstone,* Demerara contributed substantially to the future British Prime Minister's financial independence, though he protested at the time that *'this increased wealth so much beyond my needs with its attendant responsibility is very burdensome, however on his part the act be beautiful'*.

The meaning of *Vreed-en-Hoop* is 'Peace and Hope'. One hundred and fifty years ago it helped to bring both to the Gladstone family; but neither to the children of slavery and indenture who were its compulsive progenitors.

On the final division of Gladstone's estate in 1848, the house in Carlton Gardens went to William. John Gladstone had never resided in British Guiana but the sale of *Vreed-en-Hoop*, and later Plantation *Success*, was, in a sense, his act of retirement from Demerara and the West Indies. He left behind, however, the legacy of indenture which he had begun with the 'Hesperus' in 1838, and which resumed in 1845 despite the earlier protestations of Lord John Russell. For 80 years after that first arrival, indenture would tread the same circle towards abolition as slavery had done before emancipation.

CHAPTER 4

A Shared Heritage

In 1929, the Rev. C.F. Andrews, Mahatma Gandhi's friend and emissary, visited British Guiana – and spent an evening in my parents' humble home in New Amsterdam. My father had managed the Berbice end of his visit, and he in turn was interested in 'J.I.'s efforts for the education of Indian girls. It is now part of family lore that their conversations were continually disturbed by a mewling infant – I was not yet a year old – until the priest took me in his arms, quieted the cries and gave me his blessing. My mother always had hope for me thereafter.

In 1936, at the end of a sentimental visit to Fiji, C.F. Andrews placed his faith in the 'powers of recovery' of the indentured Indians. That power of recovery was a power and a quality which the children of Indian indenture shared with their brothers and sisters of African descent who are the children of slavery in its cruellest form. When in *'Poems of Resistance from Guyana'* Martin Carter wrote: *"From the nigger-yard of yesterday I come with my burden. To the world of tomorrow I turn with my strength"*, he spoke for all who were the victims of both slavery and indenture; he spoke of all who shared in British Guiana the common experience of bondage and, out of bondage, in the genesis of the nation. He spoke with truth of hope well justified. How the children of slavery and indenture would use their powers of recovery and what pathways the process of renewal would follow, would depend in large measure on whether slavery and indenture were indeed perceived as the unifying experience that it was. This process of renewal was crucial to Guyana's future; it, too, was part of the genesis of the nation.

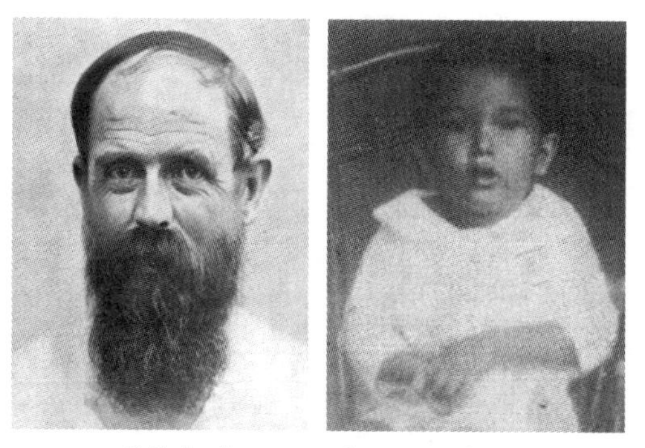

C.F. Andrews and me as a boy

But something else needs to be acknowledged. Indenture could not have thrived if the many who came had not first felt the need to leave. When everything is said about the deceit and coercion and sometimes outright kidnapping of indentured immigrants, there remains the uncomfortable reality that the great majority who crossed the *kala pani* did so because of a desperate urge to escape from destitution and despair. Crushed down by poverty, by landlessness and landlordism and, for some at least, by the hopelessness of the caste system, they were in flight from bondage. What the fraudulence and iniquity of indenture did was to lure them from one trap into another; they exchanged a familiar servitude at the base of the Indian economic and social system for the even more alienated inequality of plantation serfdom. As Tinker aptly concluded, their escape from bondage would turn out to be exile into bondage of another kind.

Yet it was not a meaningless exchange. Although the shackles of the plantation system were not easily cast off, and despite the exploitative and lifeless character of indenture, there was always the prospect of eventual release and renewal: a prospect not vouchsafed them in the ancestral home of 19th century India – as some who returned discovered. Certainly, for the generation that would follow, after the ignominy of indenture would come opportunity. There are many lessons here; among them the sobering one that the arrival of the 'Hesperus' and the 'Whitby' are worthy of commemoration for the additional reason that, in a paradoxical way, that arrival, along with slavery's abolition, was the beginning of recovery in the more ultimate sense – the sense in which together they marked the genesis of the Guyanese nation.

All I have recounted is central to my beginnings; but there is more besides that make my awareness of the shared heritage of the Guyanese people both natural and profound. While both my parents were children of Indian indenture, my mother's ancestry was more varied, and in ways that were familiar to the patterns of Guyana's demography. My mother Grace Alexandria Ramphal's maiden name was 'Abdool'. But her father was not a Muslim – or a 'Mohammedan', as he would have been described in those days. In my father's unfinished memoirs to which I have referred before, he tells the story of how Grace's 'grandfather' got the name 'Abdool' in his journey of indenture from India. It is a commentary on the whole shabby system of 'human transportation', and also on the absurdities of India's then dominant caste system. The old man's true name it seems was 'Massi Das' – a Hindu and a 'holy man'. Caught in the web of indenture, 'J.I.' writes, *"he was astounded by the thought of eating together with others"*. But he either had to do it or starve. So when he was asked his name, he said 'Abdool', rationalising necessity in an arcane culture in which only Mohammedans ate together.

'Abdool' was the name he went by for the rest of his life. He did convert; but to Christianity. Later, he became one of the prominent Indian Catechists of the Anglican Church in British Guiana. And, of course, 'Abdool' was the name he passed on to his son Norman Emelius Abdool, my mother's father. The story goes that when 'J.I.' told his father of his plans to be married to 'Grace Abdool', Daniel's exclamation was: 'Abdool, beta?' It was only when the 'Abdool' ancestry was traced for him to Catechist Abdool that Daniel Ramphal was not just appeased, but pleased. Though now a Christian, my grandfather had not lost those old Hindu biases that would have made a Mohammedan daughter-in-law unacceptable.

As it transpired, parenting was not Norman Abdool's vocation; and my mother grew up in the care of her maternal relatives – her grandmother very specially. At that time, in the late 19th Century and for a generation at least after, this was a typical social pattern throughout the West Indies: delinquent or disappearing fathers; and caring grandmothers rescuing their daughters. Grace's mother, Agnes, died in 1914 when Grace was only five years old; it was left to her grandmother Grace Elizabeth (nee Nurse) to take care of Grace, and her elder brother, Sydney.

'Granny's' husband, my mother's grandfather, was Ragunandan Singh Joseph – a product of early Indian indenture. But she herself, my great grandmother, was the product of two of Guiana's even earlier other races – white and black. Her father was Samuel Francis Nurse, born in 1813 in Barbados, the son of white parents in Barbados whose forebears had come there possibly, but not certainly, from the New England Colonies. Samuel Francis Nurse came to British Guiana as a young man in search of his fortune – and found it. He settled in British Guiana, becoming a well-established sugar planter in Essequibo, on the Islands of Leguan, Waakenam and the Essequibo coast. At one time or another he had interests in the estates of Vertrouen, Belfield, Windsor Forest, Maryville, Schoon Ord and Goed Fortune. His marble tombstone (sent out from England by his English widow, Agnes Cressall, whom he met and married in Demerara in 1854 while she was visiting her brother Paul) is in the St Bartholomew churchyard at Queenstown, Essequibo, not far from Plantation Cullen which he owned and where he died. I saw his tomb with my daughter Susan on a visit in 2010. It is Susan who diligently researched and verified most of these maternal family roots.

Early in his sojourn in Essequibo, and with slavery over, Nurse 'partnered' as we would say now, 'took up' as they would have said then, with Isabella Gilbert, with whom he had four children – one of whom was my mother's grandmother born in 1848 – my great-grandmother. Isabella was a progeny of slavery. The 1832 slave register for Plantation Vertrouen on Leguan shows Isabella as a girl of 7, born of a 'mulatto' mother and a 'black' father' – Moses and Sarah Gilbert, Creole parents themselves born in the Colony. Isabella seems never to have laboured as a slave. Nurse acquired Plantation Vertrouen and with it came Isabella. He is shown in the 1841 Census as the owner/resident of Vertrouen and Isabella as a 'domestic' there. She would have been 16. He obviously kept her on as a domestic and concubine in a fairly settled relationship. Though Nurse later married Agnes Cressall, he stood by Isabella, setting her up in a home in a respectable part of Georgetown – the 'south half of Lot 61 Brickdam' – and providing for her and their four children in an agreeable fashion. Through the mists of time are accounts of the family living a comely social life, no doubt within an emerging 'mulatto' middle class. Nurse gave Isabella (in her own name) a house and land at Plantation Vertrouen which she sold in 1861.

Samuel Francis Nurse seems to have earned a favourable name among the 'coloured' community – a fact which saved him during a post-emancipation eruption of violence when his carriage was allowed safe passage through 'black' territory. "Don't trouble him; he is a good man"' is said to have rung out in the nick of time. There must have been a down side to this 'black softness' in the planter establishment; certainly, there is no record of Samuel Francis Nurse occupying any position within it beyond being on the voters' list for the College of Electors.

And the 'Nurse' line through Isabella was to continue beyond my great grandmother. Henry Alfred Godfrey Nurse was her nephew – a grandson of Samuel Francis and Isabella – born in British Guiana on 7 July 1888. He was therefore my distant relative and was to become a worthy son of the country. At 18, in 1906, he travelled to New York and eventually, in 1914, qualified as a doctor (M.D.) at the Long Island

College of Medicine. He put down roots in New York and became a pioneer black doctor in Manhattan and particularly in Harlem Hospital where a handsome bronze plaque bearing his image today memorialises his many contributions – which included leadership in the 1930s of the successful fight for the admission of black doctors to the then 'all-white' staff of the Hospital; and founding the first School for black nurses there. And his interests reached out into the arts and politics. The Journal of the National Medical Association of the United States credits him with being a founder of the Shakespeare Theatre at Stratford, Connecticut and with twice being a member of the New York State Electoral College – the first black person to be on a Presidential Electoral College: a Democrat who helped to elect President Roosevelt. Dr Godfrey Nurse died in Brooklyn in 1968 – a relative who must be among the most notable of Guyana's Diaspora in New York.

Meanwhile, my mother's worthy grandmother discharged her matriarchal trust in full measure. Her husband 'Ragu' had been a good provider in his lifetime, but his death placed responsibility for the family finances on his daughter, Dorothy – my mother's aunt. That 'aunt', a trained nurse, was to become a celebrated midwife on Guiana's Courantyne coast. Her early ambition had been to join her cousin, Dr Godfrey Nurse, in New York; but her new local responsibilities put paid to that hope. In the event, Grace Alexandria, my mother, was admirably brought up – a Christian young lady of fine manners and values, and when my father met her in 1927, of quite exceptional beauty.

Most mothers are incomparably wonderful; mine was. As her first-born, I suppose I had an edge on my siblings; so, anyway, they complained. Suffice it that I grew up in the sunshine of her love and protection, and always mindful of it. She lived to the good age of 97 and so shared in the fortunes of my own life. They were in a small way my best recompense for all I owed to her. She died in Barbados in 2006 having lived out her later years there in the care of my sister Indrani. I shared some of those years with her too and was there to speak at her funeral service. I recall here some of what I said on 17

November in the Chapel of the Coral Ridge Memorial Gardens, for they were from a full heart:

Was ever mother, sister, aunt, grandmother, great grandmother, mother in law, matriarch – loved more? Was ever family more blessed to have had for so long – 97 years – someone so pure to love and cherish, to guide the generations she nurtured in the pathways of her ennobling life? I pay this tribute to our Mother as her first-born; but I speak for all her children, and for all our children and their children too.

How could her parents have known at her birth that there would be no name more fit for her than Grace? She exuded grace all her long life – grace and dignity and charm, and always modesty. As she grew older a younger generation – for whom these attributes were not the norm of their time – marvelled at the qualities with which she so naturally endowed the family and all whose lives she touched.

Coming out of the most humble beginnings in British Guiana almost a century ago, Grace Abdool grew into young womanhood with an angelic beauty; but even more so with an awareness from her forbears that matured into a personal conviction that the absence of wealth did not compel the absence of standards and values; did not mean the loss of dignity and refinement – on the contrary, called for greater effort toward enrichment of the spirit and strength of character.

In this she was truly the soul-mate of my father – a pioneer educator who won the respect of his community and beyond. He was a great Guianese and Mother was an important part of his greatness. Together, they nurtured and inspired generations of our family- starting, of course, with us their five children, and the others of the extended family who shared Grace's mothering wing. She never spared herself in personally ensuring that we had the best that relentless hard work could provide. I was at least 16 before I wore a shirt that mother had not personally sewn.

And for Mother the world was her family. That family now veritably inhabits the world; but for her it remained a small world of loved ones – to them, to us, she devoted her life sharing in our achievements and our disappointments, in our joys and in our sorrows. That she was there to feel proud in our modest successes, that she was there to comfort and revive us in our downside moments, were the unspoken premises of all we did or tried to do. Not to let her down became a moral duty – and gave us strength to strive in all we did.

Grace

I need to say a word about my father, J.I.'; because the example of his life had such a special influence on my own; more often than not in indirect and unseen ways. His life is a story in its own right and his unfinished memoirs only whet the appetite. But a segment of his life has been the subject of dispassionate research that is a commentary not only on my father's quite extraordinary efforts in the field of education in 1920s British Guiana, but a window on the evolving colonial society. Professor Clem Seecharran, then of the London Metropolitan University, published a book in 2011 entitled *'Mother India's Shadow Over El Dorado'*. It is a work of great scholarship and meticulous research in a field hitherto unexplored. For me and our family generally, it brought to light in three Chapters devoted to

'J.I. Ramphal' information and insights precious in family terms; and especially pertinent to the story of my life.

His father, Daniel, my stern grandfather, the boy of 9 who had come with his widowed mother on the '*Ellora*' from India in 1881, had attracted the attention of the Canadian Presbyterian Missionaries who were prominent in education in the Colony. They took him from the cane field into their schools, converting him to Christianity in the process. Later, he was to become a 'Catechist' (a lay preacher) in the Church. In turn, he brought up his son James Isaac ('J.I.') as a pupil, then as a teacher in the Canadian Mission's school system which encompassed a variety of primary schools in the country's rural areas and the first secondary school outside the Capital, Georgetown – the Berbice High School in New Amsterdam, Berbice: the town and county of my birth. Jimmy Ramphal was among the first students to be enrolled there, and, in 1918, he was the first student to secure the Cambridge School Certificate from it.

Daniel

However, both father and son were to endure turbulent times with the Church's hierarchy, essentially through their refusal to be subservient to the authoritarianism that accompanied the Mission's good deeds. But my father was bright, articulate and principled and by 18 he was already in charge of the Mission's Bush Lot Primary School. He was to go on to be Headmaster at many of their Schools most of which were Government aided and integrated into the Colony's school system. This experience won him wide respect in the rural Indian communities in which the Mission's work was concentrated. It also imbued him with a special passion over what was to become his earliest cause – his campaign for the education of Indian girls: the daughters of indenture.

Catering to a planter desire for cheap child labour (not unknown in India) and an orthodox Hindu antipathy to their daughters attending racially mixed schools, the colonial administration – in what became known as the Swettenham Circular (after the Governor (1901-4) who had issued it) – shamelessly exempted Indian girls from the legal obligation to attend school. 'J.I.' saw this as complicity in the illiteracy of Indian women – a death sentence on their personal development and their participation in the country's evolution. He made it a personal crusade and mustered others to his cause. One of these was an enlightened Indian businessman, Francis Kawall, whose grandson Kenrick (trained as a dentist in the United States) was later to marry my sister Sita.

My father's crusade for the repeal of the Swettenham Circular was pursued relentlessly in the media through a column which he wrote regularly in the *'New Daily Chronicle'* newspaper and the periodical *'Indian Opinion'* under the pseudonyms of *Akbar Shah* and later *Lala Rajpat.* It eventually brought him into contact with the rising radical politician A.R.F. Weber (editor of the Newspaper) who championed the cause deeming it (in the Legislative Council) *"the greatest blot on the literary statistics of the colony"*. By early 1933, with public opinion effectively canvassed against the Circular, the colonial Government, and its planter and orthodox Hindu supporters, retreated. After a Conference of what we would today describe as 'stakeholders', the Government on 15 July 1933 announced the withdrawal of the Circular. To the end of his life, my father considered this the greatest of his achievements – and he was still only thirty.

In pursuing the path of teaching and the vocation of education in the wider sense, and in accepting a Christian affiliation (although not Christianity as his practising religion) my father was striking out on a path that led away from the sugar plantation – the fate of most of the children of indentured Indians in the 1920s – and therefore joining the emerging multicultural colonial society at a very early stage. He went on to leave an eternal mark on the nature and quality of education in British Guiana which for a generation was respected throughout the West Indies for the high quality of its educated sons and daughters.

J.I. Ramphal was at the apex of a pyramid of private secondary education which broadened out into that base of excellence. In August 1929, when I was not yet one year old, he left rural Berbice, went into the City and opened the Modern High School (MHS) in Georgetown – a pioneer private secondary school. From the most modest start, with my mother boarding students from the country, the MHS grew to be the premier school of its kind; but this time, unlike those Canadian Mission schools that catered primarily for the children of Indian indenture, it consciously cast its net across all of Guyana's races. Perhaps the most telling commentary is that within two decades, most of the colony's secondary schools were headed by scholars from the 'Modern High' – J.C. Luck, Clem Yansen, R.B.O. Hart, Joseph Castello, and Doodnauth Hetram – a truly multi-racial base to a secondary school system of which any community could be proud.

'J I', MHS staff, seniors and me (1932)

It was in this environment that I grew up, accepting naturally my country's many people as my fellows: the names of school-day friends that remained friends for life come to mind, 'Bryn' Pollard, Eric Sam, Bertram Collins, Harold Edgehill, – and there were girl-friends too. The point I am trying to make is that from my earliest years, spent mainly in the capital, Georgetown, the link with sugar and its plantations that had brought my forbears to the 'wild Guiana coast', or with the religious cultures that bound many of the sons and daughters of indenture together in ways that made multi-racial assimilation harder, had been lost. I did not carry into life – in Guyana or the Caribbean or my global home – the stress and baggage of such cloistered beginnings. For that, I give thanks to my father, most of all. 'J.I.' died in 1966. He did not live long enough to see how much I had benefited from that up-bringing.

* * *

My generation, and the one that followed, are heirs to a formidable tradition of individual effort for recovery. That effort gathered momentum in the end years of the nineteenth century and reached a high point in the 1920s and 1930s as the capacity of the children of slavery and indenture for self-improvement enlarged directly through education – education which they rightly prized almost above all else. In the families of each of us is that record of striving upwards, of working assiduously, often quite modestly, but always steadily towards the goal of self-improvement – a generation for whom the work ethic became an almost natural element of the process of survival.

We have a lot to retrieve from those years, and from the traditions of our parents' generation. Unless I am much mistaken, we are in danger of going in another direction – making a culture of the 'pork-knocker's' materialistic dream. Yet El Dorado always was a city of the mind.

And there are other victories for human fulfilment still to be won in Guyana, as in many countries. In the last decade in particular, international economic conditions have been cruelly harsh for developing countries and have taken a heavy toll on vulnerable economies. But we must admit also that mistakes have been made. The richness of our natural resources, good levels of education and the resourcefulness of our people should have provided greater resilience. Venturing out boldly in largely unchartered waters and remembering the exploitation and repression that was so much a part of our history, we had to be pioneering and, therefore, to risk making mistakes. But we would be bad pioneers if we fail to admit to such mistakes, and to learn from them – as others are doing throughout the world, including major nations like Russia and China. To fail to do so is to fall far behind, and it will be of little comfort then to applaud our consistency, if it be consistency in error.

But the need not to fall behind is even more pointed now, because the challenge that faces developing countries is not merely the challenge of economic development, but the fact that in failure lies the danger of returning to a new dependency – a new kind of colonialism – deriving from economic weakness: a return along the path from whence we have come. We cannot afford such retrogression; and circumstances surely are now propitious for renewal and a real leap forward. The vision of a prosperous Guyana is not an empty one. It is attainable with sustained effort at economic and political reform; with continuing endeavour to liberalise the environment so that Guyanese can give of their best; with positive action to resolve insecurity and fear on the part of all sections of our society. But leadership and good direction are not enough. Much must be contributed by the people of Guyana in a great movement of change and reconstruction.

Relevant to that process of rebuilding is a cardinal lesson from the events of 150 years ago: the lesson that a special obligation devolves on the children of slavery and indenture and colonialism. It is the obligation to ensure that no trace of servitude lingers or re-emerges in our society under whatever guise. The legacy of bondage is a continuing one; it is one which only a vigilant society can eradicate. Wherever racism, oppression, intolerance, authoritarianism, dominion of whatever kind, encroaches on human freedom it stalks in the shadow of slavery and indenture. We must never allow ourselves the complacency of believing that their shadows have been lifted for all time from our country or our region; we must be vigorous in ensuring that they never fall again upon us from any quarter

In truth, slavery and indenture have left Guiana a legacy of challenge. Almost everything about them – about the systems themselves and about the linkages between them – emphasised difference and prompted division. How else but with resentment could newly-freed African slaves react to immigrants arriving to deny them the right to the economic betterment which should have been the first fruit of freedom? Yet, how were the new arrivals to escape the fate of being pawns in a game of life and death they endured but scarcely understood? *'You make human beings the subject of your commerce, as if they were merchandise, and you refuse them the benefit of the great law which governs all commercial dealings – that the supply must ever adapt itself to the demands':* thus Brougham (quoting Pitt) inveighed in vain at the very start of Indian indenture to Guiana. Slavery, apprenticeship, indenture were ingredients of a poisoned brew which left a toxic residue of race. From that cup, Guyanese must decline to sip; for to do so would be to stage the final act in a tragedy of others' making played out by themselves. Far better, to create a propitious denouement – one that denies a victory to "otherness", and makes Guyana's national motto of unity reflect not just a pious hope, but a present living reality.

The real challenge that events 150 years ago have bequeathed to Guyana is truly to make those events the genesis of a nation. It, and other countries like it, will be able to do so only when it is truly understood that slavery and indenture were a continuum, that their victims shared a common experience of bondage, that the same history which tempts their people to mutual alienation created a primordial kinship – a heritage of oneness they are prone to squander but need ceaselessly to cherish and enlarge. Beyond genesis, that surely must be the final revelation.

I am a child of all I have narrated; a child of histories near and far. I have been moulded by them all; and my global life that these 'glimpses' conjure are but the unfolding of these beginnings.

The family with 'Granny' (1933)

Guyana's national motto, adopted at independence in 1966, is *'One People, One Nation, One Destiny'*. I had a hand in shaping that formal affirmation; but years before I had taken on others who were for treating British Guiana as a communal state. In 1951 the Waddington Commission on Constitutional Reform produced its Report making recommendations for constitutional change in British Guiana. Its proposals were quite far-reaching, measured by prevailing constitutional arrangements in the region. But reactions to its proposals were mixed – and for different reasons. *The Times* in London was among them, taking the editorial line (on 20 October 1951) that the new Constitution ought to recognise the existence of racialism in Guianese politics and to provide for a system of representation in some way related to the pattern of existing racial groups. I was only just 23 and at the Institute of Advanced Legal Studies in London, but I was outraged and felt constrained to write in refutation. My letter to the Editor was published on 23 October 1951. It acknowledged that the 'gospel of race' was being preached in the country, but went on to assert:

> *Responsible elements in all racial groups in Guianese society are devoting their energies toward crushing the evil influence*

> *of racialism wherever it rears its ugly head and throughout the country men and women of diverse races are working together in all the fields of social and political activity, sublimating, in the process, conflicting racial loyalties to a comprehensive and overriding loyalty to Guiana. It is only the irresponsible and the political opportunist who attempt to retard and reverse this process...It is the avowed policy of such agencies to divide; surely it is not the office of the Constitution to assist in their design. To propose a system of communal representation is to grant to the cause of racial separatism the argument of constitutional validity and to concede to such elements of social disorganisation a victory which few Guianese would be prepared to accept as inevitable. To refuse to assist the force of an evil is not necessarily to ignore its potential danger; very often it is the surest method of ensuring its defeat. The Commission has faced the problem with courage, and many generations of Guianese may well be grateful for the 'optimism' of their decision.*

I recall this here because, while Guyana has not attained the aspirations of its national motto, the shared heritage I have narrated has trumped the divisiveness of the history of slavery and indenture and there is emerging, admittedly all too slowly, a multiracial society in which the oneness of being Guyanese is gradually prevailing over the separateness of the past. Not everyone will share this summation; but in the glimpses of my global life that this book offers I suggest that there shines the light of an identity not shaded by the past. Guyana has to ensure that that light continues to shine.

For one thing, the offspring of slavery and indenture are not Guyana's only people. Its original people, the Amerindians are now between 10 and 15 per cent of the population. And there were others who were brought in quasi indenture: Portuguese from Madeira, Chinese from Canton. Their offspring are part of Guyana's six peoples – as are the ever increasing numbers of mixed race who adorn our multi-racial society. I am one such; and my children and grandchildren even more so. Guyana's national motto must be Guyana's living credo. If the children of slavery and indenture in particular do not ensure that the oneness of their beginnings smothers any temptations to separateness, they will not do justice to the generations, their forbears, who bore the burdens of the past.

In the over 60 years since I wrote to *The Times*, those temptations have not been entirely smothered. Political leaders in particular bear a special responsibility to inspire, motivate and encourage Guyana's people to ensure that they are. The colonisers imposed on Guyana a policy of racial division as an instrument of control. Some of the leaders who replaced them adopted the same policy for their own political ends; a few even proposed partition. All this has left the country as one nation in name, and one people save only in politics. All Guyanese must summon the joint history of struggle to inform the joint future of prosperity to which they aspire. This is why I have begun this book with glimpses of that past – reminders of a shared heritage that compel a future shared in harmony.

PART II

BECKONING WORLDS

CHAPTER 5

Starting Out

It is conventional wisdom rigorously imparted to young people that they should develop clear goals in their lives and earnestly pursue them. I do not doubt the rightness of this precept, and would not urge against it. I have to admit however to not ever having followed it myself – not by any conscious reasoned rejection; but simply by not being so oriented. I suppose that means I was rather casual about the future; but that too would be wrong. The truth, as it so often is, was more complicated. As a young man, I took my cue to the future from my father, without any vestige of demurral or resentment. It was, of course, a different time – the 1940s. I did not grow up in a culture that asserted the right of the young 'to do their own thing'. Paternal guidance was not confused by us with unwanted dictation. It was a natural process, and save in some special situations would be the normal experience of my generation.

And, in my case, there was another factor reinforcing the absence of self-assertion. My father was my teacher too. He was in fact an acknowledged pioneer educator held in high repute in the community – the kind of person to whom many a parent came for advice about the future pathway their own children might pursue." 'J.I.' would know best", was an environment that enveloped me. And from the earliest time I can recall any mention of my future, it was always in a context of my father's assertion that 'Sonny will do law'. I took that as settled. Looking back, I suppose my meek acceptance would have been reinforced by the lack of options for me in any kind of professional pursuit. I had not done science in any serious way and mathematics was never a strong suit. In a colonial context, where medicine or law were the safest routes to professional self-employment, that did not leave me many options with which to flirt. 'J.I.' did know best.

Of course, that assumed I would do well enough to qualify for University abroad and that the family's finances could see me through – neither of which could be taken for granted. In the West Indies at that time, and quite prominently in British Guiana, standards of secondary education right up to the level of University entrance were high, certainly as high as in England. But there the educational system ended. In 1946 and 1947, when I did my 'A' Levels, there was one Scholarship available for University training in Britain – for the entire Colony; and that was the pattern throughout most of the West Indies. In 1946, I passed my 'A' levels in English, History and Latin. In 1947 – my final 'A' Level year- when I should theoretically have had my best shot at the Guyana Scholarship there were others doing Pure and Applied Mathematics and Latin. I assessed my chances of being first in the Colony, as minimal. I abandoned its pursuit and spent my final year at Queen's College in Georgetown co-editing the School's Annual Magazine (with Frank Pilgrim) and taking part in a joint production with the counterpart girl's school (Bishop's High) of *'A Midsummer Night's Dream'* – and doing 'Economics' as a single 'A' Level subject on the side. I have always been grateful for my father's wisdom in not insisting on another course. It was a very satisfying year; not a wasted one. It even included touring with a Queen's College cricket team to Barbados (photograph below) – my first trip beyond Guiana's shores.

British colonialism was not notable for its advancement of tertiary education; colonial administrators seemed to regard it as antithetical to their mission. So, in the West Indies, as elsewhere in the 'Empire', Africa in particular, tertiary education, like decolonisation itself, was a post-war development. The University of the West Indies, (initially, the University College of the West Indies) admitted its first undergraduates in 1948; and then they were restricted to medicine and natural science, which were admittedly the areas of greatest need. Law was not to start as a discipline at UWI until 1970 by which time I had already qualified in London, served in the Legal Department in British Guiana and could actually lend a hand in designing and launching the Law Faculty at the University and its attendant Law Schools. It has always been a matter of much personal pride that I should have been allowed to serve the University as its Chancellor for 14 years (between 1989 and 2003) and to have been dignified as 'Chancellor Emeritus' when I left.

The process that took me to London and back is worth recalling mainly for its reminders of the nature of that unique time of overlap between the fading of Britain's colonial passion and the strengthening of West Indian ambition for local autonomy. In 1947, I had my minimum requirement for University entrance in Britain – four 'A' Level passes – nothing more. The process for entry from British Guiana was an application to the Colonial Office through the local Education Department. It was the Colonial Office who did the processing in those early years after the War and secured placement for 'colonial scholars'. And, of course, it was my father who handled the process at the Georgetown end. We were notified in due course that I had secured entrance to the University of Leicester. I don't know what I had expected. With my four 'A' level passes I had certainly never aspired to Oxford or Cambridge. I was content with having got into University. My father had explained to me his hope that I would have a broader University education than the strict discipline of law; that I would read history and only after that law. And this was to be worked out with the University.

I have admitted to being without goals; but in this I was not my father's son. All his life he had been driven by goals and by the need for personal betterment through their attainment. Among these was the desire to be a lawyer – the one profession that was attainable through study locally and at home and only minimal presence at the Inns of Court in London. By 1942 he had been lured by the Colony's Governor, Sir Gordon Lethem, a liberal Scotsman, to give up education – he was at the time Principal of his own Secondary School, the Modern Educational Institute – and to join the Civil Service in a senior capacity in the newly established Labour Department, bringing to it his by then widely acknowledged skills as a conciliator. The war was raging; peace on the industrial front was a priority even in small West Indian colonies. 'J.I.' rapidly made a name as a peacemaker in the sugar and bauxite industries and more widely, becoming eventually the Commissioner of Labour – Head of the Department – the first 'local' man to do so.

Meanwhile, he kept pursuing his goal of becoming a lawyer. He joined the Inns of Court as an overseas student and studied by correspondence courses through Wolsey Hall. Over a number of years he sat and passed the specific subjects in Part 1 of the Bar examinations. As I said earlier, when I went to London in 1947 to study Law, my father went with me. He came not as an escort but fulfilling his own life-long ambition to be a lawyer himself. He had already over the years, amid all his other preoccupations, done most of the first part of the Bar examinations in British Guiana. In the six months it took me to settle down in London and tackle one subject at the Bar, he had passed his finals. I was 19; he was 44. He hardly practised law, and I would guess that he was a better teacher than he would ever have been a practising lawyer; but he had fulfilled that driving urge for further education – for betterment, for fulfilment of potential. And that was typical of his generation.

My father's example of self-improvement had inspired others – among them a cousin, Ronald Jailal, who was 12 years my senior and who had grown up with us and joined the Civil Service after School. He soon joined my father in writing the Part 1 Bar Examinations over the years, and like him was ready for the final stretch in 1947. Ronald was later to become a much respected Judge in British Guiana. The three of us travelled on the *SS Enid* – a cargo boat which took a few passengers – to Liverpool in late October of that year – already late for the University term. It was a tedious voyage, lightened only by Ronald's sense of humour – much of it at the expense of a rather old-fashioned female passenger from Guyana's white establishment who insisted on standing to attention whenever 'God Save the King' was played on the radio before the BBC news. We lost a rudder in a storm off the Azores and had to put in at the port of Funchal. It was a bitterly cold London that eventually welcomed us on 20th November; but one bedecked with flags and warmed by an enveloping air of celebration. Forty years later, I was to remind Prince Philip at an Anniversary Dinner in London that I had arrived in the capital on his wedding day, sequestering the flags as my welcome.

We stayed in modest rooms in Brunswick Square, learning how to keep warm under layers of clothing and with an unbroken flow of shillings to keep the gas fire alight. It was well before the days of central heating – at least in Brunswick Square. That night, or it could be the next, we had a visitor. My father had a close 'school-days' friend from Georgetown who had qualified in medicine in London many years earlier, Philip Jaikaran - the eldest son of a well-known Georgetown family and a cousin of Ronald's. Philip had remained in England through the war years and was now a highly respected surgeon. He was a redoubtable Londoner. After greetings and reminiscences among my elders the conversation got around to me and Philip asked his friend where I would be going to read law. My father explained about Leicester. I have never forgotten the explosion that followed. "Good God, Jimmy," bellowed Philip, "you cannot do that to the boy. He must remain in London". I had the feeling he might have said the same thing had Dad said 'Oxford'. His point was the importance of being in the metropolis. My life changed in that moment.

It turned out anyway that I could not then study History at Leicester and stay on to do Law. We talked with the Colonial Office about alternatives; the term had started and nothing seemed possible. Exeter University entered the frame briefly. But it became clear that it would be better for me to do some Part I subjects at Gray's Inn and on the strength of my four 'A' Levels (which amounted to an 'Inter BA') to try to enter Second Year Law the following year at a College of London University. King's College, London, to my great relief, and some surprise, accepted me. I had had an interview with the eminent and rather fearsome Dean of the College, Professor Harold Potter, who had a monocle which in a practiced routine he let fall occasionally and caught before it could shatter – by which time his visitor was completely nonplussed. I remember him asking me trenchantly: "Why do you want to do Law?" Beyond stupefaction, I do not remember what I answered – the facts would have been just too much. I told my Mother when I got home that King's could be taken off the list of possibilities. My mother had joined us in London with my sister, Sita, who enrolled in a hairdressing course. We had all moved into a small furnished house in Clapham.

Father and son (1946); undergraduate at King's (1950)

King's College, London, sits between the Embankment and the Strand, and in 1948 an 'invisible menders' and a wine bar were on either side of the College's wrought iron gates on the Strand. Beyond the gates, in what was the forecourt of the College, was a colossal bomb crater, larger than anything I had ever seen. The offices of the Faculty of Law occupied rooms above the 'invisible menders' and looked out onto the crater. I suppose that was one of my first lessons in London – that learning did not demand ancient towers or gilded campuses. Today, however, with the ravages of the war undone, King's College is an ornament of the Strand. The invisible menders and the wine bar have gone – as has the bomb crater – and the College has expanded to take in the east wing of Somerset House. Lectures in Law were on an inter-collegiate basis with the London School of Economics and University College; so we shared a larger community of students and lecturers.

Despite the less than inspiring surroundings, the atmosphere of learning at King's electrified me. Almost from the beginning, my attitude to scholarship was transformed. I had not come to King's trailing clouds of scholastic achievement. I was to do my best work at University. I was not a bookworm by disposition; but my situation was conducive to study. There was no Campus and no Hall of Residence for me. I lived in 'digs' in the suburbs. I took a small part in Student Union activities; but my principal interest was in the Photographic Society – of which I became Secretary. I remember now our puritanical approach to the arrival of 'colour film' on the market. It was retrograde. We would continue to pursue our laborious dye transfer process. We did not hold out for long. I had enjoyed photography from the beginning and was proud of my photographs of the 1948 Olympics in London having managed to get tickets for the Stadium events – at Wembley. My ritual travel to College was the 'Underground' from Morden on the Northern Line to the Strand (no more a Station) and a walk up the Strand to King's – and back again. In effect, I commuted.

The Olympic flame at Wembley (1948)

When I went to London in 1975, in very different circumstances, one of my very first 'honours' was to be made a Fellow of King's College. It was a particularly heart-warming moment for the boy who did that walk up the Strand to King's so many times so many years before. And, later, I was to be just as proud of my membership of the Board of King's. With modesty but equal pride I must record that King's has erected a collage of some of its graduates over the centuries whose faces now look onto the Strand from the northern façade of the College, and that mine is among them – between Lord Owen (David) and Michael Morpurgo – the whole cavalcade led by the 1st Duke of Wellington who founded King's. In 2010, I took a delighted granddaughter, India Hennessy, to see it.

I have often reflected on that moment in 1947 when Philip Jaikaran's outburst in Brunswick Square shaped my future as if I was about to take a wrong turning in life and was deflected compulsively by wise intervention. Much of my life has been like that, with unexpected events taking a decisive hand in the path I would travel.

I did well in my LL.B. I was second in the University, and the boy who was first was from King's. What is more, his was the only 'First'. It was explained to me that I had missed out on a 'First' because I had done my first year externally. I was bitterly disappointed and that steeled my resolve to do my Master's. No one in British Guiana had yet secured an LL.M. It would make up for that missed 'First'. But there were formidable difficulties – mainly financial. My parents had struggled to keep me in London to see me through Law. I simply could not ask them to cover another two years – which the LL.M would involve. And, well as I had done, it was not a time of Scholarships, although the College was keen that I should stay on.

Then, out of the blue, came a most unusual solution – or, at least, a possible one. I saw – as I recall, in *The Economist* – an advertisement by the Colonial Office of what was called a new Colonial Legal Probationership Scheme. I remember the tone, if not the actual words of the notice, to this day. The British Government was seeking to attract to the Colonial Legal Service 'a new type of Barrister'. To this end, a chosen candidate with a good degree would receive from the Colonial Office a modest stipend for a period of two years during which time he would be required to serve periods of 'pupillage' in London in the Chambers of practicing Barristers – one year in 'Chancery' Chambers, the other in 'Common Law' Chambers. The Scheme would pay the pupillage fees. In return, the 'Probationer' would give a commitment to serve for a minimum of three years anywhere in the Colonial Legal Service at the end of the Probationership. I must have jumped for joy; but sober reflection kicked in. Was this intended for the likes of me? Or for English Barristers who traditionally staffed the Colonial Legal Service – though, ironically, less so in the West Indies than elsewhere. The College urged me to apply, whatever my misgivings. I did so, and was successful. I was awarded a Colonial Legal Probationership.

This was manna from heaven. The stipend, I believe, was around thirty pounds a month – certainly far in excess of my allowance from home over the last three years. Moreover, the pupillage requirement was a huge opportunity which few lawyers from the colonies enjoyed – apprenticeship in the practice of the law for which the University degree or even the Bar examinations did not prepare the English law graduate. But, of course, best of all, the two years would allow me to do my LL.M – which did not require daytime lectures. I could not have asked for more. I didn't give much thought to the commitment of three years in the Colonial Legal Service – it would surely be in the West Indies.

There were still some hurdles. Probationers were expected to find their pupil masters – Barristers who would take them on as pupils. I knew of none; I was not preparing myself as my English colleagues were for practice in England. I turned to the Colonial Office. Sir Kenneth Roberts-Wray was the Legal Adviser of the Colonial Office and I appealed for guidance. I was reminded that finding Chambers was my responsibility; but Sir Kenneth was kind and called his friend Dingle Foot (not yet Sir Dingle) and asked whether he would consider having me in his Chambers. He could not have helped me better. Dingle Foot, the brother (as he often reminded me, the 'elder brother') of Sir Hugh Foot, then Governor of Jamaica, later Lord Caradon, was then a major figure in British politics. He was Chairman of the Liberal Party, Head of the Observer Trust, a towering figure on British television, but most of all, for me, a leading practitioner at the Privy Council Bar.

Dingle Foot was a man of rare quality; a 'liberal' in the truest sense of the word; an internationalist to the core; a passionate humanitarian, anti-imperialist in thought and action; and a caring man. I felt at home in his Chambers as he told me of Sir Kenneth's introduction of me. His response was unequivocal. Of course, he would have me as a pupil; but there was not a place right now. He suggested that I do my year in Chancery Chambers first and then, the next year, 1952, come to 2, Paper Buildings. He had thought of everything. He said he had contacted Sir Henry Salt Q.C., the Head of highly respected Chancery Chambers in Lincoln's Inn. Sir Henry could offer me a place in his Chambers immediately as a pupil of Hugh Francis – later a Treasurer of Gray's Inn. I spent a year in Hugh Francis' Chambers at 9 Old Square, Lincoln's Inn.

Hugh Francis, my pupil Master, encouraged me to write the Gray's Inn Examination for the prestigious Arden Scholarship. He did not tell me at the time that he had himself won the Scholarship in 1931. To the 'Arden' had been added, two years earlier, the Atkin Scholarship. It was a monetary award for pupils in Chambers; but the prestige was even more important. I did not get either; but I must have come close, since the Inn decided that year to award a special 'Arden and Atkin Prize' – valued then at the not insubstantial sum of £30. The Prize was awarded to me. That was 1951. As far as I am aware, it has not been awarded since. I was naturally disappointed; but Hugh Francis was quite upset; it was only later that I understood why. I had long wanted an electric razor; I spent the prize-money on a good one – a 'Kobler' made in Switzerland; and of course I cherish to this day the one and only Arden and Atkin Prize awarded to me.

Paper Buildings and Old Square

To the uninitiated, let me explain that the Chancery sphere of English law practice is regarded as the less flamboyant part of the law: wills, trusts, corporate affairs and such like; but assuredly the more intellectually exacting aspects of law. Common Law practice involves criminal law and such civil law issues as contract disputes, defamation, matrimonial issues and exotic appellate work like Privy Council cases – though the latter is restricted to a few specialist Chambers, of which Dingle Foot's was one. As it turned out, doing the Chancery pupillage first was absolutely the right order. I came to 2 Paper Buildings in 1952 with a solid legal apprenticeship behind me, and a readiness for the broader practice that lay ahead and was to continue as in an unbroken stream from Dingle's Chambers. Privy Council Appeals were all from Commonwealth countries – many, like my own, still colonies.

Nothing was more emblematic of this Commonwealth link than the connection of the Chambers with Herbert Chitepo. Herbert was a pupil in the Chambers in 1953 – the year I left; but he had been around it while I was there. He was in quasi exile from white-ruled Rhodesia. I had got to know him well. He was the first African from Southern Rhodesia to qualify as a Barrister and he went back there in 1954 after his pupillage in the Chambers. In Harare, he defended many African nationalists in court and was Legal Adviser to Joshua Nkomo at the Southern Rhodesia Constitutional Conference in Salisbury in 1961. In constant peril of being detained by the Ian Smith regime, he went into voluntary exile in Tanganyika (not yet 'Tanzania') in 1962.

The next year, in the wake of the Sithole/Nkomo split, Herbert Chitepo became the first President of ZANU – having sided with Sithole. For ten years, then living in Zambia, he was the respected face of the Liberation Movement in world capitals. But in a particularly dark period of liberation politics in 1975, Herbert Chitepo was assassinated by a car bomb outside his home in Lusaka. Following his death, there was extensive blood-letting between ZANU's ethnic and ideological factions and a comparatively unknown ZANU militant emerged as Herbert Chitepo's successor – Robert Mugabe: the man with whom I would have so much to do in the making of Zimbabwe. It has never been definitively established who killed Chitepo – Rhodesia intelligence, or Zanu activists. However, Mugabe was certainly the political beneficiary of his death. I was later to work with Herbert Chitepo's widow, Victoria, as a Minister in Mugabe's Government. I have often wondered how different my own experience as Commonwealth Secretary-General in the 1980s might have been had my interactions then been with my fellow pupil of 2 Paper Buildings; or what Zimbabwe itself would have been had Herbert Chitepo lived to become its first Prime Minister.

There is another continuous line, invisible then, stretching from those days in London, that was to emerge later in life. When I made my application for the Colonial Legal Probationership I assumed that I was the only 'colonial' scholar who was doing so. Many years later, when I was a Legal Officer in the Federation of the West Indies, I found out that the Solicitor-General of the Federation, Harvey DaCosta, my senior colleague in the Chambers of the Federal Attorney-General, had shared my experience. A Rhodes Scholar from Jamaica, Harvey had read law at Oxford and, not ready for home, had been attracted by the same Colonial Office advertisement I had seen. He applied for and got the Probationership, did his two years in Chambers, and was posted to Jamaica. Neither of us knew of each other in those same years of pupillage, but they were to lead us both to Trinidad – the Federation's Capital, eventually as Attorney-General and Assistant Attorney-General respectively of The West Indies. The Colonial Office had been casting their net more widely than I had thought. Later, Harvey and I would go into practice in Kingston, Jamaica, setting up a London style set of Chambers, hitherto unknown in the Region – drawing, of course, on that unknowingly shared experience of Chambers in England. Intriguingly, Harvey had done a part of his pupillage under Leslie Scarman – the later Lord Scarman I was long after to succeed as Chancellor of Warwick University.

There is a footnote to my side of this shared experience without which this story would not be complete. Late in 1952, as my Probationership and my year of pupillage with Dingle Foot, were ending, I received a formal letter from the Colonial Office reminding me of this and notifying me that I had been posted for three years as a Magistrate in Kenya. I was shocked, both by the office and the place. The 'Mau Mau' crisis was at its height in Kenya, and I had visions of being an outsider adjudicating crimes in a colonial conflict. I went to Dingle and put my predicament. I made it clear that I accepted my commitment for three years of service; but was this really what my pupillage best equipped me for?

Dingle was horrified. His first thought was to call his friend Sir Kenneth at the Colonial Office and plead for a less invidious posting. But he had a fall-back. He was willing to offer me a permanent seat in the Chambers in my own right. We would have to repay the Government all they had spent over the two years of my Probationership. He would do that himself, and I could repay him over time. It was magnanimity beyond measure. The offer of a seat in the leading Privy Council Chambers was the best I could wish for if I was going to live and practise in London. It was both generous and complimentary. But could I repay my parents thus? A three-year posting elsewhere was one thing, but making a decision to live in London, not to go back home, was quite another. I thanked him profusely, but explained the family angle. We decided to try the first option of pleading with Sir Kenneth.

But Dingle did not plead; he called his friend and exploded. It was a little like Philip Jaikaran in Brunswick Square five years earlier. "How could you squander this young man's talents in doing your dirty work in Kenya? I will not allow it. He is conscious of his commitments; but before he is consigned to Kenya I will repay all you have spent on him and give him a seat in my Chambers". That was the nature and tone of his explosion. I trembled a little. But Sir Kenneth merely said that he would look into it, and that meanwhile I should do nothing. I waited. Eventually, toward year-end, I received another letter cancelling the first one and appointing me to the office of Crown Counsel in the Chambers of the Attorney-General in British Guiana. I could not have been more pleased, or more grateful – especially to my Master in Chambers. Again, that wise intervention. What would my life have been had I started as a Magistrate in Kenya at the height of 'Mau Mau'?

Beyond all that there was a more compelling urge to get back to the West Indies. It started with my basic wish to find the means to do my Master's and developed through the nature of that post-graduate experience. With the chance that the Probationership allowed, I chose to do the LL.M by dissertation – and my subject was all important. It was *'Constitutional Aspects of Federalism in the British West Indies'*. So, over the two years of pupillage, I was simultaneously immersed in the issue that most occupied political minds in the region – a federation of the West Indian colonies. The issue itself was well advanced when I settled my subject, but almost nothing had been done by way of academic work, historical or comparative or of a functional nature. I would be breaking new ground. But, my efforts would not be research for academe only. By then, I was myself consumed with conviction that this was the right constitutional path for the West Indies to follow toward decolonisation.

I was just over 21, when I embraced the cause of federation – a stripling law student from British Guiana. How did it happen? It must have started with identity. I came to London as a Guyanese with little knowledge of what we now call 'the Caribbean'. A family visit to Trinidad and that schoolboy cricket team visit to Barbados were my sole acquaintance with the wider region. But as with everyone else from the region in London, while that homeland tag remained, a larger identity subsumed it; I became a West Indian. It is as with a man from Yorkshire who is a 'Yorkshireman' in England, but an Englishman in France. England made you a West Indian because the logic of your historic oneness made it treat you as one. And you began to understand and accept that oneness. The petty insularities of home were put away in face of the need to occupy a space in the metropolis. For a young man brought up in the naturalness of a multicultural environment, the larger West Indian identity was an easy fit. Federation, for me, from the beginning, was about the oneness of our West Indian home. Sixty and more years later – by whatever name we call that unity now – it still is about that oneness. Thirty-five years ago (as I write) I expressed this candidly as I received an honorary degree from the University of the West Indies on its St Augustine Campus in Trinidad:

> *In that sense of being that derives from within and is assured and unchanging, I have been a West Indian from the first moments of my rational awakening. The land of my birth, the country that I was privileged to bring to sovereign statehood, commands my devotion and my loyalty, but in a further dimension of belonging, the West Indies is, also, my native land.*

Those first moments of rational awakening had been stirred by my first encounter with Norman Manley of Jamaica – Michael Manley's father. In 1950, Manley was in London and came to the LSE to give a lunchtime talk to West Indian students at London University. He was already the leading figure in the 'federal movement' which was then for him inseparable from the thrust for constitutional reform in the West Indian colonies. He was Jamaica's leading lawyer and a polished and passionate advocate. I had already been moved by his speech two years earlier at the Montego Bay Conference of 1947 in Jamaica – the prelude to the federal negotiations in which I would later play a part. Norman Manley said there, in words characteristically eloquent and penetrating:

> *How to marry expectation with reality; how to create a larger field for ambition; how to overcome the disadvantages of being too small to be heard in a world where silence means stagnation; how to make a real culture and a real unity out of all the richness of our diversity, how to show the world that differences of origin and colour can come together on a level of tolerance and oneness; how to overcome distance and poverty: these are the challenges that federation faces and may meet to make a worthy end.*

It was one thing to read these words as I had done; it was another thing altogether to hear Norman Manley speak of his vision of the future West Indian nation that federation would fashion. I was totally captivated by the man and the cause. My academic work in federalism was now suffused with a passion for its utility to the future of the West Indies. His talk with us that lunchtime in the London School of Economics was redolent of something else he had said at Montego Bay:

> *I put first, and I put above all other things, the desire to see in the future a West Indian nation standing shoulder to shoulder with all other nations of the world. Is that a large ambition? I say it is the smallest ambition that responsible people can utter in the face of history. I say that we in the West Indies can prove one great thing to the world – and that is that a people, none of whom are native to these territories, all of whom have for one reason or another been torn from their countries and brought*

here, partly willingly, partly by compulsion or by distress in their own homelands, that we with our many strands, from Africa, from India, from China, from an assorted variety of European territories – we are capable of welding the power of that diversity into a united nation.

A major part of my life has been spent in pursuit of that ambition. The journey began in earnest that lunchtime.

Norman Manley

At the end of the LL.M process, I was awarded the Degree 'with a Mark of Distinction'. I had made up for the missed 'First'. But, more pertinent to the future, I was the only West Indian lawyer now specifically equipped for the legal challenges of federalism. My personal agony was that my own country, British Guiana, was excluding itself from the federation. Nevertheless, as I returned to British Guiana early in 1953, it was with a sense of fulfilment in my legal studies, but most especially in my capacity to contribute to the fast developing process of federalism. region-wide.

And as relevant as anything else to that future, I was returning to 'BG' with a wife and infant daughter who, with siblings to come, would be my anchor in the very peripatetic life that lay ahead. Quite early in my London years I had met Lois King, a lovely young woman from the English Midlands who was training to be a State Registered Nurse at St Helier's Hospital in Carshalton, Surrey – the same area outside London in which I had found lodgings with a most caring English couple (Basil and Elsie Aperios) with no children of their own, as a live-in student. But Lois and I did not meet in Carshalton; we met in London at a function welcoming new overseas students, and only afterwards discovered that we were neighbours – both of us students away from home. It was 1949, just in time for my modest 21st birthday party on 3 October at which, of course, Lois 'cut the cake' with me (photo below). Over sixty years since, I still have the gift she gave me: *'The Albatross Book of Living Verse'*, inscribed: *"To wish you happiness on your 21st birthday"* – a wish and later a promise. I learnt many years later that, on receiving the photographs in Georgetown, my mother said reflectively: *"that is the girl Sonny will marry"*. I had no such thought then, but so, in due course, I did, in 1952 – after I had done my Master's and Lois had completed her SRN.

Over my years at King's, Lois and I were constant companions, exploring the Surrey countryside and sharing each other's company, and love, on the shoestring allowances we each had. I would not swap that time for the 'Facebook' life of today's young people. The letters we wrote each other then, over three years, may not be 'on line', but they are a precious memento which would never have been composed were we 'texting' each other. Susan, our first born, arrived two months before we left England on 14 April 1953 by the *'S.S. Ariguani'* for my posting in British Guiana and the global life that awaited us.

Lois and Susan on the *S.S. Ariguani*

CHAPTER 6

Regional Demands

British Guiana was not Kenya, and Cheddi Jagan was not Kenyatta; but my assumption of duty as Crown Counsel in Georgetown coincided with a torrid political crisis which was to lead to the suspension of the 'BG' Constitution by the British Government only 6 months after I had assumed office. Those events are by now extensively documented and the analyses vary between glorification of Jagan as a valiant nationalist crushed by imperialist machinations, and excoriation of him as a naïve Marxist who allowed the cause of local autonomy to be sacrificed to Cold War politics. The net result was to set back Guyana's independence by four years and to leave a legacy of ethnic polarisation in the country's politics.

But these domestic issues and encounters are not what these memoirs, *Glimpses of a Global Life,* are about. British Guiana's internal politics justify monographs of their own (which have not been lacking); but for me they would not be memoirs so much as commentaries. Certainly, over the years ahead – first as Crown Counsel then as Legal Draftsman, I became more and more occupied with the rise and fall of federalism in the West Indies than with Guyana's constitutional enigmas – and this despite the fact that as early as 1951 the British Guiana legislature had resolutely opposed joining in a federation.

By 1954, however, with the constitutional stalemate in British Guiana persisting, the Government was less opposed to federation and agreed to be an Observer at the 'federal negotiations' which were then occupying the region quite rigorously. I was assigned the rarefied role of 'Adviser' to British Guiana's 'Observers'. This meant that I was present at the principal Conferences in the negotiations between 1954 and 1958. My experience with federalism (though essentially academic) ensured that I was drawn – almost in a personal capacity – into the core negotiations. This reached a high point when the Standing Federation Committee was established in 1956 to settle the final details of the federation. Guyana was still an Observer, and when the SFC appointed a Legal Committee to finalise the Federal Constitution I was invited to join it. In Sir John Mordecai's authoritative account, *'The West Indies: The Federal Negotiations'*, he described the Legal committee thus:

> *Meantime, off-stage, the Legal Committee chaired by Mr Douglas Judah and combining the Colonial Office experts with West Indian Attorneys-General, threaded their way through the draft Constitution in day and night sessions.*

The photograph of the Legal Committee above is testament to my very satisfying involvement in this crucial stage of the Federation's establishment. Though not an Attorney-General, and still a mere Adviser to an Observer, my work on federalism in London – and my obvious personal commitment to the federal project – had earned me a place of significance at its birth. When the Federation was actually established in 1958 I was appointed to the position of *First Legal Draftsman* in the Office of the Federal Attorney- General. I was there only eighteen months, working in what were the 'stables' of *Whitehall* – the initial Headquarters of the Federal Government in Trinidad – when a crisis in the Legal Department in Georgetown led to my being appointed Solicitor-General of British Guiana in 1959. But I was not there long before I returned to the Federal Government as Assistant Attorney-General in 1961 working with the new Attorney-General, Harvey DaCosta Q.C. It has always been a matter of quiet gratification that the rest of the West Indies never, at any level, treated me as anything but a West Indian in those early days when British Guiana so ingloriously excluded itself from the West Indian struggle for federalism.

But the Federation was not to survive. It was formally dissolved on 31 May 1962 – the actual day on which it was to become an independent member state of the Commonwealth. It was a terrible moment for me, made worse by the fact that the Federation had died as a result of a referendum called in Jamaica by the same Norman Manley who had so fired my passion for federalism in the West Indies twelve years before at the LSE in London, and who now as Premier of Jamaica would take his country to a separate Independence. My disillusionment with West Indian politicians was not helped by the position adopted by Dr Eric Williams, the Premier of Trinidad and Tobago: the sham arithmetic that '1 from 10 left 0' – effectively ensuring that nothing could be salvaged from the ashes of the Jamaica referendum. Like Manley, Williams took his country to a separate independence – both, in a matter of months. It was ironic that I should be asked, in the interest of a tidy unwinding of the Federation, to stay on after the formal dissolution on 31 May 1962 as Legal Adviser to the Commissioner (Sir Stephen Luke) for the Dissolution of the Federation.

It was a low point in my regional journey. I had expected more of West Indian political leaders – especially of Manley and Williams, who were without question the two most erudite politicians of the Region. I had not lost faith in federation or in West Indian unity by whatever name; but I was angry that a failure of political leadership had shattered the dream of thousands of West Indians for unity in governance responsive to their common identity. And I was, of course, ashamed of my own country for standing aside from the federal project, convinced as I was, and am, that enlightened leadership from British Guiana would have saved federalism.

I will come back to this story of Caribbean hope and effort and disappointment; a story of faith forever challenged; a story of thwarted identity – and of my part in it all. At the time, I wanted to get away as far as I could from the West Indian scene. I left Trinidad on 30 August 1962 – the day before Independence. I could not join in a rejoicing which for me was the embodiment of a West Indian disaster. With my family, I left for Boston where on a Guggenheim Fellowship to the Harvard Law School I would revive my flagging spirits by reminders of the example of other federal founding fathers who had overcome trials much greater than ours, and more traumatic, through sustained vision and leadership.

That year in Boston was one of my happiest ever. I was enrolled in the Law School which was a delight in itself with Faculty that included legal giants like Erwin Griswold, Paul Freund, Arthur Sutherland, Derek Bok, Milton Katz, Roger Fischer, Albert Sacks and, rather special to me, Joseph Leninger, with whom, as a Guggenheim scholar, I was specially engaged. Because it was a feature of my Fellowship that I was not to be "encumbered by examination anxieties" I could pace myself. I attended the Lectures I chose; and I wrote to my own timetable – a paper I eventually called *'Constitutionalism in the West Indies: Two forms of a Bill of Rights'*. It was in essence an appraisal, against the backdrop of US Supreme Court jurisprudence, of the prospects for 'judicial review' under the new and different West Indian Independence Constitutions. It ended with these words:

> *If there is some truth in these generalised propositions of the experience of judicial review in the United States, we must surely be on guard against dewy-eyed optimism when appraising its chances of success in the more limited area of manoeuvrability offered by the very different West Indian constitutional arrangements.*

It was ten tears since I had left London and I had lived a satisfying but heavily demanding professional life. The Guggenheim was a sabbatical. Beyond the files which occupied the previous seven years of my life, I could read books again – among them I recall specifically *'The Holmes-Laski Letters'* which in some measure were appropriate to my new American experience after early years in London. And I saw more of the family than I had done for years. Lois who had grown to love the Caribbean was happy in Boston; and so were the children revelling in their changed environment and new excitements not yet a Caribbean experience – like Halloween, as the 1962 photograph below confirms.

I had more time with my camera again. The children (Susan and now Ian) spent a happy year in school in Belmont where we lived; Mark was only four, and too young for school. The sojourn left its own little marks: for months after we returned to the West Indies, Susan could not resist placing her hand on her heart (which she had learned at school in the fashion of Americans) when she stood for the playing of our own national anthem.

I had no idea what I would do after Harvard; but early into the Fellowship – before I could begin to worry, I received a letter from Philip Sherlock, the Vice Chancellor of the University of the West Indies. Philip Sherlock is remembered now as an icon of the University – indeed, of the Caribbean; but even then, in his stewardship of the University he was more than ordinarily respected in academic circles. His message was that the time had come for the University to plan for Law in its Curriculum. His idea was to approach the development gradually, starting with a Legal Research Unit which would be as well the planning workshop for the development of Legal Studies at the University. The Research Unit would be modest and be housed at the Mona Campus of the University in Jamaica. The University would provide accommodation on the Campus for the Head of the Unit who would be appointed at Senior Lecturer level. Would I be interested in the job?

I did not need to ponder long about it. It seemed tailor made to my situation. I realised, of course, that it could mean committing my future to academia; but with federalism entombed and private practice not within my purview, that left only judicial service or academia. The former I had already in Guyana declined as a pathway of boredom. I had not thought of academia because there was not yet Law teaching at UWI and I always assumed a career in the Region. But here was a real possibility. Moreover, it was exciting: planning and building for Law at the Regional level. I replied to Philip Sherlock expressing interest. His response was enthusiastic and he said we must take advantage of my presence in North America to visit Foundations which he knew would be interested in supporting the development of Law at UWI. He attached importance to their becoming acquainted with the person who would be heading the programme. In due course, the Vice Chancellor and I met in New York and visited the Ford and Carnegie Foundations with good effect. All was now set. I received shipping instructions for my belongings to Jamaica. It was July 1963; we were packed, our modest belongings labelled (for UWI), and ready to go to our new life in Jamaica.

Out of the blue, I had an emergency call and then a visit from Philip Sherlock. The arrangement had to be cancelled. He needed my understanding. Dr Eric Williams, the Prime Minister of Trinidad and Tobago had earlier 'assumed' the role of Pro-Chancellor of the University (an on-the-spot Chancellor, given Princess Alice's health and distance from the University). But Williams' concept of 'Pro Chancellor' was more hands-on than most would assume. Apparently, when Sherlock told him of his plans and my role in them he exploded.

"I am not having a Guyanese heading Law at UWI. Instead, I am going to ask Sir Hugh Wooding to head a Committee to design the Law Programme. Nothing will be done until they have reported. Cancel your arrangements with Ramphal". It was a forlorn Philip Sherlock who asked for my understanding. Although this was not in the purview of a Pro Chancellor, he could not fight Williams. Of course, I understood – both Williams' unworthy, but not uncommon, eruption, and Sherlock's helplessness. I understood; but I was shattered. To whom could I even talk?

From Harvard I had maintained contact with my federal colleague Harvey da Costa and I had told him in confidence of my plans. He was in the process of settling into private practice in Jamaica and was looking forward to my being at the Mona Campus quite close to where he lived. I wrote to Harvey for counsel in my predicament. He responded instantly – and rather differently from my expectation. He was outraged by Williams' actions; but he had encountered them before in the Federal negotiations and in Williams' dealings with the Federal Government. He went on: *"Come and join me in private practice in Jamaica; I am here, and you can help me set up a proper set of Chambers as we knew in London. Come on down to Jamaica as you planned; I will make all arrangements here. I can assure you of a welcome at the Bar"*. That was the purport of his response. It was a magnanimous offer, but I had not thought of private practice anywhere. All my professional life I had been a government lawyer. I wondered whether I could cope with the less sheltered space of private practice. But, if private practice, could there be any better way than in a Chambers situation with Harvey, respected as he was in Jamaica? Lois knew Harvey from Federal days in Trinidad and trusted and valued his friendship. Besides, where else? British Guiana was in political turmoil. Racial tensions were ascendant. If I was to stay in the Caribbean, as I wanted to, Jamaica in the context of Harvey's offer was irresistible.

I went to Jamaica with the intention of settling down. The family had been dragged behind me from British Guiana to Trinidad back to 'BG', back to Trinidad, to Boston and now Jamaica – all in ten years.

Jamaica was wonderfully hospitable to us at every level. Personally, over the years, I have never felt as much at home anywhere in the Caribbean as in Jamaica. The family was happy, too. But I suppose most important of all, I was received welcomingly by the legal profession in Jamaica. The terrors of being new to private practice were quickly banished in Harvey's Chambers at 201/2 Duke Street, Kingston. I was ten years from 'call' – a senior 'junior' in the profession – and, of course, without political affiliation, The leading 'silks' in Jamaica, apart from Harvey, were all politically branded. There was a niche at the Jamaica bar for someone like me. And I rapidly filled it. I enjoyed practice in Jamaica where I was well briefed by capable Solicitors. Practice was a joy; and it was well remunerated. For the first time in my life, we were not financially strapped. In the photograph below are my colleagues in Chambers: from the left – Norman Hill, Bruce Judah, Peter Judah, Harvey da Costa, 'Joey' Cools-Lartigue, myself and Robert Randall.

* * *

Alas! It was short-lived. In just over a year, without seeking to, I was on the move again. In 1964, the political turmoil in British Guiana, which had seen widespread violence with racial overtones, was quieted in the wake of a political settlement at a Constitutional Conference in London. General elections under a new system of proportional representation to which all parties had agreed, would lead to a substantially autonomous Government whose central task would be to lead the country to Independence. In the elections that followed, conducted under the authority of the British Governor, a Coalition of the Centre and Right Parties won a clear majority over the Leftist Party led by the Indo-Guianese, Cheddi Jagan. The winning Coalition was led by an Afro-Guianese lawyer Forbes Burnham and Peter D'Aguiar, a Portuguese businessman. Burnham became Premier. I had not known him save in the legal profession; indeed, my chief recollection of him was as counsel in a civil action we appeared in, when I was Solicitor-General, in which his client had sued the Director of Education for wrongful dismissal. He was a polished Q.C.; but I won the case. It was, perhaps, his chief recollection of me too. The mood in the country, and indeed in the Caribbean, was one of hope that 'BG's worst problems were ended and that the country could return to a constructive role within the region as an independent State. I shared that mood with West Indians beyond British Guiana.

The election was in December 1964. It was not long after that I received a personal call from the new Premier. He said that if 'our' country was to advance it had to break out of the racial politics that threatened it, and he wished to head a truly multi-racial Government. That was partly done with the Coalition with Peter D'Aguiar's 'United Force' party; but he needed to go further. He was calling me, he said, to invite me to become the country's Attorney-General, with a special responsibility for drafting the Independence Constitution. He told me that he did not intend to be his own lawyer, but to rely for legal advice on his Attorney-General. My first reaction was one of shock, and I did not conceal it.

I told Forbes Burnham that I had never dabbled in politics and I did not wish to do so now. His answer was that he was not asking me to do that. In fact, he said, he had talked with his Coalition partner and he too was keen that I should come. The Attorney-General would be a technocrat without political affiliation. I said that apart from such matters I was just settled into practice and was doing well financially for the first time in my life. Moreover, I felt a responsibility to Harvey who had opened these doors for me and would feel that I had let him down. But, critical, was the family, who were settled and happy. I could not think of such a move without their concurrence.

Forbes Burnham was not easily put off. He invited me to come down to Georgetown to feel the mood of hopefulness for myself and talk some more with him. I declined, saying it was too near to Christmas to leave the family. He countered with another invitation for me to come with my wife for New Year's Eve when we could talk some more. I promised to talk to her and get back to him. I told Harvey of the conversation; indeed, within the Chambers he was within earshot of it. He was saddened; but he said that perhaps it was a summons I could not decline. That thought had been nagging me from the first moment of Burnham's phone call. I talked to Lois and we agreed to go for New Year's Eve – but without commitment. We did; and of course Burnham agreed to all my conditions. I would not join his or any political Party. If I had to sit in the Legislature for technical reasons, it would be on the basis that I had no vote, and was answerable to no whip. We went back to Jamaica without giving him a final answer, but I believe that both he and I knew that it was a summons, not just from him, but from my country, that I could not refuse. Recently, the former Prime Minister of Jamaica, P.J. Patterson, reminded me that he was my courier nearly fifty years ago who took my letter of acceptance to Georgetown. It was one of the hardest decisions of my life and, of course, it was life-changing.

'BG's' *Daily Chronicle*, May 1965

I assumed office in Georgetown in May 1965 and was immediately immersed in regional affairs. Forbes Burnham, who I believed should have spoken out more clearly in support of federation in difficult earlier years, for that very reason came to office three years after the Federation's dissolution without 'federal' baggage. He immediately set about with his friend Errol Barrow, then Premier of Barbados, reinvigorating regional unity. I was a willing recruit, and one of my first roles was working on what became the Caribbean Free Trade Area Agreement signed at Dickenson Bay, Antigua, on 15 December 1965. Barrow had tried to salvage a Federation of the 'Little Eight': Barbados and the seven Leeward and Windward Islands of the British Caribbean, but gave up in frustration.

With Burnham in power in Georgetown, a Free Trade Agreement between Antigua, Barbados and British Guiana (CARIFTA) – inspired by Barrow, developed by Burnham and hosted by Vere Bird Snr of Antigua – seemed a more practical revival of unity. Burnham's idea never was a CARIFTA of three, and having engineered the deferral of the coming into force of the Agreement for a year (against Barrow's inclination), it fell to Guyana to lead the effort to bring the others on board – particularly Jamaica and Trinidad and Tobago. The legwork was mine. The hardest hurdle was Jamaica where the anti-federal Jamaica Labour Party (JLP) was in power, but the Jamaica Manufacturers Association was more hard-headed, and the Trade Minister, Robert Lightbourne, was less ideologically anti-regional than his Party. The Government yielded to pragmatism. I was back in Caribbean regionalism in a central way. But more of this later.

My main task over the next year was managing the independence process through drafting the Independence Constitution. From federal days, including the pre-federal Legal Committee, I was no stranger to the constitutional experts of the Colonial Office – particularly Sir Hamish McPetrie, a kindly and learned Scotsman – a successor to Sir Kenneth Roberts-Wray of my Legal Probationership days. Their help was invaluable and though much of the Constitution was conventional, we were innovative too. From the outset, Burnham wanted the independent Guyana, the new name of the country, to be a Republic, and this was of course agreeable to his leftist Opposition. It was his rightist Coalition Partner who would not have it. The compromise was to place in an annex to the Constitution all the amendments that would be required to turn it in into a republican Constitution, and have in the Constitution itself a clause that any time after five years from independence would allow those amendments to be activated by a simple parliamentary process. In effect, the Constitution promised the Republic of Guyana five years from independence. It was a unique device in Commonwealth experience.

In the same vein, the Constitution took the lead in the Caribbean in abolishing appeals to the Privy Council. It is one of the reasons why Guyana was an early champion of the Caribbean Court of Justice as the final appellate court of the Region. It was a good workman-like Constitution. I remain proud of it. It was the primary reason for my return; yet it was to become one of the principal areas of my disagreement with Burnham when he later wanted to go beyond the parliamentary Republic, for which the Constitution provided, to an Executive Presidency. The Constitution came into force on 26 May 1966. Guyana was an independent state, a member of the Commonwealth, a member of the international community; and I could be happy with my contribution to Guyana's organic instrument.

I had come back to an Attorney-General's Chambers that I had earlier helped to shape in my brief stint as Solicitor-General. I was supported in particular with the professionalism of Mohammed Shahabudeen and Brynmor Pollard still in place. They were both unique talents. Shahabudeen was a prodigy. He was a country boy from Essequibo who never went to University but achieved every relevant law degree of London University externally by correspondence courses: the B.A., LL.B, LL.M, Ph.D, LL.D Degrees – and his Bar examinations similarly. When he came to my notice he was languishing as a country magistrate, but had already done the LL.M. I lost no time in bringing him into the Attorney-General's Chambers, which he never left – eventually succeeding me as Attorney-General, and then going on to be a much admired Judge of the International Court of Justice in the Hague. He was truly learned; and never lost his quiet, retiring, methodical, and always industrious manner in his extraordinary transition from Essequibo to The Hague.

Brynmor Pollard's talents lay in another direction: in legal drafting. It is a scarce gift among lawyers; but I know from experience that it is one of the most professionally satisfying branches of legal work for the few who can embrace it. And to be a good Legal Draftsman, you had first to be a good lawyer. So much importance did I attach to legal drafting talent that I had his post upgraded to that of a High Court Judge when elevation to the Bench became Brynmor's logical promotion. He later became a respected member of the Inter-American Commission on Human rights. The routine work of the Attorney-General's Chambers was in good hands; which was just as well, as the end of my preoccupation with the Constitution ushered in a wholly new role for me – one that was to shape all of my future life beyond Guyana.

With Independence came 'External Relations', and for Guyana this was no token addition to governance. Burnham, as Prime Minister, kept the Foreign Affairs portfolio; but a Foreign Ministry had to be set up and a Foreign Service, however modest, established – and for Guyana there were substantive external relations to be attended to – unlike the case of most new countries. It was not long before Burnham asked me to take charge of this new field of governance. He would remain titular Foreign Minister. Would I manage the Foreign Ministry and our external relations generally? It was beyond our Agreement, but I was pleased by the prospect. What is more, it was a field I could enter without being drawn into domestic politics. In a sense, I was already in the field at the level of the Caribbean, with CARIFTA on its way and Guyana leading the process for its evolution into an economic community. That was the logical path back to Caribbean unity from which we had strayed with the break-up of the Federation; and this time Guyana was a player. Additionally, Georgetown was the early hub, with the regional Secretarial that would drive the process located in Guyana's Capital. I would be designated 'Attorney-General and Minister of State for External Relations'. My school-days friend, Rashleigh Jackson, later much respected in the international community as Guyana's Permanent Representative to the United Nations and thereafter as Foreign Minister, was Permanent Secretary of the fledgling Ministry. Together, we began the process of fashioning Guyana's foreign relations. In the photograph below are our first diplomats with me, including Sir John Carter, Shirley Field-Ridley, Sir Lionel Luckhoo, Winifred Gaskin, myself, Anne Jardim, Hubert Jack (Minister), Pat Thompson, E.R. Braithwaite and W.O.R. Kendall.

Guyana's first diplomats

* * *

Most new countries enter the international community without much by way of a road-map. Not so Guyana. As early as 1962 our neighbour to the West, Venezuela, had taken advantage of Guyana's pending Independence to try to reopen with Britain a long-settled border controversy involving more than half of Guyana's land area. It was a spurious and, in some ways, a sinister contention. Three months before Guyana's Independence, in early 1966, Britain invited the 'about to be independent' Guyana to join in its conversations with Venezuela. The outcome was the Geneva Agreement between Venezuela and the United Kingdom, to which on attaining independence, Guyana became an additional party. It was our first international foray; and Burnham and I attended. For me, as my life has unfolded, that was the beginning of its international phase – my global life.

Guyana entering the UN

Let me, therefore, say some more about this Venezuela issue. Guyana's boundary with Venezuela was formally settled over a hundred years ago by an International Court of Arbitration under a Treaty freely signed by Venezuela. It was the days of the Monroe Doctrine and the United States had pressured Britain into signing the Treaty under threat of war – so fierce was America as Venezuela's patron. That was 2nd February 1899. It was a Treaty to settle for all time the Boundary between Venezuela and Britain's colony of British Guiana. Venezuela and Britain undertook in solemn terms "to consider the results of the proceeds of the Tribunal of Arbitration as a full, perfect and final settlement of all the questions referred to the Arbitrators".

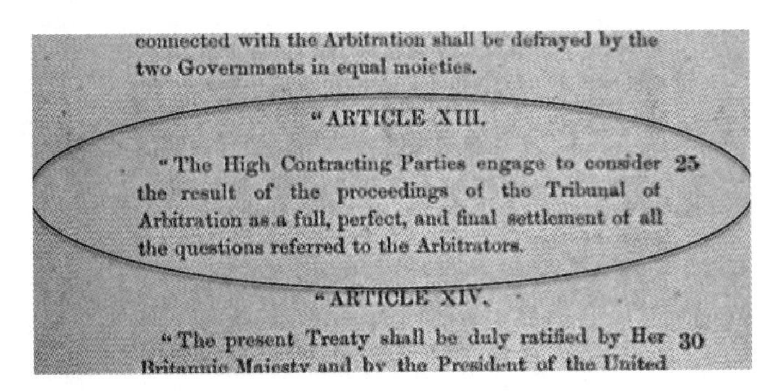

connected with the Arbitration shall be defrayed by the two Governments in equal moieties.

"ARTICLE XIII.

"The High Contracting Parties engage to consider 25 the result of the proceedings of the Tribunal of Arbitration as a full, perfect, and final settlement of all the questions referred to the Arbitrators.

"ARTICLE XIV.

"The present Treaty shall be duly ratified by Her 30 Britannic Majesty and by the President of the United

The Tribunal went into the most elaborate examination of the history of the occupation of the territory. The arguments took four hours each day, four days each week and covered a period of nearly three months. The verbatim records of the hearings occupy 54 printed volumes – with cases and counter-cases, and additional documents, correspondence and evidence. The Tribunal was presided over by M. de Martens, Professor of International Law at the University of St Petersburg. The other judges were: on the part of Venezuela, US Chief Justice Weston Fuller, nominated by the President of the United States; Justice David Josiah Brewer, nominated by the Justices of the US Supreme Court; and, on the part of Great Britain, Lord Russell of Killowen (Lord Chief Justice of England) and Sir Richard Henn Collins, a Lord Justice of Appeal of the English High Court. It is these four Judges that together chose Professor de Martens as the President of the Tribunal

On 3 October 1899 (exactly 29 years before my birth) the International Court of Arbitration presented its Award. In the words of the law firm handling Venezuela's case, written in the American Journal of International Law as late as 1949 (Vol 43, Issue 3): *"The Award secured to Venezuela the mouth of the Orinoco and control of the Orinoco basin, these being the most important questions at issue"*. It was a success that adorned the law firm's credentials. The government of Venezuela was represented by a plethora of jurists led by an ex-President of the United States Benjamin Harrison, General Benjamin F. Tracy and James Russell Soley respectively Secretary and Assistant Secretary of War during President Harrison's administration.

And there was a continuum of satisfaction with the Award. In its immediate aftermath, on 5 December 1899, the President of the United States, Venezuela's champion, actually alluded to the Award in his annual State of the Union Message to Congress. President William McKinley said:

> *The International Commission of Arbitration appointed under the Anglo-Venezuelan Treaty of 1897, rendered an award on*

> *October 3 last whereby the boundaries line between Venezuela and British Guiana is determined, thus ending a controversy which had existed for the greater part of the century. The award, as to which the arbitrators were unanimous while not meeting the extreme contention of either party, gives to Great Britain a large share of the interior territory in dispute and to Venezuela the entire mouth of the Orinoco, including Barima Point and the Caribbean littoral for some distance to the eastwards. The decision appears to be equally satisfactory to both parties.*

As required by the Treaty and the Award, the boundary as determined by the Award was demarcated on the ground by Commissioners for both parties and an official boundary map was drawn and promulgated. Satisfied with its achievements, Venezuela proceeded toward fulfilment of the destiny which the vast mineral wealth of its land yielded. Through most of the first half of the 20th century it found no quarrel with the Award; and when in 1962 it chose to reopen it with Britain – some 60 years after it had insistently closed it – it did so with restraint and circumspection in the manner of equals. But time was on the side of those in Venezuela for whom, with national wealth assured, eastward expansion had become an imperial crusade. And the ground was well prepared.

At the first sign of Guyana's movement to independence Venezuela initiated a vigorous boundary controversy on the most tenuous of grounds. The single source of these grounds was, and remains to this day, a memorandum written by an American lawyer, Severo Mallet-Prevost, who was one of the junior counsels for Venezuela during the Arbitral Tribunal's hearing. It was written in 1945 just after he had received from the Government of Venezuela the Order of the Liberator for his services to the Republic. The memorandum was given to his law partner with strict instructions to be opened and published only after his death. He died in 1949 – when every other participant in the arbitral proceedings had long since died. The posthumous memorandum contended that the Arbitral Award of 1899 was the result of a political deal between Britain and Russia carried into effect by collusion between the British Judges and the Russian President of the Tribunal and agreed to in the interest of unanimity by the American Judges – after they had consulted with the American lawyers who were Venezuela's chosen counsel.

It was on this flimsiest pretext of an old and disappointed man's posthumous memoirs set down some 45 years after the events – these shreds and patches embroidered with speculations, ambiguities and allusions to new but undisclosed evidence; these calumnies against five of the most eminent jurists in the world of their time – that Venezuela mounted its international campaign against Guyana as we approached independence. As the date drew nearer the agitation grew fiercer threatening in veiled and indirect ways the advance to independence itself. Hence, the British conversations in Geneva.

But there was more, and American State Papers (both White House and State Department papers since declassified) have revealed a darker plot. In the 1950s and 1960s, in a 'cold war' context, there was serious western concern, mainly driven by the United States, that Guyana's independence under a Jagan-led Government would see another Cuba, this time on the South American Continent. In 1962, the then Venezuelan President Rómulo Betancourt chose to take advantage of this fear of 'another Cuba' in an independent Guyana by proposing a plan to develop the Essequibo by US and British investors under 'Venezuelan sovereignty' – a pretext for intervention and acquisition under guise of curbing the spread of communism.

A despatch of 15 May 1962 from the American Ambassador in Caracas (C. Allan Stewart) conveyed to the State Department Betancourt's views on the *"border question"* as gleaned *"during the course of several meetings"* with him. He wrote:

> *President Betancourt professes to be greatly concerned about an independent British Guiana with Cheddie Jagan as Prime Minister. He suspects that Jagan is already too committed to communism and that his American wife exercises considerable influence over him... This 'alarm' may be slightly simulated*

> *since Betancourt's solution of the border dispute presupposes a hostile Jagan. His plan:*
>
> > *Through a series of conferences with the British before Guiana is awarded independence a cordon sanitaire would be set up between the present boundary line and one mutually agreed upon by the two countries (Venezuela and Britain). Sovereignty of this slice of British Guiana would pass to Venezuela...*
>
> *Of course, the reason for the existence of the strip of territory, according to the President, is the danger of communist infiltration of Venezuela from British Guiana if a Castro-type government ever were established... It would seem logical that Venezuela will from now on pursue the idea of the cordon sanitaire to protect itself from a commie-line independent British Guiana rather than send support to the Jagan opposition.*

A year later, on 30 June 1963, President Kennedy was meeting Britain's Prime Minister Macmillan at Birch Grove in England and, on the American side, the issue of British Guiana was the *"principal subject the President intend(ed) to raise with Macmillan"*. So wrote Dean Rusk (the American Secretary of State) the week before in a secret telegram to Ambassador Bruce (the U.S. Ambassador in London) seeking his thoughts *"on how best to convince our British friends of the deadly seriousness of our concern and our determination that British Guiana shall not become independent with a Communist government."* The commonality of motivation between Kennedy and Betancourt was quite remarkable.

Of course, this was never revealed to the Venezuelan people whose patriotism was infused with the simplistic fallacy that Venezuela was 'robbed' by Britain of the Essequibo region of Guyana. On their maps, and in their minds, it was the 'Zona Reclamation'. As it was, it was Jagan's political opponent Burnham who led the Independent Guyana. But by then, driven by Venezuela, the 'controversy' had taken on a life of its own, certainly for the chauvinistic forces that had nurtured it.

The young, and powerless, Guyana faced this 'David and Goliath' harassment from birth. Its only defence was diplomacy: an appeal to the international community to save the infant state from the machinations of its large, wealthy and powerful neighbour. And in those days, Venezuela pursued its territorial ambitions shamelessly. It kept Guyana out of the Organisation of American States (OAS), and. within months of independence it brazenly breached the border (on Ankoko Island) in defiance of the Geneva Agreement. The same year it began interfering in Guyana's internal affairs through attempted subversion of Guyana's indigenous people. In 1968, as Guyana's Prime Minister paid an official visit to Britain, Venezuela bought advertising space in the London *Times* (of 15 June), announcing its non-recognition of concessions granted by Guyana in the area it 'claimed'. Later that year, contemptuous of international law, it issued a Presidential 'decree' purporting to annex a strip of territorial waters adjacent to Guyana's coast. It refused, of course, to sign the Law of the Sea Convention – one of the few countries in the world to exclude itself from '*the Constitution for the Oceans*'. The young Guyana faced fearful odds, indeed. Surmounting them became my mission.

Speaking for Guyana in the General Debate of the 23rd session of the United Nations General Assembly (on 3 October 1968), I devoted my entire Address to the issue of Venezuela's attempts to stifle Guyana at birth. I called it: *"Development or Defence: the Small State threatened with Aggression"*. There was an interesting footnote to the occasion. Lord Caradon (Hugh Foot) was Britain's Ambassador to the UN. He was Dingle Foot's 'younger' brother. He sent me an immediate note of congratulation. But more than mere congratulation, he said it was one of the best addresses he had heard in the Assembly. That encomium meant a great deal, coming from him – regarded as he was as one of the Assembly's best orators. But there was more. Aristides Calvani was Venezuela's Foreign Minister shortly after. He was a Minister of Venezuela's conservative Party COPEI and so not in tune with Guyana's left of centre politics; but I had always found him a responsible and respectable colleague. His personal response to my Address to the UN was more in sadness than in anger. It made his life difficult everywhere, he said, with colleagues asking him why Venezuela kept up its harassment of its small neighbour. Of course, by proclaiming reality, that is precisely what it was intended to do – expose Venezuela's aggressive intent.

Speaking in the UN General Assembly

I do not propose to provide a narrative of the evolution of the Venezuelan issue over the nearly 50 years of Guyana's independence. It is still a matter of contention. The point I seek to make is that it was the central issue on the agenda of Guyana's formative Foreign Ministry and it was central to every facet of Guyana's foreign relations; indeed, it drove Guyana's resolve to be activist in all fora where our cause could be advanced. That meant, of course, in the Caribbean and the Hemisphere, but also beyond in UN agencies everywhere, in the Commonwealth, in the Non-Aligned Movement, in our economic arrangements with the fledgling European Community and, of course, bilaterally through all the doors that this activism opened to us.

* * *

And as if this was not aggravation enough there was tiresome contention on our eastern boundary with Suriname – a legacy from unfinished work by British and Dutch colonisers who had all but concluded the boundary treaty between their colonies when the Second World War intervened and independence followed some decades after. Nationalistic elements within the new Suriname then behaved as if history began with independence and, on both the land boundary and in the maritime area, asserted claims more rooted in aspiration than in law. Within the last decade, Suriname (through the use of force against an off-shore exploration rig) forced Guyana to have recourse to the International Convention for the Law of the Sea and settlement by an Arbitration Tribunal of the maritime boundary. Though long past my time of formal advocacy I represented Guyana (with others) in the Arbitration which I wholly enjoyed and which found the maritime boundary to be as Guyana had contended.

That ruling should have ended as well Suriname's further but related ambition to a land area of Guyana – the 'New River Triangle'. In my 2008 book, *A Triumph for UNCLOS,* I explained why this is so: given the prolongation of the river boundary to the tri-junction border point of Guyana and Suriname with Brazil, a southern border point marked as the Tribunal found the Northern point to have been marked, in the same 1936 operation of border demarcation. Reinforcing this, was the Tribunal's inclusion of the New River Triangle (like the Essequibo region) within the overall land area of Guyana. The 'shape of Guyana' as settled by the earlier 1899 Award had been respected over 100 years later. Yet some elements in Suriname (as in Venezuela) persist with illicit claims.

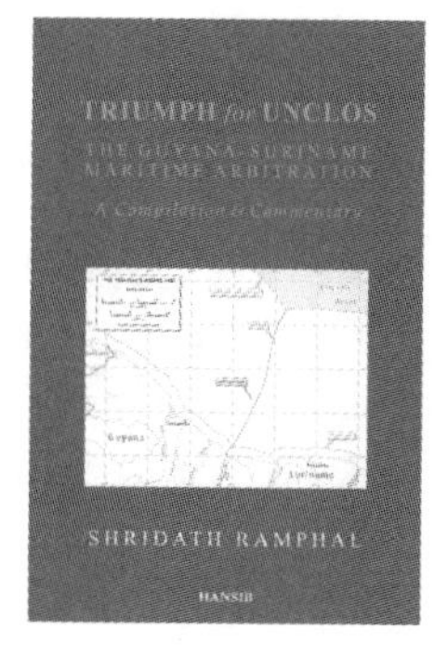

Decades earlier, I had been witness to a timely *modus vivendi* between Guyana and Suriname when the then two Prime Ministers (Burnham/ Sedney) on 10 April 1970, (under the good offices of Prime Minister Eric Williams of Trinidad and Tobago) *"agreed in principle that there should be an early demilitarisation of the border area of Guyana and Suriname in the region of the Upper Courantyne"*. It was an agreement, only "in principle", it is true; but it in effect defined the border as the Upper Courentyne or Kutari River where it meets the agreed – and marked – tri-junction boundary point between Guyana, Suriname and Brazil, and it called for *demilitarisation of the border area.* Yet the same nationalist excesses that led Suriname to international lawlessness in the maritime area continue to be urged in relation to Guyana's 'New River Triangle'. Guyana did 'demilitarise' west of the Upper Courantyne (Kutari) in the *border area.* I am not certain that Suriname ever did to the east i.e. in Suriname's *border area*. Still there are signs now that more mature policies may yet prevail.

With these challenges at birth, the Guyana Foreign Service had to grow up quickly – as did I in the diplomatic world.

CHAPTER 7

A Global Life Begins

In that world beyond our shores, I was ever mindful, that we had to win the respect of colleagues and their Governments; we had to be genuinely involved in a principled way in furthering the highest purposes toward which the institutions reached; and we had to contribute through being labourers in the vineyard. That was our credo in CARIFTA/CARICOM, in the Non- Aligned Movement, in the Group of 77, in the Commonwealth, and of course in the many aspects of our involvement in the work of the United Nations, like the evolution of the Convention on the Law of the Sea, the work of the Committee on the Definition of Aggression and the establishment of the Council for Namibia (of which we were the first Chairman). It meant also being willing to serve. Although, for example, Jamaica and Trinidad and Tobago were members of the UN four years before Guyana, we were the first Caribbean country to be elected Vice-President of the General Assembly and, more importantly, to membership of the Security Council – not for reasons of national vanity, but of national self-interest.

Ireland is one of the world's smaller states. It was a member of the Security Council in 1981-82. In his memoirs of that time, *A Small State at the Top Table – Memoirs of Ireland on the UN Security Council,* Ireland's Ambassador to the UN, Noel Dorr, wrote with much insight:

> *Large and powerful States can fend for themselves but small states like Ireland have a greater interest than most in the*

creation and maintenance of a peaceful, orderly international system. We cannot just stand back and hope this will happen – Ireland and other small States in the system must play their part and take their turn in helping to make the international system, imperfect as it is, work better.

Standing in the international community, especially in solidarity with good causes, like disarmament, is, for example, a small state's necessary armoury against aggressive forces. I presided over the meeting of the Security Council in Panama – the second such meeting held outside of New York – as one of my last acts as Foreign Minister.

Presiding in UN Security Council

Presiding in the UN General Assembly

I was personally always conscious that Guyana needed a quality Foreign Service. It could never be big; but, because of that alone, it had to be better than average. If we were to make a mark in any sphere of international activity we would be judged by the quality of our representatives. This meant a minimum of political 'interference' in Foreign Service appointments, not only Ambassadors but Foreign Service personnel. I give credit to Prime Minister Burnham in those early days for the restraint he displayed in this regard. It helped that he had a personal regard for intellect and welcomed it in young Foreign Service officers; and I was always conscious that these precepts held true for the Ministry's back-up of our handful of Missions.

In much of this I was mindful of British methodologies – they were part of our inheritance. More relevant, however, were the ways in which developing countries made their way on the international scene. From our limited vantage points the developing countries that most commended themselves in 1966 were India, Brazil and Egypt. We kept them in focus as Foreign Service role models, conscious that we could not match them in size. But it was not only structures and procedures that new countries needed as they groped their way across unfamiliar international terrain. Even more vital, was policy. I remember one of our new Ambassadors asking me at an early briefing Session. 'Minister, what is our foreign policy?' I said, in essence: Our foreign policy will emerge from a whole series of specific policies that you and your colleagues would contribute to developing. What was important were the principles that should guide us going forward. One clearly must be our identification with the developing world in the North-South divide that worked so strongly against us.

Another, I said, was being unequivocal in our stand for the principle of 'non-alignment'. The cold war was raging and everything pointed to Guyana's non-involvement in it. Our Caribbean colleagues at that time had adopted the then typical hemispheric posture of being at best sceptical of non-alignment. The West was hostile. But 'non-alignment' for small countries that wished to preserve some real independence was crucial to them. It was to us. And we needed like-minded friends. I went so far as to say to our Ambassador to the UN: *'If in doubt on the Non-Aligned position on specific global issues, vote with India'*.

A third, I ventured, was our resolute stand for Caribbean 'integration' as we were beginning to think of it. That meant working closely with Caribbean colleagues in their policy positions and wherever possible forging common positions. This was not idle counsel. Barbados became independent five months after Guyana. Our High Commissioner to London was Sir Lionel Luckhoo. He was well known to the new Prime Minister of Barbados, our old friend Errol Barrow. We put it to Barrow that we might break new ground by jointly accrediting Sir Lionel to London and having one Residence and one Chancery. He agreed. For a few years, while Sir Lionel was there, he was High Commissioner for Barbados and Guyana. In diplomatic circles in London, it is still remembered as a worthy arrangement. I enquired from Canada's Secretary of State for External Affairs, Paul Martin – the wise 'Prime Minister Canada never had' – whether Ottawa would accept a similar arrangement. His answer was enthusiastically positive. He expressed the hope that we would do it, and set an example to the developing world. He went on to say that many a time when arguing in Ottawa for more aid to developing countries he had been reminded of the life style of their Diplomats. Examples of economising, like this, were welcome. Alas, Barrow and Burnham could not agree on a name for Ottawa; nor could they again when Sir Lionel left London. It remains, however, the right path for many small countries to follow in many places.

A major part of diplomatic relations is the body of relationships that Heads of Governments build up among themselves and sustain by communications, prominently, of course, the friendships and confidences they develop. Forbes Burnham served Guyana well in this regard as its first Prime Minister. Commonwealth Summits were especially suited to this purpose by virtue of the interactions they made possible, certainly in the time before their duration became truncated. They were particularly useful to the growing number of new developing country leaders making their global entrances. Guyana's first Commonwealth Heads of Government Meeting was at Marlborough House, London, under the Chairmanship of Harold Wilson. It was September 1966 and our first outing. I accompanied the Prime Minister (as most 'foreign ministers' did). We made no grand entrance; but Burnham started friendships that were to be central to our foreign relations for years to come. I remember Julius Nyerere, Indira Gandhi, Kenneth Kaunda, and Milton Obote as his early friends. They were friendships that were to be at the core of many of Guyana's external relationships. They were friendships that I would personally inherit.

That photograph of Guyana's first Commonwealth Summit (above) is nostalgic in another context. In it, I am sitting behind Burnham – a novice Minister. Diagonally across the table, in the centre, is Arnold Smith the Commonwealth's first Secretary- General. Nine years later, in 1975, I would succeed him. The photograph following is of Arnold and me in that same room in Marlborough House at the moment of handover.

* * *

I will write of the Commonwealth later. My point here is to emphasise the importance of these occasions when world leaders can meet in informal interaction and develop personal relations. The Non-Aligned Summits were another such, though, of course, essentially confined to the world's developing countries – in the early days, excluding Latin America. They were occasions of leadership encounter – not as intimate as the Commonwealth Summit offered – which broadened the scope of a young country's external outreach. At that time, Guyana took greater advantage of these occasions than did other Caribbean countries. This was especially true of the Non-Aligned Movement. I remember particularly the Summits in Lusaka in 1970 and Algiers in 1973 and of course the Meeting of Non-Aligned Foreign Ministers in Guyana in 1972.

I have explained how from the beginning a policy of 'non-alignment' was part of the credo of Guyana's foreign policy. In practical terms, however, it affected mainly how we voted in the UN. It certainly did not mean that Guyana was at arms-length from the United States on a routine basis. That would have been absurd. The US and Britain were Guyana's largest aid donors and certainly the political opposition in Guyana would have asserted that Guyana's Government was subservient to the United States. This was not true; but I mention it to explain that non-alignment for the young state was more of a shield than a sword.

1970 was the year of the Non-Aligned Summit in Lusaka. Zambia (formerly Northern Rhodesia) had gained independence in 1964 with Kenneth Kaunda as head of government. The 1966 Commonwealth Summit at which he and Burnham met was his first too; they were to meet again in 1969 at the next Commonwealth Summit in London. When in 1970 Kaunda chaired the Non-Aligned Summit in Lusaka, he ensured that Guyana should be the Meeting's Rapporteur. Our Ambassador, Pat Thompson, filled the spot. By then, Burnham was leading the Caribbean in solidarity with Africa in the struggle against Ian Smith over his regime's Unilateral Declaration of Independence for white-ruled Southern Rhodesia, and also in the wider struggle with South Africa over apartheid. What was most important, however, was that Kaunda knew that he had in Burnham and in Guyana a reliable friend and ally. And what was true of relations with Kenneth Kaunda was true for all the 'Frontline States'. Tanzania's Julius Nyerere's relationship was as close; perhaps more intellectual, less emotional; but permeating it the same confidence in a friend and ally. Seretse Khama of Botswana had been Burnham's chum in London in the 1950s. That bond lasted, though sadly Seretse died before the struggle was over. The point I am making is that in foreign policy issues of this kind, it is not only an articulated policy that matters; it is the personal confidences between leaders that give the policy quality and substance.

Guyana and I, as its functional 'Foreign Minister', were beneficiaries of these quality relationships and mirrored them in all we did. I was personally recognised as the functionary who 'carried the ball' for Guyana; an acknowledgement that was to be a significant factor as I moved from Guyana to the Commonwealth Secretariat. But well before that it manifested itself in a wholly unplanned way. It was the practice of the Non-Aligned Movement to convene a Meeting of Foreign Ministers in the three years between summits. At Lusaka, however, a Standing Committee of 16 Foreign Ministers was established to manage the Movement's affairs on an on-going basis. Not surprisingly, Guyana was a member. Ambassadors at the UN did the routine work of the Committee, but a meeting of the Committee at Foreign Ministers' level was required. Recognising that we could not aspire to ever hosting a Summit and that even a full Foreign Ministers' Meeting was beyond our capacity, I persuaded the Prime Minister that hosting a Meeting of the Committee of Foreign Ministers was something we could do, and that doing it would be good for Guyana. Our offer to do so was accepted and in 1971 we did so; not on a grand scale, but efficiently.

It was not a good time in the Non-Aligned Movement. There was a major row over the seating of Cambodia under the Norodom Sihanouk Government and over membership of the 'People's

Revolutionary Government of South Vietnam' – with whom the Americans were at war. The latter issue, in particular, was incendiary with South-East Asian members like Indonesia, Singapore and Malaysia strongly opposed to the Non-Aligned position. And there was a fierce dispute between Algeria and Sri Lanka over the hosting of the next Non-Aligned Summit. Ours was a two-day meeting and I chaired it as the host Minister. We were not expected to take decisions on the most contentious matters, but we had good discussions of them. Our last item was a decision on the venue of the forthcoming Foreign Ministers Meeting the following year. There were no invitations on the table. Apparently, however, there had been conversations among the Foreign Ministers on the Committee, and a proposal came forward, without prior consultations with us, for the full Meeting to be held in Guyana. This was a genuine surprise. Sometimes such things are orchestrated, but this was not. We were genuinely astonished. We would be looking at a Conference of close to a hundred delegations. I asked for time to consult the Prime Minister and did. He asked whether we could do it, and at what cost? I said that almost certainly it would be beyond our means judging by other such meetings – and probably beyond our capability as well. I said also that there would be hemispheric sensitivities, but that there could be big gains if we could manage it. His answer, typically decisive, was: "*Let's do it*".

The Preparatory Committee was not empowered to take a decision at their Georgetown meeting on the venue of the next Foreign Ministers Meeting, but they were sure of their recommendation and needed an indication from us. We gave it in confidence. A month later (17 March) a special ad-hoc meeting of the Preparatory Committee held in New York decided to invite Guyana to host the Foreign Ministers meeting. We accepted, recognising that we would need to do it our way.

In Georgetown today, near to a cluster of Government Departments and the City's major hotel, is a very large thatched cathedral-like building. It is a replica of an unusually large 'meeting place' of the *Wai Wai* tribe of the indigenous people of Guyana. We chose it as the single structure we would erect for the meeting, and that we would have it erected in the manner of the *Wai Wai* with their forest materials, and by the tribe itself. Its construction was a major spectacle for city-folk; and the engineers among them were sceptical, for it went up without a nail. Yet, it remains in place more than 40 years later, as a monument to those who built it and our indigenous culture generally. We called it *'Umana Yana'* – the *Wai Wai* words for 'meeting place of the people'. It was the central lounge of the Foreign Ministers' Meeting where much of the work got done.

Umana Yana and a Waii Wai who helped construct it

For the rest, we made do with what was there. The hotel could not accommodate all delegations but we made its ballroom the Plenary Hall of the Meeting. We asked Civil Servants in nearby departments to take their annual leave over the Meeting's duration; and we used the departments as Delegation and Committee Rooms. A housing scheme of middle-income dwellings was nearing completion; and we were able to let delegations be the first occupants – with Georgetown housewives volunteering as house-mothers. We imported cars for use by Delegations and sold them immediately after at duty free prices – with no cost for their use to government. In these and other ways we managed. We had turned this exotic meeting of Non-Aligned Foreign Ministers into a Community affair – not something happening outside the community. The Delegates responded to this community-style with great warmth; and for years after referred to it with appreciation. For our own part, we hoped it would give confidence to small countries to host such occasions – within their means and cultures.

Umana Yana is not the only structural remembrance of the Conference. In the heart of Georgetown – in the much loved old

'Company Path Gardens' – we constructed a simple Memorial commemorating both the founders of the Movement and the holding of the Conference. It took the form of a collection of jasper boulders from the hinterland of Guyana set against the backdrop of a curved wall. Mounted on the wall are bronze busts of Egypt's Gamal Abdel Nasser, Ghana's Kwame Nkrumah, India's Jawaharlal Nehru and Yugoslavia's Josip Broz Tito. Set in the wall is a plaque bearing a dedication to these four men who more than any others inspired and shaped the early years of the Non-Aligned Movement. The busts were given by the respective Governments. The words of dedication were composed by Lloyd Searwar of the Foreign Ministry, who became the Conference Secretary. Some of its lines are as follows:

Having led their peoples to freedom
They did not rest
But taking the whole earth for their nation
And all peoples for their brothers
They sought to free the world from war
Gave to the oppressed a sense of dignity
And the hope of justice...
With them through the Movement of Non-Alignment
our human race took a major step forward towards
a world of peace, of justice and of progress.
They began the dialogue of all mankind

With Nyerere at the Non-Aligned Monument

But of course the logistics of the Meeting were one thing; the politics of the agenda was quite another. Many thought that if the impasse over the 'Cambodia' and the 'South Vietnam' issues could not be resolved, the Movement would face dangers of self-destruction. Conscious of this, the Prime Minister and I had developed a strategy to give the Meeting a substantial economic dimension drawing the meeting away from the traditional monopoly of political concerns and guiding the Movement itself into greater preoccupation with economic development issues – which were in any event in the ascendancy on the international scene. To this end, we had convened a Group of Experts from Non-Aligned countries under the Chairmanship of William Demas, the respected economist from Trinidad, who then headed the CARICOM Secretariat in Georgetown. In developing and carrying forward this strategy we were helped by Yugoslavia and India in particular – old Non-Aligned hands.

The Expert Group had laboured hard in Georgetown before the Foreign Ministers Meeting and had produced a draft Action Programme for Economic Co-operation among Non-Aligned Countries. At its core was insistence on 'self-reliance'. The Ministers devoted time and attention to their work before adopting the Action Programme as a central feature of the Conclusions of the Meeting. It was to serve the Non-Aligned Movement in good stead well beyond Georgetown.

On the political issues there was vigorous and heated debate on some procedural matters. They were 'procedural' only in form; they had substantial 'cold war' overtones. They were, firstly, the upgrading of the status of the Provisional Revolutionary Government of South Vietnam (the North-backed forces) from 'Observer' to 'Member' of the Non-Aligned Movement. And second, the occupation by the delegation of the National Union of Cambodia (the Sihanouk delegation) of the Cambodia seat.

From the Chair I avoided matters being taken to a vote and my strategy was to avoid a ruling which focussed on the issues but rather on the technical meaning of the concept of consensus. I used the adjournment to draw-up a Chairman's ruling on 'consensus'. It was this that I would put to the meeting and, based on it, a ruling on the discussion. By the next day, I had drawn up a series of points on which the Chair would be guided in the matter of 'consensus' and I recounted them to the Meeting as the Chairman's ruling on 'consensus'. They included these:

- *the overwhelming, though not unanimous, support expressed for the application;*
- *that of the States which had expressed misgivings concerning the application, some at least had stated their positions in terms of a reservation;*
- *that of the remainder opposed to the application some were States belonging to the region involved and entitled therefore to special attention;*
- *that the application itself, while seeking membership generally, placed particular emphasis on participation in the work of the present Conference;*
- *finally, that consensus – while signifying substantial agreement at group level on any particular occasion did not require or imply unanimity and committed no member to discontinue (his) efforts for a reversal of that consensus on some future occasion.*

Applying these precepts to the discussion we had had, I concluded that the Meeting had agreed that the Delegation of the Provisional Revolutionary Government of South Vietnam should occupy its seat as a member of the Non-Aligned Movement. I asked the Meeting to endorse this conclusion by acclamation and it did resoundingly. But Indonesia, Malaysia and Singapore protested, and announced their withdrawal from the Meeting. They disagreed with the ruling on 'consensus' and they disagreed with the procedure adopted by the Chairman. As the senior and much respected Foreign Minister of Indonesia, Adam Malik, passed my Chair on his way out, he whispered to me: *"You understand, my brother"*. I did. Following a debate on the Cambodian issue, I was able to similarly announce that there was an overwhelming majority in favour of inviting the Government of the National Union of Cambodia (Sihanouk) to occupy Cambodia's seat.

Ahead of me still lay the rambunctious contest between Algeria and Sri Lanka over the hosting of the forthcoming Summit of the Movement. It was really a contest between President Houari Boumedienne of Algeria and President Sirimavo Bandaranaika of Sri Lanka and each had made it a matter of great personal moment – for very different reasons. President Boumedienne has assumed a political leadership role in the North-South debate internationally and saw a Non-Aligned Summit in Algiers as an endorsement of that leadership and a strengthening of his authority in that role. For Mrs Bandaranaika, it was quite different. She had succeeded her husband as President. He had been prominent in the Non-Aligned Movement and had been assassinated. She conceived of the Summit in Colombo as a memorial to her late husband. Neither of course presented their invitations in that way. Both had lobbied extensively and though our view was that on a vote Algeria would win, a debate would be very divisive and not in the best interests of the Movement. Our strategy was to avoid its coming to the floor and somehow negotiate an agreement.

I told the Foreign Minister, Abdelaziz Bouteflika of Algeria, who was anxious to do battle, that Prime Minister Burnham was working to bring Mrs Bandaranaika around to withdrawing in favour of Algeria on the basis of his assessment that on a vote Sri Lanka would probably lose. On that basis, I needed his co-operation in not forcing a debate. Bouteflika (later the President of Algeria) was a wily fighter – going back to his early days with the National Liberation Army in the Algerian war against the French for independence. He was not easily convinced. He told me that he was fully 'mobilised' for the contest and I was asking him to 'demobilise'. I said I was thinking of the Movement and he must 'trust me'. I told him that he will win in the end, but a battle would do the Movement no good. He stared me in the eye as if assessing whether he could trust me, then said: *"OK, I will hold my hand for 24 hours".* The Prime Minister was communicating with Mrs Bandaranaika by telephone and she was implacable. Eventually, however, she agreed to his proposal that the next Summit would be in Algeria, but it would be decided now that the one after that would be in Sri Lanka. That was the proposal I put to the Meeting, and asked for its acceptance without debate. Bouteflika was pleased, but I felt sure he would have preferred to have won after a battle.

The main political and economic work of the Meeting was done in the Political and Economic Committees who sent forward to the Plenary for endorsement what became *'The Georgetown Declaration'* and *'The Action Programme for Economic Co-operation among Non-Aligned Countries'*. Both went forward to the UN General Assembly the following month where they received more than usual attention – especially the *Action Programme;* and, of course, to the Algiers Summit the following year.

Within the Non-Aligned world, the Meeting was hailed as a great success for Guyana and for the Non-Aligned Movement. There were many plaudits for me as Chairman. I would have liked to say to many who congratulated me what had been said to me before the Meeting began by the Foreign Minister of India. He was Sardar Swaran Singh, India's wise and respected Foreign Minister of many years. *"Young man"*, he had said, *"we will be electing you Chairman of this important Meeting. We do not expect you merely to occupy the Chair; we expect you to lead this Meeting. We will support you"*. I have chaired many an international meeting in the forty plus years since then. I have never forgotten Swaran Singh's wise counsel – or failed to follow it.

* * *

The Non-Aligned Meeting in Georgetown in 1972 had significance of many kinds, but there is one area that was – and is – very special to Guyana and the Caribbean. It is to do with Cuba. Inviting Cuba to the Meeting was never an issue with us. Cuba was a member of the Non-

Aligned Movement and would be invited and welcomed in the normal way. Besides, it had already been agreed by the Region that Cuba would participate in the first Caribbean Festival of Arts (CARIFESTA) due to be held in Guyana in the month after the Non-Aligned Meeting. Still, we were mindful that it would be the first fully international meeting in the Hemisphere that post-revolutionary Cuba would be attending outside the UN. Anti-Cuba sentiment was pervasive in Latin America as was adherence to the more formal diplomatic embargo under which, with the blessing of the Organisation of American States (OAS), the countries of the Hemisphere (with the exception of a principled Canada, Allende's Chile and an ambivalent Mexico) did not 'recognise' the Government of Cuba.

It was in this environment that, in inviting Cuba to attend the Foreign Ministers Meeting, Prime Minister Burnham signalled to Havana (via our High Commissioner in Ottawa, where Cuba had an Embassy) that when the Foreign Minister came to Georgetown he would like to 'discuss' with him the matter of Guyana's diplomatic relations with Cuba. The Cuban Delegation was led by the experienced if somewhat volatile Foreign Minister Dr Raul Roa. With him was Ambassador Ricardo Alarcon (later President of the Cuban National Assembly) with whom West Indian Missions at the UN had worked very closely.

No sooner had I greeted Raul Roa on his arrival at Timehri Airport (photograph below) than he intimated to me that, following on our signal through Ottawa, he had brought with him a draft 'Diplomatic Relations Agreement' and Plenipotentiary powers from Fidel to conclude it. We agreed to 'talk' in Georgetown. I needed time. Guyana was serious about 'diplomatic relations' with Cuba, but we had not contemplated formally establishing them at the Non-Aligned Meeting itself. We were already skating on thin diplomatic ice. I told Raul Roa as much. He was understanding, but measured me quizzically. Was the signal from Georgetown 'diplomatic courtesy', he asked with his eyes? I assured him it was serious and substantive and that after the Meeting, and separate from it, we would conclude a Diplomatic Relations Agreement with Cuba.

In all this I was conscious of the national interests of Guyana, but I was conscious too of the interests of Caribbean integration. We were in the process of moving from 'first steps' CARIFTA to the more ambitious Community – to a Caribbean Community and Common Market (CARICOM). Two months away lay the Chaguaramas Summit at which such decisions would be taken by the Heads of the English-speaking Caribbean countries. I asked Raoul Roa to 'trust me'- as I was later to ask Algeria's Bouteflika. Guyana, I told him, will establish diplomatic relations with Cuba, but we would prefer to give the three other independent English-Speaking Caribbean countries the chance to join us in doing so. *"Give me three months"*, I said, *"and we will have a multiple diplomatic relations agreement. That would be good for the Region, for Cuba and for Guyana; and it would make a dent in the hemispheric embargo"*. Raul Roa was disappointed, but he 'trusted' me; and for that I paid him tribute when I later reminisced on the event with President Fidel Castro in Havana. Immediately after the Foreign Ministers' Meeting, Prime Minister Burnham contacted Dr Eric Williams (the doyen of Caribbean Prime Ministers), Errol Barrow (his old CARIFTA buddy), and Michael Manley (his friend from London student days and newly elected Prime Minister of Jamaica). Ministers Kamaluddin Mohammed of Trinidad and Dudley Thompson of Jamaica and Ambassador 'Boogles' Williams of Barbados (as an Observer) had been at the Meeting in Georgetown and were all briefed.

I followed up the 'Cuba' discussions in Georgetown with visits to the three Prime Ministers on behalf of Burnham, inviting them to join us in recognising Cuba – but making it clear that we were committed to doing so in any event. My itinerary was Kingston, Port of Spain, Bridgetown; my appeal was to justice, to history, to regional solidarity. The order of our approach was not haphazard; it reflected our judgment of the Prime Ministers most likely to agree. All three Prime Ministers agreed, and agreed further that their collective agreement, as Heads of government of the independent English-speaking Caribbean countries, would be signalled when they met at Chaguaramas in Trinidad for a Summit meeting of the member-states of the Caribbean Free Trade Area. Burnham read an agreed Statement at the Conference. Its substantive paragraph was as follows:

> *The independent English-speaking Caribbean States, exercising their sovereign right to enter into relations with any other sovereign state, and pursuing their determination to seek regional solidarity and to achieve meaningful and comprehensive economic co-operation amongst all Caribbean Countries, will seek the early establishment of relations with Cuba, whether economic or diplomatic or both.*

On 8 December 1972, I delivered on my promise to Raul Roa when Oliver Jackman and Neville Selman signed the Diplomatic Agreement for Barbados and Guyana in Ottawa with Jose Fernandez (later Cuban Ambassador in London); and Maxine Roberts and Eustace Seignoret signed for Jamaica and Trinidad and Tobago with Ricardo Alarcon at the UN in New York. The establishment of diplomatic relations with Cuba was announced simultaneously in all five Capitals at 1500 hours on 12 December 1972. The effect of this sovereign collective Caribbean act of principle was immediate. The hemispheric diplomatic embargo of Cuba was not just dented; it collapsed. Today, Cuba has formal diplomatic relations with 160 countries.

On 8 December 2002, at a Cuba-CARICOM Summit arranged by President Fidel Castro, to which I was invited in a personal capacity, the then Prime Minister of Antigua and Barbuda, Lester Bird, quoted Pablo Neruda in his intervention. Pablo Neruda is the Chilean poet who won the Nobel Prize for Literature in 1971. In *'Cuba Appears'* (published in 1960 in *Song of Protest*), he wrote these words which the Prime Minister quoted:

And so History teaches with her light
that man can change that which exists
and if he takes purity into battle
in his honour blooms a noble spring.

8 December 2002 was the 30th Anniversary of the signing of the Diplomatic Agreement between Cuba on the one hand and Guyana, Jamaica, Trinidad and Tobago and Barbados on the other. Eventually, other Caribbean English-speaking countries, when they became independent, followed the lead set by the original four. These were historic developments. Cuba has never forgotten the acts of solidarity, and courage, which they represented in those now far-off days of 1972. It was important also for Caribbean countries to reflect with Pablo Neruda that small as we are, we too once changed that which existed – and existed for much of the world. I felt our commemoration should be more regular and advanced the idea of a Cuba-CARICOM Day each year. It was eagerly taken up on all sides – and has been observed each year since then on 8 December.

Greeting Fidel Castro

By the 1970s my burden of responsibilities had shifted almost entirely to foreign affairs. Shortly before the Non-Aligned Meeting the Prime Minister in effect signalled this by formally designating me 'Foreign Minister'. It must have become apparent to him that this was only proper if I was to Chair the Meeting of Foreign Ministers. Since I had been functioning for years as Foreign Minister it did not make a significant change in my life, but I was pleased that what had been an anomaly was rectified. After the Meeting, however, I talked with Burnham about my roles and suggested that we take the logical next step of my formally giving up the office of Attorney-General and being simply Foreign Minister. I reminded him that Shahabudeen and Pollard had been effectively in charge of the Chambers for years, so the change would be more titular than substantive. He agreed, but only partly. He said it was important that I should have an oversight of legal affairs even if not responsible for professional advice and invited me to be 'Minister of Justice'. I became in 1973, Minister of Foreign Affairs and Justice – still essentially technocratic.

All I have said about the Non-Aligned Foreign Ministers' Meeting may give the impression that my role as Minister of State for Foreign Affairs had been played mainly on the international stage. That was not so. It had been very substantially concerned with Caribbean affairs. For this, of course, I had a passion and a personal vision; that vision of Caribbean unity was one shared by Burnham. I have already bemoaned the fact that in the days of 'Federation' he had not spoken out for it and had not forced Jagan to a more regionalist posture. As Prime Minister, however, his regionalism could not be faulted. Political analysts have tried to explain the change away: the point was, however, in the 1960s and 1970s – the years of independence – there was need for the Caribbean to get its act together, and Burnham stepped forward and gave that lead. In doing so, he gave me an opportunity to help to pursue my own dream of one Caribbean. And the times were particularly propitious. Relations with the outside world constantly reinforced the case for economic integration in the Caribbean and for united action in our dealings with the world beyond. The next part of these glimpses is devoted to this Caribbean odyssey which has occupied so much of my global life.

PART III

CARIBBEAN ODYSSEY

CHAPTER 8

The Federal Dream

Mine has been a global life; but within it has been a Caribbean odyssey. Any glimpse would be too fleeting if it did not reveal it, and its linkages with so much else beyond it. And to do so I must explain who we in the Caribbean are, and our hopes and trials and failures; and such successes as there have been, for in my lifetime I have been entwined with them all – quite often centrally. My role with the federal project I have already explained. But as the early story of the start of CARIFTA hinted, I did not end there. Indeed that was but the beginning of a long journey.

The Caribbean is an archipelago. We are an archipelagic people. Even when we include the larger islands of Cuba, Dominican Republic and Haiti, and Puerto Rico we are archipelagic; but exclude them, and what is left: the 'island chains' of the Leeward and Windward Islands of the Eastern Caribbean, Jamaica and scattered habitations of descending size. With Belize, Guyana and Suriname, the Caribbean Community (CARICOM) within our archipelago speaks three languages, has a population of 19 million (almost half in Haiti) and includes 14 sovereign member-states of the United Nations. In our separateness, six of our island-states are among the world's smallest countries. Indonesia is our counterpart in the Indian Ocean, but could not be more different: 17,508 islands in the Malay Archipelago, but one country, the Republic of Indonesia. Formerly the Dutch East Indies, Indonesia's population in 2010 (the last census) was 237,424,363 and the people of its 27 provinces speak over 60 languages. Indonesia in its unity is one Member State of the UN, and is one of the world's largest countries.

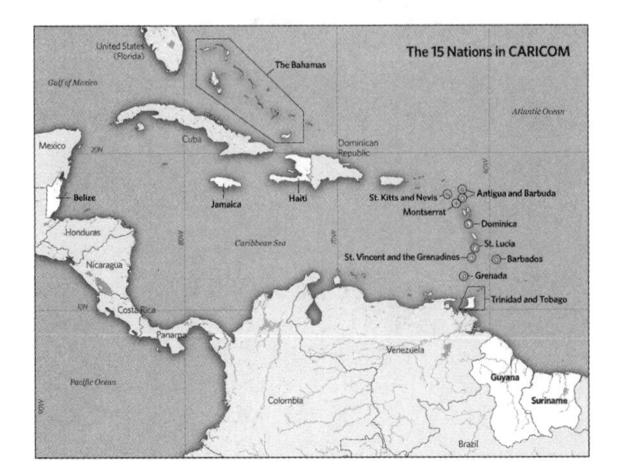

What do these comparisons connote? Certainly, that a dividing sea does not compel regional divisiveness, and where there are factors making for unity, does not preclude it. If we, the people of the Caribbean, are flawed regionalists, the fault lies not in our sea but in ourselves. And if proof be needed that the fault is not the sea, look no further than the Bahamas. There, within our own region, a Commonwealth of some 700 islands, lying off the south-east coast of America, is one state – so administered for over 300 years. The Bahamas is larger in size than any single island state of CARICOM, and its population bigger than any of the seven Leeward and Windward islands that constitute the Organisation of Eastern Caribbean States (OECS). It is still small, but in its conscious and deliberate oneness, it has overcome the separateness that the sea could have engendered. In the result, with meagre natural resource endowment, its GDP is higher than every other member state of CARICOM.

Of course, the sea is a separating influence, just as is an historic land boundary; but no more than the latter is it fatal to cultivated unity. It is a challenge to be faced; a *Rubicon* to be crossed; but once there is a need to succeed and a will to overcome, vision and leadership will close the gap between barriers, and bridge separation and unification, ambition and achievement.

There is another side to our Caribbean reality that unites, not separates, us; and it too is part of our natural state and our heritage. It is the unmistakable, unchanging fact of a Caribbean identity – circles of synonymy rippling outward from an inner core of West Indian oneness. In 1722, nearly 300 years ago, a French Dominican monk living in Martinique, Père Labat, wrote of his travels among the islands of the Caribbean. In a lyrical passage of his *'Nouveau Voyage aux iles de l'Amerique',* he invoked a vision of that Caribbean identity in what Professor Gordon Lewis was later to describe as *"his plea for the rhythm of history which, as he saw it, held all the islands together in a common destiny".*

Père Labat wrote:

> *I have travelled everywhere in your sea of the Caribbean from Haiti to Barbados, to Martinique and Guadeloupe, and I know what I am speaking about.... You are all together, in the same boat, sailing on the same uncertain sea... citizenship and race unimportant, feeble little labels compared to the message that my spirit brings to me: that of the predicament which History has imposed upon you. I saw it first with the dance... the meringue in Haiti, the beguine in Martinique and today I hear, de mon oreille morte, the echoes of calypsos from Trinidad, Jamaica, St Lucia, Antigua, Dominica, and the legendary Guiana.... It is no accident that the sea which separates your lands makes no difference to the rhythm of your bodies.*

For three centuries that included new arrivals like my forbears, the rhythm of history has carried the message of the region's common destiny; but never without obstruction by the offsetting spirit of separatism, and its concomitant claim of 'local control'. For a while, particularly during the world wars of the 20th Century, that synergy was broken when regionalism seemed to offer a route to real local control, namely, political independence and when West Indian identity saw federalism as the pathway ahead. It was the time when my own belief in a federation of the West Indies was stirred by Norman Manley's lunchtime passion in London in 1950. Since West Indian unity, in all of the many ways by which it has been pursued, has been central to so much of my life – and still is – an account of the rise and fall of federalism in my early years is essential to an understanding of much that came later in my life.

The natural state and heritage of the Caribbean people is the unmistakable, unchanging fact of a West Indian identity. We see it in what Père Labat described almost 300 years ago as the rhythm of our bodies. It attaches to us ineluctably when we leave our island cloisters – (and Guyana and Belize in this respect are islands too). We know it as we face a world beyond that knows us as West Indians first – and sometimes only. We know in our minds that in an ultimate sense we need each other for survival on any tolerable basis. And we know it more and more as the world turns around us and changes our prospects. We know deep in our hearts and minds that our oneness must overcome our separateness.

It was this growing awareness, made more acute by frustrations at home that led progressive elements in the 1940s and 1950s who recognised the need for constitutional reform as a precondition of economic improvement to reach together to Federation. That linkage between political change at home and federalism in the wider regional home is fundamental.

Inevitably, the call for political reform grew louder and more insistent throughout the 1930s. The economic depression brought to maturity the growing working class movement and the demand for economic justice was unceasing. The initiative in political agitation passed to these hands and the call for constitutional change dominated the political scene.

The war years drew the West Indian colonies much closer together. United, in a common cause, they achieved a new identity of purpose and of action that went a long way towards destroying the psychological barriers which Major Wood (later Lord Halifax) in a 1921 British Commission had found obstructive to 'federating an archipelago'. These developments gave added vitality to the federal movement. The ramparts of separatism and prejudice had been breached; contact produced understanding; association revealed how unfounded were many fears. A West Indian consciousness had developed to the point where West Indian nationalism had been born.

On the other side, the inadequacies of ad-hoc expedients born of necessity had been painfully demonstrated, and recognition of the need for federation now replaced in many minds an appreciation of the advantages of co-operation.

But if the experience of the war years reinforced one aspect of the case for Federation it weakened it in another. Political frustration had enhanced the attractions of Federation. Now for the first time since the 1860s the West Indian colonies really began to advance politically. 'Representative' government, which was the goal of the 1920s, was now firmly established. 'Responsible' government, which even in the 1930s must have appeared largely unattainable, was by the 1950s within the grasp of Barbados, Jamaica, Trinidad and British Guiana. In all but Trinidad reform of the legislature was virtually complete: universal adult suffrage prevailed in all the colonies. The reforms were long overdue and, having come at last, everything changed. Federation, in particular, which possessed an appeal as a possible alternative to improbable local self-government, began to be suspect for that very reason. Much emphasis, therefore, was laid in the post-war period on the need for a guarantee that Federation would not in any way prejudice political advance in the individual colonies. It was a sentiment evident in many of the speeches at the 1947 Montego Bay Conference of West Indian leaders drawn from politics, labour and community development. The destiny of the West Indies was now moving into West Indian hands.

Montego Bay itself was preceded by a meeting of the Caribbean Labour Congress which was really a meeting of leading West Indian political parties (other than Bustamante's Jamaica Labour Party which was in office in Jamaica) asserting, as it were, their right to be heard and heard in support, at the very outset, of the federal process. The names of those present tell their own story: Grantley Adams of Barbados, V.C. Bird of Antigua, Robert Bradshaw of St Kitts, Hubert Nathaniel Critchlow of Guyana, Albert Gomes of Trinidad and Tobago, T.A. Marryshow of Grenada, and Norman Manley himself among many others, 'knitting together', as Rex Nettletford put it, 'the ideas of federation, nationhood and self-government.'

Founding Fathers (I am in the back row, second from right)

The larger political gains of Federation still mattered. Manley, who led the Jamaica delegation, put the issue thus: *"I put first, and I put above all other things, the desire to see in the future a West Indian nation standing shoulder to shoulder with all other nations of the world"*. But he added, importantly, *"if we federate, we must federate as self-governing units and voluntarily surrender some of the power which each has over his own to the common whole"*.

The truth is that a race had begun which no one could have foreseen even ten years earlier between independence on an island basis and West Indian nationhood fulfilled through an independent West Indian Federation. It was a race Federation was to lose. For the time being, however, even at Montego Bay, there were few who imagined that independence was achievable at the level of the individual islands; and most of the Eastern Caribbean islands would be among them. For them, Federation was acquiring a justification of its own. Norman Manley could state the federal aspiration in terms wholly compatible with Jamaica's national political goals and he did so in words characteristically elegant and penetrating – words that were to inspire a generation: *'How to create a larger field for ambition'*. And Manley said something else that was as pertinent to the Federal Project – and was fatal in its unfolding:

> *The vested interest of ambition in power is the most dangerous of all the vested interests. It is in the history of every Federation that there have always been found men who were unwilling to*

> *give up any local rule of power for the creation of a larger centre of power itself, and I think we should warn ourselves of the danger and – dare I say? – that we should search our own breasts to discover if there lurks underneath the rationalisations that may be paraded for public consumption that malady which would be, and may yet prove to be, the greatest obstacle.*

Professor Gordon Lewis was to write in coruscating terms ten years later in *'The Growth of the Modern West Indies'*.

> *It was the supreme irony of Mr Manley's public career that he himself after 1958 should have provided the leading example of that temper. For his decision not to enter federal politics not only brought him the loss, almost overnight, of the veneration and respect that he had enjoyed in all the West Indies, but drove him with relentless logic into a path of ultimate desertion of the federal idea. He was thereby trapped in a situation in which he became, in the style of high Greek tragedy, the author of his own misfortune ... The great federationist would fight the Napoleons of Notting Hill. But he would not fight the Confederate rebels of Jamaica.*

That may have been a harsh judgment; he did fight them in his way – his democratic way; but was he right to put at risk the fortunes of the entire region in his struggle to prevail within Jamaica? It may be answered in his defence: '1 from 10 leaves 9, not 0.'

Many years later in Jamaica when I was briefly at the bar and Norman Manley – then retired from politics – had his Chambers nearby in Duke Street, I reminded him of that lunchtime address and told him how it had affected my life. He was pleased; he was still a West Indian regionalist and sad about the outturn of the referendum and the dreams it shattered – including mine.

Years later still, I was moved by the tender reminiscence of his grand-daughter, Rachel Manley, as she recalled her encounter with him at 'Drumblair' (the family home) hours after the results of the referendum had come in. *"Did we win, Pade?"* the little girl asked. *"No Pie; we didn't win; everybody lost"*. And in this at least he was right. Everybody did lose, including generations of West Indians not yet born. But given Jamaica's primary goal of self-government, Jamaica's loss, even in Manley's reckoning, was only partial. Within 70 days of the date on which the Federation was to have become the independent nation of The West Indies, Jamaica – on 6 August 1962 – itself became independent; and Trinidad & Tobago also later the same month. It is worth reflecting on this reality and how the Federal Project became entrapped in Jamaica's domestic politics.

The Federal flag: blue background, white waves, yellow sun

The Federation came formally into existence on 3 January 1958. It was dissolved on 31 May 1962. In the four and a half years of its life, most of which I spent within it, in the Federal Public Service, almost all activity of significance in the Federation – in the Federal Parliament, in communications between the Federal Government and the Governments of the territories, and in 'federal' discussions within the territories – centred on the issue of distribution of power between the centre and territories in wrangles conducted essentially between politicians and the public servants entrusted with the unenviable task of fulfilling their masters' contradictory mandates.

What did the West Indian people think of all this? I believe people throughout the region were caught up in the excitement of this new venture. Many travelled the Caribbean for the first time on the *Federal Palm* and the *Federal Maple* – two ships that were Canada's thoughtful gift to the Federation. It was a time of discovery of their Caribbean heritage – everywhere, including Jamaica – until their leaders started squabbling with nationalistic fervour. Save for issues like 'freedom of movement' – which it is interesting to recall was then mainly about 'small islanders' in Trinidad – the West Indian people were generally unimpressed by the antics of their political leaders until, that is, it all became too real for comfort.

The distribution of powers which the 1958 Federal Constitution ordained provided for a weak central authority; weak in constitutional status *vis-à-vis* the British government; and weak in functional authority *vis-à-vis* the constituent territories. Specifically, the most important revenue sources were left with the Territories – in particular, a federal income tax was prohibited during the first five years. For those years, the Federation would be financed by a Mandatory Levy paid by the territories on an agreed basis. This was a complete reversal of a basic principle agreed on ever since the 1947 Montego Bay Conference.

This departure from basic federal principles was to be the 'Achilles heel' of the Federation. Only eight subjects were assigned to the Federation's exclusive authority. They included such matters as defence, exchange control, migration and emigration, public services and the University College of the West Indies. The concurrent list, in which authority was shared, was much longer consisting of 39 specific subjects, including industrial development. Everything else was exclusively territorial. Provision was made however for a mandatory constitutional review within five years.

These characteristics, this built-in weakness reflected the underlying geographic, demographic, economic and political realities of the region. Agreement on Federation could only be reached on the basis of numerous compromises which satisfied no one entirely. The alternative would have been no Federation, and most of the region's leaders, in 1957, were of the view that what was of overriding importance was to launch the Federation as soon as possible; they recognised already that federation would slip beyond their grasp the longer the delay. In 1956 Eric Williams asserted that 'any Federation is better than no Federation'; but once Federation began to function his was the loudest voice against 'this weak and anaemic Federation'. He was to go on through the life of the Federation to argue forcefully – and with outstanding technical analysis – against the financial straitjacket that the Constitution imposed. It found expression ultimately in the technically brilliant but politically incandescent *'The Economics of Nationhood'* – the nearest we came to argumentation of the quality of Hamilton in the Federalist Papers.

'The Economics of Nationhood' collided head-on with Jamaica's philosophy, objectives and structure. As John Mordecai noted in his excellent book, *'The West Indies: the Federal Negotiations'*:

> *... In simple language the document (Jamaica's MP No. 18) pronounced the motive which dominated all the Jamaican proposals, namely, to ensure that Federation would in no way injure or impede the development of Jamaica. The Constitution was unsatisfactory. It was not only colonial in character, but gave the Federal Government too large powers to interfere with the industrial development of the Units and their powers of taxation.*

That view threw down a challenge which *'The Economics of Nationhood'* took up. In the ensuing battle, Federation itself was to be the victim – but not before Jamaica had prepared the way for life after death.

The battle lines were clearly drawn as early as two years after the decision to federate. They were not so unlike those faced by other federations and ways might have been found to pacify the warriors. The Inter-Governmental Committees, through their sub-committees, 'Alpha' and 'Orion' were working away at the most critical issues and were making slow but steady progress; but the old issue of Federation as a means to an end, especially for Jamaica, held the ultimate key – the primacy of 'islandness' over 'regionalism'.

In 1948, and even in 1957, Federation's driving force still was Dominion Status and Commonwealth membership for a federated West Indies against an uncertain future as isolated Islands – even the bigger ones. By 1960, the *realpolitik* had changed; the political holy grail of independence was within grasp – even alone; certainly by the larger members. Federation might no longer be compelling. It was in that context that Norman Manley went alone to London in January 1960, for bilateral talks with the British Government.

Ministry Paper No 3 was an official Jamaican account of that visit. The final crucial discussion, which would decide the future of the Federation, took place not among West Indian leaders but between Norman Manley and Iain MacLeod, the British Minister for 'decolonisation' – between Jamaica and the UK. The Federal Government was told of the visit in advance, but not of the full range of the discussions. John Mordecai describes this as "a momentous stage in the federal chronicle". And so it was.

For Norman Manley the discussions sought to find out (in the words of Ministry Paper No 3) "what would be the attitude of the British Government to a demand by Jamaica to be allowed to leave the Federation and to seek Dominion status on her own, in the event it did not prove possible to achieve an agreement in respect of the …differences of opinion (in the Region)". Manley's interpretation of the assurance he received was that, as he announced on his return to Jamaica... "the way is open for Jamaica to secede if she wants to and no obstacle will be placed in her way by the British government". That was the crucial message to the people of Jamaica and the Region.

Everything that followed took place against the backdrop of that assurance. Four months after the London visit, amid a heated political scene in Jamaica with Sir Alexander Bustamante announcing the Jamaica Labour Party's 'irrevocable decision to oppose Federation; and to do everything in their power to secure Jamaica's withdrawal, Manley and the Peoples National Party announced that 'a referendum on whether or the not Jamaica should remain in the Federation would be held as quickly as possible.' It was not to be that quickly. One effect, however, was to completely side-line the Federal Prime Minister, Grantley Adams, and his Government. With Adams' injudicious talk of 'retroactive' federal taxation, they had become part of the problem and could not broker a solution. Conciliatory discussions did take place – but between Manley and Williams – notably in Antigua on 7-8 August 1960, and earlier with Iain McLeod on 7-19 June 1960 in Trinidad. But it was all too late. Much was done, too, in the federal negotiations to try to save the federation, including the work of the Inter-Governmental Committees, an Inter-Governmental Conference in Trinidad in May 1961, and the Lancaster House Conference on 31 May 1961 in London. By the end, Manley had got most of what he wanted – but at a high price to the viability of the Federation.

Eighteen months after the crucial London visit, and a triumphal return from the Lancaster House Conference in June 1961, Manley announced on 3 August 1961 that the referendum would be held on 19 September. In making the announcement, the Premier added that if the referendum were successful he himself would stand for election. "As simply as I can, and with a full heart, I must state that when the first election for a new West Indies comes, I shall offer myself as a candidate'. That election for 'a new West Indies' never came.

The story of the Federal Project is at once the story of the West Indies at its best and at its worst. In his Epilogue to John Mordecai's Book, Sir Arthur Lewis lists 11 'if onlys' on the basis of which the Federation would have been saved, but then he asks the question: 'How did these highly intelligent men, all devoted to Federation, come to make so many errors in so short a period"? Perhaps, Mordecai had answered the question when he wrote, bemoaning the disregard of diplomacy: *"At all points the rough handling of the problems of this Federation is more extraordinary than the problems themselves".*

Williams, Adams and Manley at the Federal Flag Raising in 1958

All this was my life in those years of political acrimony as we toiled uneasily at the coalface of West Indian federalism. I was personally engaged in the drafting of the Federal constitution based on the 1961 Lancaster House decisions when the referendum was held in Jamaica. 'Federal' friends had gathered in our home in Federation Park in Port of Spain to follow the results. When they came through to us that night, the general feeling was precisely the one Norman Manley was conveying to his granddaughter Rachel – *Everbody lost!* But there were Government elements in Port of Spain that night that were not sorrowful; Jamaica would take the blame in history for what they themselves had come to want – hence the swiftly announced new arithmetic '1 from 10 leaves 0'. Had the maths been right, the Federation of nine that was left would certainly have needed Trinidad and Tobago.

How pertinent to our condition were Brutus' words in Shakespeare's *Julius Caesar* before going into battle at Philippi:

> *There is a tide in the affairs of men,*
> *Which taken at the flood, leads on to fortune,*
> *Omitted, all the voyage of their life*
> *Is bound in shallows and in miseries.*

Is it any wonder that on 30 August 1962 – the day before Trinidad and Tobago's Independence – I wanted to get as far away from West Indian politicians as I could?

CHAPTER 9

Re-Building Regionalism

On 15 December 1965 at Dickenson Bay, Antigua, a pebble fell in the Caribbean, and the ripples from it reached shores across the archipelago – their sweep strengthened by the currents that were flowing. What were those currents, and what the pebble? The currents were the currents of unity that had begun to swirl again in the aftermath of island Independence. As early as 1963, within a year of the dissolution of the Federation in an environment of resentment on all sides, Eric Williams, not the least of the contributors to acrimony, had taken an initiative to convene the First Conference of the Heads of Government of the Commonwealth Caribbean – only four, the Prime Ministers of Jamaica and Trinidad and Tobago and the Premiers of Barbados and Guyana. Forbes Burnham of Guyana was later to have complimented him saying: *"It required some courage to have thought of the idea, let alone formulated it immediately after the break-up of the West Indies Federation"*. Williams, at that first Conference, pointed to a need which Independence on an island basis could not solve: the need to unite in the face of other emerging economic groupings. He said this:

> *As our countries achieve Independence or proceed to Independence, we enter into a world dominated increasingly by regional Groupings, both economic and political. Western Europe has succeeded. Africa is succeeding and efforts are being made to translate the political association in the Western*

Hemisphere into regional economic Groupings – the Latin American Free Trade Area and the Central American Common Market. Small countries like ours encounter great difficulty in establishing their influence in a world dominated by power and Regional Associations.

These compulsions were to drive Caribbean economic integration for years to come, but Williams advanced no proposals for meeting them.

The mood, however, was changing. The case for Caribbean economic co-operation, at least, was palpable. Less than two years later, with Burnham now in office in Guyana, Barrow and he (old friends from London student days) decided to act. It was Barrow who initiated action, as he testified with becoming modesty in his speech at the signing of the Treaty of Chaguaramas eight years later on 4 July 1973:

"Occasions for making disclosures of this kind are not frequent. I can now disclose that it was on 4th July 1965 that the Prime Minister of Guyana met with me in Barbados, at my invitation, to discuss the possibility of establishing a free trade area between our two countries in the first instance, and the rest of the Caribbean at such time as they would be ready to follow our example".

I was only just on the scene in Guyana as Attorney-General, but time enough to become involved in drafting what was to become the Caribbean Free Trade Area Agreement – CARIFTA.

Errol Barrow and Forbes Burnham were both committed West Indians for whom economic integration needed no advocacy. Even so, in approaching CARIFTA initially, their emphasis was slightly different. Barrow had given up in deep frustration on the 'Little Eight' – the effort to salvage mechanisms of unity between Barbados and the seven Leeward and Windward islands – helped (as he was) by Sir Arthur Lewis, St Lucia's Economics Nobel Laureate. His main aim now was to enlarge Barbados' 'domestic' market; Guyana was the most likely candidate; perhaps, even Antigua whose Premier, V.C. Bird, was a trusted friend; Trinidad and Tobago, with its greater manufacturing capacity, would be counter-productive. Burnham's vision was larger, more political, less immediately economic. A start, he felt, had to be made in rebuilding regionalism and, with Barrow in office, the Barbados-Guyana axis was reliable, as was Antigua under V.C. Bird. Hence the pebble cast at Dickenson Bay on 15 December 1965.

A Free Trade Agreement between Antigua, Barbados and British Guiana – (CARIFTA) – inspired by Barrow, developed by Burnham and hosted by V.C. Bird was a microcosm of unity; but it was a practical revival of regionalism. Burnham's idea never was a CARIFTA of three, and having engineered the deferral of the coming into force of the Agreement for a year (against Barrow's inclination), it fell to Guyana to lead the effort to bring the others on board – particularly Jamaica and Trinidad and Tobago. The leg-work to secure this was mine. It was not exactly easy.

There were some who felt at the time that CARIFTA was a precipitate step and, far from marking the beginnings of unity, would set back those beginnings. Indeed, as late as 1967 there were rumblings of this kind from more than one West Indian capital. But Burnham was not dismayed; he had taken a calculated risk, and such reactions were within his calculations. What Guyana had done was to give notice of our intention to proceed with CARIFTA – and we were certain that before the Free Trade Area actually started the movement toward unity would develop momentum. Moreover, we had deliberately given time for this development by retarding the start of the Free Trade Area – even at the vexation of initial colleagues.

When Eric Williams decided that this was not an invitation for Trinidad and Tobago to turn down, and when the six Leeward and Windward Islands (by then States in Association with Britain but responsible for all their affairs except foreign matters and defence) came on board, it did not take long for Jamaican manufacturers to persuade the country's Minister for Trade, Robert Lightbourne, that Jamaica should not stand aloof – or for him as Trade Minister of the region's largest economy to persuade his colleagues, in an anti-regional Government, that regionalism after all had a plus side. When the CARIFTA Agreement actually became operational in 1968, eleven Caribbean countries had become signatories. The rebuilding of regionalism had begun.

Against the back-drop of the decade that preceded it, 1965 to 1975 was to be a decade of extraordinary Caribbean vision and action, regionally and beyond the Region: a time which has not been replicated since save in spasms of enlightenment. I was privileged to be active in the Caribbean in those years and to share in those 'glory days'

In Guyana, we believed that there existed a new and favourable climate for West Indian unity. No one could be sure exactly what patterns that unity might take and, certainly, we did not attempt to draw up blueprints at that stage of transition when so many new constitutional relationships were just being established. But that there was now a climate propitious to regionalism we felt certain. If we were to be responsive to it and sensitive to the many and changing moods of the area; if we all tried harder to understand the special problems of our several countries and to be tolerant of each other's behaviour in the search for solutions to them; if, above all, we could suppress suspicion and replace silence by dialogue, there was perhaps much that we might yet achieve that had eluded the West Indies for so long.

With CARIFTA everything had changed. The ice that had hardened over West Indian unity with the dissolution of the Federation had, at last, been broken. The dialogue that had started with the Caribbean Heads of Government Conferences in 1963 now had an agenda of action. And with that came the rest – sensitivity to the new moods of the area, an understanding of each other's special problems and a tolerance with each other's actions. Above all, we began to suppress suspicion and to act again like members of a family. True, we were to have many a semantic argument about 'co-operation' and 'integration'. All the same, when the time came to establish the Caribbean Development Bank – a crucial integration institution, as we saw it – Jamaica (under the Prime Ministership of Edward Seaga, the protagonist of 'co-operation' not 'integration') was a strong contender for its location. It was right to start when there was a will to do so, even among a few, especially a few who knew that what they were beginning had to grow inclusively.

There are few things in life that are the result of pure accident, but Governments cannot proceed on a philosophy of vacuous expectation of something turning up. Much work was done in quiet patient ways in the years before a refined CARIFTA became operational. As a result, when the Fourth Commonwealth Caribbean Heads of Government Conference convened in Barbados in October 1967, a climate for West Indian unity was found in fact to exist and it was possible for agreement to be reached on the important resolutions of that meeting – resolutions that have since shaped the programme of regional economic integration.

I have dwelt upon these beginnings for two reasons. First, because it is good to recognise how much had been achieved in the years after Dickenson Bay. Second, because it is necessary to take note of the lessons of the early years in determining the patterns of action in the years ahead – in particular, the lesson that progress will follow if courage and inventiveness lead the way.

The Free Trade Area had been established and the Council of Ministers that charts its course had begun, through its quarterly meetings, to function in pragmatic ways substituting practicality for dogma and acknowledging the inevitability of compromise and concession. The Regional Secretariat under the leadership of Trinidad and Tobago's William Demas had begun to establish an identity of its own and to put into high gear the machinery of integration. The region was fortunate in having Demas at the helm in those early days. He made an immense contribution to the scholarship of integration; but beyond scholarship, he contributed to the enduring strength of the West Indian spirit by his absolute faith in its triumph over the wayward ways of a dividing sea. He was succeeded in due course by Alister McIntyre (now Sir Alister) who was in these respects his mirror image. The Caribbean could not have been better served than by these two technocrats whose vision and industry matched their learning.

Demas, McIntyre and their successor Edwin Carrington

Meanwhile, the Charter of the Regional Development Bank was signed by all the parties by the end of 1969 – the target date Guyana had suggested at the Heads of Government Conference in Trinidad earlier that year. It was a target met despite the doubts of those who felt we were pushing rather too hard; that we were running risks with the establishment of the Bank in order to meet an unrealistic deadline. Suffice it that the Bank was established and that we were able to start the 1970s with this important trinity – CARIFTA, the Regional Secretariat and the Regional Development Bank – established and functioning.

Many contributed to this achievement including others besides Governments – particularly the voluntary organisations, groups like the Incorporated Commonwealth Chambers of Commerce and Industry of the Caribbean, like trade union organisations throughout the region, like manufacturers associations everywhere, like the media of the region – all helped by their own enthusiasm to carry the movement along; they all deserved of the region its gratitude.

Still, we had barely laid the foundations of Caribbean integration. Very much more remained to be done; and it is well that, at the beginning of the 1970s, we should have set our perspectives and understood the enormity of the undertaking ahead. We recognised that it had to be for the Caribbean a decade of decision – a decade that would settle, perhaps this time for all time, whether we move on in ever narrowing circles to unity in cohesion, or spin off into separate orbits like so many wayward stars lost in the constellation of the world community. What were some of these decisions?

We had to decide, first of all, to consolidate the new institutions that had been established, and to ensure that they worked as instruments of integration. CARIFTA, the Secretariat and the Bank are instruments of integration. As instruments, they have to be applied – and applied by West Indians – if they were to make economic integration a reality.

There was a long way yet to go with CARIFTA itself. For example, the Agricultural Marketing Protocol was not yet working effectively, and it was this aspect of CARIFTA that could determine whether we moved ahead or not. Guyana believed that our future must be bound up with agriculture to a very large degree; and we were certain that CARIFTA would fail to achieve its goals of promoting the integration of the economies of the region unless we could demonstrate that there was in it a place for the primary producers of the region; unless we could demonstrate effectively that CARIFTA was something more than a confederation of manufacturers' associations. We wanted to secure for its implementation the same enthusiasm and practical support that had already been given to the establishment of the free trade arrangements at the level of manufactured products. It was particularly necessary that this enthusiasm and support should be demonstrated and given in the bigger countries; for from CARIFTA itself the Associated States (the smaller islands) had little to gain unless the Agricultural Marketing Protocol worked effectively. We knew that they were looking to see whether it was the intention that CARIFTA should work for them too.

We needed also to consolidate the Regional Secretariat. In making William Demas available as its Secretary-General, the Government of Trinidad and Tobago had demonstrated the importance it attached to integration, and set a notable standard of self-sacrifice for other West Indian Governments – not all of whom had been willing to make corresponding gestures to the success of regional institutions. Guyana saw the Regional Secretariat emerging in the 1970's as a central agency for regional action, working closely with the Regional Development

Bank but having a wide area of activity that went well beyond economic development in its narrowest sense. We saw the Shipping Council and the 'Regional Carrier', the Universities and the Examinations Council, all coordinated at the regional level within the Secretariat; and we saw the Secretariat, through this role of co-ordination, helping to fashion the programme of integration that Governments would promote.

And perhaps, as great as anything else, was the need to consolidate the Regional Development Bank as a West Indian institution. Although 40 per cent of the Bank's equity was contributed by non-regional Governments, we believed that none would say that their contribution was anything other than a contribution towards making this vital West Indian institution an effective instrument of integration and of West Indian economic development more generally.

In Guyana's vision of the 1970s we saw in the skies of the Caribbean, and beyond, a regional airline staffed by West Indians and flying a regional banner. We saw, too, in the seas of the Caribbean, and beyond, a West Indian shipping service providing a more effective sea link within the region than we had and, through extra-territorial services to our principal trading ports outside the region, freeing us from arbitrarily manipulated freight rates that could have so crippling an effect on that economic development towards which our other efforts were directed. Work of this kind was in hand within the Secretariat with assistance from the University of the West Indies and agencies of the United Nations. That work included attention to a common external tariff; a location of industries policy; harmonisation of fiscal incentives, and a regional fishing policy – to identify the most prominent. It was a monumental process, but undertaken at all levels from Heads of Government down with an astonishing measure of regional commitment given all that preceded it in the years before 1965.

In the decade that followed – and particularly in the 1970s – all the matters I have outlined, and more, engaged the attention of regional Ministers under the overall policy decisions of regional Prime Ministers (there were no Presidents yet). I spoke on them and cerebrated on them for Guyana – but always with a regional outlook. In due course, our multitudinous deliberations led to the essential clutch of practical agreements.

As important as anything we did in those years was our articulation of the policy of regional integration and the philosophy of Caribbean oneness that would sustain it. I did a good deal of public speaking in those years in the Caribbean and beyond, building a constituency for West Indian unity. I spoke, for example, to the National Press Club of Trinidad and Tobago in March 1970 and I said with regard to economic integration:

> *It will not be enough for us to consolidate the present and to secure and improve upon the past. As we stand on the threshold of the 70s we must project ourselves into the decade and devise those new institutions of integration that will be necessary if the goal of economic integration is to be achieved.*

That same year I was to speak twice more in Trinidad and Tobago. The first address was at the Institute of International Affairs in May which I titled '*WEST INDIAN NATIONHOOD: Myth, Mirage or Mandate*'; the second was at Chaguaramas in November to the Caribbean Ecumenical Consultation for Development which I called '*DIALOGUE OF UNITY: A Search for West Indian Identity*'. In January 1973 I spoke to the Royal Commonwealth Society in London on '*The Prospect for Community in the Caribbean*', where I said:

> *You will appreciate from all I have said that in these first years of our own independence, the Caribbean has been for Guyana an area of concentration. Our immediate pre-occupation is to implement the decisions taken last October for the establishment of the Caribbean Community, including the Caribbean Common market. Our objective is to maximise the economic strength of the Region. Our vision is that of West Indian Nationhood. I like to think that we have made some amends for defaults of a decade ago.*

In June 1975, in a farewell address to Caribbean colleagues in Montego Bay, Jamaica, which I called *'To Care for CARICOM'*, I said this:

> *... we must respond to the self-generating momentum of integration. No matter how much care and consideration we demonstrate, CARICOM will not survive merely by standing still. It will survive only if we generate the political will to constantly renew it with relevance to the aspirations of the West Indian people and to pursue continuous process of upgrading the mechanism of integration so as to ensure their potential for fulfilling the practical needs of the West Indian region.*

The point I make in referring to these statements is that in these years of activism in the cause of West Indian unity it was necessary to fulfil a quota of advocacy in furthering its cause; and that I was much engaged in doing so. It was a task that would never end.

In the evolution of CARIFTA and CARICOM there were many players over many years; but I need to mention here some of those who worked at the furnace of those meetings that changed the fortunes of the integration process at the innumerable Council meetings in Georgetown that engaged the issues I have described. There were some Premiers like Robert Bradshaw of St Kitts and Edward LeBlanc of Dominica, and, among the pioneering Ministers were Grenada's Derek Knight, Jamaica's Robert Lightbourne, St Lucia's George Mallet, St Vincent's James 'Son' Mitchell, Trinidad and Tobago's Kamaluddin Mohammed, St Kitts' Paul Southwell and Lee Moore, Jamaica's P. J. Patterson, and Barbados' Branford Taitt – and they were only some of those whose labours paved the way for CARICOM – all sustained at meetings in Guyana (as those who attended will recall) by Mrs Ting-a-Kee's 'crab-backs' – and much more. And the CARIFTA Secretariat itself – with William Demas and Alister McIntyre combining world class professionalism with passionate regionalism – was not a passive agency keeping the records. On the contrary, the Secretariat drove and inspired the process by its dynamism and technical excellence.

Heads agree on CARICOM, April 1973

It took all this and more, including camaraderie at all levels among decision-makers – camaraderie that took many forms besides solidarity around the conference table – many forms of togetherness of which friendships were built and confidences strengthened. Sailing in the Grenadines, duck shooting in Guyana, feasting on curried goat in Antigua, not to mention carnival and cricket and carousing on ferry boats on the Demerara River – all this too was part of the story of CARIFTA and its transition to CARICOM – and I was a part of most of them.

The journey from CARIFTA to Community has been well chronicled by William Demas in '*From CARIFTA to CARICOM*'. One of the lessons the journey teaches is the importance, sometimes the essentiality, of starting on a regional course, even if only a few in the region are ready to begin the journey. This may be valid in many contexts; it has a compelling logic in the context of our scattered archipelago. Where would we have been had CARIFTA not been started in 1965?

In an interdependent world, which in the name of liberalisation makes no distinctions between rich and poor, big and small, unity is a Caribbean compulsion. West Indian states – for all their separate flags and anthems – need each other for survival – the way villages do within a wider whole. With village affairs under 'local control' they could experiment with non-political forms of co-operation; and this they did after the more ambitious federal project was abandoned by some and lost to others. The leadership now came from Guyana (alas, too late), where the vision of an integrated West Indian people loomed large with a new political dispensation carrying none of the baggage of 'federation'. It was a dispensation that allowed me space and a supportive environment to push on the new boundaries of unity.

CHAPTER 10

Leading a Wider Unity

To say that the seeds of the Lomé Convention were sown on the lawns of the Guyana Prime Minister's residence in Georgetown is perhaps going too far; but there is more than a grain of truth in it. We shall see. It was 1972 and the Caribbean was not only preparing to advance from CARIFTA to CARICOM within the region, but also to venture forth into Europe. I was prominently involved in each process as Guyana's functional Foreign Minister – and perhaps even more so as Guyana's 'Caribbean man'.

The first thing to note about those times was our relative freshness and creativity. 1973 was a time of awareness of the need for a wider unity. Developing countries had found strength in their new spirit of oneness at the level of the Group of 77, and confidence in their global pursuit of a new order – primarily a new international economic order. At the United Nations in New York, at the UN Conference on Trade and Development (UNCTAD) in Geneva, in international gatherings around the world the theme of the South was 'unity'; and in the North-South dialogue that dominated the global scene developing countries gave intellectual leadership at diplomatic and technocratic levels.

The Caribbean played an active part in these global efforts; and regionally it showed courage and resolve in moving its own integration efforts towards 'community', and using its new political independence in progressive ways – like the ending of the diplomatic embargo of Cuba through their joint act of recognition. In unity they found strength, and courage to use it. And nowhere was that regional unity more manifest than in the negotiations with Europe for a new post-colonial trade and economic regime – the process which became known as the 'Lomé negotiations', taking its name from the capital of Togo where the Lomé Agreement was signed. Caribbean countries played a leadership role – politically and professionally – in those negotiations between the fledgling European Community of nine members and their erstwhile colonies in Africa, the Caribbean and the Pacific. So far as the Caribbean was concerned, they were negotiations effectively compelled by Britain's membership of the European Community.

I was the Caribbean's spokesman for the negotiations – chosen by regional Governments. But, of course, our policy positions in the negotiations were shaped continuously by a regional Council of Ministers, some Foreign Ministers, most Trade Ministers, prominently Jamaica's Trade Minister, P.J. Patterson – later to be Prime Minister. In essence, we first consolidated the Caribbean's unity, and then moulded the diverse countries of Africa and the Pacific with us into the ACP – the African, Caribbean and Pacific Group of countries. Caribbean unity made that wider unity possible.

The reference to the lawns of the Prime Minister's Residence in Georgetown with which this chapter began is apposite to this process. It was the time of the Non-Aligned Foreign Ministers Meeting, and all the Foreign Ministers attending were on those lawns for a reception. But, important as were the issues engaging the Meeting, I knew that ahead of us lay the negotiations with the European Community, which I was chosen to lead for the Caribbean and in which we would be interacting with African and Pacific countries. I knew that securing the maximum degree of unity possible with them was going to be important. Perhaps, I thought, this was a good moment to begin the process of exploring the possibilities of unity. So, shortly before the Foreign Ministers met, I told my colleagues on the CARIFTA Council of Ministers the following:

I intend to make use of the meeting of Non-aligned Foreign Ministers in Guyana to talk with all our colleagues from the Commonwealth about the EEC. I hope that we can involve all

> *our colleagues from the Caribbean in those discussions. These are not formal discussions. They are not secret discussions. They are just talks to see if we can get other people to pool their resources with ours in relation to the negotiations that lie ahead.*

To this end, I persuaded Prime Minister Burnham to allow his reception to accommodate a meeting of relevant Ministers, in a short discussion chaired by me. It was a large reception and we were able without disruption to corral the Ministers into a nearby room for the discussion. I ensured that our principal technicians were on hand. It was the evening of 9 August 1972 and I have been reminded that on those lawns we were almost equidistant from Africa to the East and the Pacific Islands to the West.

That informal discussion was the beginning of a process that led eventually to the pooling of the resources of all the African, Caribbean and Pacific States – 'Associates' and 'Associables', 'French-speaking' and 'English-speaking', 'AASM' and 'Commonwealth Members' – in the negotiations with the EEC that ended in the Lomé Convention.

The upshot of the ad-hoc Meeting was a warm reception for the idea of close collaboration between the African, Caribbean and Pacific countries taking part in the negotiations with Europe and agreement on how the interaction might begin. The Meeting decided that a team of Caribbean officials would visit Commonwealth African capitals for more comprehensive technical discussions. That CARIFTA mission went in September 1972 to East and West Africa, holding talks in Arusha with officials of the East African Community and their counterparts in Lagos, Accra and Freetown – apprising their colleagues of the preparatory work already being undertaken in the Caribbean. What was clearly needed, however, was concerted action among African states, and at Lagos, Nigeria, in February 1973 a start was made in this direction with a meeting of Commonwealth African Ministers hosted by the Government of Nigeria. It was characterised by a bold and purposeful approach to the questions whether there should be negotiations with the European Economic Community (EEC) as it then was and, if so, on what basis, and with what objectives.

At Lagos, it was agreed that a further meeting of Ministers should be convened in Nairobi to pursue these issues. Building on the international links forged earlier in 1972 the Lagos meeting authorised a team of Commonwealth African Ministers to visit Georgetown to hold discussions with Caribbean Ministers at CARIFTA Headquarters. This meeting, held on 19 March 1973 provided an opportunity for a comprehensive exchange of views on the approach to any negotiations with the EEC and on the essentials of any possible relationship. A refusal to be confined within the negotiating straight-jacket imposed by the “options” in Protocol 22 to the Treaty Accession and a determination to resist European overtures for a free trade area arrangement involving ‘reciprocal preferences’ emerged clearly and with unanimity from these discussions. Caribbean officials were invited to attend the Nairobi meeting as observers and did so in continuation of the inter-regional dialogue that was now fully established.

The Nairobi meeting allowed the Governments concerned to further elaborate and refine their approach to the negotiations and it prepared the ground for the next major step forward – namely, a deepening of the dialogue to encompass a political mandate for Africa as a whole to negotiate a unified relationship. Until these developments, the AASM States – the Francophone ‘Associates’ – were preparing for the re-negotiation of the Yaounde Convention (due to expire at the end of 1974) and there was a real danger of the perpetuation throughout the negotiations of the separateness – and, indeed, the potential conflict of interest – which the status of ‘Associates’ and ‘Associables’ tended to imply and develop.

As these separate preparations unfolded it became clear that a wider African unity was the prerequisite to any effective negotiations with the EEC. This was accomplished at Abidjan, Ivory Coast in May 1973 at a Ministerial meeting convened under the auspices of the Organisation of Africa Unity (OAU). Out of that meeting came a united African approach to the negotiations – an approach founded on the ‘eight principles’ hammered out as the essential requirements of African States. More than once in these pioneering efforts at working together, Commonwealth and Francophone countries recognised the clear absurdity of preserving – as if decolonisation had never taken place – the biases, the suspicions, the sometimes wholly imaginary barriers to understanding that were the inheritance of colonialism itself. The Caribbean's partnering role assisted this mutual recognition. At Addis Ababa these principles were endorsed by African Heads of State at the 10th Anniversary Summit Meeting of the OAU. They were to become the corner stone of the negotiating structure erected by the ACP in Brussels.

All this had taken place against the background of not inconsiderable pressure from the EEC for the urgent commencement of negotiations and their being channelled into the pre-determined contours of Protocol 22 – contours that themselves tended to highlight distinctions between the 'Associates' and 'Associables'. As it transpired, these divisive 'options' under Protocol 22 (for inclusion in a revised Yaounde Convention, for a separate Arusha-type Convention under Article 138 of the Treaty of Rome, or for a simple Trade Agreement with the Community) were never exercised by the 'Associables' – despite Community mythology to the contrary. What eventually emerged at Lomé was the *sui generis* Agreement for which the ACP initially contended.

At Brussels, in July 1973, the first meeting took place between Ministers of the African, Caribbean and Pacific States and the Ministers of the Community. For the Europeans, it was the beginning of the negotiations; for the ACP it was 'talks about talks'. But whether it was the one or the other, a much more significant trend was discernible – a trend which the negotiations later confirmed and which had a decisive influence on their outcome. The European statement, relying heavily on generalisation, if not indeed ambiguity, bore all the marks of internal Community conflict. The ACP statement – three separate statements delivered by spokesmen of Africa ('Associates' and 'Associables' making a single speech) the Caribbean, and the Pacific – revealed clearly perceived objectives and bore all the marks of internal coordination and consistency.

From that time onward there was no turning back to separateness. At the next joint ACP/EEC Ministerial meeting in Brussels in October

1973, the ACP case presented by three voices in July was now urged by one voice – that of the then current Chairman of the African Group. This was in response to a specific Caribbean offer that the demonstrated unity of the ACP Group be symbolised and formalised by such a single presentation. Thereafter, throughout the discussions, extending over a year, the ACP never negotiated otherwise than as a Group and spoke always with one voice. It was often an African voice, sometimes a Caribbean or a Pacific voice; but always a voice that spoke for the ACP.

In the first statement I made on behalf of the Caribbean at the opening of what we called the 'ACP-EEC Conference' on 28 July 1973, I made a point that was to permeate the subsequent negotiations and bears repeating here. It was that as regards trading arrangements with the Community, we did not consider it appropriate that the negotiations should proceed on the concept of a free trade relationship; and we rejected entirely the notion that the price of duty free entry into the Community for the main products of developing States with whom the arrangements are concluded should be the reciprocation of trade benefits. Reciprocity between those who are unequal in economic strength was a contradiction in economic terms. In contemporary economic relations, I concluded:

> *Aristotle's dictum that 'justice requires equality between equals but proportionality between unequals' must surely mean that as between those who are unequal in economic strength, equity itself demands non-reciprocity. We are, therefore, strongly opposed to the incorporation in the new arrangements of anything on the lines of article 3, paragraph 1, of the Yaounde Convention.*

The reference to Aristotle was a contribution of Barbados' Foreign Minister, Cameron Tudor, a Greek scholar who had been President of the Oxford Union. It virtually ended argument, and the Lomé Convention did not require reciprocity. The Convention which was to govern trade and economic relations with the evolving Europe for two decades, and dictate the fundamentals of ACP-EU relations for two more, has now been replaced by Economic Partnership Agreements (EPAs) between the European Union and the several parts and sub-parts of the Group of African, Caribbean and Pacific countries. At the heart of EPAs is 'reciprocity'. Ironically, it is the Caribbean countries who were the first to accept the new EPA dispensation in 2008 by each of them individually signing the Agreement with the 27-nation European Union collectively.

The sustained unity of the ACP in the Lomé negotiations naturally called for immense preparatory work. In large measure, this was done by the ACP Ambassadors in Brussels, meeting in regular session. Their monumental efforts prepared the ground for Ministerial Meetings held successively in Dar-es-Salaam, Dakar, Kingston and Accra at which ACP positions and approaches were discussed and settled. The meeting in Kingston, Jamaica in 1974 represented a high point in ACP solidarity. Up to then, meetings with the EEC Ministers had all taken place in Brussels. It was important to the ACP that this pattern of movement to Europe be broken and, in July 1974, the next joint ACP/EEC Ministerial Meeting convened in the Caribbean. ACP unity was both manifest and insistent and negotiations moved forward appreciably, but with discernible signs of mounting Community resistance to some of the more 'sensitive' demands of the ACP – such as those on 'rules of origin', or the character of 'most favoured nation treatment', or access for products covered by the Community's 'Common Agricultural Policy'.

Meanwhile, the ACP had been developing its machinery of unity. Reference has already been made to the Committee of Ambassadors in Brussels and the Meetings of ACP Ministers. Underpinning all these was the ad-hoc Secretariat of the ACP Group headed by an Executive Secretary, supported by staff permanently based in Brussels and supplemented by a continuous flow of ACP technicians working closely with it. Nothing did more to forge the ACP into a disciplined united working group at all levels than this regime of joint effort directed toward concerted goals.

In the end, at the final negotiating session in Brussels, the Ministerial spokesmen of the ACP on whom rested the responsibility of negotiating with European Ministers on behalf of the entire Group, came from such varied backgrounds as Gabon (Financial and Technical Co-operation), Mauritania (Institutions, Establishments, etc.), Guyana (the Trade Regime), Fiji and Jamaica (Sugar) and Senegal (Coordinating ACP Chairman). Guyana's responsibility for 'the Trade Regime' meant that I was the central negotiator.

My Caribbean colleague, P.J. Patterson of Jamaica (photo above) played a major role in leading for the ACP the negotiations on 'sugar' – a commodity of major importance to many of our countries. The credit for the resulting 'Sugar Protocol' was largely his. I was pleased that on 12 February 2009 the European Commission honoured P.J. Patterson and me by the naming of a special room in the EC headquarters in Brussels after us – for our "historic contribution to Caribbean-European co-operation". In matters of trade, the Pacific Islands looked more to Australia and the Pacific Rim countries than to Europe, save for Fiji whose sugar exports to Britain were important to its economy. Prime Minister Ratu Mara of Fiji led generally for the Pacific, and was a shared spokesman on sugar. The 'P' in the ACP was never forgotten.

The unity of interests of the ACP became more manifest as the negotiations lengthened and, as was dramatically revealed in the ultimate stages when, rum, a product of interest to only one region – the Caribbean – threatened to frustrate the eventual consensus. Neither regional nor linguistic affinities, neither separate national interests nor past associations, neither personalities nor cultural patterns, were allowed to supersede the interest of the Group as a whole. Rum was a Caribbean product. Africa – Francophone and Anglophone – was willing to forego its hard won gains in the negotiations if the Caribbean's needs on rum were not met. They made that clear to Europe. Caribbean needs were met. For me, that was the finest moment in the negotiations; for it was a moment of solidarity that had truly begun on the Prime Minister's lawns in Georgetown two years before.

The Lomé Convention was not perfect; it did not meet all the aspirations of the ACP as a significant segment of the developing world. At the signing of the Convention in Lomé on 28 February 1975, I stressed that it was in the potential of the Convention that its great value lay – being true to the ideals of co-operation which it proclaims:

> *It would be an essay in self-deception, I said, for us to believe that the document we sign today fulfils all those ideals of co-operation, and it would be a dangerous pretence for us to imply that it does.*

Nonetheless, the Convention was a point of departure in the relations between the developing and the developed States. The negotiations were then the most effective negotiations on a package of comprehensive economic arrangements ever conducted by developing countries with any major sector of the developed world. That it was such an innovation and represented such a promise derived in the main from the process of unification described above – a process that brought together what were then 46 developing States in a uniquely effective manner to meet the challenge of negotiating with the European Economic Community – a significant segment of the developed world that had itself so rightly turned to integration in answer to the challenge of survival. The Lomé Convention was to last for 20 years – renewed three times with improvement.

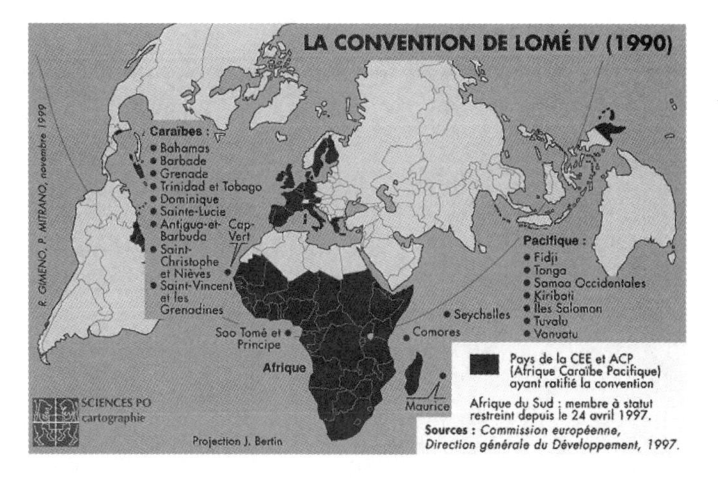

I took personal satisfaction in the conclusion of the EU-ACP's Convention; but more in the evolution of the ACP. Yet, I felt that my work was not complete. As the negotiations proceeded and the ambition for unity grew, I began to see the ACP as a group whose genesis was in the negotiations with Europe but which had to have an existence outside of those relations – the largest inter-continental group of developing countries working in functional unity. To consummate this I invited the Ministers of the ACP, who had bonded through the negotiations, to meet in Georgetown to formally establish the ACP in its own right. In June 1975 – at what was to be my last conference as Foreign Minister – the ACP Ministers signed the *'Georgetown Agreement'* establishing the ACP in its own right with objectives beyond the implementation of the Lomé Convention. The ACP now has its own headquarters in Brussels. In those pioneering days much of the effort was hands-on. Creating the ACP meant designing a logo; it was done in my office with our occasional graphic artist Cicely Godette working with me. It has served us well for four decades now,

None of this would have been possible without the progress we were making at home in developing the fledgling CARIFTA structures into the much larger, more ambitious framework of Community. Indeed that evolution of the 'CARICOM' negotiations proceeded side by side with the negotiations with Europe. Before we journeyed to Lomé in February 1975, four Caribbean countries had journeyed first to Chaguaramas in July 1973 to sign the Treaty establishing the Caribbean Community. Within a year, another eight had joined the group. These processes of ambitious activism at home and abroad were mutually reinforcing. It helped us abroad that we were working together at home; it helped us at home that we were working effectively abroad. Neither was without difficulty, for all that. But in each area of effort it became easier to overcome.

The second compelling lesson is how critical it was to pool our resources – political, economic and intellectual in negotiating with countries beyond ourselves: globally, in Europe, in the Hemisphere, and within the wider Caribbean. As regards the Lomé negotiations, the process of unification – for such it was – added a new dimension to the Third World's quest for economic justice through international action. Its significance, however, derives not mainly from the terms of the negotiated relationship between the 46 ACP States and the EEC, but rather from the methodology of unified bargaining which the negotiations pioneered. Never before had so large a segment of the developing world negotiated with so powerful a grouping of developed countries so comprehensive and so innovative a regime of economic relations. It was a new, and salutary, experience for Europe; it was a new, and reassuring, experience for the ACP States.

* * *

The inescapable lesson of the CARIFTA/CARICOM years is that West Indians need each other. All else is illusion and mirage. The Caribbean must not yield to siren songs of separateness. Nor must it be afraid to stand up for principle whether it is with Europe with the Lomé negotiations or America as we did over diplomatic relations with Cuba.

A small episode in 1974 in the area of US-Latin America relations reaffirmed to me that for small states without conventional power, principle offers diplomatic clout and earns respect. That 1972 action with which I had been so closely involved of breaking the diplomatic embargo against Cuba through joint action by Barbados, Guyana, Jamaica and Trinidad and Tobago had lifted the self-esteem of West Indians; not as an ideological statement, but as an independent stand on the side of justice – American anguish notwithstanding.

Two years later I was involved in another such assertion of universal values at the Conference of Tlatelolco in Mexico in 1974. It was a time of Henry Kissinger's ascendancy in world affairs and he had chosen a meeting of Latin American Foreign Ministers to unveil, and secure approval of, a scheme for 'A Community of the Western Hemisphere'. He had apparently squared the proposal with the Mexican Foreign Minister, Emilio Óscar Rabasa Mishkin, but with no one else. I represented Guyana and Foreign Minister Dudley Thompson, Jamaica. Kissinger spoke at the public opening and 'announced' his proposal – of course in the name of the United States. Dudley Thompson was a blunt and fearless Jamaican, who as a young lawyer had been on Jomo Kenyatta's legal defence team in Kenya during the Mau-Mau period. He and I were equally troubled by Kissinger's proposal and astonished at the manner of its presentation for decision. To make matters worse, Canada to whom we were very close was not then a member of the Latin American group and was not, therefore, at the Meeting; and Cuba was neither there nor did the US intend it to be in the 'Community'.

When the matter came to the floor for discussion (in closed session), I was surprised by the lack of Latin American complaint. Apart from Thompson and me the only other strong objection came from our Venezuelan counterpart Aristides Calvani. I spoke in a fashion Kissinger had to respect making the case that a 'Community of the Western Hemisphere' was not on, since, in an association of such unequals, 'community' would inevitably mean hegemony. Moreover, I objected to the exclusion of Canada and Cuba. I drew again on Aristotle's '*Ethics*' (to Kissinger's obvious astonishment) saying:

> *Aristotle's dictum has application beyond the field of economics, and we would do well to acknowledge its validity in these areas also. Is it not true that all history bears out the proposition that at the level of political relations between States of unequal strength, 'unity' has invariably involved hegemony? And, does it not follow.... that as between unequals, 'community' might so easily imply dominion. Do not the political realities of our time dictate that even the possibility of such an unintended implication should make us pause and approach the concept of a 'Community of the Western Hemisphere' with caution and with reserve?*

Dudley Thompson followed the same line, rather more robustly, and was particularly trenchant over the exclusion of Cuba – "treating Cuba as a four-letter word" was how he admonished Kissinger. When we were finished, Kissinger, visibly surprised, asked for an adjournment and sought out Dudley and me in the coffee-room asking, without rancour, in his bluff way: "Who the hell are you? I thought I was coming to meet a bunch of Spaniards, and you turn up. I am going to withdraw the proposal". And on the resumption, he did just that. Rabasa Mishkin was crest-fallen; but I believe that most Latin American Ministers were relieved that we had 'belled the cat'.

In the third volume of his memoirs, *Years of Renewal,* writing of the Tlatelolco Conference, Kissinger conceded: *"I had perhaps used a too grandiloquent phrase for what was really a system of closer Western Hemispheric consultation"; and* he acknowledged that *"What troubled them* (the Latin American Foreign Ministers) *was the concept of 'community'.... clearly they feared that the United States had found a new formula for its traditional hegemonic aspirations"*. It was a gracious withdrawal. But there was more. In concluding his account of the Tlatelolco meeting Kissinger wrote:

> *Gibson Barbosa (the Foreign Minister of Brazil) proposed that the English-speaking members of the conference try their hand at a counterdraft and that Foreign Minister 'Sonny' Ramphal of Guyana and I serve as the drafting committee.*

It was an extraordinary proposition. Guyana was invariably on the side of the radicals in Third World forums. Like all the successor states of Europe's Caribbean possessions, it was not part of the historic inter-American system and was not even a member of the OAS. Tlatelolco was, in fact the first meeting of Western Hemisphere foreign ministers to which Ramphal had been invited. On the other hand, Guyana had border disputes with Venezuela, with respect to which United States goodwill might prove useful. Above all, Ramphal, whose command of English was awe-inspiring and who was as charming as he was eloquent, hugely enjoyed his pivotal role. In the end, he and I managed to produce a draft more compatible with the original intentions of the New Dialogue.

Later, when I saw the UN Secretary-General (Kurt Waldheim) at the meeting of the UN General Assembly that followed Tlatelolco closely, he told me that Kissinger had recounted the episode to him and warned him not to 'tangle' with Ramphal. Altogether, it was good for Caribbean self-confidence – and for our standing in Latin America.

In friendlier times

CHAPTER 11

The Caribbean Vineyard

A. THE PROMISE OF GRAND ANSE

The year 2012 was the 50th Anniversary of the independence of Jamaica and of Trinidad and Tobago. Together, those anniversaries marked the first 50 years of West Indian 'freedom' in its larger sense. But there are ironies to share and questions to be asked in the context of my life and beyond it.

In 1962 I lived in Trinidad; in Port of Spain, my West Indian Capital. 'The West Indies', with a capital T, the Federation for which West Indian leaders had struggled, intellectually and politically, for 40 years: Trinidadians like Captain Cipriani and Uriah 'Buzz' Butler, Jamaicans like Norman Manley, Grenadians like T.A. Marryshow, Dominicans like Cecil Rawle, Guyanese like Hubert Nathaniel Critchlow, Barbadians like Grantley Adams – and for which its people had yearned – that Federation was about to become Independent on the 31 May that year. In 2012, Caribbean people should have been celebrating the 50th anniversary of the Independence of the West Indian nation.

That is how close the Caribbean came to reaching the 'holy grail'. Instead, on that same day (31 May 1962), the Federation was dissolved. The immediate cause of the dissolution was, of course, Jamaica's referendum and Dr Williams' inventive, and now notorious, arithmetic that "1 from 10 leaves nought". But these were only the proximate causes. Federation's failure had many fathers as I have described in

Chapter 8. As Assistant Attorney-General of the Federation, I had actually been drafting the Federal Constitution. My vision, my mission, was regional – an independent West Indies. I left Port of Spain for Harvard, where I would be reassured by the example of other federal founding fathers who had overcome their trials – trials much greater and more traumatic than our own – through sustained vision and leadership. That reassurance has helped me to sustain faith in Caribbean unity as our regional destiny.

Nor, did everyone lose faith. In the last pages of *'From Columbus to Castro: The History of the Caribbean, 1492-1969'*, completed while still Prime Minister of Trinidad and Tobago, Eric Williams wrote this:

> *The real case for unity in Commonwealth Caribbean countries rests on the creation of a more unified front in dealing with the outside world – diplomacy, foreign trade, foreign investment and similar matters. Without such a unified front the territories will continue to be playthings of outside Governments and outside investors. To increase the 'countervailing power' of the small individual units vis-à-vis the strong outside Governments and outside companies requires that they should aim at nothing less than a single centre of decision-making vis-à-vis the outside world.*

He had earlier written in those same pages:

> *Increasingly, the Commonwealth Caribbean countries such as Trinidad and Tobago will become aware that the goals of greater economic independence and the development of a cultural identity will involve them in even closer ties one with another – at economic and other levels. For the present disgraceful state of fragmentation of the Commonwealth Caribbean countries makes it extremely difficult (although not impossible) for a single country to adopt a more independent and less 'open' strategy of development.*

This statement perhaps explains why within months of its writing, he would send me a copy of *'From Columbus to Castro'* inscribed as follows:

> *My dear Sonny. We are both labourers in the vineyard. It is in this spirit that I send you this book. Bill.*

From Columbus to Castro: The History of the Caribbean 1492—1969

ERIC WILLIAMS

André Deutsch

The vineyard was economic integration: the new variety of unity, after 'federation' had withered. It was his hope that the efforts of the 1960s – the drive from CARIFTA to Community and the fulfilment of the integrationist dream of Chaguaramas could ameliorate *"the present disgraceful state of fragmentation of the Commonwealth Caribbean countries"* – a state of disunity he so palpably deplored, but had countenanced with the arithmetic, "1 from 10 leaves 0".

From all this, two questions invite answers: one speculative, the other more definitive. The first is whether West Indians would have been better off in 2012 were we celebrating the 50th Anniversary of the Independence of The West Indies? The second, given that we abandoned federation, is whether we have rectified what Eric Williams called (in 1969) our *"disgraceful state of fragmentation"*.

The first question is uniquely appropriate to 2012; the second is imperative at all times. As to the first, would we have been better off had the Federation not been dissolved? Any answer to this must make some assumptions; but there are good clues. The first is that the patchwork Lancaster House Constitution agreed to in 1961 would have been the basis of Independence – i.e., a very weak central government but with a constitutional review in 5 years. But another assumption is more positive. Norman Manley had pledged that if he won the referendum, he would offer himself for election to the Federal Parliament. His actual words were: *"As simply as I can, and with a full heart, I must state that when the first election for a new West Indies comes, I shall offer myself as a candidate"*. In other words, Norman Manley might have been the Prime Minister of the independent Federation – a circumstance of indubitable strength, given his superior capacity to inspire confidence and respect throughout the region and beyond it.

The new Federal Government would have minimal, indeed miniscule, powers. The *Economics of Nationhood*, by which Eric Williams placed such store, but whose strong central government so frightened Jamaica, would be in cold storage. The Government would be essentially a vehicle for mobilising the people of the West Indies to nationhood – and with Manley at the helm inspiring in them, and in the international community, confidence in the maturity of the new Caribbean state. Five years later, constitutional review, against the backdrop of those first years of nation-building, would give confidence to a process of endowing the Federal Government with more substantive but still limited powers. Perhaps, most important of all, would be the gains in the deepening of our West Indian identity and the enlargement of a West Indian patriotism.

And they would be years of the West Indian people getting to know each other as never before. *The Federal Palm* and *The Federal Maple* would carry them where only their West Indian spirit had been before in their inter-island travels.

Independence for all of the islands would be achieved within the framework of the federation, and each of the Island States would be autonomous within their substantial powers. On the international stage, The West Indies, though still small in world terms, would have become a sizeable player, not least because of the quality and spread of our human resources. One West Indies respected in the world would carry immeasurably more weight that fourteen miniscule and uncoordinated units each reliant on its separateness. And would Guyana, which had inexcusably abstained from the federal project, not have been inexorably drawn into its revival? It would, I believe, have become its unavoidable pathway to independence.

On the eve of its 50th Anniversary our national Federal State (with Guyana and Suriname in it) would have comprised more than 6 million people; it would have had vast resources of oil, gas, gold, diamonds, bauxite, forestry, uranium, manganese, tourism, and financial services; importantly, it would have had an educated and talented people who have shown by their global accomplishments, and the demand for their expertise, that they could compete with any in the world community. It would have been a State that commanded our national pride – and respect of the international community – while keeping alive our several island cultures and values.

Against what might have been, has to be placed what has been. Independence on an island basis (and I regard Belize and Guyana as islands for this purpose) with our one West Indies formally fragmented into separate states, with many flags and anthems and seats in the United Nations. But, most of all, independence in the context of very small communities without the checks and balances that larger size brings. In his frank Epilogue to Sir John Mordecai's invaluable record, *'The West Indies: The Federal Negotiations',* Sir Arthur Lewis, after asserting that "*the case for a West Indian federation is as a strong as ever",* concluded his reasoning with the following:

> *Lastly, Federation is needed to preserve political freedom. A small island falls easily under the domination of a boss, who crudely or subtly intimidates the police, the newspapers, the*

> *magistrates and private employers. The road is thus open to persecution and corruption. If the island is part of a federation the aggrieved citizen can appeal to influences outside: to Federal Courts, to the Federal police, to the Federal auditors, the Federal Civil Service Commission, the newspapers of other islands, and so on. If the Government creates disorder, or is menaced by violence beyond its control, the Federal Government will step in to uphold the law. These protections do not exist when the small island is independent on its own. So far West Indian governments have a fine tradition for respecting law and order, but in these turbulent days traditions are easily set aside. The West Indies needs a federation as the ultimate guardian of political freedom in each island.*

That was 1968. By 2012, we had up to 44 years of experience of separate independence to say whether he was right – not only in Jamaica and Trinidad and Tobago but in all the independences that followed, in Barbados and then in the smaller OECS islands – and, of course, in Guyana and Belize. Judgement will not be uniform, but I believe that many West Indians, in many parts of our region, will say that Sir Arthur was right – and is – and that the answer to my speculative question is 'Yes', we would be better off as West Indians, had we celebrated the 50th Anniversary of the Independence of the Federated West Indies in 2012.

But, besides Sir Arthur's particular questions are others which we cannot avoid; questions not only for Jamaica and Trinidad and Tobago, but for all of CARICOM; questions which probe whether as independent countries we have done as well individually as we might have done collectively.

To mention only a few:

- Would we have been in a better position to feed our growing populations by mobilising the land resources of Guyana, Suriname and Belize, the capital of Trinidad and the skills of Jamaica, Barbados and other countries to create a viable food economy that reduces our import bill of over US $4.5 billion (in 2014)?

- Would we have been better able to manage the security of our borders, and to exploit the possibilities afforded by the Exclusive Economic Zone authorised by the United Nations Convention on the Law of the Sea, by the establishment of a seamless maritime boundary across much of the Eastern Caribbean island chain?
- In the UN Climate Change negotiations, and at the Rio+20 Summit on Environment and Development, would we have been listened to with greater respect and attention, speaking as a single voice from a bloc of island states and low-lying countries whose very existence is threatened by climate change, and having a common climate change mitigation and adaptation regime governed by a common political authority?
- Would the Federation not have created a larger space for the creativity, productivity and advancement of our people, especially the youth? And, could we not have done better in keeping at home the over 60 per cent of our tertiary educated people who now live in the OECD countries?
- Would not our Caribbean companies have been more competitive in the global community than our locally placed nano-industries?
- Would not our single Caribbean state have been able to bargain more effectively in the global community – including with the World Bank, the IMF, and the WTO; with the European Union and with Canada and China – for better terms and conditions for trade, aid and investment than our individual states with their smaller resources have been able to do?
- With its greater resources and larger pool of human talent, would the Federation not have given us a wider field of opportunity and greater protection and prospects than our individual states have provided?

Of course, not all will agree on the answers. Separatism has its beneficiaries: in political establishments, in commercial sectors, among anti-social elements that prosper in environments of weakness. That has always been the allure of 'local control'. But what of the West Indian people – the ones for whom Norman Manley spoke when he looked to federation as providing *"a wider field for ambition"*?

Whatever our speculation – and it can be no more than that – in 1962 the moving finger of history wrote out 'federation', and having 'writ' moved on. But in writing out solutions, history does not erase needs. What about those needs of which Eric Williams wrote in 1969, within seven years of Independence? How have we done in our separate independences in responding to the *"real case for unity"* that he saw in *"the creation of a more united front in dealing with the outside world – diplomacy, foreign trade, foreign investment and similar matters"*.

How have we responded to his view that *"to increase the countervailing power of our small individual units... requires nothing less than the creation of a single centre of decision-making vis-à-vis the outside world"*?

How have we acted to change *"the present disgraceful state of fragmentation of the Commonwealth Caribbean countries"*? Having disposed of Federation for better or for worse, have we retrieved through economic integration the gains we had hoped for from Federation? What success has attended our labours in the vineyard? Have we been labouring? These are all aspects of the second question; and our answer can, indeed, be more definitive.

* * *

When Eric Williams inscribed *From Columbus to Castro* to me in 1970, the Caribbean Community and Common Market was on its way to being agreed. The vineyard was being planted, but the labour of nurturing would continue. Work on the Treaty to formalise and fill it out was in hand under the guidance of William Demas at the Secretariat as he toiled in the vineyard of regional economic integration and inspired a generation of West Indian regionalists: economists and others. The Treaty was signed at Chaguaramas on 4 July 1973 – the original Treaty of Chaguaramas – signed initially by Prime Ministers Errol Barrow, Forbes Burnham, Michael Manley and Eric Williams. The signing of the Treaty has been described as *"a landmark in the history of West Indian people"*; and so it was.

Signing the Treaty of Chaguaramas, 1973

And it was a highpoint of regional unity and confidence. In that same year we were negotiating with the still new European Community as one Caribbean – with our own Community – and using our oneness to forge the unity of the African, Caribbean and Pacific countries (the ACP) – reducing the developing countries negotiating the Lomé Convention with Europe from 46 to 1. And we were holding our own at the UN in New York and Geneva in the international 'make-over' debate on a New International Economic Order. And just months before the signing of the Treaty, on Guyana's initiative, as I have explained, Barbados, Guyana, Jamaica and Trinidad and Tobago had defied hemispheric opinion and broken the diplomatic embargo against Cuba in December 1972. And there was more. Long before US President Ronald Reagan's Caribbean Basin Initiative we had advanced proposals for an Association of Countries of the Caribbean Basin, with Trinidad and Tobago offering to host the defining Summit Conference.

But we had flattered to deceive. Within years, we had relapsed into inertia and worse. For seven years, from 1975 to 1982, the Heads of Government Conference – with the Common Market Council, CARICOM's 'principal organ' – did not meet. This is not the place for an inquest into Caribbean dissipation. The excuses were multiple: the enlarging economic disparity between Trinidad and Tobago and Guyana and Jamaica in particular; the virus of 'ideological pluralism' that infected the integration process; the divisive effects of the emergence of Grenada's Revolutionary Government specifically and the threat of a return of the region to external power rivalries; the deterioration of personal relations between Caribbean leaders to the point of incivility. By the end of the 1970s it was realised that an impasse had been reached in Caribbean affairs and the CARICOM Council turned to William Demas and a team of regional experts to 'review the functioning of Caribbean integration... and prepare a strategy for its improvement in the decade of the 1980s'.

The Group's findings were blunt and worth recalling:

> *"although gains were registered in many aspects of functional co-operation and to a lesser extent with respect to inter-regional trade, inadequate progress was made in production integration and coordination of foreign policies... The misunderstandings... that characterised certain initiatives taken by some member countries in the field of external economic relations also gave a poor public image to the Community.*

Their conclusions contained seeds of hope:

> *The fact, however, that the institutional framework of the community remains intact, that an inter-governmental dialogue was and is being sustained and that intra-regional trade and functional co-operation continue to show resilience and in some cases growth, indicate that the foundations of the movement are still intact.*

But hope was misplaced. The Grenada invasion in 1983 effectively put paid to any 're-launch' of CARICOM. As Professor

Anthony Payne commented in his indispensable 2008 *'Political History of CARICOM'*:

> *It was not just that the region disagreed about what to do in Grenada once the internal coup had taken place, but that the countries that actively supported and promoted the idea of a US Invasion (Jamaica, Barbados and the OECS states) deliberately connived to conceal their intentions from their remaining CARICOM partners – Trinidad, Guyana and Belize... No mention was made of such a commitment during the CARICOM discussions, which focussed exclusively upon the sanctions which could be brought to bear on the new military regime in Grenada.*
>
> *In these circumstances, the other leaders – especially George Chambers and Forbes Burnham... understandably felt that they had been made to look foolish. Bitter recrimination followed... Many commentators wondered whether CARICOM would finally fall apart.*
>
> *The critical factor was whether anyone would actually work to destroy it... A number of (leaders) came increasingly to suspect that (the then Prime Minister of Jamaica) Edward Seaga's real aim was the replacement of CARICOM with a looser organisation embracing non-Commonwealth countries and excluding any existing member state that was not willing to accept US leadership in regional affairs. He fuelled these fears by speaking of the possible creation of CARICOM Mark II, arousing the suspicion in Trinidad and Guyana that he was making a threat directed mainly at them. ... The Region was left in no doubt that during the 1980s CARICOM matters were a much lower priority in Kingston than the question of Jamaica's dealings with Washington.*

I have quoted Professor Payne at length because we need to remember how, at that time, we used our separateness, some will say our sovereignty, against each other.

No wonder that CARICOM languished during the 1980s as well. But towards the end of the decade fortunes changed. Michael Manley replaced Seaga in Jamaica and in Trinidad A.N.R. Robinson entered the vineyard lamenting CARICOM's lack of "*not only political but philosophical underpinnings*". Manley brought Jamaica back to its Caribbean roots; but it was Robinson who helped CARICOM return to its intellectual moorings. His Paper addressed to the 1989 Heads of Government Conference at Grand Anse, Grenada, which he entitled '*The West Indies Beyond 1992*' was a 'wake-up' call to the region. The year 1992 was 500 years since Columbus's mis-named voyage of 'discovery'. Though I was in London at the time his Paper was being prepared, the Prime Minister consulted me on it. I was enthused that a new leadership was emerging. The response of his colleagues at Grand Anse was equally encouraging, and among the conclusions embodied in the '*Grand Anse Declaration and Work Programme for the Advancement of the Integration Movement*' was:

> *We are determined to work towards the establishment in the shortest possible time of a single market and economy for the Caribbean Community.*

As I write, it is more than 25 years since that assertion. West Indian technicians took their leaders to the brink of implementation with the Revised Treaty of Chaguaramas. But there was no action – no political action, no political will to act. In all the years, over two decades, nothing decisive has happened to fulfil the dream of Grand Anse.

Vision and leadership were present again – 14 years after Grand Anse – at the Montego Bay Summit in 2003 under Prime Minister P.J. Patterson's watch. It was the 30th anniversary of CARICOM and the Prime Minister, who had remained steadfast to the regional cause, submitted a counterpart to the Robinson Paper of 1989 entitled '*CARICOM Beyond Thirty: Charting New Directions*'. It offered the vision and leadership CARICOM so greatly needed, and the Summit duly adopted '*The Rose Hall Declaration on Regional Governance and Integrated Development*' in which Governments agreed 'in the context of *"CARICOM as a Community of Sovereign States"*, to *"the development of a system of mature regionalism"* under the rule of regional law and with an executive mechanism to facilitate the deepening of regional integration. It was a great achievement of Jamaica's Prime Minister, P.J. Patterson.

But it was an agreement 'in principle' – words of qualification deliberately inserted to minimise the agreement the Rose Hall Declaration otherwise implied. Had our political leaders followed the lead 'PJ' had given, many of our countries would not be experiencing the extent of the terrible economic misfortune and uncertainty they now endure. Unbelievably, nothing came of the Rose Hall Declaration. Why? Because it offered, as it said, 'a mature regionalism' – a regionalism which, for all its checks and balances against supra-nationality, was still too much for the cloistered immaturity of a political culture fixated by the obsessive compulsions of 'local control': the same fixation that had held innumerable configurations of West Indian regionalism at bay for 300 years. They agreed to take the right road – but only 'in principle' – not in practice.

Those words of the Rose Hall Declaration: *"with an executive mechanism to facilitate the deepening of regional integration"* were resonant of the efforts made in the years since Grand Anse to fulfil its promises – efforts in which I was centrally engaged.

B. THE WEST INDIAN COMMISSION

The Grand Anse Summit of 1989 had done something more concrete than its declaration of promises. It passed a Resolution *on 'Preparing the People of the West Indies for the Twenty-First Century'*. By that resolution Caribbean leaders established an **"Independent West Indian Commission for Advancing the Goals of the Treaty of Chaguaramas"** (emphasis as in original) and appointed me its Chairman. Prime Minister Robinson had consulted me before the Summit Meeting on this possibility, and I had agreed that I would chair the Commission if this was the collective wish of the regional Heads of Government. My third term as Commonwealth Secretary-General was coming to an end and the Commission could have my full attention.

We were given two years in which to work, and those two years were among the most intensive of my regional life. The Commission itself was a comingling of some of the finest West Indians.

Every CARICOM country was 'represented' – but only in the sense of 'belonging'. Every member was independent, and acted independently. All the Heads of Government were consulted and only in one case did a Prime Minister vary my proposal: the person I put forward, I was told, 'was not native born'. I made up for that by inviting the Governor-General of Barbados to be our Patron – the splendid Dame Nita Barrow. It was an excellent Commission, and I acknowledge the gratitude of the Commission to all those who helped us with a real sense of being part of an historic process.

Commission with Dame Nita Barrow

The Commission's team

When I was invited to chair the Commission I felt reassured by the fact that Alister McIntyre, UWI's dynamic Vice-Chancellor, would be with me as Vice-Chairman as would Roderick Rainford and Vaughan Lewis ex-officio members as Secretary-General of CARICOM and Director-General of the OECS Secretariat respectively. But I could not know at Grand Anse in 1989 how handsomely we would together be supported by the team of Commissioners yet to be assembled. It was support of a truly superlative order, and I pay tribute to my colleagues for their impressive blend of skills, their professionalism with a practical touch; their humanism with a West Indian bias; their intellectual rigour not constrained by ideology; and not least for their staying on a rugged course with steadying good humour. In the end, chairing the Commission was not a task but a great privilege to have shared such an exciting experience with so worthy a team. The full list of Members of the Commission is set out in Appendix 3.

There was more to that privilege than our own interaction as Commissioners. For all of us, I feel sure, our consultations with the people of the region rank among the most stimulating and rewarding experiences of our lives. We tried in our Report to convey the flavour of these 'groundings' with fellow West Indians. I hope we succeeded, because the richness of those encounters still needs to be shared with all West Indians. The fact that our compatriots came forward in such numbers, no less than their written submissions to us; the frankness, often passion, sometimes anger, that characterised their presentations; the good humour that was ever present; the element of 'picong' (badinage) directed to the Commission; and, always, the underlying message that they cared about their West Indian-ness, about their 'Caribbean-ness' (as some preferred) – cared enough to come forward to 'tell it to the Commission'. All this was not just an unforgettable personal experience, but a soulful process of enduring value in our evolving regionalism.

Each member of the Commission will have high-points of recollection of these consultations with people and with Governments in CARICOM, in the wider Caribbean and with West Indians abroad. For me, a few recollections conjure up their immemorial quality:

- a poignant moment in Georgetown's City Hall with a young woman of Guyana's Amerindian Community speaking plaintively, but scoldingly, of the needs and hopes of the first peoples of CARICOM;
- our evening in Barrouallie, a fishing village in St Vincent, in a dimly lit school hall, and the people, pleased that we had come to talk with them, telling us of their concerns: about unemployment, about teenage pregnancies, about the falling off of fishing catches and production of their famed 'black oil' (of aphrodisiac quality) that was their speciality;
- our public meeting in the Titchfield High School on a bluff overlooking one of the lovely bays of Jamaica's east coast; a school established 200 years ago where all kinds of linkages confirmed for us our oneness. One Commissioner had been trained nearby at a Methodist Seminary and had married a teacher of the school. The Principal had been at the University of the West Indies with at least three other Commissioners; there were eight Guyanese teachers on the staff; one of the ladies in the audience had married an Antiguan and yearned aloud for the return of the 'Federal ships' so that she might travel through the Region;

- our meeting with sixth formers in Port of Spain when young people spoke with us about their anxieties, including anxieties about the emergence of ethnicity as a factor in national life – and our dialogue with them on the value of a transcendent regionalism that subordinates ethnic origin to an overarching West Indian identity;
- the Saturday morning I spent with Rex Nettleford and Alan Kirton talking with Rastafarians and others in Temple Yard in Barbados, as we reached out to them to hear at first hand of their grievances and to witness their industry and determination to overcome;
- the throbbing West Indian-ness of our meeting in Birmingham in the English Midlands when the diaspora spoke with us of their sense of being forgotten and neglected and their worry that their homeland – they were in no doubt that they were all West Indians there from a West Indian homeland – was falling behind in responding to contemporary needs;
- a late night in Cuba which the Commission shared with Fidel Castro: his view of the present economic problems that Cuba faced and his resolve that the Cuban people would overcome them; and the chance it gave us to explore with him our own ideas of a wider Caribbean ultimately embracing all the countries of the Caribbean Basin – ideas which he welcomed;
- the irony of a visit to tiny Carriacou when 'an old timer' asked us – not mockingly, but in serious vein – what was 'in it' for Carriacou "joining up with all those poor people in Jamaica and Guyana and even Trinidad": recalling to our minds an earlier time at Montego Bay in 1947 when those same sentiments were aired but with the countries reversed, Carriacou then among the 'pauperised' – as it seemed from Jamaica in 1961.

There were messages for us in all those encounters – as in all the consultations everywhere. Messages of 'today for you, tomorrow for me'; of ignoring only at our grave cost that integration is about people and their everyday concerns which go beyond such matters as 'trade regimes' and 'rules of origin'; of being mindful of how much we have to grow beyond our English-speaking communities into the wider multilingual Caribbean; and many, many more messages. Our Report came to be about those messages and about needed responses to them. It was something of a regional manifesto for the nineties and beyond, as we had been asked to provide by the Grand Anse Declaration. We called it *'Time for Action'*.

As the Commission faced the many problems that were at hand and the others that lay ahead of the Region, we reminded ourselves of the strengths and achievements of the West Indies. They lay principally with our people. We had produced by the time of the Commission a Nobel Prize winner (there were to be two others), a Judge of the International Court of Justice, two under-Secretaries-General of the United Nations (one of them a woman), an Assistant Secretary General of the UN, a Secretary-General of the ACP – and one of the Commonwealth. Our political leaders had won the respect of their peers in the world community. At the level of the UN, Commonwealth Summits and in Third World encounters the world beyond had glimpsed Caribbean excellence. Caribbean achievements at diplomatic levels – from negotiating the Lomé Convention to contributing to Zimbabwe's freedom – were widely acclaimed. Our writers and musicians were among those that twentieth century history would acknowledge as among the most brilliant and creative. We had produced academics of sterling quality who were in the front line of research and teaching in universities abroad, and increasingly at home. Our women, of whom our patron, Dame Nita Barrow, was such a shining example, commanded respect for their leadership all around the world, and not only in advancing the cause of women. As a community of five and a half million we were contributing beyond our numbers in the wider world.

But our achievements had not only been on the world stage; they would not be enough if they were. The overall story of governance in the post-war period had been one of credit to West Indian Governments. Despite occasional reverses, we had increased significantly over the previous decades basic levels of literacy; cut infant mortality rates; improved life expectancy and advanced health care in significant ways. Our region's political culture held fast to democratic traditions through all those years. There had been lapses, it is true, and the Commission spoke out about them and expressed the hope that, where they still remain to be remedied, such aberrations would soon be behind us.

In sport, we had made a dramatic impact; on track and field our small countries had mounted the medal-winners podium at successive Olympic Games; indeed, in per capita terms, West Indians held the foremost place among the winners of Olympic medals in the post-war years. All this was only to rise higher in the pantheon of sport. To the Commission at that time, all our achievements seemed to come together in cricket, which remained in those 'glory days' the living example of the successes we can achieve when we act together as one.

There was much more besides. But, overall, this was a substantial record of achievement. At the centre of *'Time for Action'* was the conviction that we could translate these qualities more widely across the board of regional life as the West Indies entered the 21st century – a new period, with new challenges, and with many new opportunities.

What we must not do, felt the Commission, is to run out of steam. The Moyne Commission's report 50 years before – a British Royal Commission – had led to many changes: to an input of capital for social development, to new possibilities for local autonomy and eventually for full freedom. The region received substantial help and, for the greater part, turned it to good account for the benefit of West Indians. Now, the region faced a time of threat to those achievements; social concerns that we could be falling back; new economic problems like shortages of foreign exchange which had not been a part of past experience. And with all our gains for democracy over the years there were deep anxieties about the quality of governance – indeed, disaffection with the entire political process. On top of it all was the emerging menace of the drug problem.

The West Indies, the Commission believed, needed to recapture some of the strengths of earlier years and knew that they must come from new generations. When, at our public meeting in Washington, a West Indian Professor of Political Science called for an end to 'heirloom politics' in CARICOM, we knew what he was urging – basic change in our political processes. Yet we were learning to change without being pushed. When Michael Manley stepped down from the Prime Ministership of Jamaica shortly before the Commission's report was released he was setting an important example. What was needed was a will to blend experience with change, that we could draw on all the political talents of the Region as we moved into the new time, finding roles for all who have roles to play; learning how to use political talents even when they may be for the time being on the other side. In some of the structures of unity proposed in the Report were opportunities of this kind.

As we came to the end of our work, we were conscious that there was unlikely to be another Commission of this kind for many a year, perhaps for many a decade. That awareness enlarged our responsibilities, but we were encouraged as well that a process of change had already begun. When CARICOM leaders accepted our interim proposals to ease the 'hassle' of travel in the region, to create a single line at airports for 'residents and CARICOM nationals'; when they accepted that graduates of the University of the West Indies and other skilled West Indians, as well as West Indian media personnel, should be the start of a process of freeing up the right of West Indians to live and work anywhere in the region; when they agreed to establish the Caribbean Investment Fund and to take steps towards a common currency – in addition to quickening progress towards their goal of a Single Market and Economy – something, we felt, had begun to happen in the region.

So, we were convinced of our potential to do much better in the future. There was enough that was positive in our domestic, regional and external circumstances to make us feel hopeful. But there was much to be done, and time was not on our side. The global system was becoming more competitive and many nations were making great efforts to be more efficient in economic organisation, and in resource, product and services markets. We must not be left behind – and many of our recommendations offered the means to go forward. But, the Commission was unequivocal: we must go forward in unity. Regionalism and integration are at the heart of getting our act together. As we moved to what we hoped would be the early adoption and implementation of our central recommendations, that process would acquire momentum and help to give faith to the people of the region that the end years of the 20th Century and the advent of a new millennium could be a period of hope, not of hopelessness.

One aspect of that process underlined in the Report was that the region must not proceed at the pace of the slowest; that those who are ready to move must do so, reserving a place for the others when they are ready. That was how the integration process started. The CARIFTA Agreement at Dickenson Bay was between three countries. We would not be where we are today, with the prospect of going further forward, had they not had the courage to begin and to lead. It follows that CARICOM must always leave space – under the CARICOM roof – for even closer integration among some of its members. However, the proviso of not diluting commitment to CARICOM in the process is, the Report stressed, an absolutely crucial one. The integration cup must always be more than half full. CARICOM cannot be true to itself if it becomes a group of groups held together by string, each doing its own thing.

The Commission called the report *'Time for Action'* to dramatise how necessary it was to speed up the process of integration – of acting together in a systematic way. Whether we are dealing with Europe or North America, Latin America or the Caribbean Basin, or with deepening our own integration in meaningful ways, we have to act now, said the Report. And we have to enlarge our capacity for action. The Commission recognised that many of its policy and programme recommendations would require technical work and negotiation within CARICOM and with others. What cannot be postponed, it urged, is putting in place an effective process for doing so.

Hence our central recommendation for the early establishment of a permanent CARICOM Commission, a small but high level authority in CARICOM working at the interface between political decision and practical action; a Commission with confidence to initiate proposals, update consensus, mobilise action and secure implementation of CARICOM decisions in an expeditious and informed manner. A small group of some of our best people drawn preferably from public and political life, engaged upon that task of making regional things happen and making things happen regionally – engaged in that task twenty-four hours a day, seven days a week, unencumbered by the burdens of office at the national level and freed of the technocratic and administrative roles that are the valid and valued domain of the Secretariat. We said in *'Time for Action'* that we regarded this as the single most important decision West Indian leaders can take. Indeed, we said that if they took only one decision, we believed it should be this. We said so because we were convinced that without the Commission, or some such executive authority, we would not make progress regionally – and in our view that meant not stagnation but unravelling, not ticking over but falling apart.

And we urged it because, correspondingly, the Commission could be the essential means by which the region could make the progress Governments had already agreed on in strengthening regional integration and in responding in an enlightened and energetic manner to the challenges of a changing international environment. Those changes impacted on the Caribbean in direct and practical ways; they had meaning for the future of banana growers, of rice farmers, of those who work in sugar and citrus industries and in tourism and services of many kinds – in short, to the future of all West Indians. The machinery we were inviting regional governments to establish was not grandiose, but the issues at stake were not small ones.

We proposed a Commission of four: a president, two commissioners and the CARICOM Secretary-General, and separately in our working paper, we put forward preliminary ideas in relation to a budget for the Commission and its priority work programme. We believed we had demonstrated in that way, not only the absolute necessity for the Commission, but that it could be financed in a manageable way. We were convinced, moreover, that demonstrating our determination to proceed in this manner would attract significant international assistance, not as a matter of largesse, but as a contribution to enlarging the prosperity and stability of our region, which are matters of importance beyond ourselves.

We underlined that our proposal was for a Commission that is modest in size but high-level in capacity and drawn from persons with standing in the public and political life of the region. Our democracies we felt were strong enough to enable the region to draw on its human resources in an optimal way creating, in a sense, a larger field for endeavour in public and political service. And we said that without reservation because, as we stressed publicly and privately, members of the Commission envisaged no roles for ourselves in that new machinery. Stressing that was important, because we knew well the West Indian penchant for avoiding the message by discrediting the messenger.

The CARICOM Commission should be supported, we proposed, by the CARICOM Secretariat whose Secretary-General would be a personal and institutional bridge to the Commission. CARICOM Heads had indeed, only a few years before, envisaged a CARICOM Commissioner. The Commissionership system had actually been proposed by Alister McIntyre when he was Secretary-General over fifteen years earlier. Our ideas for the Commission took this proposal to its logical evolution. What we needed desperately was not a larger number of technical experts, and the studies and reports they would generate, but a new dynamic to mobilise the expertise we have and to tap and energise our response to immediate demands. CARICOM needed a faster engine – not a longer train.

We believed that with the Commission in place – giving regional leadership on a day-to-day basis within the framework of CARICOM as 'a Community of sovereign states' – there was a chance to implement the manifesto of change. Without that process, if we merely titivated with our separateness and let slip the opportunity we had at that moment to act collectively in those areas that demand a shared response, we would be in danger of drifting along – only now towards rapids and waterfalls; drifting separately towards a single desperate fate. As it looked to the 21st Century the West Indian Commission's

Report recalled the warning of Jose Marti over a century ago in a Caribbean context: *"We must save ourselves together or together we will disappear"*.

At the Port of Spain Summit, on 30 June 1992, the Commission presented the Report to Heads of Government collectively outlining the principal recommendations and the Commission's thinking, with special emphasis on the need for timely action. Among the concluding words of my presentation as Chairman were these:

> *History has a few moments for every community when what we do or fail to do changes the future in decisive ways. In presenting our Report to you, the West Indian Commission believes we are at such a time... CARICOM Heads of Government sensed all this in 1989. In the Grand Anse Declaration and related documents you acknowledged as much. That is why you asked us to work. We have worked, talking to the people as we did so, and we have confirmed your worst fears -but confirmed as well that there are opportunities – and hope if we seize them. One way or another, this moment, these months, your decisions, will irrevocably change our regional lives – and by necessary extension, our national lives as well.*

In their response in June, CARICOM Heads noted "the central recommendations in the Commission's Report concerning basic and fundamental changes in the structural arrangement for decision-making and implementation processes in CARICOM, as well as the many wide-ranging recommendations on numerous sectoral and policy issues affecting the life of the Community". They acknowledged that once again, as at the Chaguaramas Summit in 1973, CARICOM was at "a defining moment" in its evolution, and agreed that it was "time for action". They decided to meet again in a Special Session on 28 October 1992 to consider the Commission's Report and to determine the action to be taken on its recommendations.

In the four months from July to October 1992, there was much activity. The Report was widely disseminated both in the Region and among the West Indian diaspora abroad and much discussed. To facilitate consideration of the Report at the Special Summit in October, the Commission prepared a Working Paper highlighting a limited number of recommendations for priority decision. Additionally, the Commission held a special meeting with the regional media in Jamaica in the first week of September at which Commissioners briefed regional journalists extensively on the Report and encouraged wide-ranging discussion of the recommendations following that regional encounter. The Commission accepted the invitation of the Inter-American Development Bank – whose President, Dr Enrique Iglesias, had been a special guest of CARICOM at its June Summit at Port of Spain, to a Symposium on the Report at the IDB Offices in Washington. This was attended by a group of eminent persons from the Hemisphere, including representatives of the principal multilateral institutions. It was clear from the discussion that the Hemisphere believed that CARICOM was, indeed, at a defining moment and that it was ready to help once the basic political decisions were taken within the region itself.

As we approached the Special Summit at the end of October, we felt that as a Commission we had done all in our power to discharge the mandate placed on us by CARICOM Heads three years earlier in the Grand Anse Declaration. We might have added, as Brutus did at Philippi:

On such a full sea are we now afloat,
and we must take the current when it serves,
or lose our ventures.

In September 1992 the Report was discussed in the Parliaments of Jamaica and Barbados and the Commission was invited to a two-day symposium with parliamentarians in Trinidad and Tobago. It became clear from both debates that the spirit of resolution that had been so evident at Grand Anse in 1989, at Basseterre in 1991, and at Kingston and Port of Spain earlier in 1992, was unlikely to translate into political will at the special Summit convened to take decisions for action. That, in fact, was precisely what West Indians had predicted during the Commission's public consultations.

At the opening of the Port of Spain Special Summit, I explained this to Heads of Government in the following terms:

> *It is a symptom of what ails our regional processes that the most pervasive mood we have encountered among West Indian people is disbelief that anything – anything serious, anything effective, anything lasting, anything fundamentally different, anything that can anchor ambition in a West Indian future – will come out of our efforts and yours. They have grown inured to high flown declarations, they have grown cynical about bureaucratic delays, they have grown disdainful of the instinct to protect small areas of turf leaving the wide West Indian pasture fallow. They will not be surprised if in this time for action you do not act; if at this moment of decision you differ and defer.*
>
> *I must say this in all candour, because you have asked us to consult the people; and we have done so, imperfectly perhaps, but as best we could and in larger measure than they have been consulted for fifty years. You have asked us to help to prepare our Region for the twenty-first century. Everything in that preparation turns on the faith of West Indian people in our regional processes. This is therefore not only a time for decision; it is a moment of affirmation. If regionalism falters now, it will not easily recover. That might sound stark, even alarmist; but after three years as West Indians working together, looking towards the future, we believe it is a simple truth.*

In the Working Paper that the Commission offered to the Special Summit, the recommendations proposed for priority decision came down (as we explained) to a small cluster, namely: a regional process that goes forward as a Community of Sovereign States; the deepening of CARICOM through the Single Market and Economy (on which CARICOM had already agreed) being made a reality; the widening of our vision of the Caribbean by encompassing not just our enclave of English-speaking countries, but the wider Caribbean Basin which needs to be reclaimed – not a lake that is Spanish, or English, or French, or Dutch, or American – but, at last, 500 years later, a Caribbean lake; and, to make all this happen in practical ways and with a qualitative flavour that touches West Indian lives, a CARICOM Commission that can energise the process of regionalism and a CARICOM Charter of Civil Society that can help to keep us on course for enrichment beyond the economics of regionalism.

In taking stock of the Port of Spain Summit, it is pertinent that the Working Paper prepared by the Commission, and used by the Chairman in recording the Summit's conclusions, invited initial decisions on just 19 of the Commission's 200-plus recommendations, and acceptance of one overall proposition. The proposition was that CARICOM Heads "approve the broad thrust of the West Indian Commission's Report". They did not adopt that language. The Port of Spain Protocol says that the Conference considers the Report "as a landmark document in charting the course of Caribbean integration and accepts the challenge that it is 'time for action'".

The Heads of Government accepted some of the 19 recommendations, but the exceptions were critical ones. The three recommendations for the CARICOM Commission were not accepted. The recommendation for a Charter of Civil Society was agreed to "in principle" and the reference to "greater public access to information" was dropped. The recommendation for the CARICOM Supreme Court with original jurisdiction was "noted" and mention made of the "need for careful study". The Record of Conclusions states that the recommendations for the Court and the Charter "would be further studied and developed for consideration at the next regular meeting of the Conference"

Reflecting at the time on this largely negative response of CARICOM Heads I wrote:

These were the conclusions of the October meeting. What the outturn will be, how the decisions taken (and not taken) will affect the lives of West Indian people, are matters for the future. If the Commission's analysis is even partly right, that future will be for our Region an excessively difficult one. If CARICOM is seen by decision-makers (including others besides Heads of Government) as an occasionally convenient but mainly peripheral facility, not as a central, creative, energising force for development, it will forever fall short of the highest hopes for regionalism that we found among West Indian people. At the end of the Commission's experience, this must be the lingering fear that while everyone will buy the concept of CARICOM as a "Community of Sovereign States', for people the emphasis will be on community, but for the political and bureaucratic establishment the emphasis could be on sovereignty and turf in general. Governments were inevitably in the forefront at Port of Spain; their conclusions, however, were actually the preferred options of the CARICOM Secretariat on the one hand, and those opposed to the very notion of genuine integration on the other. Such were the contrarieties of our time and circumstance.

I signalled these fears at Port of Spain when I suggested that *'Time for Action'* fell victim to "insularity and insecurity". In doing so, I was echoing much that Arthur Lewis had written 30 years before in *'The Agony of the Eight'*. If, 500 years after Columbus, we were unable to overcome these ancestral separatist urges or at least hold them in check, balanced against the contemporary claims of realism and rationality, we would be in deep trouble. Regionalism itself (I ventured to suggest) may be questioned next; 'marginalisation' (foretold in the Grand Anse Declaration) could then come to be rationalised as the virtue of 'subsidiarity' – copying once more the trimmings of European fashion while the Europeans themselves move on, not allowing their own insularities and even insecurities to override reason and realism as they prepared for the twenty-first century.

In November 1992 I had an opportunity to touch briefly on these wider issues at the University of the West Indies Graduation Ceremony at the St Augustine Campus at which Prime Minister Manning was the Graduation Speaker. What I said then, as Chancellor, after calling for an end to separateness within some of our countries, was this:

> *In our Caribbean homeland, it is no different; we are one people too from Belize to Guyana, and beyond CARICOM from Cuba to Suriname; we have to give meaning to that oneness in tangible ways. Sometimes our West Indian contrariness gets in the way; but despite disappointments neither vexation nor opting out is a valid response. In Guyana we have a saying: 'na mine how bird vex, he caan vex wid tree'. The Caribbean is our tree; for us it will ever bloom. Attachment, commitment, hope, and effort must ever be sustained as well. When we stumble and seem about to collapse we have to recall that that, after all, is how on the whole we play our West Indian cricket; disaster is ever imminent, glorious recovery is almost always round the corner.*
>
> *But adventurism is one thing; recklessness is another. We cannot make a habit of coming to watersheds and failing to cross over, of being at defining moments and opting for the old terms. In the new world that is upon us we cannot count on second chances. If our countries are to respond to the character and environment of the new age, we have to jettison smallness and meanness and preoccupation with self, and find ways of not being held to the pace of the most inert among us.*

On 15 December 1992 Prime Minister Manning (who had chaired the Port of Spain Meeting as A.N.R. Robinson's successor) wrote to Commissioners from Georgetown, as he chaired the first meeting of the new Bureau. It was a letter which assured us that it was the *"firm determination"* of CARICOM Heads of Government to *"continue to give most serious consideration to all aspects of the Report"*. No consideration, serious or otherwise, has ever been given collectively to the Commission's proposal for a CARICOM Commission.

There was an exception. Speaking at the time to the theme of *'Building a Caribbean Nation'*, the Prime Minister of Antigua and

Barbuda, Lester Bird, spoke out in solitary support of the Commission's main proposal:

> *The rejection of the CARICOM Commission and the adoption of the Bureau of Heads of Government have set us back in the Caribbean. For with all the vast changes in the world, and with all the blows to which our economies are now subject, there was no more opportune a time to be bold in addressing our difficulties than now. Instead Heads of Government opted not to protect national turf, for the Commission was no threat to the individual sovereignty of states; they chose to protect what they saw as their own authority.*

And there have been valiant efforts much later by individual leaders, most notably, P.J. Patterson and Ralph Gonsalves, to resume the journey to unity; but to no avail. *'Time for Action'* remains the unused Caribbean road map.

Telling it to the Commission, left, and listening to West Indians

* * *

As I predicted in 1993, following the rejection of the West Indian Commission's proposal for an executive authority for the Caribbean Community, the emphasis of the political and bureaucratic establishment has been on 'sovereignty' and turf in general – a cloistered immaturity; because now, in the era of globalisation, 'local control' has so little content. How, for example, has the individual sovereignty of Caribbean countries insulated them from the power of external forces: the World Bank has graduated them from concessional financing; the OECD has imposed criteria for financial services that are enforced by the IMF; the WTO has refused to accord special and differential treatment to the small and vulnerable economies of the region; the 27-nation EU demanded reciprocity with each of the Caribbean countries individually under an Economic Partnership Agreement; and several of the region's governments individually entered economic and financing arrangements with China which lack any real negotiation.

Powerlessness, not power, is the political reality at every island level. Sovereignty, still touted, has lost much of its meaning. Yet West Indian governments unable to assert it in the wider world seek fulfilment in asserting it against each other.

In a time that marks over 50 years of national independence and over 50 years of stagnating regionalism, it is well to remember that in the Introduction to his *'History of the People of Trinidad and Tobago'*, which Eric Williams published on Trinidad and Tobago's Independence Day, he wrote of the continuing challenge with respect to the *"integration of the separated Caribbean Territories"*. He said:

> *Separation and fragmentation were the policy of colonialism and rival colonialisms. Association and integration must be the policy of Independence.*

His counsel applies as well to all West Indians – governments and people. Independence and integration are not alternatives. For West Indians, labouring in the vineyard of unity knows no rest. So has it been for me all my adult life.

PART IV

THE COMMONWEALTH

CHAPTER 12

Becoming Secretary-General

It's a forest fire! Those are the words I recall most vividly in the context of leaving Guyana for London in 1975. Much had preceded their utterance; much that accounted for them. Looking back, the decade since I came to British Guiana as Attorney-General was as astonishing as it was unplanned; and it led by its own logic and with similar self-propulsion to the best years of my life. When I came back home in 1965, I was by local standards a travelled son; but, objectively, my experience was within the cocoon of the Caribbean and in such compartments as the Federation and the Jamaican Bar. That experience beyond borders was to multiply exponentially in the decade that followed. Some of it has been unfurled in earlier chapters, but altogether it had meaning best understood in recollection.

The journey from CARIFTA to CARICOM gave me an intimacy with Caribbean political leaders – not only Prime Ministers, but Ministers who would later replace them. My lead role in the Lomé negotiations, not only solidified those relationships but widened them to leading Ministers of some 46 African and Pacific countries – new relationships deepened by my role in the creation of the ACP Group. The Georgetown Meeting of Non-Aligned Foreign Ministers in 1972 had already established a base of relationships at the level of Foreign Ministers and Foreign Ministries of the 70 countries there. Not less significant were the Commonwealth Heads of Government Meetings between 1966 and 1973 in London, Singapore and Ottawa, which I attended with Prime Minister Burnham, and the Commonwealth Law

Conferences over that time in which I played modest roles. And there was more, especially in a United Nations context where Guyana was prominent in the 'New International Economic Order' debates and in such internationalist enterprises as the 'definition of aggression' and the Convention on the Law of the Sea. There were, more personally, my annual addresses to the General Assembly each year from 1967. For a small new member State these annual occasions are invaluable. If used to good effect, they provide an otherwise unobtainable entry point to the international community. I remember how pleased I was when the World Federalist Movement assessed my address to the General Assembly in 1973 as the most 'internationalist' Statement in that year's General Debate. It was an address I had entitled: *The Need for Answers: Wither Internationalism?* Someone had taken note of Guyana.

The point I am trying to make is that from my small perch in Guyana I had, by 1974, come to the notice of the international community – and, it seems, favourably so. A substantial element of this good opinion was a reflection of the standing Guyana itself was acquiring in all international theatres – especially as a reliable and effective advocate of the causes of developing countries. But it went beyond economic issues. On matters like apartheid in South Africa and Namibia's independence, on the rejection of a 'two China' policy, on resisting the Cuban diplomatic embargo I earned respect for Guyana's principled positions. I was inseparable from Guyana and, in the international community, Guyana was recognised as being progressive but not extremist, non-aligned in a principled way, internationalist but of the 'South' – and not only in its coterie of small newly independent countries, but also in a wider world. Hence that 'favourable notice'.

In 1974, Sir John Carter, an urbane and enlightened man who had failed in domestic politics because he was not hungry enough for power – was Guyana's much respected High Commissioner in London. He was older than me and I treated him as a trusted senior colleague. I need to explain that it is part of the Commonwealth mystique that Ambassadors from one Commonwealth country to another are called

'High Commissioners' and in London enjoy a somewhat favoured diplomatic rank. It hails from the time when the British sovereign was Head of State of each Commonwealth country and so the King (later, the Queen) could not accredit an ambassador to himself. All that ended in 1949, when the modern Commonwealth emerged, but this quaint tradition survived. Commonwealth High Commissioners are accredited from Prime Minister to Prime Minister (or President as the case may be), but with the Queen as 'Head of the Commonwealth' they enjoy a special status with Her Majesty, and a special place in Palace protocol.

But to continue: Commonwealth Heads would be meeting at the end of April 1975 in Jamaica, and the second five-year term of office of the Secretary-General – the Canadian Arnold Smith – would be coming to an end then. He was the first Secretary-General of the Commonwealth Secretariat and there were no precedents or protocols regarding succession. It seems, however, that Commonwealth High Commissioners in London had begun talking informally among themselves about a successor. Arnold Smith was widely acknowledged to have done a capable job in establishing the Secretariat and managing the transition from administration of Commonwealth affairs by the British Foreign and Commonwealth Office.

In mid-1974, I received a phone call in Georgetown from John Carter in London. He was clearly excited. He told me what had been going on in London – of which I was entirely unaware. He then said that in the High Commissioners' informal discussions of a possible successor my name had come up from several quarters, and it was his impression that if I was interested in the post, it could be mine. He said that he had been careful to say that he had no idea whether I would be interested, but was pressed to explore the situation. I was totally taken aback. And as he talked to me the imponderables mounted in my mind. I needed time to think. I told John Carter that *he should take the temperature* among his colleagues on the assumption that I could be interested, but without any suggestion that I was. Two days later he called back and said: *"Minister, you asked me to take the temperature; I have done so; it's a forest fire"*. I asked him what was the Secretary-General's position on going for a third term? He said he had not indicated a position, but the High Commissioners were proceeding on a two-term basis. More than a little dazed, I thanked the High Commissioner, but asked him to give no indication to anyone, either way, until I had time to think, talk and come back to him.

On my mind were these imponderables – the family, the Prime Minister, and the position of the Canadian government. As to the family, my intuitive feeling was that Lois would welcome London. We would have been in Georgetown for ten years; not like the move from Jamaica in 1965. As to the Prime Minister, his blessing of the move would be crucial to its actually happening. He would have to give it his personal support. Would he? I felt he might. I believed he valued my several roles, but there was the matter of the 'Executive Presidency' on which he knew we would disagree so fundamentally that it would be a parting. Perhaps, my moving on would have the bonus for him of freeing up the way for this major constitutional change, though I was sure he would never say so.

And then, the position of the Canadian government. I had grown quite close to Pierre Trudeau and his Assistant Ivan Head. At the Singapore Commonwealth Summit in 1971 I had worked with Ivan Head (and Zambia's Mark Chona) in drafting the *'Singapore Declaration'* which saved the Summit from disaster given the obduracy of Britain's Prime Minister, Ted Heath, on the matter of arms sales to South Africa. At that meeting, I had encouraged Trudeau to offer to host the next Summit and use it to change the structure of the Meeting along lines he had indicated at Singapore. He had done so, and I had been in close consultation with Ottawa as they overhauled the style and format of the forthcoming Summit to make it more inter-active, more relaxed and more of a meeting of minds between Heads of Governments than an exchange of positions between states. All in all, if Canada, i.e., Trudeau, was backing Arnold Smith for a third term, I could not see myself in a contest with him.

And what about me? Did I really want this? The truth was I did not know. I was clearly enjoying the roles that had fallen to me as Foreign Minister, and some were in need of nurturing, like the ACP.

The aftermath of the Non-Aligned Foreign Ministers Meeting in Guyana was heady, and my standing in the 'club' of the world's Foreign Ministers was moderately high. Would going to the Commonwealth be stepping down from a larger world stage, however large a step up it was from Guyana? On the other hand, perhaps this was like Philip Jaikaran's deflection of my going to Leicester, or Dingle Foot's prevention of my going to Kenya – a wise unplanned intervention that could change my life for the better. Sooner rather than later, I knew, I would face a showdown over the 'Executive Presidency' – which I would lose; and then what? Neither politics nor the Bar in Guyana had any attraction for me. Should I not see this as a 'godsend'? Trudeau's Summit had turned the Commonwealth in progressive directions; so, certainly, would Michael Manley's Summit in a few months' time. Would this not be a real challenge to make the Commonwealth more activist in enlightened ways. Would this not be a chance for its first 'Third World' Secretary-General to make the Commonwealth Secretariat a development hub? The more I thought about it the more persuaded I became. Or was I subliminally persuading myself? Looking back on that time of balancing options, it is curious that the only thing that never crossed my mind was the practical one of 'terms and conditions'. I suppose I simply assumed that for such an office they had to be acceptable.

Lois agreed that it might be time to move on: Susan who had come to Guyana as a baby in 1953 was now engaged to be married and the boys (Ian and Mark) would benefit from further schooling in London. Only Amanda, born in Guyana and now nine, would face disruption. Lois' minor doubt was whether I was sure that leaving was what I wanted? But, by then, I was surer than when I first spoke to Sir John.

I went to see Burnham and outlined all that had passed between John Carter and me in the last few days – including my awareness that nothing on these lines could happen without his blessing and support. He asked me directly what I wanted. I said that I had thought hard and long and concluded on balance that it might be a good time to move on, and a good place to move to. We talked about it for a while and eventually he said that if I was sure that I wanted it, he would give me every support. In that moment my life changed again. I mentioned my reservation about Canada, but he did not think Ottawa's view should be a deterrent in the light of John Carter's report of overwhelming support. I left reassured; I could go forward with the blessing of Guyana. Of course, none of this was public – and would remain so for months.

When I told John Carter of my talk with the Prime Minister he was overjoyed. He now told me that he was supportive of it from the outset and would work to make it happen, but he assured me again that in his view it would not be a fight. I asked him to speak candidly with Burnham to give him the assurance that he would not be gambling his political credits with Commonwealth colleagues in soliciting their support for me.

I continued to believe that I still needed to check with Ottawa. I called Ivan Head. He was personally pleased that I might be willing to go to the Commonwealth, but he said they had not had an indication from Arnold Smith of his own inclinations; he would take soundings – which I interpreted to mean he would talk with Trudeau. He assured me that he himself could not think of a better successor. Arnold Smith must at this time have been 'taking the temperature' himself – I suppose in both London and Ottawa. He later wrote of his own uncertainty at this time. By the summer, diplomatic correspondents in London were on to the 'story', and it was not long before Arnold Smith let it be known that he would be stepping down after the Jamaica Summit. As he wrote much later:

> *At the end of a trip to Canada, in October 1974, I suffered a heart attack, and realised that I was not in shape to carry on for a third term with the energy the post deserved. The same month I notified Heads of Government of my decision, which was made easier by the fact that a first-class statesman, Sonny Ramphal, was available to replace me.*

Soon after, Ivan Head let me know that Arnold was not standing after the Kingston Summit, and I would have Canada's support as his successor – and with Prime Minister Trudeau's personal good wishes. I understood, and felt much relieved. I would need Canada's support not only to win, but also to succeed in the job.

With Pierre Trudeau at Kaieteur Falls, Guyana

But there were others of whose support I also wanted assurance, and prominent among them was the Commonwealth's largest member – India. Indira Gandhi was Prime Minister. She and Forbes Burnham had good personal relations; they were fellow political beings and she approved of Guyana's stand on international issues, and he, very specially, of her defiance of the then nuclear powers. But I felt I needed to talk to her myself. When I eventually raised the Commonwealth possibility with her, Mrs Gandhi was thoughtful, and then somewhat questioning. She alluded to the roles I had been playing on behalf of the 'Third World' – particularly in the Non-Aligned Movement (which was close to India's political heart) – and asked whether I would not have more opportunities of service as Foreign Minister of Guyana than in the rather 'old-fashioned' Commonwealth. I told her that as the first 'Third World' person to be Secretary-General of the Commonwealth, I believed there would be an opportunity to vitalise the Commonwealth whose membership, following India's example under Nehru, was now predominantly developing countries. She reflected on this, and eventually said: *"Yes, I suppose that is true; but when you go there you must be sure to 'shake it up'. You will have India's support"*. That settled the issue for me.

With Indira Gandhi, New Delhi

I have said this was the first succession; there were no settled procedures. But some steps were obvious. The first and most important one was for the Prime Minister to write to his Commonwealth colleagues. This was easier once Arnold Smith had indicated that he would be retiring after the Kingston Summit; but, particularly since I was Guyana's Foreign Minister, the Government's advancement of my candidature would be expected. Burnham did so without delay; and of course Guyana's Foreign Service was mobilised to follow up. At a personal level, it remained for me to call the Secretary-General and tell him of my hope to succeed him. We had long been on good terms, and I believe he was genuine in welcoming my probable succession. We remained friends. He died in 1994, but not before publishing an important book on his period as Secretary General: *'Stitches in Time: The Commonwealth in World Politics'* – an authentic account of the transformative first years of the Commonwealth Secretariat's existence, when under his leadership it established its independence and shed its 'British' trappings.

By the time of the Commonwealth Summit in Kingston, Jamaica, in 1975 it was generally assumed that I would be appointed there to be the next Commonwealth Secretary-General. But as I accompanied Prime Minister Burnham to the Meeting I was mindful of other things as well. I had been personally involved in encouraging Michael Manley to offer Jamaica for the next meeting after Ottawa in 1973. That had been his first Commonwealth Summit and while he fitted comfortably, and easily, into the 'Club', he was more than a little reticent about taking on the hosting of the very next Summit. What I helped to organise was a commitment by all Caribbean countries there to lend a hand to Jamaica – treating it as a Summit hosted by them all: a Caribbean Summit. This helped Michael Manley to come forward and offer Jamaica – though the help eventually given was more psychological than functional. Even so, I personally felt obliged to lend a hand as he chaired the meeting, and I did so in modest ways.

Michael Manley and Forbes Burnham were personal friends, but Michael had an easy relationship with me as well and would often talk to Burnham through me. In the context of his hosting of the Kingston Meeting, I recall his calling me some months after the Ottawa Meeting to say that I had not told him then that hosting the Commonwealth Summit meant that he had to host a Royal visit as well. Michael was cultivating a radical posture in Jamaica and was uncertain whether a visit from the Queen with 'imperialist' connotations was not at odds with his political image. I told him it was a necessary part of the process, but that he should not worry: the Queen was a celebrity and the people of Jamaica would warm to her (and him as her host). He remained uneasy. But, of course, the Queen's visit was a towering success. He lost no 'radical' credits; in fact, I think he rather enjoyed escorting the Queen about Kingston to the applause of rapturous crowds.

* * *

At the Summit itself, I had a particular role. In preparing the Meeting, the Secretary-General had identified lead speakers for the principal agenda items. 'International Economic Issues' was a major agenda item at all Commonwealth Summits, but recent years had seen the North-South divide grow sharper; the debate on *'A New International Economic Order'* dominated UN discussions with developing countries nailing their flag to its mast. At Kingston, Guyana was invited to lead the discussion for the 'South' and Britain to lead for the 'North'. This meant lead-offs by Forbes Burnham and Harold Wilson. Though we were not to know beforehand, Wilson had taken on the task personally as an economist, and he made a major presentation informed, as he said, by his 'lifelong' involvement with the problems of commodity trade. I, of course, had a 'hand in preparing the Guyana case and the debate was for me a central feature of the meeting. Kingston was not just a matter of waiting to be called.

In the context of the North-South debate which was raging internationally, Harold Wilson prefaced his remarks by an important affirmation. He wanted to make it clear that in what he was now about to propose, his Government fully accepted that the relationship, the balance, between the rich and poor countries of the world was wrong and must be remedied. That was the principle on which his proposals rested: the wealth of the world must be re-distributed to better benefit the poverty-stricken and the starving. That meant a new deal in world economies, in trade between nations and in the terms of that trade. He believed that this could be done. But it was fundamental that there should be more wealth; more wealth to be shared more equitably; shared more equitably within nations and between nations and peoples. What the British Government had in mind was that they set as their objective a general agreement on commodities. A generation after the General Agreement on Tariffs and Trade he believed the time had come to balance it with a General Agreement on Commodities. Indeed it was long overdue.

In his response, Forbes Burnham made it clear that he was speaking from the position of the developing world. The issues confronting mankind were planetary in their range, whether they concerned the abolition of hunger and poverty, or the management of the resources of the sea or the environment, or devising a new monetary system. But this particular moment in history was also characterised by divisions and discontinuities, and by preoccupations with the interests of regions or ethnic groups or the preservation of an ideology or system. There was need to take immediate steps towards the creation of a rational and equitable international economic order which had as one of its primary objectives the redistribution of wealth in favour of the poor countries.

In view of the complexity, range and inter-related nature of the issues involved, Burnham proposed to his colleagues that the Commonwealth appoint a small group of eminent individuals, selected from the Commonwealth on the basis of their personal capacities and their expert knowledge of contemporary problems of international economic development, and invite them to identify measures of a practical nature which were amenable to effective implementation. The Expert Group should, as far as possible, be assembled in a way which would enable the perspectives of the different regions of the Commonwealth and the different national development strategies to be brought to bear on problems. He contemplated that the British Prime Minister might wish to refer the proposals he had outlined for consideration by the Expert Group.

The upshot of the Wilson-Burnham encounter at Kingston was the Commonwealth's agreement to establish an independent Expert Group of eminence and distinction and from North and South in the Commonwealth chosen by the Secretary-General after consultation with Governments. The Group's mandate was to "draw up for consideration by Commonwealth Governments, in the context of the current international dialogue, a comprehensive and interrelated programme of practical measures directed at closing the gap between the rich and the poor countries". Its Chairman would be Alister McIntyre, Secretary-General of the Caribbean Community.

This was to be the first of 13 'Expert Groups' the Commonwealth would establish under my watch on the thorniest issues on the international agenda. Among them were Groups (always of eminence; always independent; always on a North-South basis) on, for example: *the negotiating process, reform of the Bretton Woods system, commodity markets and the Common Fund, the debt problem, protectionism, technological change, the vulnerability of small states, women and structural adjustment and climate change and sea level rise.* In every case the Commonwealth's work was in the forefront of international thinking. We will encounter them as these glimpses unfold. The point is, however, that coincident with my appointment, the Commonwealth at Kingston established a process that would place it in the front rank of internationalist effort on global issues. The Commonwealth had begun a turning away from a narrow agenda, and the new direction was wholly in tune with my own conception of what the Commonwealth was and what the Secretariat's mission should be. I faced the future with confidence.

There was another highlight of the Kingston Summit that would set the stage for my priorities over the next 15 years. It was the matter of 'Southern Africa', as the Agenda listed it; but at that time *'Rhodesia and the Unilateral Declaration of Independence (UDI) by the minority government led by Ian Smith'* more specifically. There will be space later to tell the full Commonwealth story, but here I recount how the stage was set for me at that Summit Meeting at which I was appointed Secretary-General.

Michael Manley, from the outset of taking office as Prime Minister of Jamaica in 1972, had been militant in his denunciation of Ian Smith's 'UDI' regime in Rhodesia. Hosting the Commonwealth Summit gave him an opportunity (however unorthodox) to go beyond words. Unknown to anyone at the Summit he invited the 'liberation' leaders in Rhodesia at that time to come to Jamaica on the occasion of the Summit. As he himself put it in his Address of Welcome at the public Opening Ceremony, *"as I announced yesterday, the Government of Jamaica has invited Bishop Muzorewa, and Joshua Nkoma and Chief Sithole of the African National Council to be present at our gathering and we will be asking the Conference to permit them to address us on the latest turn of events in the struggle which they lead"*. It was clearly his intention to orchestrate from the Chair a session where they would have an opportunity to address Commonwealth leaders.

But not everyone was compliant; some were uneasy by the Summit being 'hi-jacked' in this way. Pierre Trudeau took a stand on principle and insisted that the 'session' they would address would not be a session of the Summit. This was the compromise eventually brokered – that the meeting would be adjourned to hear in informal session, an address by Bishop Muzorewa on behalf of the African

National Council of Zimbabwe. At the informal session Trudeau emphasised his point by dramatically turning down Canada's name-plate when the Bishop and his colleagues came in. All the same, it was a victory for the liberation forces in Rhodesia, and a triumph for Michael Manley. Most of all, it stamped the Commonwealth's credentials in the epic struggle that was unfolding in Southern Africa and would dominate my years as Secretary-General. As with North-South issues, so with Southern African issues, the Commonwealth Summit that appointed me to the office of Secretary-General was clear about the direction they expected the Commonwealth to take – a direction that matched my every disposition. The Official Communiqué of the Summit contained no reference to the 'informal session', but the press, of course, was fully briefed.

There was another 'off the record' matter of some significance. In June 1975 Harold Wilson was due to face a referendum on Britain leaving the European Common Market (EEC). It was an 'open vote' in party terms; and some members of Wilson's Labour Party were hostile to the EEC and had actually lobbied Caribbean Governments to express opposition to it in a 'Commonwealth' context. I remember Fred Peart (later Lord Peart) a former Labour Minister of Agriculture, leading an 'anti Common Market' delegation to the Caribbean without much success. Commonwealth sentiment was broadly supportive of Britain being in, not out, of this emerging economic giant.

At Kingston, Wilson was keen to have an expression of Commonwealth support for Britain remaining in the European Community. Tactically, however, he did not want to seek it. Jim Callaghan was his Foreign Minister and foot soldier at the Conference, and he shared Harold Wilson's wishes with me (and, I expect, others). I helped to orchestrate a move whereby at an appropriate point in the consideration of the draft Communiqué, Forbes Burnham would allude to the pending referendum and, in careful language that avoided overtones of 'interference' in Britain's domestic processes, propose that the Commonwealth express its hope for Britain remaining in the Community. He was immediately supported by Trudeau. There was general approval and it was eventually agreed that the sentiment would be expressed by the Chairman in his Press Conference introducing the Communiqué. And so it was – to everyone's satisfaction. It is ironic, as I write nearly 40 years later, that Britain should once more be in confabulation on the 'in/out' issue and again having voices that raise a 'Commonwealth' argument in support of leaving the European Union. I suspect that for the Commonwealth nothing much would have changed since Kingston.

* * *

But, of course, at a personal level the Kingston Summit was specially significant as the Commonwealth Meeting at which I was elected to the office of Secretary-General. News of my probable succession had been out in the London press for some time. As early as 7 October the London *Daily Mail* carried the following in its 'Mail Diary' under the heading, *'Step up for 'Sonny'?:*

> *A colourful Caribbean, Sir Shridath 'Sonny' Ramphal, the 45-year-old lotus-eating Foreign Minister of Guyana has become the runaway favourite to take over as Commonwealth Secretary-General next year.*

I wasn't sure if I should be happy with this introduction in the British Press. Three months later, on 18 January 1975, the more staid *Economist* reported, under the headline *"Shoo-in"*:

> *Barring accidents, the Commonwealth heads of government will announce at their meeting at Kingston, Jamaica, at the beginning of May that the next Head of their joint Secretariat in London will be the foreign Minister of Guyana, Sir Shridath Surendranath ("Sonny") Ramphal... A 46 year old lawyer with a very lively style (and an English wife), Sir Shridath has lately proved an eloquent spokesman for Commonwealth "associables" in their bargaining with the EEC and enjoys warm personal friendships in many quarters.... his engagingly*

> *buoyant personality will help to publicise the work of the secretariat despite the fact that much of that work is necessarily unspectacular.*

A week before, on 12 January 1975, *The Observer Review*, under the headline *"Sonny times ahead"* commented flippantly as follows:

> *A new ebullient figure is, barring accidents, about to take over in Marlborough House, Queen Mary's old home with its four Gainsboroughs, revolving summerhouse and poignantly stocked pets' graveyard. The Commonwealth is set to get its first non-white Secretary-General.*
>
> *Sir Shridath Surendranath Ramphal, universally known as 'Sonny', Guyana's brilliant 46 year old Foreign Minister, will almost certainly be confirmed in April as head of the 220-strong multinational Commonwealth Secretariat, which works from Marlborough House (lent by the Queen). Sonny (called to the Bar at Gray's Inn in 1951) combines sharp-witted ability with a reputation as an enthusiastic party-goer – he and his English ex-nurse wife are famed for their lively 'jump-ups' with steel bands, and barbecues, adorned by Sonny's gorgeous cocktail shirts brought back from his travels abroad.*
>
> *Ratification of his appointment at the Heads of Government get-together in Jamaica in April seemed a forgone conclusion – he was, after all, the only candidate. One snag: last week, a telegram arrived formally nominating another candidate. President Idi Amin proposed a man he commended for his wide knowledge of Commonwealth affairs – none other than his predecessor, Milton Obote. They could hardly believe it at Marlborough House, but Sonny is nevertheless expected there.*

Amin's proposal was made in a telegram to the British Prime Minister, and was regarded as facetious. Milton Obote was the man he had deposed in a military coup d'état while Obote was attending the Commonwealth Heads of Government Meeting in Singapore in

1971, and had been in exile in Tanzania ever since. The 'proposal' was regarded as a characteristically Amin 'prank' and was not pursued – even by his representative at Kingston.

John Carter had been right all along. There was no other candidate at Kingston. Appointment of the new Secretary-General would be a matter for the Chairman to orchestrate. What Michael Manley did, was to make a statement from the Chair at the start of the Meeting referring to the matter of the selection of a new Secretary-General and his assumption that the Meeting would wish to arrive at a consensus on the succession. He proposed that he would hold informal consultations during the week so that the matter could be concluded by the weekend when some Heads of Government had to leave. The Meeting readily agreed to this procedure.

When the Meeting convened on the morning of Friday 2nd May, Michael Manley paid tribute to Arnold Smith's ten years of "distinguished and devoted service to the Commonwealth". As far as the choice of a successor was concerned, he said, he was *"happy to announce that there was a consensus among his colleagues that the Foreign Minister of Guyana, Mr Shridath Ramphal, would be an entirely worthy person to succeed to the office".*

It was received by acclamation. My words of acceptance which followed were as follows:

> *It is with profound gratitude that I acknowledge the confidence you have all reposed in me through this decision and it is with great humility that I accept the responsibilities you have collectively entrusted to me as Commonwealth Secretary-General.*
>
> *In so doing, I am fully conscious of the great potential of the Commonwealth association as a forum for advancing the wider human dialogue on which our planetary survival may now depend and for deepening the process of understanding between peoples which is such an essential underpinning of that dialogue. It is a potential, therefore, which obliges the Commonwealth steadfastly to continue to serve the international*

community by retaining its character as an outward-looking association of States.

I am mindful also of the great capacity of the Commonwealth as an instrument of functional co-operation between its member states – a capacity already well demonstrated, yet one sufficiently ample to remain responsive to the enlarging and changing demands of succeeding generations and, in our time, to the specially urgent needs of its developing member states.

But my awareness of these possibilities is tempered with an appreciation of the limits of Commonwealth action and a perception that just as the Commonwealth must not be restrained in the fulfilment of its true vocation by any lack of vision or courage or inventiveness, so too we must not distort or diminish it by excessive expectations or by untenable roles.

As has been so eloquently demonstrated at this Conference, and those that have preceded it, the great strength of the Commonwealth has been its quality of striking the balance of practicality, of melding formalism with reality, of accepting the challenge of change. It is really an on-going challenge that the Commonwealth must always remain ready to meet – a challenge to prevent this unique association of nations and peoples from ever becoming a relic of yesterday; a challenge that can only be met by constantly endowing it with the relevance, the freshness and the promise of tomorrow. It is with these perceptions and understandings, and with the commitments that derive from them, that I approach the office of Secretary-General.

The Commonwealth Secretariat is a young institution, but already its achievements have been immense. The work of foundation-building carried out with such dedication and distinction over the last ten years by its first Secretary- General has been of enormous importance to the Commonwealth as a whole; but it is work of which I, as his successor am a special beneficiary. The tasks ahead of me will be rendered immeasurably lighter by the pioneering efforts of Arnold Smith and his colleagues and I wish to acknowledge this special indebtedness to them.

But, for the way ahead, let me acknowledge also that no effort of mine nor any achievement of years past will suffice to meet the demands of the future without the support and sustenance that the Commonwealth requires of its member states – and which therefore it will be my constant concern to deserve of Commonwealth Governments and of the people of all our States – to whose service I now commit myself.

For 15 years I would devote my life to being faithful to these assurances and commitments. I could hardly do otherwise. The torrent of good wishes heightened the duty that election imposed. One message I recall from my Caribbean friend, the poet and writer Ian McDonald, intoned compulsion:

All best wishes to you when you take up the appointment. It will surely be a formidable job full of challenging times. I recently read an article on Brian Urquhart's book on Hammarskjold. "The United Nations", Hammarskjold apparently once remarked, "was not created to guide man to heaven, but to save him from hell". I suppose the Commonwealth is somewhat like the United Nations, but I believe you are still idealistic enough to feel in the job of Secretary-General of the Commonwealth that you will not only be helping to save us all from hell but also perhaps leading us a little way along the road to heaven.

Another message, among many from Commonwealth leaders, that gave me strength was the one from Pierre Trudeau, Canada's (and my predecessor's) Prime Minister. He had stopped over briefly in Guyana on the way to the Kingston Summit and, afterwards, he wrote to this effect:

This note is for two purposes, each of them equally sincere and equally deserved. The first is to thank you without reservation for your contribution to a memorable and enjoyable day in the interior of Guyana. The second is to congratulate you wholeheartedly on your election as Commonwealth Secretary-General, to wish you well in that endeavour and to promise you every measure of Canadian support for a successful term of office.

The congenial relationship which you long since established with me, with Ivan Head and with so many Canadian officials has served well the interests of our countries and of the Commonwealth in the past, and will unquestionably make more effective your work in the future. It was a pleasure being with you in Guyana and in Jamaica; I look forward to many more occasions in the future in London and elsewhere.

From Africa, Asia, the Pacific, the Mediterranean, the Caribbean and Britain where I lived thereafter, that congeniality was to be ever my pursuit within the principles and precepts of the Commonwealth.

Family gathered at Hill Street residence

CHAPTER 13

1949: The Queen and the Commonwealth

In April 2009, my successor Secretaries-General of the Commonwealth and I were photographed with Her Majesty Queen Elizabeth II in Buckingham Palace. The photograph was taken at exactly the same spot where her father King George VI had been photographed in April 1949 with the Prime Ministers of seven Commonwealth countries and the Foreign Minister of Canada. No one person is in both photographs; but while I was in the second, certainly, for me, there is a link to that first photograph of which I must offer a glimpse. I must do so, too, of the role of the Queen in the Commonwealth in my 15 years at her 'grandmother's House' (Marlborough House where her grandmother Queen Mary lived).

The occasion of the second photograph was a Reception given by the Queen to mark the 60th anniversary of the 'April Declaration' of 1949 – and the emergence of the modern Commonwealth. The first photograph was on the occasion of the Declaration itself in 1949. The story of it is fascinating in the light of unforeseeable coming events.

1949 Heads and George VI

There are two other photographs following them. They are photographs of Commonwealth Prime Ministers. The first, taken (I suspect) in the garden of No 10 Downing Street, is of Winston Churchill and four colleagues: Mackenzie King of Canada, Field Marshal Jan Smuts of South Africa, Peter Fraser of New Zealand and John Curtis of Australia. It was May 1944; and this was the old Empire club. But the war was ending and with it – ironically for 'the victor' – so was *pax Britannica*. 'Winds of change' were beginning to blow, and were acknowledged to be transforming Empire into Commonwealth. The rules of the club were changing.

The other photograph was also in a garden, but arranged more formally. It was June 1957, thirteen years later, and a new and larger coterie of leaders. In the front row were Kwame Nkrumah of Ghana, Jawarharlal Nehru of India, John Diefenbaker of Canada, Harold Macmillan of Britain, Robert Menzies of Australia and Huseyn Suhrawardy of Pakistan. Behind them were Ministers of Sri Lanka, New Zealand, South Africa and the Federation of Rhodesia and Nyasaland. In the time between these two photographs the modern Commonwealth had emerged. Great vision had made the transformation possible – the vision of great men.

Between those gatherings, in April 1949, Britain's post-war Prime Minister, Clement Atlee, hosted his Commonwealth colleagues at a special meeting at No.10 Downing Street. It was to be the end game of Britain's withdrawal from the Indian sub-continent. In the 5 years since the 1944 photograph the 'British Commonwealth of Nations' had been challenged. Did it have the enlightenment and will to respond to the palpable need for change? India, Pakistan and Ceylon had become independent Dominions; but for India, in particular, independence on 15th August 1947 (independence by virtue of an Act of the British Parliament) was not the end of change. Before 1947 began, the Indian Constituent Assembly had already met to draft a Constitution for the proposed new Dominion. In February 1948, barely six months into independence, the draft of India's home-made Constitution was published. As expected, it provided for India to be an "Independent Sovereign Republic". Alive to the implications of this intent, the Constituent Assembly acknowledged with great delicacy that the relationship between the new Republic and the British Commonwealth of Nations was a matter "to be subsequently decided". Put bluntly, the problem was: how could India as a Republic, with its own Head of State, remain in a Commonwealth where all the members owed allegiance to the British Crown.

It was in furtherance of this that on 22nd April 1949 (and for six days thereafter) the leaders of the still 'British' Commonwealth laboured to find a consensual way forward. With Atlee, were the Prime Ministers of Australia, Ceylon, India, New Zealand, Pakistan, South Africa and Canada's Foreign Minister. It was not an easy task that faced them; and had it not been for men of the very special quality of Atlee and Nehru and Canada's Lester Pearson that way forward might never have been found, nor anything like the present Commonwealth ever have emerged.

India had both precipitated the problem and offered a solution. On 3rd April, before leaving for London, Nehru (speaking in Lucknow) had expressed the hope that "without restricting our freedom, India may form some sort of link with the Commonwealth which will benefit and enable us to contribute to the peace of the world". In short, India would become a Republic and wished, as a Republic, to remain in the Commonwealth. Until Nehru raised the matter thus, the proposition for most people was an oxymoron; republican Ireland had left the Commommwealth only months before, at least ostensibly, on the issue of 'allegiance'. In reality, India's proposition was a challenge to the British Commonwealth to adapt or wither on the vine – a challenge that could not be refused if the Commonwealth was to be significant in the aftermath of decolonisation. Indeed, if the Commonwealth had not accommodated republican India, it is unlikely that it would have survived in any meaningful way. Clement Atlee understood this well.

But not everyone saw it that way. Smuts, for example – and he spoke for many – emphatically denied any possibility of accommodation: "There is", he said, "no middle course between Crown and Republic, between in and out of the Commonwealth".

Menzies, then Leader of the Opposition in Australia, speaking to the Canadian Club in Ottawa on 21st October 1948 said he did not think a formula by which a Republic could be included with the Dominions in one political organisation could be devised, adding: "If we spread the butter of the British Association until it is too thin it will disappear". He failed utterly to see that it was precisely 'the butter of the British association' spread too thick – the issue of allegiance to the British Crown – that was the problem.

Fortunately for the Commonwealth, and for the post-war world, wiser counsels prevailed. Great vision charactertised the Declaration that issued from Downing Street on 26 April 1949 – one must assume, not without consultation with the Palace. It was:

> *The Governments of the United Kingdom, Canada, Australia, New Zealand, South Africa, India, Pakistan and Ceylon, whose countries are united as Members of the British Commonwealth of Nations and owe a common allegiance to the Crown, which is also the symbol of their free association, have considered the impending constitutional changes in India.*
>
> *The Government of India have informed the other Governments of the Commonwealth of the intention of the Indian people that under the new constitution which is about to be adopted India shall become a sovereign independent republic. The Government of India have however declared and affirmed India's desire to continue her full membership of the Commonwealth of Nations and her acceptance of The King as the symbol of the free association of its independent member nations and as such the Head of the Commonwealth.*
>
> *The Governments of the other countries of the Commonwealth, the basis of whose membership of the Commonwealth is not hereby changed, accept and recognise India's continuing membership in accordance with the terms of this declaration.*
>
> *Accordingly the United Kingdom, Canada, Australia, New Zealand, South Africa, India, Pakistan, and Ceylon hereby*

declare that they remain united as free and equal members of the Commonwealth of Nations, freely co-operating in the pursuit of peace, liberty and progress.

Professor S.A. de Smith, the much respected constitutional lawyer of that time – and my tutor in constitutional law – was later to describe it as *a declaration which may well prove to be one of the great constitutional documents of modern times.* The critical paragraph was, of course, the second, which stated that India is soon to become an Independent Sovereign Republic, but that she still desires to retain her membership of the organisation – now described as 'the Commonwealth of Nations' – and is prepared to continue to accept the "King as the symbol of the free association of its independent member nations and as such the Head of the Commonwealth". It was a supreme example of enlightened statesmanship and consummate political skill – and a masterpiece of drafting.

But, again, not everyone shared that judgment. Writing in the *Times* the next day L.S. Amery – an influential Conservative politician and journalist, born in India of the British raj – suggested, predictably, that the effect of the Declaration was that "it has changed in respect of India alone the historic conception of allegiance as an element of our unity". How often those timid of change minimise great moments of transition when they come.

In that same year, in 1949, with these momentous events unfolding, I was a law student at King's College, London. With the brashness of youth, I offered an article on the 'April Declaration' for *King's Counsel* – the Journal of the Faculty of Laws. It was written as a constitutional law answer to the 'Amery' view. I called it "The Second Commonwealth of Nations", and it was published in *King's Counsel,* April 1950. In it I asserted that the concept of 'allegiance' as a basis of Commonwealth membership had gone; that the Commonwealth was now a free association of nations, independent in form as they are in status, each free to go its own way in regional and international affairs; but united by common ideals and common interests.

The article rejected the Amery view as shying away from the full implications of the Declaration, which, it suggested constitutes a much greater achievement so far as the future of the Commonwealth is concerned, than the narrow compromise implied by Amery. On the other hand, it pointed out, Field Marshal Smuts, one of the few Commonwealth figures to have expressed grave doubts about the wisdom of the decision, had himself recognised its general implications: *Instead of treating India as a special case,* he said, *the Prime Ministers so worded their declaration that other Commonwealth countries are free to go the way India has gone.* Dr Daniel Malan, the Prime Minister of South Africa, himself an old Republican and a strong nationalist, had already spoken of South Africa's *rights to become a Republic within the Commonwealth.*

As regards the statement in the third paragraph of the Declaration that the basis of the membership of the other countries of the Commonwealth has not been changed, the article contended that other Dominions still owe allegiance to the Crown as they all did before the Declaration; but whereas before such allegiance was obligatory, it had now become voluntary; but voluntary only in the sense that it exists until constitutionally renounced. The difference between India and the other members of the Commonwealth, it suggested, *is the difference between actual and potential Republicanism.*

The second pillar of the British Commonwealth of Nations as represented in the first paragraph is that the King was the symbol of the free association of the member nations. The second paragraph does not ostensibly alter this basis as India has declared her *acceptance of the King as the symbol of the free association of the independent member nations and as such the Head of the Commonwealth.* But here also, the article suggested, *great changes lie concealed behind these vague and modest phrases—where before stood a pillar of solid rock now stands a column of hollow clay.* Prior to the Declaration this acceptance of the King as the symbol of the free association within the British Commonwealth produced quite positive manifestations.

The King possessed and exercised important functions. The theory was that there was one King and different Governments, different

Legislatures and different Courts throughout the Dominions, who all acted in his name and on his behalf. He was the sole repository of power and no legislation could be enacted unless assent was given by him or in his name. Although it is true that these functions affected matters of form only, and not matters of status, in them lay an important concept of the Commonwealth relationship – the Unity of the Crown. In respect of these formalities the Declaration is silent; but the Indian Prime Minister had been extremely outspoken. His statement in this respect in the Constituent Assembly on 18th May, 1949, being at once important and authoritative: *"In this particular Declaration nothing much is said about the position of the King except that he will be a symbol; but it has been made perfectly clear – it was made perfectly clear – that the King has no functions at all. This was cleared up in the course of our proceedings; it has no doubt been recorded in the minutes of the Conference in London."*

Accordingly, the Article asserted, so far as India is concerned, henceforth its Government, its Legislatures and its Courts will act in the name of the President of the Republic who will be the representative of the sovereign people of India. The King of Canada and of Australia and of South Africa will no longer be the King of India; but merely the head of an organisation of which she is a member. *So far, therefore, as India is concerned, the Unity of the Crown has passed into the shades of legal history to accompany the ghosts of fellow fictions who all outstayed their welcome.* And the article reasoned:

> *It seems quite clear that any other member of the Commonwealth can at any time follow the path India has chosen. What is there to prevent South Africa or Australia from becoming a Republic – from severing the bond of allegiance and eliminating the King from any functional part of that Dominion's Constitution – and at the same time preserve her membership of the Commonwealth? Nothing we suggest, but a genuine desire to remain a member, and willingness to adopt and to employ the constitutional processes which*

unquestionably exist. This made all the difference between India being in and Eire being out of the Commonwealth of Nations. In an institution founded on principles of mutual co-operation, unilateral action is at once unconstitutional and unwise.

And so it has been. Sixty-four years (as I write) after the April Declaration, of the Commonwealth's 54 Member States, 33 are Republics, while five have their own Monarchs: Brunei, Lesotho, Malaysia, Swaziland and Tonga. In constitutional terms, there is no such thing as 'the unity of the Crown' – so redolent of Empire. My Article had ended with these words:

This being the position, therefore, how can we say that the basis of the Commonwealth conception has remained unimpaired? The old concept of allegiance, the keystone as it were of the Commonwealth arch cracked and scarred through years of pressure and strain – has at last fallen away and the structure it supported has collapsed in the dust. But even as it fell a new structure arose, as it were from the same pressure that had split the cracks wide open. It is this we call the Second Commonwealth of Nations – and its features we have already noted. It is a free association of nations: independent in form as they are in status, each free to go its own way in regional and international affairs; but united by common ideals and common interests. It. may well be that this new bond will prove more acceptable and so more lasting than the now rusted links of allegiance; if that is so, the April Declaration augurs well not only for Commonwealth harmony, but for world peace as well.

I was in good company. Years later, Lester Pearson, who went on to become one of Canada's great Prime Ministers, wrote in his memoirs of the 1949 Delcaration:

So began the new 'Commonwealth of Nations': British Empire to British Commonwealth to Commonwealth of Nations.

> *Emperor to King to Head. This was one of the most important landmarks in the history of the Commonwealth. It was the critical moment in her post-war development.*

The Declaration did augur well – the voluntary acceptance by members of the Commonwealth of the British sovereign (King or Queen) *"as the symbol of the free association of its independent member nations and as such the Head of the Commonwealth"*. That it is an acceptable formula is palpable. If it needs to be supported by logic, the British Sovereign is Head of State of more member countries of the Commonwealth that any other Commonwealth Head of State. But the culture of the Commonwealth does not seek such rationalisation. And there is something else: Immemorial changes are not made by parchment only. 'Declarations' are statements of intent and promises of change; they may light the way 'less trodden by'; but it is people who ensure that it is the path actually taken. Queen Elizabeth has given that 'symbolic' role of which the Declaration spoke a quality that has enhanced its acceptability to, and strengthenend its enduring character with, the people of the Commonwealth.

Nothing manifests this more than the presence of the Queen in Commonwealth countries where she is received rapturously – hosted by leaders of Asian, African, Pacific, Caribbean and all other Commonwealth countries. I have recounted earlier Michael Manley's experience as host to the Queen in Jamaica. Correspondingly, the Queen is always a happy Head of the Commonwealth on these occasions as if delighted to be with the 'family'. Occasions of the Commonwealth Games exude a special quality of that 'family' spirit; and the Queen glories in it. I have always been moved by the account of the then young Queen insisting to her lofty designer, Norman Hartnell, that her Coronation gown had to be embroidered with the floral emblems of the then Commonwealth countries: the English tudor rose, the Scottish thistle, the Welsh leek, the Irish shamrock, the Australian wattle, the Canadian maple leaf, the New Zealand silver fern, the South African proteas, the lotus flowers of India and Ceylon, and Pakistan's wheat, cotton and jute. It mattered to her.

Nehru had emphasised to the Indian Constituent Assembly after the 1949 'April' Declaration "that the King has no functions at all"; and in a constitutional law context, as Head of the Commonwealth, that is so. It is so, therefore, of the Queen. But there is a great difference between 'constitutional functions' and 'informal roles'; and the absence of the former does not preclude the latter; indeed, it is the absence of formal binding functions that endows the informal roles with the acceptability they enjoy. Commonwealth countries acknowledge the Queen as Head of the Commonwealth and, as it were in return, the Queen extends to the Commonwealth a measure of caring for it and about it that expresses itself in innumerable ways.

* * *

That sense of caring about the Commonwealth infused the Queen's influential roles to a degree that made them an invaluable Commonwealth asset. Most knowledgeable commentators agree that the Queen's presence in Lusaka at the time of the 1979 Heads of Government Meeting was conducive to its success. Hers was no small contribution: the Lusaka Accord which the Commonwealth agreed – and which was not likely to have found agreement otherwise – paved the way for the Lancaster House Conference, the end of 'UDI' and Zimbabwe's independence. But the Queen was in Lusaka despite several stratagems to keep her away – by the British Prime Minister and others, including the Prime Minister of New Zealand. She was there because she understood the influence of her presence to the Commonwealth finding accord. The story of those efforts to keep the Queen from being in Lusaka, and her determination not to be kept away will be told in a later Chapter dealing with the Lusaka Conference. Suffice it here that her resolve prevailed.

Another example of that influential role was in the most critical days of the Commonwealth's efforts to end *apartheid* in South Africa. The Commonwealth's path-breaking mission to South Africa had ended in June 1986, and the Group of seven Commonwealth Heads of Government designated at Nassau to assist the process were about to meet in London, in Marlborough House, to consider their Report. The Group's final message to the Commonwealth was:

> *The question in front of Heads of Government is in our view clear. It is not whether such measures (sanctions) will compel change; it is already the case that their absence and Pretoria's belief that they need not be feared defers change. Is the Commonwealth to stand by and allow the cycle of violence to spiral? Or will it take concerted action of an effective kind? Such action may offer the last opportunity to avert what could be the worst bloodbath since the Second World War.*

It was well known that the British Prime Minister, Mrs Margaret Thatcher (later Baroness Thatcher), was still in iron-clad opposition to sanctions against South Africa. The mini Commonwealth Summit which included, as well as Mrs Thatcher, the Prime Ministers of Australia, the Bahamas, Canada, India and Zimbabwe, and the President of Zambia, would convene on 3 August to respond to the Report which had attracted attention and support world-wide. The Commonwealth was on the line. The Queen moved on her own initiative.

She invited the assembled Heads, and me, to meet with her in a working dinner in Buckingham Palace on the eve of the Meeting. She invited Mrs Thatcher to bring her Foreign Secretary with her. It was not a social occasion; and it served the purpose of breaking the ice before the formal meeting. The Queen's message was simple: the Commonwealth must not be in discord on this matter. Mrs Thatcher was palpably uneasy with the occasion; but it was a clear message to her that the Commonwealth must close ranks against *apartheid.* It was also a reminder of the Commonwealth's oneness, which British intransigence was threatening to render. It was a call for unity at a critical moment. The mini Summit that followed produced only partial agreement; but Mrs Thatcher had moved on sanctions. The Head of the Commonwealth, not the Queen of the United Kingdom, had gone the extra mile to help the Commonwealth to agree and to act.

The Commonwealth has been fortunate in the quality of caring that Queen Elizabeth has brought to her role as Head of the Commonwealth, an essential element of which is caring for the collectivity of the Commonwealth, its integrity, its organic unity – its very existence. Time and again, as over the existential threats to the Commonwealth posed by *apartheid* in South Africa, the Queen has acted to remind the Commonwealth, including the British Prime Minister, of its obligation to retain its integrity by the triumph of agreement over discord. They were never 'interventions' in the formal sense; they could not be – but they were reminders which the Commonwealth's respect for her endowed with quiet insistence.

That sense of caring which the Queen has brought to her role as Head of the Commonwealth is rooted in an understanding of and empathy with the aspirations of the Commonwealth's once young leaders – of Africa in particular – with whom the Queen grew up in her capacity as Head the Commonwealth. I think of Julius Nyerere and Kenneth Kaunda in particular who were young Commonwealth leaders in the 1960s as the Queen was herself a young Queen. She had exposure to them and their hopes for the young countries they were nurturing, long before others who came later. And they in turn valued their opportunities of interaction with her. Those opportunities arose, of course, in various ways: on country visits; on their visits to London; and on their little known 'audiences' with her at Commonwealth Heads of Government meetings (CHOGM). Let me say a little about the last.

An observer of such a CHOGM in my time (although, of course, there were not such observers) would notice individual Heads, Prime Ministers and Presidents, slip away from Meetings – sometimes at quite surprising moments in discussions – and return some 45 minutes later. They had gone to have their scheduled conversation (their 'audience', protocol would insist) with the Queen – on the Royal Yacht *Brittannia*, or the local State House, or wherever she was staying during the Meeting. It was an opportunity away from the discords, or vigorous attempts at accord, of the larger Meeting, for a quiet, off the record, conversation with the Queen. What I know, because many of them told me so, is how much each valued those moments. This did not mean they were closet 'monarchists' – many were among the world's most radical leaders.

Nor was it a 'courtesy' call. Universally, they never ceased to be impressed with how up to date the Queen was on their situations at home – their efforts, their successes, sometimes their failures; and how freely they could share with her their hopes for their countries and, of course, the Commonwealth. She was not in those moments the Queen of the United Kingdom; though one can conjecture that from time to time they did not refrain from sharing particular disappointments with this or that position of their British colleague – but never to the point of embarassment. The cumulative effect of these several conversations was inevitably to draw the Queen ever closer to an understanding of the Commonwealth environment. No wonder every Secretary-General valued the Queen as a Commonwealth resource; not just an embellishment, but a functional asset. I know I did in substantial measure.

The countries and leaders of the Commonwealth had long ago ceased to be regarded by the world as 'anglophile'; the decolonisation process with many a bitter struggle against Britain ensured that; but so too did the roles played by Commonwealth developing countries on both the economic and political divides in the post war world. The deep intellectual differences that characterised the arguments about a new international economic order in the 70s; the role of non-alignment in the 'cold war' era, all served to remove from new Commonwealth countries an image of 'Britishness'. Having the Queen as Head of the Commonwealth posed no political problems.

No reflection on the role of the Queen as Head of the Commonwealth would be complete without acknowledgment of the largely unseen hand of her Private Office and of her Private Secretaries in particular. I recall from my time Martin Charteris, Philip Moore, William Heseltine and Robert Fellows. They would reject a description of being powers behind the throne; but they were repositories of wisdom and good judgement indispensable to the exercise of the Queen's many-faceted roles. For me they were essential interlocutors, and no glimpse of my Commonwealth days could be complete without avowal of my gratitude to them and their colleagues.

* * *

My article about the Declaration whose 60th Anniversary the photograph with the Queen in 2009 celebrated was written in 1949. I was 21 and had, of course, no notion how that Declaration, and the emergence of the modern Commonwealth along the lines I ventured to predict, would shape the course of my own life. Twenty- six years later, in July 1975, I would arrive in London to take up my appointment as Secretary-General of the Commonwealth – the modern Commonwealth which that Declaration of 1949 had made possible. As I recounted in Chapter 1, my family and I would go in a strange circularity to the Secretary-General's residence at 5, Carlton Gardens – the address Sir John Gladstone had made his London residence with the proceeds of sale of his Demerara sugar plantations – to which my forebears had been bound as indentured labourers just over a century ago.

My appointment as Secretary-General took effect on 1 July, 1975. On that day, I was actually in Jamaica, having left Guyana on 30th June en route to Ottawa, where my first official function was addressing the opening meeting of the McIntyre Group established at the Kingston Summit. I will reflect later on the work of this first Commonwealth Expert Group; my point here is that it was a matter of importance to me at that time that I assumed office as Secretary-General in a capital city of the Commonwealth other than London. It was a small point; but it was symbolic of the importance I attached to showing how far the modern Commonwealth – 'the Second Commonwealth of Nations' – had travelled along the path first lighted by the April Declaration of 1949.

The Jamaica and Canada routing to London served two other purposes. In Montego Bay, Jamaica, I would take leave of the Caribbean whose regional ambitions had commanded so much of my previous 10 years. I did so at a dinner held in my honour at which I poured out my soul and its anxieties in an address I called *To Care for Caricom.* In it I counselled:

> *A consequence of our relative success over the last ten years is a readiness to believe that unity is our natural state – one that will subsist despite ourselves. It is a dangerous falsehood. A history of colonialism and the geography of a scattered archepelago deny its validity. The natural state of our Caribbean is fragmentation: without constant effort, withouth unrelenting perseverance and discipline in suppressing instincts born of tradition and environment, it is to our natural state of disunity that we shall return.*

It was an address, alas, that I could make with plaintive relevance even now as I recall, nearly 40 years later, that balmy evening on Jamaica's North Coast. Beyond Jamaica, I was travelling to a new life with my wife and two younger children, Mark and Amanda. Going via Canada allowed me as well to see my widowed mother in Toronto, and to receive her blessings on this new chapter of our lives.

We arrived in London on 14 July and the next day I met the Secretariat's staff in a moving welcome in Marlborough House managed by my able Deputy Azim Hussain – who had managed as well the transition from Arnold Smith to me. I had naturally received many messages of congratulation and welcome; but the message from Arnold at that time was very special: *"I think you know how happy I am that it is specifically to you that I hand over the post of Secretary-General of the Commonwealth. I have greatly enjoyed and appreciated our co-operation over the years. I wish you great success in your new post and feel sure you will have it."*

My first formal engagement was a courtesy call on Her Majesty the Queen as Head of the Commonwealth – by my wife and me. It had been arranged before my arrival and confirmed by letter from the Marshall of the Diplomatic Corps. It was a short letter but it offers glimpses of that time, not all that long ago

> *I am writing to confirm that The Queen will receive you and your wife in Audience on Thursday 17th July at 12.40 p.m. at Buckingham Palace.*
> *Would you please arrive at the Grand Entrance at 12.35 p.m. on that day.*
> *The dress would be Morning Dress for yourself, and day dress and hat and gloves for your wife.*

There were a few problems, of course. I had never possessed 'Morning Dress'. Guyana had adopted a relaxed dress code appropriate to the tropics, so anything like 'tails' was out of the question. But our 'formal' wear was a 'Nehru' style tunic, and that I wore; 'national' dress was always acceptable. Besides, I had an aversion to 'hiring'. Lois too had been in the Caribbean for over 20 years and had neither hat nor gloves; but she conjured up both.

To the Palace

The 'audience', for all its pompous intonations was a relaxed 'gettting to know you' call – formal in its structure perhaps, but informal and relaxed in its nature. The Queen, I felt, was pleased to receive 'her' new Secretary-General; and the message to me was one of special welcome. It was also one assuring me of access as necessary. I left with a sense of the Queen as a friendly, caring and perceptive 'Head of the Commonwealth'. They were early impressions that would be reinforced over and over again in the 15 years of a working relationship that followed. Her Majesty was not yet fifty, and I specially value the framed signed photgraph of a mature but youthful Queen that she gave me on that first 'audience'.

At a different time that journey we had made to the Palace would not have been unfamiliar to the Queen and the time came when she would tell me of that. In 1971 Pierre Trudeau, still a new Canadian Prime Minister and somewhat sceptical about the Commonwealth, played a major role at the Commonwealth's Singapore Summit (which I attended as Guyana's Foreign Minister). It was not a good Meeting, as I have mentioned earlier, and Trudeau attributed some of its shortcomings to 'style and format'. In offering to host the next Meeting in 1973, he was determined to make changes and not only to the nature of the meeting. One of his proposals at Ottawa was to establish a 'Commonwealth Day' each year when member countries would focus their populations on the Commonwealth and especially on its values. It was adopted, and at the Commonwealth Secretariat it became a major annual event – fixed for the second Monday in March each year. The Council of Commonwealth Socities was responsible for a major eccumenical Commemorative Service in Westminister Abbey attended by the Queen and Prince Philip, and this was followed some hours later by the Commonwealth Secretary-General's Reception at Marlborough House, also attended by the Queen and Prince Philip. The 8th March,

1976 would be my first Commonwealth Day Reception – my first occasion to welcome Her Majesty to Marlborough House.

At the start of Arnold Smith's tenure as the Commonealth's first Secretary-General, the British Government had offered Marlborough House as Headquarters of the new Secretariat. But it was the Queen who had first linked this Royal Residence to the Commonwealth. In September 1959 she had made it available to the British Government as a 'Commonwealth centre'. When the Secretariat was established five years later, the perfect 'centre' was at hand. For the Queen, well into her role as Head of the Commonwealth, the conjunction must have been perfect.

Marlborough House has a noble heritage. Commissioned by the first Duke of Marlborough to be built by Sir Christopher Wren, the construction was really driven by his wife Sarah Churchill, whose portrait hangs in the 'Green Room', alongside two Gainsboroughs from the Royal Collection. The Foundation stone was laid in 1709 and the building finished in 1711. Over a century later it would be the venue of a wedding banquet for Queen Victoria and Prince Albert. Eventually it became the home of the Prince of Wales (later King George V). When he died in 1936, his widow, Queen Mary – Princess Elizabeth's grandmother – moved to Marlborough House, where she died in 1953 – the year I left London for Guyana. It was to Marlborough House as my office that I would return twenty-two years later. My own portrait now hangs there.

My Barrington Watson portrait unveiled by HM The Queen

All this was encapsulated in what the Queen said to me that Commonwealth Day in 1976 as she entered Marlborough House as my guest, explaining that "I remember this place as my grandmother's house to which my sister and I came for tutorials. It is a very special place to me". I promised to cherish it as such, explaining that my office was in what was her grandmother's sitting room. And so I did, inspired by the heritage and the constant reminders of it by the views through the windows of that room. I was later to commission a painter and art teacher in Scotland who had been at school with me in British Guiana nearly 40 years earlier, Robert Batchelor, to capture those views for all time: through the western casement – St James' Palace from which the changing of the guards at Buckingham Palace began; through the southern casement – St James' Park and across it the Houses of Parliament. Together they are precious reminders of those 15 years I spent in Queen Mary's old home.

The Queen will be a hard act to follow; but her supreme success in the role of Head of the Commonwealth will forever be confirmation of the wisdom of the 1949 design of the modern Commonwealth and the excellence of Queen Elizabeth's fulfilment of the role entrusted to her. When the time does come, I would regard the only precedent we have – that of the transition from the King to Queen Elizabeth II – to be followed. It was without contention. The Queen and her several

Heads of Government over the years have together demonstrated the wisdom and practicability of the formula their predecessors devised in 1949 for keeping the Commonwealth together. The formula's tenets, like those of a virtuous founding constitution, are a heritage to be preserved.

CHAPTER 14

Internationalising the 'Club'

On September 6, 1943, with World War II at its apogee, Winston Churchill, receiving an honorary degree from Harvard University, spoke of his vision of the world beyond the conflict. His central theme, of course, was Anglo-American unity; but the wider Commonwealth connection (the 'British Commonwealth and Empire' he called it) was central to his conception of 'fraternal association'. He spoke of the shared heritage of law, language and literature, of common conceptions of what is right and decent – regard for fair play especially for the weak and poor, a sentiment for impartial justice, a love of personal freedom. He spoke of 'basic English' (on which much work was then being done at Harvard) as the head-stream of what might well be a mighty fertilising and health-giving river – an advantage to many races, an aid to the building up of our new structure for preserving peace. *"Let us go forward"*, he concluded in words that have passed into legend, *"in malice to none and goodwill to all. Such plans offer far better prizes than taking away other people's provinces or lands or grinding them down in exploitation. The empires of the future are the empires of the mind."* Churchill was a man of empire; but his internationalism, shaped by his long crusade against the weakness of the League of Nations, and the conflict he saw looming – and by the conflict when it came – overrode imperialist ambitions. Even as he spoke of the 'British Commonwealth and Empire', he knew the club was dissolving.

The 1949 April Declaration changed the structure of the Commonwealth; but the substantive change had actually begun with the admission of India in 1947 – the first member not claiming kinship with Britain; the first non-white member. The rules of the 'club' changed in 1949 to accommodate that basic change. When Pakistan, Ceylon and Ghana became members, the transformation was palpable – as that early photograph of 1957 showed. Ten years earlier, the Commonwealth was a 'club' – an 'Empire club' of five members. South Africa, with a substantial Boer population, was always an aberration – and a problem; but it was within the 'club'. Field Marshall Smuts was a confidant of Churchill's War Cabinet. However, in the post-war world, which soon became the world of the 'Cold War', with new Commonwealth leaders like Nehru and Nkrumah being leaders as well of the rapidly developing Non-Aligned Movement, the Commonwealth 'club' needed more than even structural adjustment if it was to find a sufficient basis of commonality to bolster those historic elements of oneness that Churchill had mentioned at Harvard. In the post-war world, that had to be no less than the Commonwealth's acknowledged identity with the pursuit of man's highest purposes – with the noblest aims of the newly emerging internationalism.

Commonwealth Heads, London, 1977

The first Commonwealth Heads of Government Meeting (HGM) under my watch was in 1977. It had become established by then that the Secretary-General would submit a Report on the Secretariat's work since the previous Meeting. It would be inevitably a fairly humdrum though necessary record; but the 'Introduction' to it gave the Secretary-

General an opportunity for personal reflection on the challenges past and present. I valued this opportunity and eventually presented the Report in two parts – the Introduction and the Record. In the Introduction to my first Report in 1977 I reflected on the need for an articulated ethos worthy of a Commonwealth that had grown beyond the 'Club'.

> *Four themes have dominated the collective work of the Commonwealth since the Kingston Meeting: liberation in Southern Africa, the restructuring of world economic relationships, the more positive commitment of our association to the service of the world community, and the enlargement of its practical contribution to the economic and social development of its member states. In the first two we have, I believe, made some contribution to progress; but we are still far from success in either. This is the overwhelming reason why the third has become not only desirable, but inevitable. The Commonwealth must see itself in its global context, participating in the search for global solutions to problems that, while affecting our members with a particular intimate poignancy, are inextricably problems of the world...*
>
> *In defining more clearly the particular role that the Commonwealth itself can play in man's arrangements for his future, it is evident that we are no longer a club distinguished by the likeness of our membership. We are, instead a co-mingling of humanity in all its variety. What we have to offer the world is a special capacity for communication across the lines of geography and race and wealth – a facility by which a quarter of the world's states may enlarge understanding and advance co-operation. In this sense, the Commonwealth serves not just itself, but all the world.*

In March 1976, within months of assuming office, I discussed with Commonwealth Permanent Representatives at UN headquarters the idea of formal observer status for the Commonwealth Secretariat at the General Assembly. This would be symbolic of our internationalism;

but on the practical side it would give us entitlement to all UN documentation and to be represented in an observer capacity at all meetings of the General Assembly as well as of its subsidiary organs. The idea was warmly received as it was two months later by Commonwealth Senior Officials. It was consummated by a General Assembly consensus resolution later that year. It was a consensus resolution because the world had begun to see the Commonwealth not as an Empire club; but as a global asset in the world's search for a new way forward and agreement on taking it together. Our leadership role on Southern Africa issues and on the restructuring of world economic relationships played a major part in the international community's perception of the Commonwealth.

In 1987, I was pleased to have attestation of this from a dispassionate source beyond the Commonwealth. In that year, the West German President, Dr Richard Von Weizsacker, on a State visit to Britain, said this about the Commonwealth:

> *The Commonwealth is not against anyone, it is a source of common sense in the world where that quality is sadly lacking. It cannot negotiate on behalf of the world, but it can caution the world and help it to negotiate. The more the Commonwealth preserves its coherence across the oceans and continents, the better for all – including my own country.*

This was not a small endorsement of the Commonwealth's significance beyond itself – and all the Commonwealth was proud to be so perceived.

But there is such a thing as throwing out the baby with the bathwater; and that is a risk when we discard entirely the notion of the 'Commonwealth club'. In January 1987 I found myself speaking in Toronto to the Empire Club of Canada. My hosts were not throw-backs to earlier times. I was assured that the Club's name in no way implied veneration of things imperial. Like the Commonwealth, this club did emerge from 'Empire', and like the Commonwealth itself, it did not disown those beginnings; but both, like the butterfly, adorn the present because of a past transformed. And 'Empire', I realised, has another connotation which belongs to all time: the connotation of worthy ambition not for dominion over others, but for out-reach towards them – that connotation to which Churchill had come in his speech at Harvard in 1943. And so too does 'club'. In many minds it conjures up an image of the 'old boys' club' or of the closed inward-looking, often anti-social group. But, it too has another connotation: that of a familial group special to its members because heritage has made them so, and practice has endowed them with worthy aims to each other and to others – a worthy club.

When I came to the Commonwealth in 1975, I confess to an aversion to the very notion of the Commonwealth as a 'club' for my connotations were all the negative ones. I found, however, that there were parts of the Commonwealth where they were more enlightened – and nowhere more so than in Africa. On my first visit to Tanzania in my earliest years I was astonished to find the Commonwealth referred to extensively in the media as the 'Commonwealth club' or more simply 'the club'. The Tanzania *Daily News* of 24 June 1975 had carried the story of my assumption of office under bold headlines "CLUB: MR RAMPHAL TAKES OVER IN JULY"; and always, as in this case, the connotation was positive – our club which must certainly do better; but our club. It was an image of a club not to be disowned but to be made to perform better because it was ours. And I came to realise that in that positive connotation lay a Commonwealth asset – an asset of belonging to something new and whole.

That separateness of the club from its members – even Britain – was to be manifest early in the Commonwealth's struggles in Southern Africa when in December 1965, in the first months of the Commonwealth Secretariat's establishment, both Tanzania and Ghana broke diplomatic relations with Britain over its non-intervention in Rhodesia in the wake of Ian Smith's 'Unilateral Declaration of Independence' (UDI). There had been threats to leave the Commonwealth; but neither did. President Nyerere explained to his National Assembly that the Commonwealth 'was no longer the British Commonwealth. It is a Commonwealth of free nations'. The 'club' remained intact.

That was a decision of long term significance to the world; for one of the ways the Commonwealth could serve the international community was for member states like Tanzania, and leaders like Julius Nyerere, to struggle within the Commonwealth on global causes, taking advantage of the unique opportunities for the forging of consensus that the Commonwealth offered. Sometimes, as on Southern Africa issues, such struggles would be grim; but as we shall see they would lead in only one direction – towards victory for the forces of civilised values. On some matters, such struggles could only take place within the Commonwealth, and the international community knew it. Small wonder that President Von Weizsacker, drawing on words I had myself used earlier, acknowledged that while the Commonwealth cannot negotiate for the world, it can help the world to negotiate.

Acknowledging our limitations was as important as recognising our potential. We needed not to overreach ourselves or imply that we could do more than we really could. I was never in doubt of the importance of being aware of these limits and admitting to them. The mission of the Commonwealth association was to help human society to reach its goals – by using our very special facilities for dialogue across a spectrum of the world community in the service of those goals. That was ever the objective of internationalising the 'club'.

* * *

At my very first HGM I was confronted with this reality of the Commonwealth in its international setting. At the end of the Singapore HGM in 1971, before President Milton Obote could leave for Kampala, General Idi Amin seized power in Uganda in a midnight coup. As Arnold Smith wrote:

> *Obote in the 1960s was a true internationalist ... and a practical idealist in Pan-African affairs. But at home he was beset by many problems which the British had left on his desk at independence in 1962.*

They had become so acute by the end of 1970 that Obote was reluctant to leave Kampala for Singapore. But trouble was looming at the Conference with Ted Heath's announced plan to sell arms to South Africa; and both the Secretary-General and African leaders urged Obote to be at Singapore. Kenneth Kaunda was to tell me many years later how bitterly he regretted the pressure he put on Obote to come to Singapore. By contrast, in the wake of the coup, there was much speculation that British and Israeli intelligence operatives had helped Amin to power. It did not help that Britain moved swiftly to recognise Amin, and Heath received him in Downing Street within months of the coup.

It did not take long for Amin to show the horrific nature of his cunning and his evil. In August 1971 Colin Legum would be reporting in the London *Observer* of the massacre of Acholi and Langi soldiers loyal to Obote. And so it continued. In 1977 Obote gave details to the Organisation of African Unity (OAU) in writing of the horrible deaths of some 80,000 Ugandans under Amin's regime. But much sooner, in August 1972, had come the bizarre demand that Uganda's 80,000 Asians must leave the country within ninety days – creating displacement problems of such international proportions that Britain, while taking some 28,000 of the Uganda Asians, spoke aloud about (but did not actually propose) Uganda's expulsion from the Commonwealth. Matters continued to deteriorate; but the OAU had recognised Amin almost from the beginning, and he sheltered in this haven.

Addressing Amin's human rights abuses was my paramount concern. The Commonwealth simply could not abstain from collective action; but that would be essentially for the Heads of Government when they met in London in June 1977. I had, meanwhile, a more immediate disquiet. As June approached, the political environment in England was openly hostile to Amin coming to Britain and the Prime Minister, Jim Callaghan, was under pressure in Westminster to give assurances that he would not be allowed to. I had counselled Callaghan that on no account must he say that Amin would be prevented from attending the Meeting; but I was as anxious as he was that Amin should not have a Commonwealth platform to flout

Commonwealth principles. I assured the Prime Minister that I would ensure that he would not come. In due course I went to Uganda, with my wife, on an official visit – my object was to prevail on Amin to stay away of his own volition.

Amin embarked on a charm offensive. We were most welcome Commonwealth guests. Lois was invited to open a paint factory. We were both invited to open a new game park five hours drive outside Kampala, which he explained would be named after me. When set to depart for the park, we discovered (with some alarm) that we would be going by helicopter – piloted by the President. And so we did. Our pilot enlarged our concerns by also acting as a tour guide as he flew us over Pygmy country. We arrived to be met by an already assembled audience including, I thought, a rather dour diplomatic corps. Eventually, the German Ambassador explained to me in an aside that their melancholy had nothing to do with me, but with the fact that they had had to suffer the five-hour drive from Kampala – to which they had not grown accustomed although regularly undertaken, as the same game park was 'opened' in honour of State guests many times a year – and the Corps' presence was mandatory. The farce proceeded – Pygmy dancers and all. We subsequently learnt that the paint factory Lois 'opened' in Kampala had been opened, too, by earlier visitors.

Our programme was so packed with these fraudulent honorifics that I thought Amin was trying to avoid discussion; but eventually we did talk. I made it clear to him at the outset that he was entitled to attend the London HGM and that I would not countenance any denial of that right. I explained, however, that his policies in Uganda had made it difficult for his colleagues to be with him in the intimacy of the Commonwealth Summit and not be seen to be critical of him. I said the situation at the OAU and the UN was different, and I felt it right to warn him of the dangers of an onslaught on him in London not limited to non-African leaders. Far better, I urged him, in his own interest, and that of the Commonwealth, that he should stay away of his own volition. It was tempestuous for a while after that; but he seemed to reflect on what I was saying and said in the end that he would take my advice; but I was not to say so to anyone; he would make his own announcement when he was ready. I told him that I was sure that would be a service to the Commonwealth and Her Majesty the Queen as its Head – this latter, an appeal to his distorted military instincts of which he spoke openly.

Returning to London, I felt emboldened enough to tell Jim Callaghan that I had done my best to dissuade Amin from coming and was reasonably sure that he would not. The Prime Minister was far from reassured; but said that while he would not say so publicly, I should know that if Amin did try to come he would not be allowed to land in Britain. Amin did not make life easier by announcing through the media (without saying he was coming to the Summit) that he was coming to England 'to see Queen Elizabeth II, his Commander-in-Chief", and would be bringing a troupe of Pygmy dancers with him. This murderous tyrant was a consummate manipulator of the media. I still felt fairly confident; then the day before the Summit opened Jim Callaghan summoned me to 'No 10'. There, a visibly troubled Prime Minister told me that the media was reporting that Amin was in a plane over Ireland en route to London. I pleaded with him to hold his peace – at least until he had confirmation of the 'report'. Of course it was not confirmed; it was another Amin conjuring trick using a gullible media as his prop. In the end, he didn't come; but no one had said that he couldn't. Uganda was not represented at the Meeting.

Many African nations were of course ashamed of events in Uganda and outraged by Amin's atrocities; but they felt constrained from acting against him – even within the OAU. Why? Because of the principle of 'non-interference in the internal affairs of states' enshrined in the OAU Charter (Article 111 (2)). And that was a principle of greater vintage and of global authority, and the reluctance was not limited to Africa. The UN itself was similarly inhibited; however strongly its member states felt about what today we would call 'crimes against humanity'. Article 2.7 of the United Nations Charter says:

> *Nothing contained in the present Charter shall authorise the United Nations to intervene in matters which are essentially*

within the domestic jurisdiction of any state or shall require the Members to submit such matters to settlement under the present Charter; but this principle shall not prejudice the application of enforcement measures under Chapter VII.

Did that mean that the Commonwealth could do nothing on the evils of Amin? As Secretary-General, I believed it my duty to encourage the Commonwealth to stand by its principles on basic issues of human rights – principles reflected in its own Declaration of Commonwealth Principles. I knew that the Commonwealth accepted as axiomatic the universality of human dignity and the sanctity of human life; that the dignity of man is everywhere affronted when the human personality is anywhere degraded; that justice must be given a worldwide dimension if injustice is not to debase our civilisation and threaten the peace of the world. I knew too that gross violations of human rights wherever they occur in the world are the legitimate concern of the international community and of Commonwealth countries as part of it. I believed that matters ceased to be 'essentially within the domestic jurisdiction' of a state when they give rise to humanitarian issues of such magnitude that the international community must of necessity grapple with them.

The 1977 HGM in London was my first such Meeting as Secretary-General. Amin was rampant. In the Introduction to my Report to Heads on the eve of the Meeting, I confronted the issue thus:

There has been in the Commonwealth, of course, as in the international community, a long and necessary tradition of non-interference in the internal affairs of other states. No Commonwealth country (indeed, who anywhere in the world?) is above reproach in some respect or other. If these traditions were not to be respected there would be no end to recrimination and censoriousness. How to strike a balance of political judgement between the two extremes of declamation and silence is sometimes difficult – but it would be entirely illusory to believe that such a judgment could, or indeed should, be avoided

> *altogether. There will be times in the affairs of the Commonwealth when one member's conduct will provoke the wrath of others beyond the limits of silence. Any other relationship would be so sterile as to be effete. What we must work for is an ethic which constrains meddling but which also inhibits excesses of the kind that demand and justify protest from without.*
>
> *There never will be unanimity that criticism or complaint is legitimate comment, not improper interference. But the truth is that although the line may be indefinable, all the world will know when it is crossed.*

Ever since Trudeau's innovative 1973 HGM in Ottawa, the Retreat of the Heads over the weekend straddling the Meeting had proved its substantive value. Manley had used it to good effect at the Kingston meeting in 1975 and I had encouraged Jim Callaghan (who had succeeded Wilson as the UK's Prime Minister) as Chairman of the 1977 HGM to make full use of the Retreat mechanism. He needed no urging, and offered the most splendid of venues for it – the Gleneagles Hotel in Scotland. For my part, I had several stratagems for the Retreat – which for the Secretariat was an integral part of the Conference – and one of them concerned Uganda. I had discussed my ideas with Callaghan who was as aggrieved as anyone else by Amin's evil antics and their wounds to the Commonwealth's image. Essentially, I hoped to use the ideas I had advanced in my Report to encourage Commonwealth Heads to break new ground in international institutional practice by condemning Amin and his regime's inhumanities in Uganda. The world has made great progress since then in blunting, in a good way, the constraints of the 'non-interference' principle; but in 1977 it was still holy script.

I had, of course done some homework with leaders like Pierre Trudeau, Kenneth Kaunda, Julius Nyerere, Michael Manley, and Malcolm Fraser, and at the Retreat I argued the case for the Commonwealth speaking out in condemnation of one of its members. The line had been crossed; all the world knew it. The Commonwealth's own Principles had been grossly violated. Let us give a lead to the world in standing against evil. I did not have to argue. The Commonwealth's leadership was with me; African leaders prominently so. I had prepared some paragraphs as a basis for the Retreat's conclusion and inclusion in the Communiqué. With minor adjustments the Heads adopted them. There was no more discussion of this at the Retreat or in the Plenary when the Communiqué was adopted, containing the following under the heading 'Human Rights':

> *Recalling the Singapore Declaration of Commonwealth Principles, Heads of Government reiterated their belief in the fundamental rights of all men to life and liberty, to those personal freedoms that are the common heritage of their peoples and to respect for human dignity and the equal rights of all men. Mindful that the realisation of these rights the world over was a continuing if faltering pursuit, they reaffirmed their commitment to advancing respect for human rights in all their fundamental aspects: for economic, social and cultural rights no less than for civil and political rights. The effective enjoyment and protection of these rights was a cause to which the Commonwealth was resolutely committed.*
>
> *Cognisant of the accumulated evidence of sustained disregard for the sanctity of life and of massive violation of basic human rights in Uganda, it was the overwhelming view of Commonwealth leaders that these excesses were so gross as to warrant the world's concern and to evoke condemnation by Heads of Government in strong and unequivocal terms. Mindful that the people of Uganda were within the fraternity of Commonwealth fellowship Heads of Government looked to the day when the people of Uganda would once more fully enjoy their basic human rights which were being so cruelly denied.*

In an interview after the Summit with the then doyen of Commonwealth journalists, Derek Ingram (later carried in the *Round Table of October 1977)*, I was asked: *What in terms of Commonwealth history do you see as the significance of the statement on Uganda made in London?* In my answer, I said, *inter alia:*

> *Perhaps the most important of its elements of significance is the moral strength that the Commonwealth demonstrated in standing by its own Declaration of Principles, its own commitment to truly fundamental human rights, basic human dignity, life itself. I believe that it greatly strengthened the self-respect of the Commonwealth. An important consideration, although not often mentioned in so many words is the fact that it emphasised the truly non-racial character of the Commonwealth in that it spoke out in condemnation of what it regarded as tyranny, whether the origins were in a white or a black leadership. It also helped to dissolve what I regarded as a myth that national sovereignty is some kind of shield behind which every unspeakable horror can take place with the rest of the international community behaving as if it were not taking place at all – the notion that it is 'bad form', particularly among friends and within an association of nations, to recognise fundamental evil within the group. That reflection can have long-term significance for the Commonwealth and for the international community.*

In June 1977, speaking to the Commonwealth Press Union in London, I said of this achievement: "*Our association can now be seen more clearly than ever to stand for a view of international relations inspired by moral concern for the peoples of all its member states... we may have helped the world to recognise that there is a point of departure when happenings within one country become the business of all men*". Less than a year later (in April 1978) I was able to reassure the United Nations Secretary-General himself, Dr Kurt Waldheim, at a luncheon in Marlborough House in his honour, of our internationalism in these terms:

> *I place high among the obligations and commitments of the Commonwealth, and of the Secretariat that serves it, a wider*

service to the world community. We must endeavour to render that service by moulding the Commonwealth itself into a facility that is modern, outward-looking and truly internationalist, and by placing that facility at the service of the world community.

UN Secretary-General at Marlborough House

* * *

Throughout my three terms as Secretary-General it was my constant endeavour to help the 'club' become a facility that is 'modern, outward-looking and truly internationalist'. In 1985, the year in which I began my third term (and a high point in the Commonwealth's confrontation with Mrs Thatcher's Conservative government) the former British (Conservative) Prime Minister and Foreign Minister, Alec Douglas-Home, then Lord Home of the Hirsel, addressed the Diplomatic and Commonwealth Writers Association in London. It was the Association's 25th Anniversary Banquet and he devoted much of his address to the Commonwealth. After praising the 1949 'act of statesmanship' of Nehru and the Atlee Government in Britain, he continued:

One wonders – it often occurs to all of us – if the Commonwealth association represents anything in international relations which would so to speak make sense in terms of real politics. My answer is this: It is an association which starts with a prejudice in favour of friendship – and that in this modern world is a good start. It crosses the boundaries of doctrines and religions – all apt to be divisive. It has no veto on discussion and debate and that is a good thing where tolerance is in short supply. It is an association which seeks consensus and has the machinery for co-operation and is beginning to use it. Certainly, in terms of world politics it probably seems too intangible for people outside the circle. But those inside feel that we would have lost something of substance and value in terms of international harmony if the Commonwealth were to dissolve... Europe has its place because economy is our livelihood. But the Commonwealth surely will continue to have a place so long as friendship counts in international affairs and I believe that friendship does count.

The 'club' was truly internationalised.

PART V

THE ECONOMIC CHALLENGE

CHAPTER 15

The Other World

I came to the Commonwealth at the end of the first three-quarters of the 20th Century. For most of that time, and before it, international poverty had been as national poverty was throughout most of the 18th century – a matter on the periphery of the concerns of the rich. It was a cause that touched the hearts of good people everywhere – but it was all too easily put off by the affluent as a subject for Sunday reflection. It did not obtrude into their workaday national life; it did not seem to bear on the quality of that life or to have any relevance to sustained enrichment. For the developed world, international poverty was an external issue. It did not affect the price of bread; it did not influence, yet, the price of petrol; it did not threaten the value of currencies; it did not hurt.

These are not criticisms merely; they are reflections on realities at the heart of the global agenda for the last quarter of the century – years that had already begun to witness great changes. The simple fact is that by 1975 the issue of international poverty had become a matter of domestic importance to the rich no less than to the poor. It could no longer be relegated by developed countries to the periphery of national concern; it was not a matter for Sundays only.

In 1975, the Commonwealth was a Community of 35 states: one in every four of the members of the United Nations was a Commonwealth country. In population terms, its almost 1,000 million people constituted one-quarter of the human race. In geographical spread, its peoples inhabited all of the continents. All of the world's oceans touched Commonwealth shores. It was of North and South, of East and West. It had among its members, rich countries and some of the world's poorest.

It included a few industrialised nations, many countries who were primary producers only, and some island communities who were neither. It included countries that were, or soon would be, major oil producers, within or outside of OPEC, and many who were net oil importers. Its members ranked high among the world's producers of grain, tea, cocoa, sisal and rubber as well as of copper, bauxite and iron ore.

It included countries with great forest resources and some with pastoral resources that made them major world producers of meat and dairy products. And it included countries that had almost no other known resource but their people. It included countries that had been in the forefront of developing the most advanced technology, those who had just mastered intermediate technology, and those for which technological advance was still an aspiration. It included countries that had harnessed nuclear power to peaceful purposes and that had a potential military nuclear capacity. It included countries with major direct interests in the resources of the sea and the seabed.

It included economies that depended for survival on massive imports of primary and semi-manufactured products, for which assurance of supply was a critical factor; and others that depended on natural resource and secondary industry development, for which development capital and access to markets were the key to sustained growth.

It was a Commonwealth whose member states were prominent in the world's most important economic and political groupings and had influences which reached out beyond those to all other groupings of significance. It was a Commonwealth of all races and of many cultures. It was a Commonwealth of Hindus, of Muslims and of Christians in vast numbers. It was a miscellany of political ideologies and forms of government but with democracy as a central aspiration among its declared principles.

It was a Commonwealth, as we have seen, that at a much earlier stage of its development took pride in its intimacy – the intimacy of a mono-lingual, rather familial, club – but which by then acknowledged a great value and potential in its diversity while retaining an established ease of communication as an asset. It was a Commonwealth that in almost every sense was a sample of the world community. It was a Commonwealth, therefore, that could not but be concerned with all the great problems of mankind – for there was no area of global concern that did not touch some Commonwealth country intimately and directly.

For these general reasons the Commonwealth had to be concerned with the issue of change in the world's economic arrangements. But there were even more particular reasons why the Commonwealth's concern with development made these global economic challenges a matter of special priority.

In population terms – and therefore in human terms – Commonwealth countries then accounted for 44 per cent of the developing world. Nearly every other person among the world's poor lived in the Commonwealth. But the involvement with poverty went deeper. Of the world's absolute poor in 1975 – the 950 million people with annual per capita incomes of less than $200 – 760 million, lived (if indeed it could be called living) in a Commonwealth 'Least Developed Country' (LDC). Eighty per cent of the world's 'marginal' people inhabited the Commonwealth.

These figures have changed, of course; but not the general picture. By the time I left Marlborough House in 1990, the membership of the Commonwealth had grown from 35 to 50; and all the new members were developing countries – from Africa, the Caribbean, Asia, and the Pacific. Mindful of these realities in 1975, the Commonwealth would have been a mere masquerade of community were it not pre-eminently concerned with the issue of poverty and militant in its preoccupation with the promotion of development. The goal of more just and equitable human relationships – a goal which could only be achieved through development that ultimately eradicated poverty – was not a challenge about which the Commonwealth that I came to could be ambivalent.

As I saw it – and as the HGM at Kingston that appointed me had asserted – the Commonwealth could not be true to itself were it to eschew an activist role in any movement for new international economic arrangements that promised a more just and equitable human society. In the war against poverty, in the crusade for real development, in the supportive campaign for a new international economic order, the Commonwealth could not be neutral. In the years that followed, it would not be. But, clear glimpses of these efforts need a recall of the times that preceded 1975.

In 1945, the world had emerged from bitter conflict between the dominant powers – a struggle for primacy between the industrialised countries. It was a struggle, of course, that concerned important human values: freedom, democracy, the right to life itself; but, essentially, it was a struggle for dominance among the already powerful. At its end, the world set itself to rebuilding peace and security, but it was the victors who carried out this task, and the world they sought to reconstruct was the model they felt would best preserve the power and the paramountcy they had fought to secure.

Great vision inspired many of these efforts. The United Nations Organisation was the centrepiece of the new international political order. But basic to the conception of the reconstructed post-war world was the retention and enlargement of power. Even within the headquarters of peace the 'major powers' were more equal than others under the Charter. The political dimension of their power was thus assured; but real power derived essentially from economic strength founded on and sustained by the patterns of international economic relations that had dominated the pre-war world.

What were these patterns? They were the patterns of an international economic system that assigned to states and peoples predetermined economic roles and predictable economic fortunes. They were patterns that took as their starting point the economic ideology of free market forces – an ideology designed to support and advance the economic growth of the industrialised countries, but one premised upon the supportive role of those states and peoples that were primary producers mainly. For those subordinate players, economic hope was supposed to rest in processes by which the wealth of the rich would trickle down to the poor of the earth. It was an ideology that could not be written into the Charter, for among the architects of the Charter was the Soviet Union, committed not only to a centrally planned economy of its own but itself intent upon a global ideological crusade for its universality. The West, for its part, preserving the economic system despite the countervailing political processes of decolonisation, supplemented the Charter by the Agreement of Bretton Woods (setting up the International Monetary Fund and the World Bank) and, later, by the General Agreement on Tariffs and Trade (GATT). Thus was re-established an international economic system dedicated to the attainment not of global but of sectoral ends.

* * *

Henry Kissinger often urged that the system which these agreements affirmed had "served the world well". The old economic order had, it is true, served some nations well: but, indisputably, it had served many countries ill, and among these were the poor countries whose condition by the 1970s derived in large measure from the working of this system. No global economic system can be judged satisfactory that fails to serve the basic needs of the people of the planet – their needs for food, for shelter, for health, and for the development of the intellect that marks them out as human. But what was the reality of the working of this skewed economic order? How did the system serve the people of the developing world? What would be, for them, for example, the record at the end of the decade of the seventies?

After a monumental effort by the developing countries themselves; at the end of two decades of international action devoted to development; on the basis of nearly three decades of the working of the Bretton Woods and GATT regimes – the result by 1980 was estimated to be an increase of $3 per capita in the annual incomes of the poorest group compared with an increase of $900 per capita for those of the richest who were already at the start of the decade 300 per cent better off. By 1980, the developing nations would have grown relatively poorer when compared to the developed countries. The gap, in fact, would have widened.

In 1975, those whom Franz Fanon described 20 years earlier as 'the wretched of the earth' – nearly one billion of the world's poorest – subsisted on incomes of less than $75 a year (less than 20 cents per day) in an environment of squalor, hunger and hopelessness. As the President of the World Bank, Robert McNamara, said at that year's meeting of the Board of Governors of the Bank:

> *They are the absolute poor, living in institutions so deprived as to be below any rational definition of poverty. Absolute poverty is a condition of life so limited by illiteracy, malnutrition, disease, high infant mortality and low life expectancy as to deny its victims the very potential of the genes with which they are born. In effect, it is life at the margin of existence.*

At about that same time Vidia Naipaul was writing his book *India – A Wounded Civilisation* in which he described the reality of grinding poverty as he found it in a village in Bihar:

> *In the village I went to, one family out of four had land; only one child out of four went to school; only one man out of four had work. For a wage calculated to keep him only in food for the day he worked, the employed man, hardly exercising a skill, using the simplest tools and sometimes no tools at all, did the simplest agricultural labour. Child's work, and children being cheaper than men, were preferred; so that, suicidally, in the midst of an over-population which no one recognised... children were a source of wealth, available for hire after their eighth year for, if times were good, fifteen rupees, a dollar fifty a month. Generation followed generation quickly here, men as easily replaceable as their huts of grass and mud and matting... Cruelty no longer had a meaning: it was life itself.*

This was the Bihar from which my own forebears had fled into indenture a century before. Nothing much had changed. What

McNamara saw in Africa, what Naipaul saw in Bihar, was still in 1975 the reality of much of the Third World.

These were the people whom the old economic order was said to have 'served well'. The old economic order had not served them well. It had not served them at all. It was not designed to serve them. And the fault lay not in its workings, but in the system itself. The system promised order, stability and growth for the industrialised countries, for those who already wielded economic power; but it implied disorder, insecurity and deprivation for those who did not. Upholders of the system took for granted that some countries are rich and others are poor and assumed that by helping the rich to become richer they will help the poor to become less poor. They ignore the possibility that some countries may be rich because others are poor and that the price of sustained growth in the developed countries may be sustained poverty in the developing ones.

However, the developing world was convinced by hard experience that international poverty was not a mere aberration of international economic relations which minor adjustments could correct, but the unspoken premise of the old economic order. However different may have been the prospects from other casements, this was how the old economic order looked from Third World windows. This view was itself one of the realities of the contemporary scene. If it was at least acknowledged as such it would become easier to understand why the developing world called for a new international economic order.

Two Development Decades – 1960-70 and 1970-80 – had yielded bitter disappointment; five UNCTAD's (UN Conferences on Trade and development) – 1964, 1968, 1972, 1976, 1979 – had institutionalised frustration; and nearly 30 years of post-war internationalism had seen the political equality of states guaranteed by the Charter almost totally nullified by pervasive economic inequality between the world's peoples. What may be thought surprising is that the challenge to the system which preserved these economic inequalities should have come so late. In fact, it could not have come before. In the early post-war years when the old order itself was reinforced by the Bretton Woods and GATT regimes, the

Third World for the greater part was a voiceless captive of the colonial system, powerless to influence the decisions being taken about the kind of world they would inherit.

It was only in 1947 that India became independent marking the start of the process of decolonisation. It was only in 1956 that the dismantling of the French empire in Africa began, and a year later that the first of Britain's colonies in Africa – Ghana- attained freedom. Over more than a decade and a half since then the developing countries had been almost excessively patient in their trial of prescriptions for development that in retrospect served merely to mask the basic ailment, and, indeed, to worsen the prospects for a more equal world society.

Take aid, for example: the World Bank had projected that the United Nations target of 0.7 per cent of GNP of the industrialised countries in official development assistance (ODA) could be reached were they willing to commit to it a minor fraction of no more than 2 per cent of the incremental wealth – 2 per cent of further growth – they could expect to receive in the second half of the decade. Despite this, ODA relative to GNP kept steadily falling: from 0.39 per cent in 1969, to 0.35 per cent by 1978, to 0.25 per cent in 2003. It continues to decline.

In trade, the record was no better. Produce more, sell more, and earn more: that was the simple formula. With major effort, developing countries produced and sold more; but their net earnings, their terms of trade, steadily declined. The amount of cotton, or sisal, or tea or bauxite they had to produce and export in order to buy say, a tractor, or antibiotics or an irrigation pump, kept increasing – a grim reality of which President Julius Nyerere persistently reminded the world. Poor countries were 'developing' on a basis of diminishing returns. And there were other problems when they tried to diversify their economic base – efforts to industrialise, to process their raw materials and produce simple manufactured goods, led them to high tariff walls, differential freight rates and administrative obstructions to trade, all frustrating their entry into the markets of the rich countries. Despite all their effort, the poor grew relatively poorer.

It was while they were taking the measure of this predicament that the oil producers acted. Small wonder that their success in using their collective strength to win a better price for oil and to turn the terms of trade in their favour acted like a tonic throughout the developing world. For the first time in history a group of primary producers acting together had prevailed over the industrialised nations in a field in which they had traditionally dictated prices under the existing system of international trade. The success of the Organisation of the Petroleum Exporting Countries (OPEC) brought many problems for other developing countries, severe problems for some of them; but it pointed a way forward out of the development impasse, the predicament of poverty.

Despite the crippling impact of oil price increases, that glimpse of wider horizons encouraged developing countries to look anew at their collective strengths and to entertain the hope that the old rules which seemed to condemn them to perpetual penury were not immutable, and could be challenged. It encouraged them to conceive of a new world economic order that would make development probable. They had long recognised that the essential effort of development must be their own. What they sought was an environment – an international economic system propitious, not hostile, to their effort.

By 1975, also, there had emerged awareness by the developing world that self-reliance, both at the national level and at the collective level among developing countries must be an essential feature of development. Self-reliance thus conceived was not autarchy; nor was it isolation: it is not a vision of detached self-sufficiency. It was a conviction that development must come from within each society – conditioned by its history and its social, cultural, and economic strengths, founded on its resources, including its human resources, and committed to the national well-being. 'Self-reliant development' was based not on what the world could do for poor countries, but on what they could do for themselves. It sought to ensure the provision by national effort of the essentials of national subsistence – of food, of habitat, of health, of education. And, maximising complementarities, it pursued fulfilment by exploring new frontiers of co-operation between developing countries themselves. 'Self-reliance' had been the essence of the *Action Programme for Economic Co-operation among Non-Aligned*

Countries that emanated from the Meeting of Non-Aligned Foreign Ministers in Guyana that I had chaired in 1972.

It needs to be recalled that self-reliant development was rooted in a commitment to the creation of just societies; for there is no rational basis, there is no morality, in the demand for a more equal world community, unless it implies the facilitation of more equal national societies. It is a model of development, therefore, that condemns privilege within developing countries as rigorously as within the world community of states. The Third World, it was understood, had to articulate these perceptions of development and be zealous for their translation into reality. It must demonstrate both by precept and by example a commitment to national and collective self-reliance; to the dismantling of feudal structures; to the dispelling of pretences of privilege which are even more grotesque in the midst of poverty than they are in conditions of affluence. And it must prove by these advances that the creation of truly just societies, in which basic human values are respected and man's humanity is allowed to develop its potential, is the true fulfilment of the promise of development.

For some developing countries that process was already well advanced. For too many others, it had yet to begin. But, in both cases, it was wrong, and unhelpful, for developed societies to yield to the too easy temptation to escape responsibility for creating conditions of growth within the Third World by pointing to imperfections which at one time or another had been features of their own national development. The Third World did not divide up as easily as some asserted into 'the deserving' and 'the undeserving'. It did not do so any more fairly than did the Victorian poor, castigated by their overlords for their indolence and indiscipline. Some developed states have, indeed, shared with the Third World some of the humiliations of economic dominion, and had been neither the architects nor the primary beneficiaries, certainly not the primary operators, of the old economic order. These developed countries, many of the middle states – like Canada and Sweden – had, a special role to play in man's search for a better economic way for the entire world's people. They brought to the search for a deeper understanding of the aspirations of developing countries a lower level of vested interest in resisting fundamental change and, for both these reasons, a greater capability for advancing consensus on the mechanisms of change that would fulfil those aspirations. And some – like Canada and Sweden, but others too – did try.

In the evolution of a new international economic order a major responsibility rested upon industrialised Western countries. Jan Pronk, the dynamic Dutch Minister for Development Co-operation, rightly observed:

> *The new order required by the poor countries will be within easy reach when the United States and the Common Market agree it.*

Together, they dominated world trade, international finance, and industrial production. But obligation did not rest on them exclusively. All developed countries, of East no less than West, shared in the obligation to end international poverty. It was not enough for Eastern countries to say, as some did, that they had no responsibility for the colonial exploitation of the Third World. It was not merely a legal issue of restitution or reparation. It was a moral issue – then as it is now – that concerned the quality of life of a large section of humanity; it was fast becoming, for all nations, culpable and blameless alike, an issue of global survival.

If these, then, were the realities, what were the prospects for advance towards the promise of the new order? Developing countries had no option but to seek an end to poverty and deprivation. For them, the analogy of the poor within the nation-state is apposite, and the Marxist dialectic is pertinent. "The proletariat," said Marx, "have nothing to lose but their chains; they have a world to win." The Third World, or at least a major part of it, had nothing to lose but its poverty. It could have a world to win. It was important that the developed world understood this psychological reality of the human condition among the poor of the earth.

By 1975, it certainly seemed that the way forward must lie in a change of attitude on the part of the developed world. Developed states had to acknowledge frankly that the need is pressing for fundamental change in international economic relations; that the choice is not between an old order or a new one but between a new order or sustained disorder. They had to abandon petulance, and cease to deceive themselves that serious demands stemming from deep resentment of pervasive injustice was mere rhetoric. They needed to acknowledge that, together with the developing states, there is a mutuality of interest in change. Above all, in working for consensus on the nature of change, the developed world had to be prepared to give a good deal more by way of compromise than the developing can be expected to yield – remembering Aristotle's time-hallowed teaching that, as between unequals, equity demands unequal inputs.

The new order could not be installed in its entirety overnight. What was needed if the peoples of the world were to be made less unequal in their economic destinies was not so much the outvoting of a rich minority or their passive acquiescence in the promise of change, but the conversion of that minority to the need for change and to the urgency of its imperative. Such conversion cannot be expected from the processes of United Nations action only; other fora, other forms of diplomacy, other machinery for dialogue that possess a potential for promoting such conversion must render service to the cause of change.

The Commonwealth, as a representative cross-section of the world community, possessed a special capability for promoting conversion. Certainly it was uniquely equipped to advance consensus through understanding, dialogue and accommodation. In the discussions at the Kingston Heads of Government Meeting on the international economic situation; in the commitment of Commonwealth leaders, and particularly the leaders of the Commonwealth's developing countries, to the principle of *"immediate action towards the creation of a rational and equitable new international economic order";* in the instruction to the Commonwealth Group of Experts to put forward *"a comprehensive and inter-related programme of practical measures directed at closing the gap between the rich and poor countries"* – the Commonwealth was placing its special talents and facilities at the service of the international community in the cause of consensus-building.

Mahatma Gandhi saw his life's work in India as one man's response to the need *"to wipe every tear from every eye"*. He would have agreed that international poverty gives that same need a global dimension and that it demands responses from all men. Paul Eluard observed a long time ago with penetrating insight that: *"There is another world; but it is in this one."* The promise of a new international economic order was the promise of that other world here on earth. In our search for it, not only the poor, but all people and all states, and, certainly, the Commonwealth of rich and poor alike, had to be sedulously engaged; for all were now involved.

I recall these contentions – some of which are with us still – because they were at the heart of the global environment in which my life in the 1970s and beyond would be lived.

CHAPTER 16

Helping the World to Negotiate

By way of an interlude, before I turn to the Commonwealth's post-1975 efforts in helping the world to negotiate the challenges of a new economic order, let me recall an episode just before I went to Marlborough House that might have changed the world economic scene, and the nature of those challenges, had OPEC countries acted with the group solidarity they had demanded and received from other developing countries.

I have mentioned the "crippling effect' of OPEC's 1973 oil price increase on other developing countries, as well as the genuine solidarity with the oil producers which they demonstrated at the global level. But there was no avoiding the devastating consequences of the increases for poor countries. The total import bill of all non-OPEC developing countries, using 1973 volumes, rose by just over $10 billion in 1973 over 1972 and was projected to rise by between $20 and $30 billion in 1974 over 1972. This was only partially explained by direct increases in petroleum products. The indirect costs, through which developed countries recouped their oil bills, were just as real. Food and fertiliser imports by developing countries grew by more than $5 billion in 1973 and were estimated to grow by a further $5 billion for 1974.

Prices of oil and manufactures became entwined in an inflationary spiral with developing countries bearing the burden of price increases without the prospect of recoupment from increased export earnings. Non-OPEC developing countries were outside the ambit of the re-cycling process which the industrialised countries employed as the countervailing mechanism to rising oil prices; and, therefore, were its hapless victims.

To take an example I know best, but one by no means unique; in February 1974 the economy of Guyana was put on a basis of sustained emergency. Normal imports of commodities besides oil (many needed for development itself) were reduced by over 30 per cent. The country's Development Programme was cut with resulting retrenchment and unemployment. Foreign reserves were almost liquidated. By the end of February 1974 they had reached the dangerous level of two weeks of imports. A regime of austerity was instituted and all forms of foreign travel forbidden save for those engaged on efforts of economic restoration, including regional economic integration. And this was true of Jamaica also, with whom we worked closely in the Non-Aligned Movement on this matter, and of innumerable non-OPEC developing countries.

Guyanese were told without ambiguity or qualification that the OPEC policy of increasing the price of oil to the developed world was right; that the effects upon our economy were unintended consequences; and that within the family of Third World countries ways would be found to overcome these crushing difficulties. But ways were not being found. Some ameliorating steps were taken, bilaterally and regionally; but nothing of a systemic nature.

In, 1974, working closely with Jamaica, I raised the matter as Foreign Minister of Guyana *"of emergency relief to non-aligned countries facing serious and unintended difficulties as a result of recent increases in the price of petroleum products."* The Forum was the Bureau of Non-Aligned Countries meeting in Algiers on March 21, some three weeks before the Special Session of the General Assembly on Raw Materials and Development called for by President Houari Boumedienne of Algeria as Head of the Non-Aligned Movement. Michael Manley, as Prime Minister of Jamaica, had addressed a similar proposal to key Non-Aligned leaders. Its essence was that since 83 per cent of OPEC exports go to the developed world it would take very little by way of a price diversion to alleviate the distress of developing countries. The supplement we calculated would be significantly less than $1 on the price per barrel of oil; the amount would be paid by all consumers with nothing borne by oil producers. It would yield enough to offset by way of a rebate the total increment in price to developing countries. Most significantly, it would be in effect a net transfer of resources from developed to developing countries.

The proposal was well received by the Bureau which…

> *recognised the paramount need for co-operation among non-aligned countries in evolving, urgently and in a spirit of solidarity, all possible means to assist non-aligned and other developing countries to cope with the immediate problems resulting from the legitimate and perfectly justified action of OPEC countries.*

The Bureau appointed a Working Group of Foreign Ministers from Guyana, Liberia, Nepal and Sri Lanka – 'the Group of Four' – and mandated it "to hold urgent consultations with non-aligned OPEC member states". The idea was to hold the first consultations before the Special Session of the General Assembly on 9 April; but this did not happen. Eventually, we were invited by OPEC to come to Quito, Ecuador, *"to engage in discussions with OPEC designed to explore the possibilities of co-operation between the oil producing countries and the countries of the developing world".*

I was the spokesman for the Group when we met with OPEC Ministers in Quito on 16 June 1974. We had prepared a Paper which we left with OPEC setting out our proposals which, subsequent to Algiers, had been endorsed by the Council of Ministers of the OAU on 4 April 1974 in Kampala. The crux of the presentation was as set out earlier at Algiers. At Quito, addressing the OPEC Ministerial Council, I recalled this:

> *At the Algiers meeting of the Bureau of the Non-Aligned Movement that led to our current presence in Quito, there was raised for consideration the idea of a rebate scheme by which a substantial part of the increased price of petroleum products*

sold to developing countries would, in effect, be met by the price paid by developed countries.

In other words, Mr President, without impairing OPEC receipts, those members of the international community that could most afford it, would in effect subsidise oil imports that were essential to the growth of the developing world. The concept is to use the price mechanism of OPEC to achieve a net transfer of resources from the developed to the developing nations without diminishing the resources of OPEC countries.

It was an idea which was rooted in the common objectives to which we are all committed as developing countries, whether we are oil producers or oil consumers, and it was based on the belief that it was not the intention of OPEC to further aggravate the difficulties imposed on other developing countries by an inequitable international economic system and the exploitative practices of the developed countries... It was based on our confidence that OPEC would want to find ways, not merely of not hurting other developing countries, but of positively assisting them out of the quagmire of underdevelopment.

In summary, therefore, what does the situation require? It requires, first of all, it seems to us, an acknowledgement that the balance of economic justice in the world is not addressed in ways that are either satisfactory or durable if their effect over any appreciable period is to impose even greater impediments to the achievement of economic justice by others. It requires – without for one moment presuming to dictate – that the legitimate and courageous policies of OPEC be so implemented as to take account of their effect upon other developing countries and either adapted by procedures which avoid the creation of serious difficulties for them or complemented by mechanisms which will, at least, alleviate those difficulties. Some such procedures and mechanisms we have put before you.

I ended with the assurance that: *I and my colleagues remain willing to pursue these consultations for co-operation in whatever way and through whatever machinery you may consider most appropriate.*

The OPEC Ministers gave us a patient hearing, including Saudi Arabian Minister Ahmed Zaki Yamani who exercised a great deal of influence. They indicated that the OPEC Secretariat in Vienna would work urgently on our paper and its presentation, and promised that they would get back to us. There was no dialogue at Quito. The message I intuited was: *Don't call us, we'll call you.* They never did. The moment of historic change was lost.

But, of course, the devastating effects of the oil price increase on developing countries only grew worse and the scheme of relief I had initiated at Algiers was not allowed to die with OPEC's fabian tactics at Quito. Jamaica and Guyana were prominent in these efforts; but, throughout the 1970s it proved impossible to get the OPEC countries to discuss energy as a separate subject even at conferences of developing countries only, much less to adopt specific proposals designed to alleviate the impact of increased oil prices. Of major oil-producing countries, only Venezuela and Norway seemed to care.

Eventually, at the Non-Aligned Summit Meeting in Colombo in 1979, Guyana raised again the question of assistance to the non-oil-producing countries and it was agreed to convene a Conference in Georgetown on the more generalised subject of "mutual assistance and solidarity among developing countries in the context of the principle of collective self-reliance". By then, I was in London with the Commonwealth; but Guyana put forward specific proposals designed to alleviate the impact of oil price increases on the non-oil-producing countries. In a fully worked out proposal presented to the Conference, Guyana showed that its Rebate Scheme on Oil Purchases (based essentially on the one I had put to OPEC five years earlier) had the potential to provide an almost complete solution to the problem. With the benefit of actual consumption figures since 1974, the Guyana paper was able to demonstrate that a levy of 32 cents per barrel of crude exported by OPEC and other oil exporting countries would be sufficient to offset the total price increase (including the levy) devolving on the oil importing developing countries. Despite exhaustive discussions, the OPEC countries refused to accept any arrangement which, in their opinion, "could affect their pricing policy". As Professor Denis Benn concluded in his erudite book *Multilateral Diplomacy and the Economics of Change,* which contains an authentic account of these efforts:

> *The failure of the developing countries to adopt specific measures to directly offset the adverse impact of increased oil prices on the non-oil-producing countries constituted a fatal flaw in the unity and solidarity of the developing countries in their negotiations with the developed countries since it tended to weaken the resolve of the non-oil-producing developing countries in carrying out the struggle for the establishment of the New International Economic Order. The failure also proved to be a hindrance to the adoption by the developing countries of a longer term strategy of making ECDC ('economic co-operation between developing countries') an effective instrument for changing the structure of international economic relations.*

Those are polite words for what was surely the betrayal of the cause of development by the OPEC countries – despite the much vaunted talk of solidarity. In the name of justice for themselves, they were content to condemn already poor countries to prolonged destitution and to set back the cause of a more fair and equitable world order. I am proud of the stand Guyana took in this historic episode and the opportunity I had of contributing to it. A new international economic order would have to be pursued without the aid of OPEC. For me, the way immediately ahead would lie in whatever I could do through the Commonwealth.

* * *

In fact, the path had been charted. Discussion of economic issues had long been a feature of meetings of Commonwealth Heads of Government and of Commonwealth Finance Ministers. In the 1950s and 1960s, however, the concerns of these meetings were with such 'Commonwealth' issues as sterling area management and the potential impact on Commonwealth trade of Britain's entry into the European Community. The first major discussion on what came to be termed 'North-South issues' was the one I mentioned earlier – at the HGM in Kingston, Jamaica, in 1975.

There, host Prime Minister and Chairman, Michael Manley, recalling the 1971 Singapore Declaration of Principles in which Commonwealth leaders recorded their belief *"that the wide disparities in wealth now existing between different sections of mankind are too great to be tolerated"*, called on the Commonwealth to help to find *"the techniques of political management of world trade and world finance that will lead to a progressive removal of those wide disparities"*. Arguing that the world faced a choice between dialogue and confrontation on the demand for a new economic order, he urged the meeting to explore ways by which *"the scales of probability may be tipped in favour of dialogue."* By then, Manley was already a prominent, and persuasive, advocate of the need for global economic change in the interest of development, as his book *JAMAICA: Struggle in the Periphery* confirms.

At the Kingston Meeting, as I indicated earlier, Britain's Prime Minister, Harold Wilson, made a strong case for measures to promote stability in commodity markets, and to secure remunerative prices for producers, as a way of improving the prospects for developing countries. Forbes Burnham of Guyana, his counter-part presenter, wanted movement over a much wider front than commodities. But it was clear that they had a shared objective: a more secure basis for developing-country efforts to reduce poverty and speed development.

Following their opening presentations on the agenda item *'World Trade, Finance and Development',* Commonwealth leaders engaged in a frank and enlightened debate highlighted by contributions from Pierre Trudeau, Julius Nyerere, Lee Kuan Yew and Michael Manley. I remember wishing at the time that this had been taking place at the UN. But, of course, it could not; it was the intimacy of the (now internationalised) 'club' that allowed it. Trudeau supported the proposal advanced by Burnham that the Commonwealth should remain engaged on these issues through a Group of Commonwealth Experts which would *"help Commonwealth Governments prepare themselves for the special General Assembly Session in September"*. Trudeau urged that *"results were needed quickly, and the Group of Experts should be asked for at least an interim report before September"*.

As it turned out, this was a principal feature of the Kingston Communiqué. Centrally, Commonwealth leaders:

> *recognised the need to take immediate steps towards the creation of a rational and equitable new international economic order. They reaffirmed the statement included in the Commonwealth Declaration adopted in Singapore in 1971 that 'the wide disparities of wealth now existing between different sections of mankind are too great to be tolerated... our aim is their progressive removal', and acknowledged the complexity, range and inter-related nature of the issues involved.*

It was in this context that they agreed that the Group of Experts should be invited:

> *to draw up for consideration by Commonwealth Governments, in the context of the current international dialogue, a comprehensive and interrelated programme of practical measures directed at closing the gap between the rich and the poor countries. These measures would be designed to promote development and to increase the transfer of real resources to developing countries inter alia in the areas of production, distribution and exchange of primary and secondary products as well as services. (They) recognised the importance in this context of co-operating to achieve an expanding world economy and world trade.*

The Group of Experts would be appointed by the Secretary-General after consultation with Governments; but they specifically agreed that *"it would be desirable that the Secretary-General-elect should be associated at as early a stage as possible with the work of the Group".* They invited Alister McIntyre, then Secretary-General of the Caribbean Community, later to be an Assistant Secretary-General at the United Nations (UNCTAD) to be the Group's Chairman. Arnold Smith associated me from the outset with the constitution and preparations for the work of the Group. Trudeau had offered Ottawa for the Group's first substantive meeting – a mark of his seriousness about the Kingston decision – and my address to the Group at its Opening Session was my first function as Secretary-General, en route to Marlborough House.

Kissinger's statement (to which I have already alluded) that the Bretton Woods system had "*generally served the world well*" had been made in Kansas City, Missouri, exactly one week after the Commonwealth had reached, in effect, the opposite conclusion. He did so in the course of a comprehensive review of the international economic system, and his conclusion was that "*while many of the fundamental premises* (of the system) are *challenged by nations of the developing world... these contemporary challenges to the world economic structure must be overcome".*

In my address to the Expert Group I drew attention to other voices from the developed world, like the Prime Minister of the Netherlands, Joop den Uyl, who, after rejecting Kissinger's basic contention that the present economic system has served the world well, had said:

> *My second doubt concerns the central elements of the present economic system. As against the principle of open and expanding trade, we see a tariff system with low tariffs for raw materials and high tariffs for industrial products blocking the industrialisation of the poor countries.*
>
> *As against the free flow of capital, we know that capital creation and credit systems are dominated by the United States and Europe, together with a number of oil producing countries.*
>
> *As against the free movement of technology, there is a system regulating the ownership of patents which, in fact, restricts the use of patents to rich countries. Thus it turns out that the*

international economic system is not as free as has been claimed and that our choice is not one between a free system based on free enterprise and a fully centrally planned economy.

The real choice we have to make is between sticking to our present system which is largely guided and manipulated for the benefit of the rich countries, and opting for a system directed towards finding solutions to problems of an equitable division of income and property, of scarcity of natural resource and of despoliation of the environment. For that reason, the demand for a new international economic order is both relevant and timely.

And I recalled the sage words of Pierre Trudeau speaking shortly before the Kingston Meeting in the ancient Hall of the Mansion House, after receiving the Freedom of the City of London:

The human community is a complex organism linked again and again within itself and as well as with the biosphere on which it is totally dependent for life. This inter-dependency demands of us two functions: First, the maintenance of equilibrium among all our activities, whatever their nature; second, an equitable distribution, worldwide, of resources and opportunities.

The proper discharge of these functions calls for more than tinkering with the present system. The processes required must be more than global in scope and universal in application. In their magnitude, if not in their concept, they must be new. Of their need, none can doubt.

We know in our hearts what has to be done even if we have not yet found in our minds the way it can be done.

Let us begin the search, and let us do so with boldness and with excitement, not with hesitancy and uncertainty.

I reminded the Group that at Kingston, 34 Commonwealth Governments had agreed to begin that search; their leaders having accepted in their hearts what had to be done. *"They have entrusted to you"*, I said, *"the finding of the ways in which it can be done"*. And I reminded them, too, of Michael Manley's words in opening the Kingston Meeting:

> *The choice ... is inevitably between dialogue and confrontation. The challenge ... is to explore ways by which the scales of probability may be tipped in favour of dialogue. It is precisely here that ... the Commonwealth can make a meaningful contribution to the process by which it justifies its continuing existence while helping mankind to search, perhaps grope, for solutions. I believe that the Commonwealth may be uniquely blessed in this effort.*

At its first meeting, in Ottawa in July 1975, the Group prepared an Interim Report, as requested by Heads of Government, in time for the annual meeting of Commonwealth Finance Ministers in August so that governments could take account of the Group's views in preparing for the Seventh Special Session of the UN General Assembly in September. A special contribution of the report was that it represented one of the early attempts to formulate a programme of reforms for the international economic system. Although the developing countries had pressed for a new economic order they had given little attention to refining a programme of measures that could constitute such an order.

Finance Ministers gave their general endorsement to the report. They decided to make it available to the international community in the context of the Seventh Special Session, where it played a part in the emergence of a wider degree of consensus on a new international economic order than had been evident at the Sixth Special Session in 1974.

After their second meeting, in London in March 1976, the experts issued a *Further Report*. This addressed the main issues to be discussed at UNCTAD IV (the Fourth Session of the UN Conference on Trade and Development) in Nairobi in May 1976. Both reports were presented by me, as Commonwealth Secretary-General, to the plenary session of the Conference. They proved of acknowledged value to

Commonwealth delegations who held seven consultations as the Conference progressed. Given wide distribution at UNCTAD IV (and elsewhere), the reports were also seen as important inputs to the wider debate. Commonwealth Finance Ministers considered the *Further Report* at their 1976 meeting and agreed that the Group's proposals should be given due consideration in framing national and international policies on critical issues.

The Group's Final Report, prepared at a meeting in Ibadan, Nigeria, in March 1977, incorporated material from its earlier reports and extended the coverage to several additional issues. It made a large number of recommendations in several areas: commodities, food, industrialisation, finance, invisible earnings, co-operation among developing countries, and international institutions.

The recommendations were set in the context of the Group's unanimous view that *"a new and more equitable economic order must depend on progressive and radical change in the distribution of economic activity throughout the world"*, provide for *"genuine equality of opportunity and rewards between states'*, and *'bring new relationships of interdependence in place of the older patterns of dominance and dependence"*.

The report, *Towards a New International Economic Order,* emphasised that such disparities as were represented by a per capita income of $200 and one of, say, $5,000 were socially disruptive and no longer accepted within countries; they should no longer be tolerated between countries.

The overriding aim of development, the report observed, should be to ensure that all people had an acceptable level of food, clothing, housing, health care and education. Development to achieve the satisfaction of these basic needs for all mankind would require fundamental structural changes in the economies of developing countries. But these countries could not achieve the necessary transformation by their own individual or collective efforts; it would require *"a substantially different pattern of international economic relations"*.

This provided the rationale for a new international economic order. It was wishful thinking, the group said, *"to suppose that solutions to global poverty could be found in case by case adjustments of an essentially marginal character"*. The world community had therefore to demonstrate *"a new resolve for urgent and imaginative action"*.

The Group regretted that this sense of urgency had not been fully reflected in the discussions held since the Seventh Special Session in September 1975. Meanwhile the external environment was making *"questions of survival take precedence over the pursuit of development"* in developing countries. The report accordingly urged a *"comprehensive and early consensus on major issues"*, pointing out that the effective implementation of a new order would call for *"firm commitments from all parties to match rhetoric with action"*.

In reviewing developments in the global discussions on an NIEO, the Group noted that while some progress had been made, there remained a wide area in which conclusions or agreements were not in sight. Further, in many cases, the agreements reached so far had been concerned with establishing broad principles; ways to convert them into programmes of action had not been decided and, in some cases, not even considered. In this regard, the Group made a particularly valuable contribution by examining the technical validity and practicability of these proposals, and by suggesting the possible meeting ground between the developed and developing countries.

The Commonwealth's initiative in establishing the Group was, in this respect, particularly well timed: its combined expertise and North-South synthesis placed the Group in an important position to influence the course of international economic discussions. The report indicated the main areas in which decisions or action remained to be taken, and voiced the hope that the time lost in taking the basic initial steps towards the reconstruction of the world economy would be speedily made up.

A particular value of the Group's reports was the contribution they made to an understanding of the issues, especially within national administrations. For many years after its publication, the *Final Report* was treated by many Commonwealth officials as a handbook on North-South issues. A number of its recommendations remained active proposals for change long after they were made. Over the years, some significant decisions have been taken in international development co-operation, and it would be difficult to trace all the factors influencing such decisions. It is fair to say, however, that Commonwealth contributions by the McIntyre and other Groups would have played their part in the evolution of thinking and policies which led to them.

For example, the IMF Compensatory Financing Facility was liberalised in December 1975. In July of that year the Group's Interim Report had given much attention to this subject and pointed to some of the directions in which the reform of the Facility was actually undertaken. Also in areas such as indebtedness and the role of services in development, later events confirmed the perceptiveness of the McIntyre Group's analyses and recommendations. The Group's comments and recommendations on specific aspects of international economic relations were reflected in the international discussion that followed on the substantive issues in North-South negotiations – prominent among them commodity issues.

* * *

I have mentioned in some detail the process by which the McIntyre Group of Experts came into being and the nature of its Report, *Towards a New International Economic Order,* for two principal reasons. The first is the frank acceptance by the Commonwealth of its functional role in contributing to the solution of the world's economic problems. 'World Trade, Finance and Development' were global issues. The Commonwealth as a sample of global variety functioning within the intimacy the association provided had a special capacity to build consensus. It could not negotiate for the world; but it could help the world to negotiate. At Kingston, the Commonwealth pledged that help, and in the process proclaimed its global credentials.

The second reason is that it represented the beginning of a process of helping that was to become characteristic of the Commonwealth's outreach and of the intellectual credentials of the Commonwealth Secretariat. In my 15 years at Marlborough House, the McIntyre Group was the first of 13 Expert Groups established by the Commonwealth in its fashion. Their Reports bore the hallmark of the Commonwealth's enlightenment, and were all of global significance. Their influence permeated Commonwealth thought and, sometimes, action; and they all reached beyond the Commonwealth to influence in small ways or large the issues with which they dealt. The work of these Groups which brought together some of the best minds in the Commonwealth both carried a Commonwealth stamp, and stamped the Commonwealth as a progressive association, and its Secretariat as a centre of enlightened thought and action. The McIntyre Group signalled the start of what was to become a new dimension of the Commonwealth at work.

In Appendix 4, I have listed the titles of the Reports of these Groups (and their Chairmen) between 1975 and 1990. Their members had all been drawn from a representative range of Commonwealth countries selected to ensure that they themselves brought a diversity of views to bear on the issues. All members were invited to serve as individuals eminent in their own right; not as spokespersons for their countries, governments or institutions. That they would be sensitive to the national interests of their countries was strength; yet they were not under the constraint of briefs prepared in their capitals or of the compulsions of official negotiating positions. While they worked and reported within an inter-governmental framework provided by their official mandates, their Reports were unique formulations of consensual professional judgment on broad international issues and earned respect world-wide.

The calibre of the individuals serving on the Groups was of paramount importance. They were professionals from countries large and small, developed and developing, North and South who had distinguished themselves in a wide range of occupations and positions in politics and government, public administration and diplomacy, banking and finance, business and industry, international organisations, voluntary bodies and trade unions. For all of them the experience of working together in the respective Expert Groups forged links of value beyond their immediate tasks – and, of course, beyond the

Commonwealth. They became a network of Commonwealth thinkers who through their several roles beyond the Commonwealth became a global asset.

The range of subjects the Groups had been commissioned to study covered most of the major issues which had thrust themselves on the economic agenda of the world community over the time of my Commonwealth watch. They included matters of long-standing concern like commodity prices, protectionism, reform of multilateral financial institutions, and developing-country debt, as well as issues which had come to the forefront of world concern more recently, such as the impact of 'frontier' technologies, structural adjustment as it impinges on women, and the global environmental threat of climate change and global warming. Not every subject studied fell under the rubric of North/South issues or ranged developed and developing countries on opposite sides. But some of them, like high unemployment among the young or the vulnerabilities associated with countries being small, tended to be most acute in developing countries, and their amelioration clearly involved significant North/South co-operation.

Even on those issues which bore the 'North/South' label, the arguments for change within the Commonwealth had not come entirely from developing member countries. There had been a general appreciation that most of the issues did not present zero sum situations where the benefits of change would flow in one direction only. Protectionism, for instance, was seen to hold out threats to the international trading system and the global economy and therefore to all countries that live by trade, though poor countries are naturally more vulnerable to the incidence and effects of trade barriers. I have recalled Prime Minister Pierre Trudeau's enlightened contributions at the Kingston HGM on the subject of a new international economic order; and Prime Minister Harold Wilson's forthright proposals for a new international regime on commodities. The Prime Minister of Australia, Malcolm Fraser, with his 'hands on' experience as a sheep farmer, brought special understanding to the issue of the Common Fund, and on the issue of the Bretton Woods system, the case for reform was argued most trenchantly by the Prime Minister of New Zealand, Robert Muldoon, with his experience of managing the economy of a 'small country'.

While each Group's work was a discrete exercise, there were many links and continuities. Several of the issues which the first Group of Experts covered in their report on the New International Economic Order came to be explored in greater detail by later groups. The Helleiner Group (the Groups came quickly to be known by the names of those who chaired them) focused on the Bretton Woods institutions, for instance, and the Campbell Group dealt specifically with commodities. There were many strands linking the Arndt Group's report on the world economic crisis in 1980 and the work of the Cairncross Group on protectionism in 1982. Altogether these Commonwealth Expert Groups were rendering a notable service not only to the Commonwealth, but also to the world beyond it.

Over this same period, I had the opportunity of participating personally in the work of several Independent Commissions dealing with such matters as development, disarmament, environment and humanitarian issues – all of importance to the Commonwealth. They included: the Independent Commission on International Development Issues (the Brandt Commission) 1980 and 1983; the Independent Commission on Disarmament and Security Issues (the Palme Commission) 1982; the World Commission on Environment and Development (the Brundtland Commission) 1987; the Independent Commission on International Humanitarian Issues 1987, and the South Commission 1990. The years refer to the year of publication of the reports, and I will return to them later. The point here is that this international service afforded me a unique opportunity to identify the Commonwealth directly with the highest independent global thinking. On more than one occasion, the International Commissions were able to draw on work in progress within the Commonwealth's ambit. In the same way, I was able to keep the Commonwealth *au fait* with the perceptions of these high level global think-tanks. The Commonwealth framework in which our groups were created and functioned did not in any way circumscribe their broad international scope. They addressed matters of worldwide relevance and their mandates were essentially to propose measures which the Commonwealth could offer as a basis on which global consensus could be built.

In many instances, the recommendations made by Commonwealth Expert Groups have reinforced, or were reinforced by, other impulses within the international arena, and have contributed towards specific action. A notable instance was the proposal for a Common Fund to promote stability in commodity prices. The study, made by the Group of Experts chaired by Lord Campbell in 1977 led to a Commonwealth Ministerial Meeting which looked at ways of accelerating progress in the global Common Fund negotiations. That it took several years for the way to be fully cleared for the Fund's establishment in 1989 does not detract from the catalytic role the Commonwealth played in these early stages.

The Clarke report's proposals on improving the North-South negotiating process were acknowledged as timely and valuable by many participants in that process, and continue to remain relevant. It generated significant interest in other international organisations, including the UN and the OECD, and has been of great influence on subsequent reports on the global negotiating process. The Lever report on debt was among the first to highlight the particular problems of low-income debtors; a theme taken up by successive meetings of Finance Ministers and providing a background to the Toronto/Berlin initiatives on official debt a few years later. The Holdgate report on climate change and sea level rise became an important input to the work of the Intergovernmental Panel on Climate Change which was at the time preparing the ground for the Global Climate Convention.

Another example is the sequel to the Helleiner Group's report in the form of sustained Commonwealth efforts to initiate a dialogue on the Bretton Woods system and its institutions. These were undertaken at the direction of Heads of Government and Ministers of Finance, by specially constituted Consultative Groups representing Commonwealth governments, with the support of the Secretariat. They involved the Commonwealth in a series of interactions with the key policy-setting committees of the IMF and the World Bank. This is one of the several areas where the Commonwealth Expert Groups' work in clarifying issues has helped to heighten the quality of international discussion, and nudge the process along.

Not least among the achievements of the reports is that they have had important bearings on how the Commonwealth Secretariat itself would operate. The Jha report on industrial co-operation led to the establishment of the Industrial Development Unit in the Secretariat. The report on the vulnerability of small states provided powerful intellectual rationale for the operational emphasis of the Secretariat on small states' problems. It has helped to confirm a leadership role for the Secretariat in the international articulation of small states' issues. The study on structural adjustment and women emerged from, and reinforced, the work of the Secretariat on gender issues as well as on structural adjustment. The Menon report on technological change led to the establishment, after the Kuala Lumpur HGM, of the Commonwealth Consultative Group for Technology Management, a network designed to provide advisory services to governments in the field of technology forecasting and assessment and R&D management. The Lever report on debt provided a powerful stimulus to the Secretariat's technical assistance work on debt management and its bulletin on capital markets.

As Secretary-General, I had the opportunity to be associated closely with the work of all these groups. It was my responsibility to set them up; to convey to them at the outset of their work the background to their mandate and the expectations of Commonwealth governments; and then to bring the reports to wider public attention within the Commonwealth and outside it.

In all of this I had the good fortune to have in the Secretariat's Economic Affairs Division a pool of professional officers, drawn from all parts of the Commonwealth, of extraordinarily high technical calibre and an equally high level of commitment to the Commonwealth's goal of responding effectively to the challenge *'to narrow the disparities in wealth between different sections of mankind which are too wide to be tolerated'*. To the Division's four Directors in the years of the Expert Groups' work – Frank Rampersad, Bimal

Jalan, Bishnodat Persaud and Vincent Cable – the Commonwealth owes an immense debt. They set the bar high for professional excellence. I know it was a specially rewarding experience for them – as it was for me – to witness over those years the steady growth in international regard for the work of the Commonwealth and its Secretariat – to which they and their colleagues and the Expert Groups which they supported made such a substantial contribution. For many years the Economic Division benefited from the supervision of Sir Peter Marshall whose experience and wisdom I greatly valued.

Few organisations have the capacity and attributes to discharge the function the Commonwealth assumed in seeking to bridge differences between the North and the South on economic issues and be a catalyst for global agreement. Outside the world forum of the United Nations, it is the Commonwealth that reflects most of the world's diversities and disparities. It has a strong interest in international issues, especially those concerned with poverty and development. At the same time, it functions with a degree of informality and understanding, based on common traditions and language. It is thus uniquely equipped to try to build bridges between the North and the South. These factors themselves justify the Commonwealth's commitment to this function, despite what appeared to be less than encouraging progress in some areas. Indeed, that insufficiency of progress enlarged the Commonwealth's obligation to try harder.

Not all the Expert Groups looked to long term negotiations. On 9 November 1986, I inaugurated a meeting in Marlborough House, of what we called then the Expert Group on Distance Education. It was a Group I had brought together on the strength of an earlier report the year before on the Management of Technological Change in the Commonwealth. That Report had made the point that 'the combination of satellite technology and English as the common language could be used to achieve more cost effective education systems', with particular value for small Commonwealth countries. Hence, the Expert Group on Distance Education. And it was, indeed, a group of most eminent experts.

Lord Briggs of Lewes, then Provost of Worcester College, Oxford, had accepted my invitation to be Chairman of the Group and was there that morning. The names of his colleagues on the Group conjure up memories of Commonwealth co-operation in education – one of the oldest of Commonwealth activities: Akin Adesola of the University of Lagos, Anastasios Christodoulou of the ACU, Marjorie Crocombe of the University of the South Pacific, Rex Nettleford of the University of the West Indies, Ram Reddy of India's Open University, Ramon Rickett of the Middlesex Polytechnic, Ronald Watts, former Principal and Vice-Chancellor of Queen's University in Canada, Sir Bruce Williams, former Vice-Chancellor of the University of Sydney. The Commonwealth could not have been better served, and Asa Briggs was a hands-on leader.

As they embarked on their journey towards a Commonwealth of Learning – words that were to become the title of their Report – I said to them:

> *And so, if I have a single piece of advice to offer you, it is to encourage you to be bold and imaginative in your thinking, in your conception, in your design. Devise a strategy which is forward looking and points the way for decades, rather than years. Not everything can be done at once; but help to give us a vision of where we are going.*

Asa Briggs' Expert Group did just that. It gave us a vision of where we should be going. Their Report *'Towards a Commonwealth of Learning'* advanced 'a proposal to create the University of the Commonwealth for co-operation in distance education'. At the heart of the proposal, in language they used in the Report was this:

> *Our long term aim is that any learner, anywhere in the Commonwealth, shall be able to study any distance teaching programme available from any bona fide College or University in the Commonwealth. The new institution would seek to achieve this by working in a co-operative partnership with*

existing Colleges, Universities and other institutions of post secondary education.

It was a noble vision, and it has endured.

The following year, in Vancouver, Commonwealth Heads of Government, elevating the subject to one of primacy in the area of Commonwealth functional co-operation; 'welcomed' the Briggs Report; commended it 'as an imaginative and constructive approach to meeting urgent educational needs in member countries'; and recognised that 'its proposals could usher in a new era of Commonwealth co-operation and significantly widen learning opportunities for young people and adults throughout the Commonwealth'. The next year, Asa Briggs became the first Chairman of the Board of Governors of the Commonwealth of Learning. With great vision, Canada offered to host it in Vancouver. It was later to develop a Centre for Asia in New Delhi.

Today, the Commonwealth of Learning has passed its 25th anniversary and is a jewel in the crown of the Commonwealth. Commonwealth Heads had believed in the 1980s that media and technology, particularly Open and Distance Leaning, had an important role to play in advancing education, training and learning generally. Everything that has happened since indicates that they were right. Today, millions of people around the Commonwealth are involved in all kinds of technology-mediated learning. And it all began with a Commonwealth Expert Group.

As I left the Secretariat in 1990, I felt that the Commonwealth had a unique opportunity to build on its efforts to nudge the world towards better management of its economic affairs in the interests of all its people. In the absence of consensus, no change is durable. The reality of growing economic interdependence was making itself increasingly felt. The Commonwealth had the experience and capability to remain in the forefront of change. It had an inescapable obligation to help to chart the path towards the larger partnership the world so desperately needed.

CHAPTER 17

The Brandt Commission

When, in March 2003, the new President of the World Bank, Jim Wolfensohn, paid tribute to his predecessor, he said of Robert McNamara:

> *Like all great men, Bob is effective because he dares to dream – and to pursue his dreams with action: on the nexus of agriculture stagnation, population growth and environmental degradation. On the conflict between military expenditures and development. On river blindness. Above all, on poverty. His dream remains our dream.*

As the decade of the 1970s had dragged on in fruitless debate between North and South, between rich and poor countries, with rising frustration and tension, McNamara acted. In the late seventies in a world where debate was largely stylised – confined to governments and international institutions, between groups of nations shackled to inflexible positions, ideological prisoners on all sides – he sought to break the mould. In January 1977, in Boston, he launched the idea of establishing an independent Commission on international development whose members would not be official representatives of governments, but would work independently to formulate basic proposals on which global agreement was both essential and possible. The Commission was to make recommendations on ways of breaking through the existing international political impasse in North-South negotiations for global development. McNamara's emphasis was on experienced, respected politicians and economists. He wanted Willy Brandt, the former Chancellor of Germany, Mayor of Berlin through its darkest post-war period, and Nobel Peace Prize laureate, to chair the Commission – to do for development what he had done for peace with 'detente'.

McNamara returned to his proposal in his address to that year's annual meeting of the World Bank and the IMF, and on 28 September Willy Brandt announced at a press conference in New York that he was prepared to form and chair an Independent Commission on International Development Issues. Brandt made it clear that he wanted the Commission to represent as many views and interests, and to have as much political and regional balance as possible. He was insistent that a majority of Commission members should be from developing countries. He made a point of emphasising that the Commission would not interfere in any way with governmental negotiations or with the on-going work of international organisations. Rather, the Commission would have a supplementary function to present recommendations which could improve the climate for further negotiations on North-South relations.

Between McNamara's proposal in Boston and Brandt's Press Conference there had been much consultation. I had long admired Willy Brandt as a mature internationalist and a man of peace; but I did not know him. It seemed, however, that he had made enquiries about me; and he did not take long to persuade me – well before his announcement of his own acceptance – not only to join the Commission but also to help him in assembling it. Working with him and his able Special Assistants, Fritz Fischer and Michael Hoffman, I valued the opportunity of helping him to establish the Commission – conscious of the importance of its credibility in the eyes of developing countries. I helped particularly, in offering names from the South and being an interlocutor with possible members. But, as important as anything else, I had a hand in designing the Commission's mandate. In the process, I grew close to Willy Brandt, becoming something like his 'partner' from the South. For his part,

I believe he came to rely on my judgement as such. Because of the consultations in this period before Brandt's announcement, it was possible to formally establish the Commission as early as December 1977.

The full list of members of the Commission is set out in Appendix 5. It was a truly eminent group – experienced and respected political figures of North and South; politicians and those whose lives were touched by politics; liberal-minded internationalists like Olof Palme of Sweden and Eduardo Frei of Chile; hard-headed businessmen, like Peter Peterson, the Chairman of Lehmann Bros; hard-liners of the South like Lyachi Yaker of Algeria and Amir Jamal of Tanzania; men of the North who carried weight in their respective circles, like Edward (Ted) Heath, the former Prime Minister of Britain, and Edgar Pisani, former member of the French government and a member of the European Parliament; practitioners in the field of development like L.K. Jha, former Governor of the Reserve Bank of India, and the Commission's Treasurer Jan Pronk, then Minister for Development Co-operation in the Netherlands. Everyone brought something to the Commission – all nineteen members, whose names and backgrounds are set out in the Appendix 5.

Brandt Commission members with Dutch Prime Minister Joop den Uyl

* * *

I am not, of course, a dispassionate commentator on the Brandt Report. I tried so hard as a member of the Commission to ensure that our Report would respond to the essential challenge of our time that I am likely to claim success too readily. Others must make that judgement. Once, during the work of the Commission, I had cause to recall that wonderful verse by James Leigh-Hunt about Abou Ben Adhem: Abou, whose name had not made the list the angel in his dream was compiling – the list of those *who loved the Lord* – begged to be inscribed at least among those who *loved his fellow men*. In the result, in the next night's dream, Ben Adhem's name led the list of those *whom love of God had blessed*. Some of our work was not unlike that. We could not all worship at prevailing shrines; but to be counted on the side of common humanity was both duty and reward. If that insistence helped the Report to give a worthy lead to others, that is recompense enough. Someday, someone might be disposed to say of us, as of Ben Adhem – *may their tribe increase*! At the time, however, we were not without our critics, although the remarkable thing is not how few people read the Report but how many; not how much criticism there was of it, but how little and from whom.

The Commission was about development issues – not the state of the world economy. At the beginning of the 1980s it was both simplistic and facile to think that the progress of the poor depended on the prosperity of the rich. But it did not take us long to recognise that development issues could not be divorced from the major issues facing the world economy. Thus the Report acknowledged that: *"The poor will not make progress in a world economy characterised by uncertainty, disorder and low rates of growth"*. It recognised that it was equally true that *"the rich cannot prosper without progress by the poor"*. *"It will not be possible"*, asserted the Report, *"for any nation or group of nations to save itself either by dominion over others or by isolation from them. On the contrary, real progress will only be made nationally if it can be assured globally"*. The Report's conceptual framework was mutual interest in change: the joint interests of rich and poor countries in the kind of changes – and they were fundamental changes – that we recommended for the world economy. Not aid or charity in an old-fashioned sense; not a game of winners or losers that the extremists on both sides would have us play. The moral imperative for development was not lost, was not abandoned, and certainly was not rejected: but there was less in the Report than in earlier work on North/South issues of the 'Sunday' virtues of generosity and charity. There was a good deal more of human solidarity and of international social justice.

We were convinced that the humanistic urge to help the weak must always be one of the mainsprings of human actions, and that we should not cease to recall the international community to the moral imperative for development. But there was little doubt, we felt, that the 1980s would witness a movement away from a pre-occupation with aid and altruism. There would be a transition, to be sure, and a need for aid. There would be a period during which the poorest countries and the poorest within the poorer countries would need assistance of the traditional kind. But, increasingly, what should be done through international co-operation was to enable the world's poor to earn. Not welfare, but work, not handouts, but jobs. Just as developed societies recognised – or used to – that the answer to the problems of poverty within them was not soup kitchens and charity, but more employment and greater social justice; so did we feel that world society should apply the same concepts to the challenge of global poverty and the tensions it created – as it continues to do as I write.

Essentially, what the Report was urging was a new perspective of the world as a community of nations; a movement away from previous conceptions – lingering conceptions – of an adversarial international system in which the interests of nations are seen as being served mainly in opposition to the interests of others – with 'sovereignty' more often a sword than a shield, but in either form an unwieldy encumbrance in our interdependent world. *"We are looking"*, the Report said, *"for a world based less on power and status, more on justice and contract; less discretionary, more governed by fair and open rules"*.

These basic perspectives of the Commission are important to an understanding of the Report's responses to the challenge of the 1980s. An explanation for its thrust should not be sought only in the process of compromise between viewpoints. The recognition of a mutuality of interest in change led to a quantum leap in the thinking of Commissioners.

Understandably, we could not avoid touching on the issue of disarmament. It was a subject that deserved a Commission all to itself, but it was impossible to produce a report on development without drawing attention to the massive contradiction between military expenditure then of some 450 billion dollars a year compared with Official Development Assistance of some 20 billion dollars. And we did so.

We also had something to say about the international institutional system. Our starting point was, of course, support for the United Nations as an indispensable force for peace and development; but we were convinced that it needed strengthening if it was to be fully effective. We were troubled by a number of matters bearing on its functioning; at the very large number of international meetings – then about 6,000 every year in New York and Geneva and about a million pages of connected documentation; at the risk that, without a political basis for consensus on the major issues that concern meetings on international co-operation, there could be only ritual discussion and resolutions without obligation for subsequent action; at a situation in which the language of international resolutions had become inbred, specialised, imprecise and coded; at a group system in which the process of reconciling differences within groups often led to extreme positions driving out moderate ones and maximum demands eliciting minimum offers. We questioned whether the existing negotiating machinery served to facilitate development or the emergence of the political will that is necessary for major decisions; whether a negotiating format could be devised which was more functional, while fully respecting the concerns of the developing countries for maintaining their solidarity.

We called for a major effort to avert a foundering of the human dialogue; for greater experimentation with the committee system; for innovation and the exploration of new techniques of dialogue. And we called for greater public education, particularly in the North, so that ordinary citizens, especially the younger generation, could understand the implications for them of global interdependence and identify with international organisations that are meant to manage it.

Commissioners from the South were particularly anxious that the Report should not be silent on the obligations of the developing world – on those things that the Third World must do in relation to development. We tried to do so with frankness in the Chapter entitled, 'The Task of the South'. We emphasised the general point that national efforts, the domestic obligations that fall on the developing countries, should not be seen in any sense as preconditions for reform of the global system, but as valid and essential in their own right and should be undertaken and discharged by the developing countries. We recognised, of course, the great variety of conditions, of situations, of economic systems, indeed of economic philosophies in the different countries of the developing world. Overall, however, we expressed the belief that: *"In the vast majority of developing countries much more could be done to achieve equitable development"*.

While acknowledging the variations that exist in the different countries and regions of the Third World, we talked about priorities for agriculture, for land reform, for much greater assistance to the informal sector, for spreading social services more equitably, particularly between urban and rural areas, for arresting what we feared was a decline in the importance being attached to planning, and for much greater emphasis on efficient management. We drew attention to the fact that development in an ultimate sense must involve the full participation of the people. And we called not only for domestic reforms but also for greatly enhanced economic co-operation between developing countries. We hoped that that conclusion would receive serious attention in the centres of decision-making in the Third World.

Our terms of reference required us to keep *'the need for a new international economic order at the centre of our concerns'*. On this, and in the context of the totality of its recommendations, the Report observed that: "The present world economic and political environment only adds urgency to this task. We are convinced that the world community will have to be bold and imaginative in shaping that new order and will have to be realistic in its endeavours". The summary of recommendations, which was brought together at the end of the Report, represented the roads we proposed towards the new order.

It became clear to us on the Commission that while people everywhere talked about the challenges confronting them, whether immediate or in the longer term, they each had a different perception of the challenge – because, essentially, they did not share a common perception of the world. Our small planet looks very different from a boardroom in Bonn or a paddy field in Bangladesh.

If we asked an OECD economist, for example, what was the central challenge of the 1980s, he would have told us it is the challenge of inflation in the industrialised world. His priorities would have been maintaining stability through policies of restraint, even at the expense of sustained recession in the world economy. A Brazilian economic planner, however, was likely to see the principal challenge in the new protectionism of the time. He was adjusting to the non-oil era, particularly with ethanol, and saw the debt problem as one as much for the lender as the borrower, and he would have accepted that rapid industrial development required emphasis on export markets, and, therefore, would have seen the challenges of the 1980s in the contraction of world trade. A farmer in Nepal would tell us of his own energy crisis; but, for him, the challenge was to find enough firewood to cook and to be warm through a chilly Himalayan night. And if we found a villager in Mali willing to look so far ahead into the future, he would tell us that the challenge was survival – having enough for his family to eat tomorrow and next week. The Commission came to understand that these differences of perception were at the heart of man's dilemma; that their reconciliation would have much to do with the shape of human destiny.

We were not without such varied perceptions even among members of the Commission. When first I spoke in the Commission outlining my view of the disparities of wealth and poverty in the world, a Commissioner spoke quietly to a staff member saying that she *"had not heard a communist speak before"*. She was told that, *"Sonny Ramphal is regarded as a moderate by some of his colleagues, and was by no means a communist"*. She was Katharine Graham, the owner of the *Washington Post* and a sophisticated modern woman, but such 'talk' was entirely outside her 'ken'. She would discover reality in time, and be a valued member of the Commission, but such was the gap in perception outside one's cloistered circle. And it was so in much of the world.

Katharine Graham and I were to have another interesting encounter while we served on the Commission, although it was one that had nothing to do with the Commission's work. Commission meetings were held around the world. After the opening meeting at Gymnich in Germany, we met at Mont Pelerin in Switzerland (twice), Bamako in Mali, Tarrytown in the U.S., Kuala Lumpur in Malaysia, Brussels in Belgium, Annecy in France, Vienna in Austria, and Kent (Leeds Castle) in England. Each venue had its highlights. Our Fifth full Meeting was in Kuala Lumpur; but, en route, we had a Round Table Discussion in New Delhi. On 19 November, an agitated Kay Graham hailed me on the steps of the Ashoka Hotel where we were staying. Her *Washington Post* editor had called to tell her of mass suicides at Jonestown in Guyana on 18 November and to urge her to make the most of my presence in Delhi to illumine the story. I was slightly ashamed to tell her that I had never heard of 'Jonestown' or of a cult settlement anywhere in Guyana. I ventured a wild guess that it might be far down in the South near Brazil. I am not sure what Mrs Graham told her editor. Jonestown turned out to be in the furthest northwest of the country near Venezuela. I took comfort later in my ignorance which, as it turned out, was shared by the vast majority of the people of Guyana who had no idea that Jonestown existed or of the Americans who formed its bizarre settlement or of the weird Jim Jones who headed it.

Debate in the Commission was robust and protracted, but it was not a North-South ritual. We became one team striving to find a common way forward from our very different starting perceptions. Our Terms of Reference, formulated and agreed by the Commission itself, had (as already mentioned) stipulated that, *"the need for a new international economic order will be at the centre of the Commission's concern"*. Yet, when early in our work I mentioned 'the new international economic order' (NIEO), Peter Peterson chided me that, when he heard those words, they brought on in him *"the MEGO effect"*. I had not heard the epithet before, and he explained that it meant: *"my eyes glaze over"*. Such were our disparate beginnings.

By our 9th Meeting in Brussels in October 1979 we had met the most respected thinkers on North-South issues world-wide, and had reached the stage of considering a draft report prepared by the Secretariat. But discussions in the Commission were not complete and argument persisted. As it turned out, Ted Heath and I became the principal protagonists in relation to the text and Willy Brandt grew increasingly impatient with us. Eventually, at the Brussels Meeting he literally blew up and said in effect, *I've had enough, if after nearly two years we can't agree, let us give up the effort and tell the world we failed.* Both Heath and I were aghast and told him that his reaction was unjustified; the issues, we said, were profound and needed exhaustive debate; our argumentation was the way consensus would be forged. At this point he stormed: *since Heath and Ramphal are the principal offenders and they both believe consensus lies through their excessive arguments, let us leave it to them to find that consensus. We will give them two months to produce a draft Report on which they agree and can recommend to us. They should go away with a few Secretariat staff and come back to us in December.* No one objected.

Both Ted Heath and I were in London. I made room in the Commonwealth Secretariat where a small group could work. Heath arranged for Archibald McKenzie of his staff to work with economists from Marlborough House and with Robert Cassen of the Commission's staff who joined them from Geneva. As a small group we hammered away – challenged by Brandt to find agreement. And we did, aided by a spirit of co-operation from Heath that was admirable. By December 1980, Heath used his substantial British influence to get us Leeds Castle in England for the Commission's final Meeting, and we duly unveiled the draft we had agreed.

Until then, Heath and I were adversaries – North and South. At Leeds Castle, we were partners, defending the draft (over two days) against all-comers. Some of my colleagues from the South were not entirely happy. They felt I had conceded too much. Ted Heath had the same experience. But he and I held to our agreed position and convinced the Commission that we were right. The now historic Brandt Report: '***NORTH-SOUTH: A Programme for Survival***' was the result.

To this day, I wonder whether Willy Brandt's tantrum in Brussels was not contrived to get the result he got. In the discreet language of the Report's annex it is recorded simply: *"An Editorial Group advised by experts was set up under the leadership of Mr Heath and Mr Ramphal, in consultation with the Chairman, to work in London and prepare a complete draft of the Report for submission to the Tenth Meeting"*. At a Press Conference in London on 17 December 1979 Willy Brandt announced to the world that the Commission had completed its task.

While the Commission was in the first year of its work, Geoffrey Barraclough wrote a two-part article in the *New York Review* (26 October and 9 November 1978) in which he reviewed four publications on the problems of development and the world economy – by Michael Harrington, Arthur Lewis, W. Howard Higgins and the US Council of Foreign Relations. He concluded it with these words:

> *If we in the West are going to insist that we must have regular increases in our standard of living no matter who foots the bill, if we continue to rely, as we have relied in the last 30 years, on endless growth and endless consumption as a way out of our self-induced economic problems, disaster will strike us all, rich and poor alike ... That is why, contrary to appearances, the quest for a new international economic order is not dead ... Nevertheless, the choice facing us today is a choice between a NIEO and chaos indescribably worse than the world has ever experienced in the past... But we still have a slender chance that it will not culminate in irretrievable disaster. That is the central issue of our generation, as we march towards the limits*

> *of growth; and it transcends the question of rich and poor, for what is at stake is the survival of us all.*

The Commission believed that its recommendations offered that 'slender chance' to ensure that the 1980s did not 'culminate in irretrievable disaster'. That is why we called the Report: "A Programme for Survival". But its recommendations offered more than mere survival. They offered pathways towards a new order – roads along which the world could travel towards a less unequal and more stable world society. Because of the North/South character of the Commissioners, they opened up practicable and encouraging prospects of consensus in taking these new pathways, these new roads. The Report held out both a plan and a vision of hope.

Yet we had to respond to the obvious question: If all these were the recommendations that should together constitute the goals of the world community, what can we do and where should we start in the 1980s, and what should be carried through into the 1990s? The Commission's answer was the 'Programme of Priorities': the agenda of reforms that we recommended for negotiation in the decades that lay ahead which we identified and elaborated under the headings: *Priority Needs of the Poorest, Abolition of Hunger, Commodities, Manufactures, Transnational Technology and Mineral Development, Reform of the Monetary System, A New Approach to Development Finance and Power Sharing.*

But we went further. Under the heading – *An Emergency Programme: 1980-85,* we said this:

> *We believe, however, that the world cannot wait for the longer-term measures before embarking on an immediate action programme for the next five years to avert the most serious dangers, and interlocking programme which will require undertakings by all parties, and also bring benefits to all. Its principal elements – all of equal importance – would be:*
>
> - *A large-scale transfer of resources to developing countries.*

- *An international energy strategy*
- *A global food programme*
- *A start on some major reforms in the international economic system.*

In this spirit of urgency we recommended the convening of "*A Summit of World Leaders –*

a summit ... limited to some twenty-five world leaders who could ensure fair representation of major world groupings, to enable initiatives and concessions to be thrashed out with candour and boldness ... We hope that a summit could enable political leaders to take the first steps towards committing themselves and their people to a global agreement for the whole world.

We came to this conclusion not without reluctance since we were all mindful of the difficulties. But in the context of our belief that the *"1980s could witness even greater catastrophes than the 1930s"*, we were fully convinced that:

It is not enough ... to sit around tables talking, like characters in Chekhov plays about insoluble problems. We have to lift ourselves above the immediate constrictions, and offer the world a plan and a vision of hope, without which nothing substantial can be achieved.

We ended: *"Whatever their differences and however profound, there is a mutuality of interest between North and South. The fate of both is intimately connected. The search for solutions is not an act of benevolence but a condition of mutual survival"*.

The Report was translated into 20 languages, and sold a million copies world-wide. Members of the Commission from North and South became ambassadors for its proposals. I spoke widely in the Commonwealth and beyond, but so, for example, did Willy Brandt and Ted Heath. And voices were raised world-wide in support of the report. I recall a 'Mass Lobby on Brandt: FIGHT WORLD POVERTY' in the British Parliament in May 1981 attracting over 4,000 registrants and speakers from all parties in Britain, as well as Jamaica's Michael Manley. A Conservative MP wrote in his local paper that: *"The mass lobby was effective, it jolted me out of the mire of frustration on development issues that I had felt for years and I have now written to the Prime Minister (*Margaret Thatcher*) about the Mexico Summit"*. For him at least, as he wrote, *'it was a new beginning'*. 'Development' NGOs united worldwide in calling for 'support for Brandt'.

* * *

There were critics, of course, mainly of the right whose mission was to defend the status quo, and for some the new 'Reaganomics'. Heath, a former Conservative Prime Minister, and no admirer of his successor Margaret Thatcher, was just the person to speak up for the Report as he did in this typical response:

> *Lest we become too demoralised by the refusal of so many to refuse to recognise the new realities of our era, by their ferocious opposition to change, or simply by their blindness to the need for it, we can perhaps draw some comfort from the experience of history that almost every progressive idea has had to confront savage opposition, from the electric light bulb to the steam engine, from the first piece of labour legislation to the abolition of slavery. Yet once the vision is accepted it is the rationalisers of the received wisdom who are its most meticulous and earnest sponsors. We shall have to live with this reality in the future as we have had to do in the past.*

The Report was to stand the test of time. In 2010, James B. Quilligan, writing in the on-line international journal *Integral Review* under the title, *How the Brandt Report Foresaw Today's Global Economic Crisis,* had this to say:

> *Looking back from the perspective of the Millennium, it was clear that all of the basic problems that the Brandt Commission had initially addressed – food, aid, environment, energy, trade, finance and monetary reform, as well as global negotiations to find solutions to these issues – were still unresolved and had become even more urgent with the passage of time...*
>
> *Now, on the thirtieth anniversary of its publication, I wish to underscore some of the major policy areas in which the Brandt report still has something vital to say – proposals which have been largely forgotten but may yet have relevance to our present generation of politicians, economists, and global citizens. History would not be served if the significance of the Brandt Report were ignored, particularly since many of today's familiar trends and potential solutions had their origins in this book. It is widely recognised, for example that the Brandt Commission was the first international body to introduce the concepts of interdependence, globalisation, sustainable development, and alternative sources of development financing in its Report and supporting documents. Indeed there are many dimensions of the Brandt Report that were ahead of their time – yet none as prescient as its proposals for restructuring the international monetary system.*

As Chairman of the Commission, Willy Brandt's work went beyond advocacy. We had recommended an Emergency Programme and a Summit Meeting of World Leaders to agree it. He did not rest until he had enabled it, and he sustained our partnership throughout the process. President Jose Lopez Portillo of Mexico, who was anxious to present himself as a spokesman of the South, offered to host the Summit in Cancun, and Brandt encouraged his European Social Democrat friend, Chancellor Bruno Kreisky of Austria, to be co-chairman with Portillo. Kreisky, however, took ill, and between us we encouraged Canada's Prime Minister Pierre Trudeau – in whom I had immense confidence from his record in Commonwealth summitry – to join Portillo as Co-Chair of the Cancun Summit. It was called the International Meeting on Co-operation and Development and took place from 21 to 23 October 1981 at Cancun.

On 11 September, in the run-up to the Summit, Willy Brandt and I addressed a joint letter to the Presidents and Prime Ministers attending the Summit offering suggestions for the 'objectives' of the Summit based on our conviction from the work of the Commission *"that North-South issues demand from our global society a programme of urgent, concerted and sustained action"*. We ended our letter as follows:

> *Cancun is in one sense an occasion of last resort in the face of serious failures in the development dialogue. However it arises not merely out of desperation, but also out of awareness of the degree to which all parts of our human society depend upon each other and, therefore need to agree with each other on the essential elements of a tolerable existence for all people. Cancun, in this sense, is not an end but a beginning.*

Between that letter and the Summit, the Commonwealth HGM was held at Melbourne, Australia. There, Commonwealth leaders – seven of whom would be at Cancun (Burnham, Indira Gandhi, Nyerere, Abdus Sattar Shagari, Margaret Thatcher and Trudeau) – expressed the hope that the Summit *"would make a bold start by putting international economic co-operation on a new and constructive course, and that it would unequivocally reaffirm the commitment to Global Negotiations"*. They specifically asked their colleagues attending Cancun to provide them, through me, their assessment of the Cancun meeting. Not all did; but Prime Minister Trudeau's letter to me as Co-Chairman was especially important. I circulated it, along with a personal letter from President Reagan, to Commonwealth leaders. Some extracts from Pierre Trudeau's letter are:

> *In my view, the Cancun Summit should be seen as a success. A number of credible achievements can be pointed to. Perhaps, most obvious, yet still significant was the very fact that the*

summit took place. That leaders from some of the world's most influential, yet very diverse, countries were prepared to attend the Cancun Summit clearly demonstrated the seriousness and gravity with which they view North/South economic relations as well as the importance they attach to enhanced international co-operation...

What struck me as particularly important in all our discussions was the recognition of the depth of interdependence of our economies. While it could not be expected that approaches to problems would be identical, we did share, to a large degree, basic objectives and priorities...

Finally, I believe we can be pleased with the agreement that was reached on the desirability of achieving consensus on the launching of the Global Negotiations. I was somewhat disappointed that a Canadian proposal, which suggested a more specific way of moving forward with a firmer time frame, did not in the end prove acceptable to some participants. I believe, however, that the momentum toward the launching of global negotiations was maintained and that the positive atmosphere of Cancun will make an important contribution to the efforts which are once again underway in New York to reach agreement on an appropriate framework.

I take particular satisfaction in the participation of the Commonwealth Heads of Government at Cancun. We all carried our recent experience in Melbourne, and I feel this added significantly to the substance of our discussions as well as to the informality and frankness with which they were conducted. I would not wish to end without expressing my particular appreciation and praise for the solid support which you personally have given the Summit initiative from its very inception.

President Reagan's letter was somewhat different. While asserting that the meeting at Cancun *"was an extremely constructive and positive meeting"*, he took a swipe at the 'global negotiations', saying, *"too much time has been wasted on words and conferences. We need to turn our attention to the practical issues and institutions where real progress has been achieved and can be further accelerated",* (namely, of course, as he spelled out, the institutions that the US and its closest allies controlled) the World Bank, the IMF and the GATT; and he added:

> *I am convinced that our approach to development must emphasise two efforts – the effort to revive world growth and expand open trade, investment and financial relations, and the effort to provide co-operative assistance to achieve self-sustaining growth in the poor countries, particularly in food and energy.*

The Cancun meeting was not the success in finite terms that the Brandt Commission hoped for; 'Reaganite' policies thwarted concrete agreements, for example, on the Global Negotiations, as Trudeau's letter implied. In a booklet entitled *'Cancun: A Candid Evaluation'* published by the North-South Round Table in 1982, Manmohan Singh (later Prime Minister of India) contributed an article which he entitled *'Cancun: 'Agreement' but no Results'*. In it he wrote frankly about the rigid ideological stance of the US Government (Reagan), with its emphasis on *'the magic of the market-place and its related approaches to issues of world development'*. In my own contribution to that booklet, I wrote about the element of 'agreement':

> *I have spoken with many of the leaders who sat around the table at Cancun. I do not find among them a sense of despair over the process itself. Far from it. I have found a belief that it was a better way than many that had so far been tried; that with the benefit of hindsight they might actually have had the kind of political dialogue by which a new start could have been inspired; that in some areas they came close to practical success. This is not an apologia for Cancun. It is a hint of hope that if we can, indeed, see Cancun as a beginning, we*

> *might help to ensure that it was a start, however faltering in a long process by which our world might find the essential way ahead, in the course of which other 'Cancuns' may well be necessary".*

In his Introduction to the Roundtable booklet, after canvassing the many negatives and the few positives, Andrew Rice concluded:

> *Perhaps the lasting legacy of Cancun, therefore, is something so intangible that it is difficult to quantify even in words – a deeper awareness of all those who took part at Cancun, and also of those who observed Cancun, of the common humanity and thus the common destiny of our planet.*

But it was not enough for the Commission. Conditions in the first years of the 1980s only confirmed some of the worst fears expressed in the Report. The world's prospects deteriorated rapidly, not only for improved relations between North and South, but for the outlook of the world economy as a whole. Further decline, we thought, was likely to cause the deterioration of societies and create conditions of anarchy in many parts of the world. By the end of 1982, led by Willy Brandt, we felt it necessary to present an urgent and up-to-date version of our original Emergency Programme. Altogether we held five meetings between May 1980 and December 1982 – in The Hague, Berlin, Kuwait, Brussels and Ottawa. The old team of Ted Heath and me, working in London, with the help of a small staff – Robert Cassen from the Institute of Development Studies at Sussex University, Bishnodat Persaud from the Commonwealth Secretariat and Simon May from Heath's office – produced the follow-up Memorandum which the Commission published as the book *'COMMON CRISIS – North-South Co-operation for World Recovery'*. For my part, I was grateful for the acknowledgement in the book that: *"The Commission owes a particular debt to the Commonwealth Secretariat in London, which provided a wealth of technical and logistic support"*. We were, of course, doing no more than helping the world to negotiate.

With Willy Brandt

As today we contemplate Summits of the G20, the 1981 Cancun Summit was, indeed, a way-station in the chequered history of North-South negotiations – a milestone in a journey still on-going, and one that the Brandt Commission helped the world to reach. In the calculus of my memoirs, I count high my association with Willy Brandt and fellow Commissioners, and, strengthened by hindsight, I remain as sure today as I was at Leeds Castle over three decades ago of the worth of the Report, *'North-South: A Programme for Survival'* – and its continuing relevance to our common humanity. I am proud to have played a part in offering it to the world.

PART VI

THE 'THATCHER' YEARS

CHAPTER 18

Zimbabwe

As I began writing this Chapter on 8 April 2013, news came of the death of Baroness Margaret Thatcher, Britain's former Prime Minister. I sent a message of condolence to Prime Minister David Cameron and, at the invitation of the Editor of *The Round Table: The Commonwealth Journal of International Affairs*, I wrote a short comment about her in a Commonwealth context. The timing for me was uncannily apposite. My *Round Table* comment, under the title *Mrs Thatcher and the Commonwealth,* was as follows:

> *For eleven of my fifteen years as Commonwealth Secretary-General, Margaret Thatcher was Prime Minister at Westminster – from 1979 to 1990. Those eleven years were also the period of the Commonwealth's most intensive engagement with the political issues of Southern Africa – the unilateral declaration of independence ('UDI') by Southern Rhodesia's Prime Minister, Ian Smith, and the grotesque racism of 'apartheid' in South Africa. That there should have been Commonwealth engagement with these issues was inevitable; that the engagement was so bruising for the Commonwealth derived in the main from Margaret Thatcher's stewardship as Britain's Prime Minister during those years. This is not to say that other factors were not at work. Harold Wilson before her was less confrontational within the councils of the Commonwealth, but dalliance and obfuscation characterised*

his record on Southern Africa's afflictions. Margaret Thatcher's years, however, took Britain's posture to a new level of obduracy in the Commonwealth. It meant that my relations with her as Secretary-General, though always cordial, were never consistently warm.

The stage for confrontation over Rhodesia was set in the Conservative Party's manifesto for the 1979 elections that swept her to power. It seemed to commit her administration to 'recognition' of Bishop Abel Muzorewa's regime under an 'internal settlement' Constitution widely regarded as entrenching white minority rule. The Smith-Muzorewa 'alliance' was delighted with her victory African Commonwealth countries, however, were united in rejection of Muzorewa; Nigeria black-listed British firms and joined the 'front-line' states led by Tanzania and Zambia; and so was the Commonwealth generally – the Prime Minister of Australia, Malcolm Fraser, playing an honourable role in ensuring that Commonwealth opinion was not divided on black-white lines.

My immediate concern was the Commonwealth Summit due to open in Lusaka on 1 August where I felt the time propitious for a Commonwealth break-through on Rhodesia; but an opportunity that could be lost by a recalcitrant Margaret Thatcher. I had seen her two weeks after she came to power and urged that she change her view of the 'liberation' movement as 'terrorists', and see them instead as Britain saw the 'partisans' in Yugoslavia during the Second World War – as 'freedom fighters'. Her response was: "Well, of course, they're terrorists; they're just like the IRA". I believed she saw, however, how provocative such language could be at Lusaka. The Queen was known to value the chance of Commonwealth reconciliation at Lusaka and quickly quashed ideas of her staying away from 'a war zone' – floated by Prime Minister Robert Muldoon of New Zealand with Mrs Thatcher's encouragement.

With the stage set for Lusaka, my role was to encourage a very uneasy Prime Minister that she would not be harassed at her first Commonwealth Summit – and to deliver on it by persuading African frontline states and others to surprise her by their calm reason. For her part, Mrs Thatcher announced in Parliament before leaving for Lusaka that "the British Government are wholly committed to genuine black majority rule in Rhodesia". I was in the Visitors' Gallery to hear her say this. Julius Nyerere accepted the olive branch, and with some further orchestration at Lusaka the 'Accord' that led to the Lancaster House Conference was reached. It was a great achievement for the Commonwealth – and for Mrs Thatcher, with all save the extreme right of her Party.

But ending UDI was only the first hurdle in Southern Africa; and Mrs Thatcher was much less receptive to the demand for change in South Africa. With all of Africa and most of the world calling for an end to apartheid's inhumanities in South Africa, Margaret Thatcher threw the evil system a lifeline by resisting the imposition of any save the mildest sanctions on South Africa. Had leaders like Malcolm Fraser, and later Bob Hawke, and Brian Mulroney of Canada not taken the stand against racism that they did, the Commonwealth could have been wrecked by 'Thatcherism'. I use the aphorism, because she accepted isolation within the Commonwealth and much of the world beyond it, with ideological zeal. She avowed disapproval of apartheid but, in the eyes of most, she became apartheid's steadfast protector. Cold War considerations, the Reagan/Thatcher alliance all played a part; but she never seemed to see apartheid as the transcendent evil that it was.

Even the Commonwealth's Eminent Persons Group (EPG) to South Africa in 1986 chaired jointly by Malcolm Fraser and General Olusegun Obasanjo of Nigeria, and including Lord Barber as Mrs Thatcher's chosen member, failed to move her. They had unanimously concluded: "The question in front of Heads of Government is in our view clear. It is not whether such measures (sanctions) will compel change; it is already the case that their absence, and Pretoria's belief that they need not be feared, defers change". At the special limited Commonwealth Summit in Marlborough House to discuss the EPG Report, Mrs Thatcher faced down this damning indictment of her support for the apartheid regime and protested as vigorously as before against sanctions beyond gestures – a position she maintained to the end, when the self-destructive system became so unsustainable that Pretoria itself effectively surrendered.

Mrs Thatcher's legacies are many and varied. The Commonwealth stood with her, for example, on the Falklands. But on the Commonwealth's necessary engagement in Southern Africa, and the ending of apartheid in South Africa in particular, I am proud that the Commonwealth stood united against her view, and in the end prevailed.

Let that suffice as a prelude to what follows in the Chapters of this Part; *'The Thatcher Years'*.

* * *

By the time I came to London in July 1975 Southern Africa issues, long prominent on the Commonwealth agenda, were intensifying. Indeed, at Singapore in 1971, which I attended as Guyana's Foreign Minister, the row over arms sales to South Africa almost wrecked the meeting – and the Commonwealth itself. It derived from the decision of the newly elected British Government, with Edward Heath as Prime Minister, to resume arms sales to South Africa under the Simonstown Agreements of 1955 promising, inter alia, British co-operation with South Africa in defence of the sea-route around the Cape of Good Hope. Sir Alec Douglas Home (later Lord Home) was Heath's Foreign Secretary and both his own pronouncements and the Party's election manifesto had given clear indications that the Conservatives would lift the non-mandatory embargo on arms sales to South Africa which had been approved by the UN Security Council in 1963, and which the former British Labour (Wilson) Government had honoured. The

Heath decision was redolent of Cold War considerations and wholly insensitive to African and wider Commonwealth concerns. Although Heath stressed that any 'equipment' would be for external defence and not internal security, it was undeniable that arms for the *apartheid* regime were arms that further endangered *apartheid's* victims. Emotions ran high: Tanzania's President Julius Nyerere immediately told Downing Street that he would withdraw his country from the Commonwealth if Britain went ahead with the resumption of arms sales to South Africa. His dismay and anger were shared widely in the Commonwealth. I recall well Guyana's concerns. In Arnold Smith's memoirs is the following passage:

> *Sonny Ramphal, then Foreign Minister of Guyana, was passing through London and saw Home the next day. He put the view strongly that it would be extremely tactless for the British government to make a decision and simply inform Commonwealth countries. He urged delay until consultations could take place, and went on to press Sir Alec not to make any decision until after the HGM in January (in Singapore), when leaders would listen seriously to a genuine case about defence of the western world.*

I was trying to follow the wise advice of the old Chinese adage: *Build your enemy a golden bridge on which he may retreat* – advice which the Labour Peer Lord Chalfont later urged on Zambia's President Kenneth Kaunda in the same context. The bridge was built, Heath deferred the decision and inexorably the Singapore Summit arrived six months later. On its eve, *The Guardian* in London was counselling the Prime Minister:

> *The disasters of history suggest that governments at times have made costly blunders due to tragic misjudgements which have usually arisen from a lack of sensitivity to the realities of the outside world in which foreign policy has to operate. Consultations, if approached in the spirit of sincerity, sensitivity*

and open-mindedness, can decrease the danger of miscalculations.

Arnold Smith's assessment at the time was:

I have no doubt that if Heath had gone ahead with large sales of arms to South Africa he would have done even more damage to Britain's standing and influence in the world than Anthony Eden did through the invasion of Suez in 1956.

Singapore itself was a bruising encounter. Ted Heath's stubbornness in the face of concerted Commonwealth pressure was quite phenomenal. Towards the end, it appeared as if he was resisting the advice of his own Foreign Secretary, Sir Alec Douglas Home, to be more conciliatory: the same Ted Heath who ten years later – but out of office – was to play such a different role in the Brandt Commission.

The row contributed greatly to the Singapore Declaration of Commonwealth Principles – which I helped to refine along with Ivan Head of Canada and Mark Chona of Zambia and, of course, Secretariat officials. Zambia had come to Singapore with a draft declaration – President Kaunda's belief that the answer to these political differences should be rooted in values and principles – and his offer of a 'golden bridge' in words that Heath eventually accepted in the Singapore Declaration of Commonwealth principles, namely:

No country will afford to regimes which practice racial discrimination assistance which in its own judgement directly contributes to the pursuit or consolidation of this evil policy. We oppose all forms of colonial domination and racial oppression and are committed to the principles of human dignity and equality.

And on the practical side, the 'arms sales' came down to six helicopters for three anti-submarine frigates (earlier supplied), before Wilson returned to power in 1974 and scrapped the Simonstown Agreement.

Having had such a harsh encounter in Singapore it might be assumed that British Conservative Prime Ministers, and the Conservative Party itself, would have learnt a lesson in standing against the Commonwealth, and much of the world, in the Southern African theatre; but much worse was to come. Heath at least took his stand on issues of British security and sovereignty. The next Conservative Prime Minister was Margaret Thatcher, who came to power in May 1979; and the issues reflected in her policies were old ones of kinship and racism and 'Cold War' ideology – and all with a new passion and intensity. Between Singapore and Mrs Thatcher's coming to power, Commonwealth and international pressures had kept mounting on both the Rhodesian and the South African fronts – though most immediately on the Rhodesian front where there was the clearest argument for British accountability in the entrenchment of racism and repression.

A 'unilateral declaration of independence' (UDI) by a white minority cabal led by Ian Smith in Salisbury in November 1965 had left the colonial power (Britain) manifestly answerable. The social, political and economic reality of Rhodesia was that a 5 per cent white settler minority had seized political power, usurped 80 per cent of the country's arable land, institutionalised racism beyond land distribution – and rejected the authority of the United Kingdom. Anywhere else it would have been denounced as a rebellion against the Crown and followed by swift retribution and reversal. Britain's acquiescence in it all, through policies of studied inertia, was intolerable, not only to black Rhodesians who were its victims, but also more widely within the Commonwealth and the international community. It only made matters worse that *apartheid* South Africa, already an international pariah, was Rhodesia's neighbouring patron and protector. The specious symbol of Britain's rejection of UDI was its insistence on describing the country by its colonial name: 'Southern Rhodesia' – even after it declared itself a Republic in 1970. To 'black' Africa, and beyond, it smacked of collusion. Unapologetic pro-Rhodesia opinion in the right wing of the British Conservative Party reinforced that conclusion.

Struggle in Rhodesia did not begin with Ian Smith's UDI. The seeds of struggle were sown by the invasion of Mashonaland by Cecil Rhodes on 26 June 1890 – Mashonaland, the largest area of today's Zimbabwe. From that day, struggle was about land. Land is what Rhodes and his cohorts who dignified themselves as 'Pioneers' seized, then ruled in the name of Empire through deception and repression, unabashed by his dictum of "equal rights for all civilised men". Seventy-five years later, in 1965, when Ian Smith announced his 'unilateral declaration of independence' the same piety obfuscated the racism that claims of civilisation and Christianity masked: *"The mantle of the pioneers has fallen on our shoulders"*, he said, *"to sustain civilisation in a primitive country"*. In that context of 'civilisation and Christianity', it is worth recalling what Evelyn Waugh wrote in his *Letters* about these self-appointed custodians of higher values:

> *Rhodesia is not an interesting country... the whites are (a) old Rhodesians – that is to say, families dating from 1890 – survivors and descendants of the riff-raff who came up from the Cape with Jameson and Rhodes, dreadful people, rather stuck-up. (b) English county families who came there in 1946 to escape the welfare State. They are rapidly becoming middle-class. (c) odd persons – Hungarians etc. very poor and rather gay. (d) Jesuits and other missionaries. Black Americans who come to the Federation are labelled 'foreign natives'; white Americans are 'Europeans'... Every white man has a motorcar and a dinner jacket and goes to bed at nine. The women drink tea all day long.*

Land is what generations of the dispossessed Shona and Matabele people strove to reclaim for nearly a century. Land is what in 1975 lay behind the demand of nationalist groups for 'immediate majority rule'. In 1976, Tongagara, the last commander of Zimbabwe's nationalist forces, explained:

> *My grievances were based on the question of oppression which I had seen myself from my parents or from my own people, particularly in the deprivation of land. You know our people are naturally farmers. They like soil. They know that everything is soil, and yet they are deprived of the rich soil in Zimbabwe.*

Awareness of that basic reality is essential to an understanding of all that followed in Zimbabwe. Regrettably, it was all too often ignored by Britain. The struggle was never only about forms of democracy, as in much of colonial Africa – though for a long time it took that form – it was always, at heart, a demand for retributive justice for land taken by force from the native people of Rhodesia.

I have earlier described my encounter in 1975 with the Rhodesian nationalists at the Commonwealth Summit in Kingston at which I was elected Secretary-General – when Michael Manley had invited a delegation comprising Bishop Abel Muzorewa, Ndabaningi Sithole and Joshua Nkomo. They represented the African National Council – a vain attempt to unify the splintered nationalist forces. It had been formed in 1971 to oppose proposals for a settlement concocted by Britain's Foreign Secretary, Sir Alec Douglas Home and Ian Smith. Unfortunately, Britain was more motivated by a desire to be rid of the 'Rhodesia problem' than to close a sordid imperial chapter with honour and justice.

In the years of the Heath administration, long before Margaret Thatcher came on the scene, Douglas Home and Ian Smith had devised a constitutional arrangement which would have deferred anything like 'majority African rule' *ad infinitum.* Black Africans, of course, were not a party to the 'Agreement' – or to the discussions leading to it. It paid only lip service to the 'six Principles' which had governed British policy since Wilson's early efforts. These had evolved as:

- Unimpeded progress toward majority rule,
- Guarantees against retrogressive amendment of the Constitution,
- Immediate improvement of the political status of Africans,

- Progress toward ending racial discrimination, and
- The need for the British Government to be satisfied that any basis proposed for independence was acceptable to the people of Rhodesia as a whole.

To these, Wilson – at the insistence of Commonwealth leaders – had later added a sixth – the NIBMAR principle: No independence before majority African rule

In 1972, the British Government recognised that however much it wanted adoption of the Home-Smith Agreement, it could not skirt around the fifth principle: that *any Rhodesian settlement should be generally acceptable to the people as a whole.* The arrangement had to pass the 'test of acceptability' to black opinion; and the British Government convinced itself that in this case the answer would be 'yes'. Lord Pearce, an eminent Law Lord, led a high level Commission which found that the answer by black opinion was resoundingly 'no'.

The British Government's effort to bring Southern Rhodesia to independence before majority rule had therefore failed. It failed not because it was shown to be intrinsically wrong for the country (as it was); but because it was shown to be a violation of Britain's word on process. Had that word (in the form of the 'fifth principle) not been wrung from successive governments by an insistent Commonwealth, the wrong to Zimbabwe would have been consummated and proclaimed as a great British political success. It was a lesson to the nationalist movement, which turned with heightened intensity to armed struggle which until then had been an unconvincing strategy of the two major African parties: the Zimbabwe African People's Union (ZAPU) led from the outset by Joshua Nkomo, and the Zimbabwe African Nationalist Union (ZANU) led ultimately by Robert Mugabe. Nkomo was close to Kenneth Kaunda, had established lines to the Soviet Union, and was later headquartered in Zambia; Mugabe was closer to Julius Nyerere, and established lines to the People's Republic of China. Their military wings were respectively ZIPRA (the Zimbabwe People's Revolutionary Army) and ZANLA (the Zimbabwe African National Liberation Army).

ZAPU and ZANU remained steadfast to the armed struggle which developed momentum with the opening of an eastern front as Mozambique gained independence of the Portuguese in 1975 and FRELIMO (the Mozambique nationalist movement) openly identified with ZANU and ZANLA. The same thing happened with the independence of Angola in November allowing the opening of a western front and practical support for ZAPU and ZIPRA.

I was still Foreign Minister of Guyana, in 1975, when the Prime Minister, Forbes Burnham gave advance clearance to Fidel Castro for Cuban flights to Angola to transit through Guyana's Timehri Airport. It was a small contribution by Guyana to the struggle against *apartheid.* It was that Cuban involvement in Southern Africa that activated Henry Kissinger to himself become involved in the theatre. Angola and Mozambique were both now independent; South Africa was a close friend. Rhodesia must be his agenda. UDI was indefensible and weakened the West. Ian Smith must be made to yield to majority rule, his avowal *not in a thousand years* notwithstanding. To his credit he succeeded in getting Smith to concede majority rule in principle – and to talk of implementation in two years. This was now 1976, and a great deal of shuttle diplomacy was involved to bring Julius Nyerere, Kenneth Kaunda, and Samora Machel of Mozambique on board. Although I had doubts about Smith's 'concession', the Commonwealth, at the 1975 Jamaica Summit at which I was elected, had:

> *reaffirmed their total support for the struggle of the people of Zimbabwe for independence on the basis of majority rule and pledged to concert their efforts for the speedy attainment of this objective.*

With the frontline states insisting on a British constitutional Conference to bring Zimbabwe to legality, it was eventually convened in Geneva under the chairmanship of the British Ambassador to the United Nations Ivor Richards. There were four African delegations headed by Robert Mugabe, Abel Muzorewa, Joshua Nkomo and

Ndabiningi Sithole. I arranged for technical assistance for each delegation and for my Assistant Secretary-General, Emeka Anyaoku, to be in Geneva throughout. The Conference opened in October 1976 but collapsed in January 1977 under Smith's intransigence. By then, Kissinger had left office as Jimmy Carter succeeded Gerald Ford as President of the United States.

The baton also passed to the new British Foreign and Commonwealth Secretary, David Owen, an able and energetic Labour Minister, partnered by the new and dynamic roving Ambassador in the Carter administration Andrew Young. A passage from *The Struggle for Zimbabwe* by David Martin and Phyllis Johnson is evocative of the moment:

> *When a suave new British Foreign Secretary jogged down the steps of the Royal Air Force VC-10 at Dar-es-Salaam airport on 11 April 1977, it marked the start of yet another initiative. It could not succeed because the pressure of war was not yet sufficient to make the Rhodesians capitulate to reality, but it would add new links to the chain of events begun by Kissinger, and as it ran its two year course, the war would spread across the country ... encircling the cities and dampening white morale.*

Dr Owen put a great deal of effort into what became known as the 'Anglo American proposals' which postulated a significant role for the United States in the transition; hence their description. The proposals were much less Commonwealth oriented than might have been expected. At the 1977 Commonwealth Summit held in London in June, Britain did not elaborate its ideas. The full proposals were published in September. In the light of later developments, it is interesting that they envisaged a Zimbabwe Development Fund, jointly sponsored by the British and American governments, with a target of between $1,000 million and $1,500 million. If only these numbers were on hand 2 years later at Lancaster House in London; but while in 1979 it was still Cyrus Vance in Washington, David Owen had yielded place to the Conservative Lord, Peter Carrington.

The frontline states were never wholly on board with the Anglo-American Proposals and my anxiety throughout was damage to their unity, and that of the Patriotic Front. My fears were justified in the differences that developed between Nyerere and Kaunda over the proposals. In January 1978, when British and American representatives met the Patriotic Front in Malta (because the Patriotic Front, irked by Owen, declined to go to London), the Secretariat provided assistance to the delegations. I believed that the Anglo-American proposals had possibilities and worked to advance them; but the truth was that Smith never believed he had to capitulate. He pressed on instead with his 'internal settlement' ideas, and eventually snared Bishop Muzorewa.

The guerrilla war was now full blown; but Bishop Muzorewa, whose political naivety was palpable, allowed himself to be lured into a political settlement with Ian Smith ('the March 3 Agreement') which would allow him to win an election, boycotted by Nkomo and Mugabe, under a 'constitution' which wore the mask of change (the country was now 'Zimbabwe – Rhodesia') but left real power in the hands of the white minority. This 'internal settlement' was widely denounced as not providing for majority rule: in the UN, in the Commonwealth and, of course, in Africa. Would anyone recognise the Muzorewa government?

The 'Zimbabwe-Rhodesia' election was held in April 1979. Less than two weeks later, on 3 May, Margaret Thatcher became Prime Minister of Britain and in the saga of Southern Africa the eleven 'Thatcher years' began. As I wrote in my *Round Table* comment quoted at the start of this Chapter:

> *The stage for confrontation (with the new Prime Minister) over Rhodesia was set in the Conservative Party's manifesto for the 1979 elections that swept her to power. It seemed to commit her administration to 'recognition' of Bishop Abel Muzorewa's regime under an 'internal settlement' Constitution widely regarded as entrenching white minority rule. The Smith-Muzorewa 'alliance' was delighted with her victory.*

Their joy was well founded. The actual language of the Conservative Party's Manifesto was:

> *If the six principles ... are fully satisfied following the present Rhodesian elections, the next government will have the duty to return Rhodesia to a state of legality, move to lift sanctions and do its utmost to ensure that the new independent state gains international recognition.*

On 9 April, Francis Pym, the Conservative Party's foreign affairs spokesman, referring to the up-coming 'Zimbabwe-Rhodesia' elections told his constituents:

> *I would like to reiterate that if the election takes place in reasonably free and fair conditions and with a reasonable turnout the last of the traditional six principles which have governed British policy for so long will have been satisfied. In that case it would be the duty of any British Government to bring Rhodesia back to legality and to do everything to make sure that the new independent state receives international recognition.*

No wonder the Ian Smith regime and Abel Muzorewa in Salisbury were euphoric over Mrs Thatcher's victory. The carefully phrased Pym assurance was a clever way around the principle on which an earlier Conservative Government had stumbled in 1972. No Pearce Commission would be a spoiler now. And there was more. The Callaghan Labour Government which Mrs Thatcher replaced had refused to send observers to the Zimbabwe–Rhodesia election on the ground that doing so would imply recognition. Mrs Thatcher, in opposition, had no such inhibition. She sent a team of five observers led by Viscount Boyd (former Colonial Secretary Lennox Boyd) – the inference being that if their verdict was that the election was 'free and fair' a new conservative Government (her Government) would recognise the 'elected' government, return Rhodesia to legality and persuade the UN to lift sanctions – the absence of 'majority rule' and other shortcomings of the Constitution notwithstanding.

Lord Boyd had duly found that judging by *"the strictest Western European criteria"* the elections were *"fairly conducted and above reproach"*. However the observer group led by the Liberal Peer, Lord Chitnis, was less charitable in its report when it said:

> *The recent election in Rhodesia was nothing more than a gigantic confidence trick designed to foist on a cowed and indoctrinated black electorate a settlement and a constitution which were formulated without its consent and which are being implemented without its approval... We cannot play our appointed role in this process and endorse this blatant attempt to perpetrate a fraud and justify a lie.*

And there were more dispassionate voices. Dr Claire Palley had written the definitive work on Southern Rhodesia's constitutional history. Now, in a booklet *Should the Present Government be Recognised,* she argued forcefully that the constitution complied with none of the 'six principles'.

Despite all this, and the weight of international and Commonwealth opinion, it was Boyd to whom Mrs Thatcher and her Conservative Party looked; and there was a distinct danger at that point that her Government would recognise the Muzorewa 'government' and grant independence to the Smith-Muzorewa 'Zimbabwe-Rhodesia'.

But there were other views, and other strategies about ensuring self-determination in Rhodesia. Bishop Muzorewa had flown to London immediately after signing the 'March 3 Agreement'. That gave me a personal opportunity to counsel him about the serious flaws of the Agreement. To personalise the occasion I invited him to my 'Hill Street' residence for us to talk privately. There, on 11 June, I went over the 'internal settlement' agreement in a systematic way drawing on the work we had done in the Secretariat's Legal Division, mainly by Jeremy Pope. And beyond the specific flaws which deviated from the by now deified 'six principles' of NIBMAR, I showed him how far the agreement fell short of majority rule and would not lead inexorably to it. I urged on him the fundamental reality that the war could not be ended without the involvement in a negotiated settlement of the nationalist parties – ZAPU and ZANU, by now in alliance as the Patriotic Front. I pleaded with him to withdraw from the Agreement with Ian Smith and work instead for greater unity among Zimbabwean leaders. He heard me out; but, by now, white voices, including those of the British Conservative Party's right wing, had convinced him that he was on the right path and that a Thatcher victory, of which they were confident, would seal his success. My counsel fell on deaf ears. Nothing could prevent the election; avoidance of an 'electoral coup' in Rhodesia must focus instead on the issue of 'recognition' of a Muzorewa Government.

On 15 July, London's *Sunday Telegraph* reported Bishop Muzorewa as saying at a press conference after meeting Mrs Thatcher: *"We are very close to being recognised. You should not be surprised if Zimbabwe is completely recognised and sanctions completely removed three months from now"*. Was this self-delusion? Two weeks earlier, on I July in Canberra, Mrs Thatcher had certainly implied the non-renewal of sanctions – much to the chagrin of the Prime Minister of Australia, Malcolm Fraser, who was to play a central role, and an honourable one, in all that unfolded. It was well known, as Lord Carrington (Mrs Thatcher's Foreign and Commonwealth Secretary from 1979 to 1982) has confirmed in his memoir, *Reflect on Things Past,* that Margaret Thatcher's *"instincts were in line with those of the right-wing of the Party"*. Her view as he represented it was:

> *Alan Boyd has reported, he is a man whose judgement was worthy of our respect, we had gone through the correct motions, why not stick out our jaws and get on with it, damning much of the world for its ignorant prejudice and its double standards?*

As was to be the case many times in coming months, those *instincts* were to play a crucial role at every stage of the stuttering progression towards Zimbabwe's freedom. Of course, in this instance, Carrington claimed to have persuaded the Prime Minister against her *instincts* – which he agreed had not changed. But did that persuasion go beyond non-recognition of Muzorewa? In any event, matters were not as singular as that; there were many other factors and players; and prominent among them was the Commonwealth: Commonwealth leaders in Capitals, Commonwealth representatives in London and, not least, the Commonwealth Secretariat.

* * *

My role at the Secretariat had been clear throughout. It was to ensure adherence to the 'six principles' which were by then the Commonwealth's credo on Rhodesia; and we needed to do more than advocacy. Hence, the Secretariat's rigorous professional analysis of the 'Zimbabwe-Rhodesia' Constitution, concluding:

> *Virtually every lever of institutional power has been retained in white hands; those few surrendered have been effectively emasculated ... the people at large are bequeathed a government bereft of the power to govern effectively, and a Legislature denuded of all means either to change the status quo, or to advance the legitimate aspirations of the nation as a whole ... Taken as a whole ... (the constitution) is revealed as a carefully woven, carefully contrived subterfuge for sustaining a wholly anti-democratic regime.*

That was my message to the Commonwealth: to the Heads of Commonwealth Governments, now including Mrs Thatcher – through the Commonwealth Committee on Southern Africa. This was the old Sanctions Committee renamed, and comprising all the Commonwealth High Commissioners in London, a representative of the British Government – usually a senior official of the Foreign and Commonwealth Office – and the Secretary-General. It was standing machinery for Commonwealth consultations on Southern Africa issues and a vital element of interaction. The Committee's verdict on 18

May was that the Secretariat's analysis justified their own conclusion that *"the elections could not, and indeed were not intended to, produce majority rule"*. With the British representative dissenting, the Committee added:

> *The present situation holds little prospect for an end to the mounting suffering and bloodshed in Rhodesia; indeed, recent developments may intensify the conflict. If an acceptable solution is to come to Zimbabwe through negotiations, it is self-evident that it must be by a process involving all parties to the conflict. To proceed on any other assumption is to accept the inevitability of a military solution alone – and one that could dangerously internationalise the conflict.*

In a quite unusual move, on May 23, a delegation of Commonwealth High Commissioners, including Australia and Canada, went with me to call on Lord Carrington to deliver directly the Commonwealth's concerns as expressed by the Committee on behalf of their Governments. Mrs Thatcher was left in no doubt of the views of her Commonwealth colleagues.

There were others who reinforced those Commonwealth concerns, including Cyrus Vance, President Carter's Secretary of State. And, beyond individual states, the UN Security Council (Britain, France and the United States abstaining), the Organisation of African Unity and the Colombo Summit of Non-Aligned countries all passed resolutions calling on states not to recognise the Muzorewa administration. No one did. Nearer home, Carrington's Labour predecessor, David Owen – speaking in Parliament – described 'recognition' and the lifting of sanctions as potentially *"an error as grave as Suez"*. All this occurred within weeks of Mrs Thatcher's election.

I called on the new Prime Minister at Downing Street on 18 June – before her visit to Australia. My first purpose was to fulfil protocol – a courtesy call on Mrs Thatcher after her sweeping victory. I had met her before as Leader of the Opposition; now I looked ahead to working with her as Britain's Prime Minister, knowing, of course, that her *instincts* on many issues, but especially on Southern African issues, would pose severe challenges for the Commonwealth. All the same, I told myself, my attitude had to be one of hope; the realities of office had traditionally, everywhere, exerted influences, sometimes pressures, that transformed opposition policies. I knew that her political instincts were those of the right wing of the Conservative Party and that theirs were antithetical to much for which the Commonwealth stood. Yet, I believed as we met that first time in Downing Street that principle and realism could prevail. Our meeting did not wholly dispel my optimism. I found Mrs Thatcher a good listener to well marshalled argument. I had heard that she had no time for waffling, still less for rhetoric; though she was not above dogmatism herself.

But my visit had a substantive purpose as well. Commonwealth Heads were due to meet in Lusaka, Zambia, in six weeks' time – on 1 August, and Rhodesia would be high on the agenda, given recent developments. I believed that, taken as a whole, events were moving towards the possibility of a negotiated settlement. First, of course, was the overwhelmingly negative response to the 'internal settlement' and recognition of the Muzorewa 'government'. Ian Smith's options were closing and the civil war, which is what the 'armed struggle' had developed into, was becoming intolerable to white Rhodesians; by the end of the year, 95 per cent of Rhodesia would be under martial law. Its burden on the front-line states was heavy; on Tanzania and Zambia especially. Nigeria's new militancy on the side of the nationalist forces and its particular hostility to Britain was a new factor. Three weeks after Mrs Thatcher's election, Nigeria, Britain's largest trading partner in Africa (on 24 May) rejected all British tenders for a £101,000,000 port project. It was said bluntly: *"Until the British Government clarifies its attitude (on Rhodesia) to black Africa the Nigerian Government is not prepared to entertain any new proposals from British companies"*. Nigeria was adding economic clout which the front-line states were unable to bring to bear on Britain. It had the attributes of a 'game changer'. Together, the case for ending the status quo in Rhodesia was strong on all sides.

I did not recite all this to Mrs Thatcher. I did not need to. I tried to address what I believe drove her instinct of hostility to the Patriotic Front. Since her election she had referred to the nationalist forces in Rhodesia as 'terrorists'; I urged her to see them instead as Britons saw the 'partisans' in Yugoslavia during the war – as 'freedom fighters'; they too were guerrilla fighters who came out of the bush; and their cause too was just. Her reply was swift: *"Of course they are terrorists; they are just like the IRA"*. I urged that most of the world, and more pertinently most of the Commonwealth, saw them differently and that emphasising the difference of image did not assist the dialogue of consensus which all of Rhodesia needed. I asked her not to refer to them as 'terrorists' in the interest of our finding a way forward. She did not promise to refrain; but I felt she understood the need not to provoke.

My essential concern was the upcoming Summit in Lusaka. I knew Mrs Thatcher was worried lest she was flying into a hornet's nest. I needed to dispel that anxiety and to ensure that I delivered on the promise. I had talked about this with both Julius Nyerere and Kenneth Kaunda and told them of the need to surprise Mrs Thatcher by their calm reason and by our orchestration of the agenda to ensure a dialogue devoid of recrimination. They had accepted my counsel and promised their co-operation. On that basis, I assured Mrs Thatcher that while her known views would not be shared; there would be no 'ganging-up' on her. I pleaded, however, that she needed to send a signal that whatever else they disagreed on she, like the rest of the Commonwealth, was committed to majority rule in Rhodesia. Let the argument be about how they got there. Mrs Thatcher responded with studied interest. She saw, I believe, the good sense of my suggestions, including my promise of a 'civilised' dialogue. From that point, it was a short step to thinking positively of the Summit's outcome.

I urged on her, of course, that all these prospects would be shattered by Britain's precipitate recognition of the Muzorewa 'government'. I avoided the 'free and fair' elections discussion and focussed instead on the deficiencies of the constitution under which they were held – recalling the Secretariat's analysis and the unanimity of all save Britain on the issue. Mrs Thatcher gave me no assurances; but I left Downing Street believing that her instincts were contending with her intellect.

But other forces were at work, intent on sabotaging Lusaka. The Prime Minister of New Zealand, Robert Muldoon, was beholden to his own backwoodsmen whose kin had settled in substantial numbers in Ian Smith's Rhodesia. His instincts were for recognition of Muzorewa and against any effort at Lusaka to quash the 'internal settlement'. On 11 June, on a visit to London, he publicly expressed concern for the safety of 'the 'Queen of New Zealand' were she to go to Lusaka for the Commonwealth Meeting. On her visit to Australia at the end of June Mrs Thatcher followed the same line; implying, moreover, that she could, and might, prevent the Queen from going to Lusaka. Writing about this in *Stitches in Time,* my predecessor Arnold Smith had this to say:

> *She (Mrs Thatcher) caused a further stir by speaking of the 'final advice' she would give to the Queen on whether it was safe for her to go visit Zambia around the time of the HGM, and implied that it would be negative advice. I was shocked at her ineptness. It was, after all, not the job of the British Prime Minister to advise the Head of the Commonwealth on this matter; it was the responsibility of Sonny Ramphal as Secretary-General or of all the Heads of Government collectively, for the Queen was planning to visit Lusaka as Head of the Commonwealth. In any case, the Palace did not wait for Mrs Thatcher to return to London and offer advice. The following day it issued a statement saying the Queen had 'every intention' of fulfilling her plans to visit Tanzania, Malawi, Botswana – and Zambia.*

I had, of course, already exercised my 'responsibility' to the Head of the Commonwealth, imparting to her the strategy of 'not ganging-up' which I had already agreed with Kaunda and Nyerere – who she would be seeing soon. The Queen needed no persuading. But I had gone further. On a pre-Conference visit to Lusaka I had met with Joshua Nkomo and persuaded him to offer unilaterally a suspension of cross-border activity of his fighters for seventeen days – the period of the Queen's tour of Africa – starting from the day before it began. I had first discussed the idea with Kaunda who agreed and was sure that Muzorewa would feel bound to do likewise. He was about to leave for Washington and London to press for 'recognition' and the lifting of sanctions; he simply could not allow himself to be seen as the party that posed a threat to the Queen and 39 other Commonwealth leaders. As we had contemplated, he felt bound to do likewise. In his statement Nkomo said:

> *We have great deference to the Commonwealth and the role it plays internationally for the benefit of our struggle. Consequently we will not engage in any activities at the Zambia-Rhodesia border as are likely to prove a pretext for the Rhodesian regime to undermine the Conference.*

This effective 'ceasefire' nailed another lie which the right-wing media in Britain had been spreading. On 13 June, London's *Daily Telegraph* reported that conference halls and hotels in Nairobi had been provisionally booked as an alternative venue. Fortunately, President Daniel Arap Moi of Kenya was on a State visit to Britain and his Foreign Minister, Dr Munyua Waiyaki, joined me in publicly denying that the Government of Kenya had taken any steps to prepare an alternative site. Such were the unseemly lengths to which UDI's friends in Britain went to frustrate Commonwealth efforts to bring peace and justice and freedom to Rhodesia. As the Commonwealth at every level overcame these jeopardies, I began to believe more strongly in the Commonwealth's prospects at Lusaka.

CHAPTER 19

Lusaka

In a practical sense, the Commonwealth's Summit meeting in 1979 at Lusaka started with the visit of the Queen. She had made State visits to Tanzania, Malawi and Botswana before arriving in Zambia. Everywhere, she had received a rapturous welcome from the people of the country. They were all Republics, but she was Head of the Commonwealth; and it was well known that there was distance between herself and Mrs Thatcher on African issues. They knew that Mrs Thatcher had not wanted her to come to Lusaka; they saw her presence as a good omen. She was not a campaigner on these issues before the Conference; but where Mrs Thatcher was seen as a 'spoiler' at the Commonwealth party; the Queen was seen as bringing to it a healing touch. The day she arrived in Lusaka, a great crowd turned out to welcome her, and the local newspaper assured her that she was "the most welcome British visitor".

And that message of healing was one she would have brought to her hosts everywhere – especially Julius Nyerere in Tanzania whom she had known for seventeen years and who would play a crucial role at the Meeting. Well before Mrs Thatcher reached Lusaka, the Queen had ensured that the Commonwealth Summit would commence in a spirit that was positive to progress on the Rhodesia issue. Her presence explained why the 'Rhodesia lobby' in London did not want her to come; did not want 'Lusaka' to take place – and why I did.

Mrs Thatcher arrived close to midnight the day before the Conference opened – and uncharacteristically, in dark glasses. Despite the hour, the world's press was on hand, and inevitably, an impromptu press conference ensued – of which she later complained; but handled with her accustomed skill. She would have heard how jubilant was the Queen's reception; she knew how modest was her own. I believe she was determined not to be outdone. She had travelled with her Foreign and Commonwealth Secretary, Lord Carrington, but from the moment of her arrival she made it clear that she was in charge – a fact that was to be of great value. Her account of the journey from London, in her own words in *The Downing Street Years,* makes fascinating reading:

> *We had put the long flight out to good use, working through the precise approach we should take. I had a first-class team of advisers, and, of course, a first-class Foreign Secretary – with whom I had a lively exchange when he suggested that our mission was really a 'damage limitation exercise', at that time (as I told him) a phrase I had never even heard. I said that I wanted to do better than that; and between us in the end we managed to do so.*

'A damage limitation exercise'. That was how Lord Carrington saw the Lusaka HGM as he flew out from London – the 'damage' from disagreement – but hopefully with no bones broken. It was a wholly negative view; and one which Mrs Thatcher could not share. She had come to Lusaka having weighed all the factors. Her intellect had won the contest with her instincts and not even her Foreign and Commonwealth Secretary could deflect her now from being positive. Her role at the Lusaka Summit would be to work for agreement. She could be forced back to her instincts; but avoidance of that would depend on the good sense of her colleagues and on good conference management – the latter, my personal responsibility.

I knew that Kaunda and Nyerere would be faithful to the strategy we had worked out; and I now had a notable ally in the Prime Minister of Australia, Malcolm Fraser. He was politically close to

Mrs Thatcher; they both led Conservative Parties; but he did not carry the racial biases of his right wing. And while he was in the camp of the West in a 'Cold War' context; he was not a 'Cold Warrior'. At an early stage he had taken an enlightened view of the futility of the 'internal settlement', and had actually urged Mrs Thatcher soon after her election against 'recognition' of Muzorewa. He had done the same thing to the new Canadian (Conservative Party) Prime Minister, Joe Clarke. He visited Nigeria en route to Zambia to talk with General Olusegun Obasanjo, the President of Nigeria. He was closely in touch with Michael Manley of Jamaica. A visit by Fraser's Foreign Minister, Andrew Peacock, to Tanzania on his way to Lusaka had confirmed how much the Queen's earlier visit had done to create a mellowing of feelings toward Britain on the eve of the Lusaka HGM.

Working with Malcolm Fraser was not new. I had already worked harmoniously with him in 1977 in securing the Gleneagles Agreement against sporting links with apartheid South Africa during the London Commonwealth Summit. The chemistry was good between us – which surprised Australians who knew him at home as a bit of a snob. Many a time I was asked by Australians: *How on earth do you get on so well with this man?* The fact is I did; over a long time, he was a great Commonwealth leader. I told him of my strategy of not ganging-up on Mrs Thatcher and my promise to her that it would not happen. I told him I had 'Julius' and 'Kenneth' on board and would brief 'Michael' when he arrived. I then asked him to set the tone for agreement at Lusaka by being the first Prime Minister to speak at the formal Opening Ceremony. He agreed.

I then outlined to Fraser, what I had already agreed with Kenneth Kaunda as Chairman, namely, that though the Conference would start on Wednesday, we would hold back the item on Rhodesia ('Southern Africa') until Friday and then ensure that it was only a brief session, with only Nyerere and Thatcher and a few others speaking, before adjourning the discussion for the following Monday. The idea would be to allow for private consultations at the informal retreat over the weekend so that when the debate resumed on Monday, progress would have been made. My very private hope was that it would never need to be resumed.

This would be achieved by inviting all Heads to an outing on Saturday to Victoria Falls, one of the seven natural wonders of the world which could be accessed through Livingstone in Zambia. It was an opportunity not to be missed. Very quietly, however, a handful of Heads would be asked to miss the opportunity, to stay back in Lusaka – a handful that I believed could find a way forward if the environment was right. That environment, I hoped, would have been created by the speeches at the Opening Ceremony and the Nyerere/ Thatcher openers of the short debate on Friday – and, of course, by the presence of the Queen in Lusaka (though not at the Summit itself) and the atmosphere of goodwill already generated by her African tour. The select group would be invited to a private discussion on Saturday, in President Kaunda's study at State House, to explore the possibilities of Commonwealth agreement on the Rhodesia issue.

Those to be invited would be Malcolm Fraser (Australia), Margaret Thatcher and Lord Carrington (Britain), Michael Manley (Jamaica), Maj. Gen. Henry Edmund Olufemi Adefope (Nigeria) Julius Nyerere (Tanzania), President Kaunda and his Personal Assistant Mark Chona and myself. Adefope was the Nigerian Foreign Minister (Obasanjo did not come). Because it was important that Mrs Thatcher did not feel insecure – and because it was prudent anyway to have him there in the light of roles he might have to play thereafter – I told Mrs Thatcher that Lord Carrington would be welcome. Only Fraser, Thatcher, Nyerere, and Chairman Kaunda knew the full procedural game plan when the Conference began at Mulungushi Hall on Wednesday, August 1.

But, before it did, there was the important social side to the Conference: The photograph of Mrs Thatcher dancing with President Kaunda – both smiling and relaxed in each other's company at his State House Dinner, told a story of what each wished the Conference to be like; and the occasion helped to make it so. It was a photograph that came to be a lasting memento of Lusaka.

I was no stranger to Mulungushi Hall. It had been built ten years earlier as Zambia hosted the Non-Aligned Summit in 1970 – the Summit at which Guyana had occupied the position of Rapporteur. I had persuaded President Kaunda that the Commonwealth should occupy a smaller room than the Grand Hall for its substantive meetings, though the Opening Ceremony would be held there. And so it was; the idea being to make the Commonwealth meeting as intimate as feasible.

After initial welcoming remarks by President Kaunda and myself, there were three opening speeches in reply by Prime Ministers Fraser and Thatcher and in between them by the President of Bangladesh, Ziaur Rahman. In my own remarks, I stressed the Commonwealth's significance, both generally and in the special context of Southern Africa:

> *Had our founding fathers not developed the Commonwealth in the late 40s and 50s we would now be searching for ways of*

creating some such mechanism in response to the needs of the 80s and beyond. To care for the Commonwealth, therefore, is not just a duty we owe to ourselves; it is a trust we are now impressed with on behalf of a much wider human society – as every month I have confirmed to me by leaders of that society outside our membership...

It must be history's mandate and a more personal challenge that as a result of our work in Lusaka no shadow shall hereafter fall between the conception and the reality of Zimbabwe's freedom. It is a task of fulfilment that will tax all your talents and your will. You will have to be assiduous in the pursuit of principle and unyielding in your accommodation to its supremacy...

I am certain, for example, that despite conflicting interpretations of the quality of events between our Meeting in London in 1977 and your consultations here, if the Commonwealth remains faithful to the principles which have guided its collective responses to the situation in Southern Africa over the years, you cannot fail to move closer to the goal of Zimbabwe's true independence.

I wanted to make it clear that this was the Commonwealth's moment to undo the wrongs that history had allowed to remain unrequited for so long.

Malcolm Fraser was the first Prime Minister to reply – and his speech was all I expected it to be. He said, with particular reference to Rhodesia:

First, it is vital that we recognise and build on the substantial areas of agreement which exist among us on this issue, that we not be dominated by negative aspects. No one at this meeting believes that a settlement is compatible with a constitutional situation in Salisbury which is tainted in any way with racialism. We are all in favour of majority rule – true majority rule which takes account of all the parties concerned and which is reflected not only in elections but in the underlying structure of power and authority. No one wants a solution through slaughter and bloodshed, both because it will produce untold suffering to innocent people and because it will breed new hatreds. Everyone wants to see outside interference in the Region diminish, not grow. No one wants to see the Commonwealth damaged. It is imperative that as we enter the thickets of technicalities and controversies, we do not allow them to obscure these basic points. Formidable as the differences on some issues are, I believe that, as far as those of us present at this meeting are concerned, they are differences about means and timing, not about ends. We must not allow means to dominate ends.

Malcolm Fraser had erected the stage on which Mrs Thatcher could show that she was not "dominated by negative aspects"; was not in Lusaka for "damage limitation". In her closing remarks she said:

Now, Mr President, there is the problem of Southern Africa to which you and our other colleagues have referred. We are all conscious of the ever more urgent need for a settlement of the Rhodesia problem. My colleagues and I have greatly benefited from the consultations we have been pursuing within the Commonwealth and with other African Governments. I am grateful to all those who have given us their advice and have expressed their views so clearly. I shall listen with the greatest attention to what is said at this meeting in Lusaka. The UK has pledged to exercise its constitutional responsibility for Rhodesia. The aim is to bring Rhodesia to legal independence on a basis which the Commonwealth and the international community as a whole will find acceptable and which offers the prospect of peace for the people of Rhodesia and her neighbours. As I said in the House of Commons last week, the British Government are wholly committed to genuine black majority rule in Rhodesia.

When she ended there was general acclamation led, prominently, by Nyerere. There was a sense among all present that the Conference was off to a promising start.

A report in the London Sunday Observer of 5 August by Colin Legum and others headlined *"The gentling of Margaret Thatcher"* gave credit for the 'gentling' detected in her speech to Lord Carrington and the Foreign Office:

> *The voice was Mrs Thatcher's but the guiding hand was unmistakably that of Lord Carrington. For months a debate had been going on in a secret Cabinet Committee which deals with problems of Rhodesia. In these debates, Carrington has, with patience and with skill, managed to bring Mrs Thatcher around to the Foreign Office point of view.*
>
> *He argued that if the British Government recognised Bishop Muzorewa, it would hardly have any support from the rest of the world community. It would, therefore not have much to offer Rhodesians since there would be very little it could in fact do on its own to help Muzorewa.*
>
> *In contrast, going for a settlement that would stand some chance of gaining wider international support would do far more to salvage the Muzorewa regime – and the white Rhodesians. (Someone who has closely watched the debate commented: "It is not so much that they disagree about policy matters: it is their instincts that are different').*

Was the end game, then, to 'salvage the Muzorewa regime and help the white Rhodesians'? That is not how it was understood by the Conservative right in London. The same day's *Sunday Telegraph* had headlines: "Tory dismay over 'sell-out' on Rhodesia' – Carrington and Foreign Office overrule Mrs Thatcher". Former Foreign Office Minister Julian Amery (whose father L.S. Amery had opposed the 1949 formula that made the modern Commonwealth possible) was characteristically critical of Mrs Thatcher. He had led the 116 Tory MPs who had voted against the renewal of sanctions against Rhodesia in 1978:

> *It is unfortunate that Mrs Thatcher said the Rhodesian constitution was defective and had weak-points. When you are talking in the presence of leaders of one-party states and military dictators, that is not quite the moment to criticise what is the most democratic constitution in Africa... I am deeply worried by the implication that the so-called Patriotic Front leaders might be involved in Rhodesia's future. It would give these terrorists the same veto they had under the Owen-Vance proposals.*

It took the *News of the World* to salvage sanity:

> *Britain is now paying the final price for the failure of successive Governments to put down the Smith rebellion. What two London bobbies could have put right on UDI Day way back in 1965, not all the Queen's horses nor all the Queen's men can do in 1979. Indeed, if we are foolish enough even to end sanctions too soon, we shall find every man's hand against us.*

The public Opening Ceremony was all I could have wished. It was specially important on this first business occasion, with all the world's media on hand, that Mrs Thatcher (as I had promised) was treated with courtesy, and not backed into a corner. In return she had significantly advanced the prospect of consensus. The stage was set for the private debate on Friday morning. As planned, Julius Nyerere opened the discussion on Rhodesia. As if himself setting the tone for a discussion among friends, Kaunda referred to Nyerere as the *doyen* of Commonwealth Heads – an accolade Nyerere declined in favour of Dr Eric Williams the Prime Minister of Trinidad and Tobago who was not there. Then Kaunda called on Nyerere introducing him as *Mwalimu* (Swahili for 'teacher') and saying *"Mwalimu, give us some lessons"*. Julius Nyerere was a mild mannered man with simple but penetrating eloquence and he was at his controlled best as he began what was to be the last plenary discussion at a Commonwealth Summit of Rhodesia and UDI. His remarks were a model of calm reasoning and quiet conciliation. He avoided history and histrionics. He started with a call for the necessary constitutional conference to establish 'majority rule' saying:

> *Britain had the responsibility, the experience and, he hoped, the political will to produce such a constitution and to put it to an all-parties constitutional conference. The Commonwealth might also have some local knowledge or other special qualifications to help in that exercise.*

Everyone knew that a constitutional conference would be necessary to return Rhodesia to legality; but this was the first articulate call for it. Nyerere looked to the opportunity which the present offered and presented his conditions in simple terms: a new democratic constitution, even including reserved seats for minorities, and internationally supervised elections. Against his delegation's advice, he was prepared to have a re-settlement fund for whites who chose to leave rather than stay under an African government. Nyerere stressed that it was on these three points and especially on the first two, that he hoped a Commonwealth consensus for action could be obtained. He had been encouraged, he said, by Mrs Thatcher's statement at the Opening Session that the British Government was wholly committed to genuine black majority rule in Rhodesia, and that its aim was to bring Rhodesia to legal independence on a basis which the Commonwealth and the international community as a whole would find acceptable. He was looking forward to a more specific statement of the British Government's proposals and plans. As if answering Mrs Thatcher's earlier talk of 'terrorists', Nyerere said that it was necessary to remember that *"those who were fighting for the liberation of their country were doing so not because they preferred the bullet but because the ballot was denied them"*. He concluded by saying, without threat, that *"the Commonwealth itself might be jeopardised if it failed to act immediately to bring justice to the people of Zimbabwe"*.

President Moi followed, and then Mrs Thatcher spoke. She too was calm and without recrimination or dogmatism. She stressed the recent changes in Rhodesia and said it was the British Government's view that the opportunity created by them should be exploited to see if the solution, for so long elusive, could now be found. She said her Government had consulted widely in the Commonwealth and internationally and certain 'common factors' had clearly emerged. These 'common factors', she seemed to be explaining to her Party at home, left Britain no other course. *"The first and most fundamental was the view that the constitution under which Bishop Muzorewa had come to power was defective in certain important respects"*. That put to rest the issue of 'recognition', and opened the way to consideration of alternatives of achieving 'genuine black majority rule' which she reaffirmed as her goal. But there was more:

- *it was Britain's constitutional responsibility to grant legal independence on that basis, and that only Britain could do it;*
- *the objective must be to establish that independence on the basis of a constitution comparable with the constitutions which Britain had agreed with other countries;*
- *Britain was deeply conscious of the urgent need to bring peace to the people of Rhodesia and the neighbouring countries.*
- *Britain's aim was to bring Rhodesia to legal independence on a basis which the Commonwealth and the international community as a whole would find acceptable.*

Mrs Thatcher ended: *"There was now a chance to achieve that, and it must be taken"*.

There was a sense in Mulungushi Hall that the debate was over. Certainly, the Chairman and I believed that further discussion could not improve on what had been said by Nyerere and Thatcher. Certainly, there was more to resolve: Nyerere's call for an all-party constitutional conference; what part would the Commonwealth and the UN play; would the elections be internationally supervised? And more; But we needed to hold on to that moment of accord the like of which the

Commonwealth had not known in 19 years since UDI. And we were right. In the eight short interventions that followed, the contribution by the Foreign Minister of Nigeria almost broke the mould of unity introducing scepticism about Mrs Thatcher's speech: "Nothing had moved an inch", he said; and threatening that Nigeria would have to reconsider belonging to the Commonwealth if the Conference was a failure. He seemed to have fashioned his remarks before Mrs Thatcher had spoken.

Sir Dawda Jawara of the Gambia restored the mood. *"In his view the atmosphere of the present discussion over the Rhodesia issue, which had been with the Commonwealth for so long, had been calmer, more realistic and more objective than he had witnessed before... the atmosphere augured well for the Meeting reaching decisions which would have a positive effect on the situation in Zimbabwe."* He ended saying: *"he had no doubt that after their private discussions at the weekend Commonwealth leaders would be able to see some light, leading to a fairly early solution of that crucial issue"*

On that note, the Chairman closed the discussion and adjourned the Plenary until the afternoon when Heads would discuss the issue of 'Island developing and other specially disadvantaged states'. They would resume discussion on Rhodesia on Monday morning. The debate had begun at 9.45 and ended at 1.10 – three hours and twenty-five minutes. So far, it had been the shortest discussion on Rhodesia at a Commonwealth Summit. So far, the Conference strategy had worked; but the crunch dimension lay ahead.

That Friday night in my Mulugushi Village dwelling I sat alone with the transcripts of the speeches Julius Nyerere and Margaret Thatcher had made that morning. The New Zealand Prime Minister Robert Muldoon had put into words what all who listened to them must have felt: "*... their views overlapped to such a great extent that there seemed a very real chance of achieving a positive result by the end of the Meeting."* The next step must surely be to identify the areas of overlap and give then the shape of an overall agreement – and that I felt must be my immediate task. The following morning our group would meet in the Chairman's small book-lined study. I had to have ready by then draft 'heads of accord' based on those areas of overlap. And so I did: nine short sentences; nine points of light to guide the discussion. I had them typed up on half sheets that I could pass around at the appropriate moment. It was a strategy I had long followed. As a legal draftsman in my early career, it was a practice that came naturally to me; and I found that the first piece of paper on the table – once it genuinely captured an emerging consensus – was likely to frame the conclusion: as it had done at the last Commonwealth Summit with the Gleneagles Agreement on Sporting Contacts with South Africa.

* * *

Saturday dawned with safari weather, and all the Heads and Ministers, save those who had been asked to stay back, left for Livingstone and Victoria Falls. At around 10.30 our 'stay-back' Group assembled at State House and were ushered into the President's study by Mark Chona, the President's Assistant – who was in many ways his personal Policy Adviser. I was there joined shortly by Kenneth Kaunda and Julius Nyerere, Malcolm Fraser and Michael Manley, Margaret Thatcher and Lord Carrington, and Nigeria's Olufemi Adefope – a group of eight. There was no round table; the study was too small for that. Chairs were pulled around a small coffee table and seating was informal. I made sure I was next to Kaunda.

He welcomed us all to his little office, and promised to make up for our not going to Livingstone today. Then he reminded us all how close the Commonwealth had come in Friday's plenary session to agreeing on the way forward in Zimbabwe. Between Julius who had spoken for the 'front-line states' and Margaret, 'his dancing partner', the Commonwealth had accomplished more in three hours than in nearly twenty years of often bitter argument. He said we needed to pull the threads of consensus together into a working plan in which the world could believe. That credibility was particularly important for the parties in Zimbabwe of whose destinies we had become trustees.

From there on, the discussion flowed. Malcolm Fraser and Michael Manley who had not spoken in the Meeting were prominent in their support of the combined Nyerere-Thatcher approach and both welcomed Nyerere's proposal for an all-party Constitutional Conference convened by Britain to give effect to the principles both he and Margaret Thatcher had laid out and supported. Mrs Thatcher and Nyerere spoke along the lines of their plenary remarks with Mrs Thatcher confirming Britain's willingness to invite all parties to a Constitutional Conference.

At this point I Indicated how I had spent the previous night pulling together the points that had been made in the Plenary by President Nyerere and Mrs Thatcher in particular, into heads of agreement on the way forward – using in most places their exact words. I said I had made copies for this informal meeting and would pass them around in the hope that they might help the process of developing a concrete plan. I did so; and after everyone had had a chance of reading my nine points the Chairman thanked me, saying he believed I had captured the essence of the emerging consensus and suggested that the draft might form the basis of our continuing discussion. The group agreed, and eventually, with very little change, they were to emerge as paragraph 15 of the Communiqué of the Lusaka Meeting – which was as follows:

Heads of Government
(a) confirmed that they were wholly committed to genuine black majority rule for the people of Zimbabwe;
(b) recognised, in this context, that the internal settlement constitution is defective in certain important respects;
(c) fully accepted that it is the constitutional responsibility of the British Government to grant legal independence to Zimbabwe on the basis of majority rule;
(d) recognised that the search for a lasting settlement must involve all parties to the conflict;
(e) were deeply conscious of the urgent need to achieve such a settlement and bring peace to the people of Zimbabwe and their neighbours;

(f) accepted that independence on the basis of majority rule requires the adoption of a democratic constitution including appropriate safeguards for minorities;
(g) acknowledged that the government formed under such an independence constitution must be chosen through free and fair elections properly supervised under British Government authority, and with Commonwealth observers;
(h) welcomed the British Government's indication that an appropriate procedure for advancing towards these objectives would be for them to call a constitutional conference to which all the parties would be invited; and
(i) consequently, accepted that it must be a major objective to bring about a cessation of hostilities and an end to sanctions as part of the process of implementation of a lasting settlement.

I said the nine points had emerged with very little change. That is so; but the changes were important and were all at Britain's suggestion. The first related to (g) concerning 'elections'. Following the lines of the plenary discussion, my draft had contemplated elections under international supervision. Lord Carrington made it a matter of principle that the UN must have no role. If Britain returned Rhodesia to legality, the British Government alone must conduct the pre-independence elections. The strength of his insistence caused some misgiving, and produced insistence from others that there had at least to be a role for the Commonwealth. The result was as in the final paragraph (g) *"free and fair elections properly supervised under British Government authority and with Commonwealth observers"*. As regards paragraph (h), it was a matter of great moment to Carrington that the idea of a constitutional Conference emanated from Britain and was welcomed by the Commonwealth. It was of course the other way round; but others realised it might have more to do with Tory Party politics and were happy to help Mrs Thatcher if this did. Hence the form of paragraph (h). The same was true of the reference to *"an end to sanctions as part of the process of implementation of a lasting settlement"* which Britain wanted added in paragraph (i).

I was asked to tidy up the draft with Sir Anthony Duff, a good friend from the Foreign and Commonwealth Office on Mrs Thatcher's delegation, and Mark Chona, and have it cleared after lunch with the Group. We did both without difficulty. The idea then was that the Secretariat would have copies ready for distribution at the resumption of the Plenary on Monday morning when the Chairman would explain the discussions over the weekend and invite all his colleagues to adopt the draft paragraphs (which became known as 'the Lusaka Accord') as the Commonwealth's consensus on Rhodesia. That consensus on change – after fourteen years of an illegal racist regime in Rhodesia, after years of United Nations and Commonwealth sanctions, after the escalation of war that touched not only the country itself, but also the neighbouring countries of Zambia, Tanzania and Mozambique, after threats to the stability of the Commonwealth itself – was a monumental achievement for the Commonwealth. It was an achievement to which many contributed, like the nationalist movements that bore the brunt of the struggle, like the Presidents of the front-line states who never relented in their contentions and their sacrifices, like Mrs Thatcher at the end game. But it was the Commonwealth that made the consummation of change possible when it came.

President Kaunda had laid on a modest buffet lunch on the spacious lawns at the rear of State House for those he had led to that historic consensus in his study. As they strolled though his Residence and out to the lawns, each with his own thoughts, I walked with Mrs Thatcher and I congratulated her on the political wisdom and courage that had made our consensus possible. She thanked me, then said reflectively: *"You realise, of course, that we have given it to the communist." "He is a nationalist mainly"*, I said, *"it is that which will be dominant"*. We were talking, of course, about Robert Mugabe.

The time between Saturday afternoon and Monday morning seemed like free time. The fixed events were a Church Service on Sunday afternoon in the Anglican Cathedral in Lusaka and a barbecue dinner on the grounds of the Residence of the Australian High Commissioner in Lusaka, hosted by Malcolm Fraser. At the Cathedral, Mrs Thatcher was due to read the Second Lesson and I the First. I sat on her right in the same pew. We both endured a wholly inappropriate and lengthy rant from the Archbishop who had clearly not been briefed by Kaunda that peace had broken out over Rhodesia. I duly read the First Lesson and on returning to the pew Mrs Thatcher passed me a note given her by an aide from the pew behind. It was an urgent message to her from Lord Carrington. We had a crisis!

I already knew what had gone wrong. Although the 9-point Agreement was to be kept secret until shared with all the Heads and endorsed by them on Monday morning, there had been a leak on Sunday afternoon just before the Church Service. Carrington reached me as I was leaving for the Cathedral. He was furious: *"The whole thing is off"*, he said*, "it's been leaked to the press, and we're in deep trouble. We can't live with this."* I told him I was leaving for the Cathedral but would have Secretariat officials look into it immediately and would call him as soon as I got back. At the time, I thought he was suggesting a leak by the Secretariat; and his words "the whole thing is off" troubled me. I felt sure the Secretariat had not leaked the agreement; but whoever did, there were surely ways of not jeopardising the great Commonwealth achievement with all it meant for all Rhodesians. But Carrington was not thinking of the Commonwealth or of Rhodesians. He was thinking of the Tory Party, Mrs Thatcher and himself. He had led her through a U-turn on Rhodesia and needed time to prepare the Party for it and head off the inevitable storm from the right wing. I felt his reaction was too strong. However the note to Mrs Thatcher in the Cathedral was worse.

It was to this effect: 'I am quite satisfied that the Australians gave it to press. My advice is that it's off. We have to release it as a draft which has emerged and will be considered, and we have no position on it'. I was horrified. First, that his advice amounted to abandonment of all that had been achieved; next, at how ready he was to settle for that. While Mrs Thatcher was reading her Lesson I hastily scribbled a response to her on the back of my Order of Service in these words:

> *Prime Minister, I think it would be better, in deference to the Heads outside the negotiating group, to hold a brief meeting of*

> *Heads at Malcolm's villa shortly after they arrive at 7 pm. We can then explain (with the texts before them) what has happened – seek their concurrence on the text – and secure their permission for immediate release.*
>
> *We can then get it out – as an already agreed text – before any further press briefings by leaders. Briefing on a 'draft' is a recipe for disaster; it will risk a reopening of the text on the basis of the explanations given. Perhaps we can have a private word with 'KK' before we leave here.*

Mrs Thatcher was in immediate accord. In *The Downing Street Years* she records of my *"alternative suggestion": "This seemed to me an excellent idea"*. Both she and I contacted Kaunda immediately after the Service, told him what had happened, and how we proposed to handle it that night at Malcolm Fraser's barbecue. He would have a role for which I would brief him fully. Margaret Thatcher was furious with Fraser and would only attend the barbecue for the new 'business' part of it.

It transpired that Malcolm Fraser, thinking of Australian deadlines, did break the rules in giving the Australian media on Sunday an advance briefing of the Saturday agreement – unaware that his briefing had been infiltrated by several members of the British press. In his memoirs, Lord Carrington says simply of the episode: "there were some difficulties, but they passed." This was not just English understatement; it did less than justice to Mrs Thatcher. What he might have acknowledged was that when the crunch came to save the 'Lusaka Accord' or let it die on the altar of British politics, it was Mrs Thatcher's nerve that held.

By the time for Fraser's barbecue, word was already around Mulungushi that he was in the hot seat with Thatcher, and no one enjoyed this more than Robert Muldoon of New Zealand. I had agreed with Kaunda that at the start of the evening the Secretariat would gather Heads alone in the dining room of the residence and give them there a copy of the nine points of agreement. He would then address them, narrating what had happened but calling no names and explaining the resulting need for release of the agreement immediately – providing, of course, they shared the agreement which had been reached. He did so, and then went on to commend the agreement, and specifically commend the British Prime Minister.

I had privately briefed Sir Dawda Jawara as one of the most senior Heads there to lead the responses to the Chairman, congratulating the negotiating group and proposing that the agreement be accepted by acclamation. He did so; but Muldoon intervened saying that while he agreed with Sir Dawda, he wanted to know how such a leak as the Chairman explained could have occurred. Was it known who was responsible? Of course, by then, everyone knew. President Kaunda in his best pastoral manner deflected the Muldoon inquiry, thanked Sir Dawda and invited his colleagues to adopt the agreement unanimously. There will be stressful days ahead, he said, for the Commonwealth and for all parties; it was important that the Commonwealth's accord at Lusaka, which would be the foundation stone on which the future of Zimbabwe would be built, should have unanimous support. He received it by acclamation. Mrs Thatcher left the party. It was not to be her last discord with Malcolm Fraser.

On Monday morning on the resumed item on Rhodesia the Chairman in a few words stated what had transpired over the weekend, including agreement of all Heads on the conclusions of the negotiating group that had worked on Saturday. *"It was, he believed, a victory for the highest traditions of the Commonwealth and a chance for peace with justice In Zimbabwe"*. In view of the agreement reached, he proposed that there be no further debate on the Agenda item. It had been the shortest and least acrimonious debate on Rhodesia in the long history of Commonwealth Summits. I felt I had delivered on my promise to Mrs Thatcher in London weeks before. In her final press conference in Lusaka she described me as "a superb Commonwealth Secretary-General"; perhaps she had recalled the promise too.

The Meeting had not talked directly about Robert Mugabe or Joshua Nkomo, or Ian Smith, or for that matter Abel Muzorewa; but there was awareness throughout that the Commonwealth's conclusions on how to proceed was bound up with these players; and that the processes the consensus contemplated would require not only their involvement, but also their co-operation. The British were conscious of the need for getting Salisbury (both Ian Smith and his military Commander Lieutenant-General Peter Walls) on board. The front-line Presidents were mindful that they had made agreements which assumed the concurrence of the Patriotic Front. Their co-option could not be assumed – any more than Smith's. But that was now their respective tasks; and all knew that success could not be taken for granted. The *realpolitik* of the situation dictated, however, that co-option would be accomplished. It was; but not without reminders that no one had consulted the principal parties before signing off. The answer was that, so far as Rhodesia was concerned, the Commonwealth Conference in Lusaka was in the main a conference about a conference – one in which the parties alone would be in the ring – with rules agreed in Lusaka to guide them – and with Britain as the ring-master. The Commonwealth at Lusaka made possible the Lancaster House Conference on Zimbabwe's independence.

CHAPTER 20

Lancaster House

Queen Victoria, on a visit from Buckingham Palace, is said to have commented to the Duchess of Sutherland as she entered what we today call Lancaster House: *"I have come from my House to your Palace"*. Concerning what was once rated the most valuable private house in London, the comment was not hyperbolic. The dramatic sweep of its great staircase – down a banister of which Prime Minister Pierre Trudeau could not resist riding in 1969 – is as magnificent as any in the world. It belongs today to the nation, and has played a prominent part in the evolution from Empire as successive independence Conferences have been held under its glittering chandeliers. It is here that the 'Commonwealth' Constitutional Conference on Rhodesia was held – five weeks after the Lusaka Summit from 10 September to 15 December 1979.

I am deliberately provocative in describing it as the 'Commonwealth' Conference; because nowhere has it been so described by the British Government whose policy from the moment of return from the Lusaka Heads of Government meeting – besides claiming its success a historic triumph for Mrs Thatcher and Lord Carrington – was to expunge the Commonwealth and all things pertaining to it from the aftermath of that success, including the follow up Conference that was held in Lancaster House. In his memoir, *Reflect on Things Past,* Lord Carrington went further in usurping credit.

> *The Lancaster House Conference which followed was attributed by some to a 'Commonwealth initiative' in which Britain reluctantly concurred. That was nonsense. Margaret Thatcher and I arrived at Lusaka with perfectly clear intentions of what we wanted to achieve. We knew what we wanted and we got it.*

The classic description of 'diplomacy' is: "The art of letting others have your way" – to which I add "and take credit for it". The diplomatic triumph at Lusaka was the Commonwealth's. Thatcher and Carrington 'taking credit for it' was part of the diplomatic success. So erasure of the Commonwealth was a continuing strategy. In the same memoir Carrington wrote:

> *As ever, the most trying occasions generally took place out of the conference room. I remember having to keep Sonny Ramphal, Secretary-General of the Commonwealth, from interfering. Having been present at the Lusaka conference, he thought, no doubt with the best of intentions, that he could help and had the right to try. He was mistaken, and I spent some time persuading him of the fact: totally committed to the Patriotic Front, he had no credibility as an impartial observer.*

What Lord Carrington describes as 'interfering' is the epithet most Secretaries-General (not only of the Commonwealth) must endure for being dutiful to the higher values of their organisations, when national policy threatens them. To that extent, rejection is an occupational hazard and 'interfering' a badge of honour. What a Secretary-General must not do, is bend to that national pressure – particularly when the great majority of his member states look to him to hold the line. If what Lord Carrington suggests is that I was persuaded to the contrary, history manifestly refutes it. What he describes as my being 'totally committed to the Patriotic Front' was my total commitment – and that of the rest of the Commonwealth, as we shall see – to his not bullying the Patriotic Front, the one delegation without conventional advisers. I threw the full weight of the Commonwealth Secretariat, alongside the High Commissioners of Commonwealth countries in London, behind the Patriotic Front – and I am proud that I did so. It provided one of the Commonwealth's more glorious moments – made possible, I must emphasise, by those same Heads of Government who at the Lusaka Summit had mandated the Lancaster House Conference.

There had long been a 'Sanctions Committee' of the Commonwealth which, as its mandate enlarged, became the 'Commonwealth Committee on Southern Africa' (CCSA). It was a Committee of Commonwealth High Commissioners in London and a representative of the British Government, usually a Senior member of the Foreign and Commonwealth Office, and the Secretary General. It was a high-level body, which met in Marlborough House and was serviced by the Secretariat. By convention, the Chairman was not from an African country. From the Lusaka Summit in 1979 until 1990, the CCSA held 14 formal meetings and 24 informal ones. We had some great Chairmen: Eustace Seignoret, High Commissioner for Trinidad and Tobago; Cedric Joseph, High Commissioner for Guyana; (the late) Alfred Parsons High Commissioner for Australia; and Roy McMurtry High Commissioner for Canada.

The CCSA continued to meet during the Lancaster House Conference; but less frequently, since under pressure from Commonwealth High Commissioners to be kept in the picture the British Government agreed that 'the Commonwealth would be regularly briefed on progress at the Conference by a member of the Chairman's staff' meeting at the Secretariat with Commonwealth High Commissioners. This was a major dent in the British policy of side-lining the Commonwealth, particularly since it was specifically understood that the briefings *"on how the Conference is going ... would also, of course, give High Commissioners the opportunity to make any points they wished to make."* The meetings were described as 'Briefing Sessions' and became the essential unofficial channel of communication between the Commonwealth and the Conference. I moderated the Sessions, which came to play an important role in the overall conference process. From September to December, thirty-two briefing-sessions were held. In all this, as in much else, I was greatly helped by my Deputy responsible for Political and Administrative Affairs, Chief Emeka Anyaoku of Nigeria, who was to later succeed me as Secretary-General. The Commonwealth was not in Lancaster House; but the briefing Sessions two doors away in Marlborough House resonated in the Conference and contributed in important respects to the Lancaster House outcome.

From the Chairman's point of view, the Conference was all about tactics. The Conference opened on 10 September. Just over a week earlier (on 31 August) Peter Carrington sent Margaret Thatcher a note on 'tactics' (now declassified) which makes interesting reading, for example:

> *Our task at the Constitutional Conference must be to demonstrate clearly that we are making a determined effort to achieve a fair settlement. The chances that the Patriotic Front will be prepared to accept reasonable constitutional proposals and agree to participate in new elections are slight...*
>
> *We must not however so proceed as to give rise to accusations that this was our objective from the outset. We should seek to ensure that, if there is a breakdown at the Conference, the responsibility for this is clearly seen to rest with the Patriotic Front and their intransigence on the basic issues – their demands in relation to the constitution and the arrangements for elections. We should proceed in such a way as to put maximum strain on Commonwealth Government's support for the Patriotic Front; and on relations between Nkomo and Mugabe...*
>
> *The proposal that 20 per cent of the parliamentary seats should be reserved to the white electorate will be criticised in Africa but is indispensable to retain the confidence of the white community. These proposals are likely to be rejected by the Patriotic Front (if they have not already broken off the negotiations on other issues)...*

> *We should in any event seek to avoid bringing matters to a point at which we proceed with Muzorewa alone until the civilian government has been established in Lagos on 1 October.*
>
> *We should in the meantime proceed with our bilateral negotiations with the Salisbury parties to establish the kind of Constitution we could in the end accept...*
>
> *If, as is to be expected, the Patriotic Front reject these proposals, we shall then be best placed to proceed with the internal parties with a chance of securing a measure of international support at any rate from our principal friends and allies.*

In the context of the expected final negotiations with the Salisbury parties alone, the note on tactics did say at the end *"there must be some form of test of acceptability"*. On the Note, Mrs Thatcher scribbled *"includes no provision for a referendum should that be preferable"*.

This may seem Machiavellian after all that was agreed at Lusaka; but not so to Muzorewa who at a meeting at Downing Street with Mrs Thatcher and Lord Carrington on 13 July 1979 (two weeks before Lusaka) had been assured by Mrs Thatcher (note of discussion also declassified):

> *... at the forthcoming conference in Lusaka, they would not propose to set out the constitutional changes which they had in mind in detail. This was purely a matter between Bishop Muzorewa and the UK ... If the Partriotic Front refused to attend, this would not give them a power of veto over progress to independence...*
>
> *Lord Carrington said that it was important to be able to wrong-foot the bullies. If this were done there would be a much better chance of putting an end to the war in Rhodesia.*

On 23 July, at the last Cabinet Committee (minute declassified) on Rhodesia which Mrs Thatcher attended before leaving for Lusaka, the strategy was spelled out by Lord Carrington:

At Lusaka it could be best to avoid revealing our intentions beyond announcing, at a fairly late stage, our plan for a constitutional conference. When issuing invitations to that conference, we should announce our outline plans for an independence constitution. Details would then be explained to the Bishop with a view to securing his tacit agreement at least when we tabled them at the constitutional conference which would meet in London on 4 September. The Patriotic Front would probably attend but soon walk out having rejected our proposals. We should then negotiate these with the Bishop's Government and defend them internationally as being comparable to the terms on which others of our former territories had been brought to independence. Finally we should need to persuade the Bishop to arrange a test of acceptability with our help, probably in the form of a referendum, on the basis that at its successful conclusion we would grant full legal independence.

Matters did not quite work out like that at Lusaka; nor did they at Lancaster House; but these declassified documents explain a great deal of the motives and machinations of what did happen at both.

* * *

The Conference lasted for three months – from 10 September to 15 December 1979 – and the Commonwealth's role, and my own as Secretary-General, were substantial. With the Conference ended and the election process underway, I spoke to Commonwealth Ambassadors at the United Nations on 11 February 1980 explaining this:

It is in the nature of Commonwealth business that you can play that kind of part without ever being in the Conference room: and none of us were in the Conference room ... and throughout that period Commonwealth High Commissioners in London held thirty-two (32) separate meetings ... in Marlborough House between September and December. And those meetings were very much a part of the process of the Conference. They were meetings which were partly briefings by our British colleagues, partly meetings of the Southern Africa Committee which actually makes recommendations to Governments; and, of course, they were meetings which looked to me from time to time to play particular roles in seeking to ensure that the Conference did go forward and that agreement was reached.

One of the earliest roles concerned land. Remember Rhodesia's history, and that in 1979 the statistics were that 5 per cent of the population owned 70 per cent of the arable land. In his opening statement at Lancaster House, on behalf of the Patriotic Front, Joshua Nkomo had said this:

The essential questions we have posed constantly to ourselves and which we insist must be understood by all seriously concerned with a solution include the following:

9. ... What will be the future of the people's land?

These and similar issues are those which should be placed on the agenda of the Conference and before the world if real peace is to return to our beloved Zimbabwe. The time for evasion is long past and we insist that the final phase of decolonisation be seriously pursued now by the British and by ourselves.

Of course, 'land', as such, was not on the agenda, and Lord Carrington's opening statement made no mention of it. The Conference proceeded to consider only the British Government's 'Outline Constitution' which provided, under the 'Declaration of Rights' section:

V. Freedom from Deprivation of Property

1. Every person will be protected from having his property compulsorily acquired except when the acquisition is in the interests of ... or, in the case of under-utilised land, settlement of land for agricultural purposes. When property is wanted for one of these purposes, its acquisition will be lawful only on condition that the law provides for the prompt payment of adequate compensation...

The Outline Constitution had made no provision for amendment, but on 3 October Carrington informed Downing Street (document declassified) that on the Declaration of Rights he

had reached a compromise with the Salisbury delegation on the question of the compulsory acquisition of agricultural land for settlement. This will be allowed where the land is not fully utilised, where a court order has been obtained and adequate compensation has been agreed... The protective provisions of the Declaration of Rights will be amendable only by unanimous vote of the House of Assembly for ten years. This gives added protection to the whites and others.

In opening the Plenary that day, Carrington announced this. In other words: the Constitution would guarantee for 10 years the status quo on land. That, in effect, was the answer to the Patriotic Front's initial inquiry as to 'the future of the people's land'.

Commonwealth High Commissioners, particularly from African countries, were in constant touch with the Patriotic Front and knew and understood their reservations on the land provisions. They were increasingly concerned by Carrington's pressure on the Patriotic Front to agree the Constitution without reservation. At the briefing meeting on 9 October Sir Antony Duff outlined Carrington's strong belief *"that the detailed constitutional proposals he had put before them constitute the only basis on which it was possible to reach an agreement"*.

Muzorewa had already announced publicly and in the Conference that he accepted the proposals. The High Commissioners were incensed at what they described as Carrington's 'take it or leave it' tactic. They sent a clear message of disaffection via Sir Antony, and agreed to convene the Committee on Southern Africa. They reported to their Governments, and tensions over Carrington's tactics mounted, especially in the Front Line states.

On 11 October Nkomo made a statement for the Patriotic Front reiterating their reservations: *"The issue before us"*, he said. *"is not just the 14 year-old problem of UDI, but the 80 year colonial problem of Rhodesia"*. Nevertheless, he added, they are prepared to discuss the transitional arrangements with which their reservations have *"a vital connection...if we are satisfied beyond doubt as to the vital issues relating to transitional arrangements, there may not be need to revert to discussion on the issues we have raised under the Constitution."* Carrington was not impressed and made a statement of his own on 'land' saying: *"The British Government recognises the importance of this issue to a future Zimbabwe Government and will be prepared, within the limits imposed by our financial resources, to help ... We should however be ready to support the efforts of the Government of independent Zimbabwe to obtain international assistance for these purposes"*. As reported to the briefing-session, the Chairman then said that *"the British Government could not accept the reservations of the Patriotic Front ... he had therefore no alternative but to adjourn the meeting in the hope that when it resumed in the near future he would have received an unequivocal response from the Patriotic Front"*. When the Conference resumed on 15 October, with no change in the Patriotic Front's reservation, Carrington said he *"would have to begin the discussions on the 'interim arrangements' with the delegation which had accepted the draft constitution"*; and in fact he began such discussions. It was no longer a Conference of all the parties.

To me, this was an outrageous and unacceptable breach of the Lusaka Accord and I issued a Statement saying so on the evening of 15 October:

> *It was not within the letter or the spirit of the Lusaka Agreement nor was it contemplated by Commonwealth Leaders at Lusaka that the lasting settlement towards which they agreed to work could be attained save by agreement between all the Parties to the conflict. Negotiations at the Lancaster House conference on the interim arrangements would be within the framework of that Agreement only if they involve all the Parties. It is important that there should be no misunderstanding of what was agreed at Lusaka. It would be a mistake to assume Commonwealth support for any procedure at variance with it. I hope the Conference will proceed with all the Parties on the basis agreed at Lusaka.*

At the briefing-session the next day Commonwealth High Commissioners supported the statement and spoke strongly to the same effect. In an unusual move, the representatives of the Front Line states in London made a public statement of their own, supporting mine and *"reiterating their conviction that the objectives endorsed by the Commonwealth at Lusaka cannot be achieved with the exclusion of the Patriotic Front."*

The weekend was full of stories of breakdown and the Patriotic Front was on the point of leaving. I realised that left to Carrington, his expectations would have been fulfilled, and he would conclude the Conference with Muzorewa. I had to keep Nkomo and Mugabe in London and somehow break the logjam. My first effort was to convince them not to fight the provision on 'property rights' (which was fairly conventional in Commonwealth Constitutions reflecting international conventions) but find an answer to the compensation issue which was essential to land re-distribution in Zimbabwe. On 11 October Sir Garfield Todd – a former, much respected, Prime Minister of pre-UDI Rhodesia – had written to Carrington urging that *"land provisions should be designed to facilitate the distribution of land, not to frustrate both white land owners and black farmers who wish to co-operate. Your suggestions are not designed to meet the real needs of the country."* But Carrington was in no mood to listen to good sense from Rhodesia. I decided to turn to the Americans.

Kingman Brewster was the American Ambassador in London. He was a liberal and cultivated man, a former President of Yale and a close friend of both Cyrus Vance (the Secretary of State) and the President, Jimmy Carter. I had a good relationship with him and knew he was generally worried by Carrington's high-handed tactics. By now he too was specifically troubled by developments at the Conference and offered to come and see me at home. He was there within minutes – his Embassy in Grosvenor Square was close to my residence in Mayfair. I explained the situation and said that I could not stop the Patriotic Front from leaving without finding them an answer to their legitimate concerns on land. They had understood Carrington to be determined to give the 'whites' a 10-year guarantee on their 70 per cent landholding; to accept that would be to lose the struggle. They would rather go back to the bush and fight a war they knew they would win. I said I would try to persuade them to accept the property rights guarantee in the Constitution if I could offer them the prospect of money for compensation for land (for re-distribution) acquired under it. Carrington had made a pusillanimous offer which only convinced them of his 'sell-out to Salisbury'.

Brewster was appalled at how close we were to a Lancaster House collapse – and war in Southern Africa. Could he, I asked, get Washington to intervene by offering a Fund to a new Zimbabwe Government for land redistribution under the Constitution? Kingman Brewster said he would try. He contacted Cyrus Vance immediately and Vance cleared a positive response with Carter. Brewster was back in my home within 24 hours. His answer was that the US would be willing to contribute 'substantially' to an Agricultural Development Fund which an independent Zimbabwe Government could use in its discretion, including paying compensation for lands compulsorily acquired under the Constitution – contingent, however, on a like British contribution which the US will urge the British Government to confirm. I thanked Kingman but said I needed the Patriotic Front to hear this directly from the US. Later that day, the Deputy Ambassador, Ray Sykes, met Nkomo and Mugabe in the same room in my home to convey the same offer. I told them the US would be speaking to the UK and if they shared in the assurances they should drop their reservations to the Constitution and move on. I myself contacted Carrington; if they joined the US in assurances, I told him, the Patriotic Front will accept the Constitution and move on to the next stage.

Mugabe – Kaunda – Nkomo at Hill Street

I had kept the front-line Presidents informed every step of the way; and they applied their own pressures – on the Patriotic Front to stay; on the British Government to co-operate in the US offer. They themselves had an emergency meeting in Dar es Salam on 17 October where they issued a public Statement asserting that they:

> *... regard the land issue as an important matter. They consider that the Patriotic Front are right in seeking assurance that funds for compensation will be available. The leaders of the Front Line states are satisfied that the British Government understand the need for this clarification.*

Meanwhile, Kaunda's Mark Chona was on his way to London as a Personal Envoy to join the Patriotic Front in 'back channel' discussions with the Foreign Office on the 'assurances'. The result was a Statement squared with the Foreign Office indicating the Patriotic Front's receipt of the 'assurances' on the land issue and their acceptance of them. The next day (18 October) Nkomo and Mugabe met Carrington, gave him the Statement on Land as it had evolved and released it to the Press. It was as follows:

> *When the Conference adjourned we stated that we required clarification on the fund relating to the land question to which the Chairman had made reference. We have now obtained assurances that depending on the successful outcome of the Conference Britain, the United States of America and other countries will participate in a multinational financial donor effort to assist in land, agricultural and economic development programmes.*
>
> *These assurances go a long way in allaying the great concern we have over the whole land question arising from the great need our people have for land and our commitment to satisfying that need when in government.*
>
> *In these circumstances and in clarification of our statement of 11th of October, 1979, we are now able to say that if we are satisfied beyond doubt about the vital issues of the transitional arrangements, there will not be need to revert to discussion on the constitution including those issues on which we reserved our position.*

In reporting on these developments to Commonwealth High Commissioners the Foreign Office representative said that, *"the British Government very much appreciated the help and counsel given by the Commonwealth as a whole and by the Secretary-General."* We had 'interfered' to good effect.

And there were other issues that demanded Commonwealth intervention like the presence of South African military in Rhodesia at Beitbridge in breach of the British 'assurance' under the 'ceasefire' agreement that *"there would be no external involvement in Rhodesia under the British Governor, stressing that the position had been made clear to all Governments concerned, including South Africa"*. The 'external involvement' was not terminated; but it was exposed and contained.

During all of the Lancaster House Conference, the Commonwealth through its diplomatic representatives in London, and through the Secretariat, monitored the proceedings to keep them faithful to the Lusaka Accord. When agreement on the Constitution was announced there were encomiums from the Commonwealth, none more touching that that of the High Commissioner of Tanzania, Tony Nyaki who said, at the 23rd Briefing Session:

> *The Frontline States appreciated the effort of the Commonwealth to bring about the agreement. What has been achieved might not have been realised without the support of the Commonwealth; when the history of Zimbabwe comes to be written the role of the Commonwealth would have to be acknowledged, and associated himself with the appreciation of the Secretary-General's labours behind the scenes ... The success of the Conference was a tribute to the Commonwealth, to the High Commissioners in London as well as to their respective Governments.*

But deviations from the Lusaka Accord continued to the end – none more palpable than that relating to Commonwealth observers of the elections. I have already noted Lord Carrington's insistence at the

Lusaka HGM on a free British hand in the conduct of the elections, leading to the insistence of Commonwealth leaders that there must be 'Commonwealth observers'. Point (g) of the Lusaka Accord as eventually agreed was:

> *(g) acknowledged that the government formed under such an independence constitution must be chosen through free and fair elections properly supervised under British Government authority, and with Commonwealth observers.*

Those words '*and with Commonwealth observers*' were an important part of the consensus at Lusaka, as no one knew better than Lord Carrington. Immediately after Lusaka I began planning for this essential Commonwealth role. I knew its logistics were not for discussion between Carrington and the parties; but between the British Government and the Secretariat; but Carrington showed no disposition to discuss it. Eventually, I raised it in the Briefing Session on 20 November in these terms:

> *He (the Secretary General) had written to Lord Carrington on 1 November 1979 putting forward some ideas on how they might proceed. He had received a reply on 12 November and had met Lord Carrington on Friday 16 November. Although he could not report in detail on the content of the discussions, he noted that they had been pre-empted by press comment, all of which was by no means speculative. He had therefore thought that the best course was to ask representatives to transmit to their Governments his preliminary ideas on the role of Commonwealth observers as envisaged in the Lusaka Agreement... the role of the Commonwealth was essentially one that would have to be settled by the Commonwealth itself.*

My reference to 'the press' was to a report in the *Daily Telegraph* by David Adamson under the headline *"Running Battle Over Rhodesia Poll Observers"* – as follows:

> *A discreet running battle between the Foreign Office and the Commonwealth Secretariat over monitoring the Rhodesia elections will be carried a stage further today...*
>
> *Lord Carrington's ideas have not been spelled out in detail. Basically, he wants individual Commonwealth countries to send teams which will report to their own Governments on the elections...*
>
> *Sir Shridath's position is that the Foreign Secretary has misinterpreted the mandate given by the Lusaka agreement. The Secretary General has taken as his text part of a negotiating document put forward by President Kaunda of Zambia in his talks with Mrs Thatcher two weeks ago. This in turn derived from a compromise with which the Patriotic Front hoped to break the deadlock over the transitional arrangements for Rhodesia.*

I went on to propose in the Briefing Session a discussion of the Secretariat's Outline proposals in the Southern Africa Committee. This drew out a response from the Foreign Office official (Mr Day) that:

> *following the Secretary-General's consultations with the British Government Lord Carrington had sent out instructions to British High Commissioners in Commonwealth capitals to reassure the host Governments that the British Government warmly welcomed Commonwealth observers and would give every facility needed in the execution of their duties. In addition, Commonwealth Governments had been asked whether they wished to send observers.*

The tactic was out: for the British Government, the words 'and with Commonwealth observers' in the Lusaka accord were being reworked to mean not a collective Commonwealth observer mission, but 'observers from Commonwealth countries'. Fortunately, by now, my proposal for a collective Commonwealth Mission was with

Commonwealth Governments and on 23 December I placed the matter before the Commonwealth Committee on Southern Africa making a strong plea for no deviation from the Lusaka Accord properly interpreted as requiring a collective observer role for the Commonwealth. To correct the *Telegraph's* incorrect interpretations, I released my statement to the Press.

The Southern Africa Committee was unanimous in supporting my interpretation of the Lusaka Accord and, therefore, of the independent collective Commonwealth Observer role – save for reservations by Canada, New Zealand and Britain on 'financing' – the first two being quickly withdrawn, the third by attrition. The Commonwealth Committee settled the Observer Group's Terms of Reference:

> *The Observer Group will observe and report to Commonwealth Heads of Government on all relevant aspects of the organisation and conduct of the elections in Southern Rhodesia held pursuant to the agreement at the Lancaster House Conference, Their function will be to ascertain in their impartial judgement, whether, in the context of the Lusaka Accord and the Lancaster House Conference, the elections were free and fair. In furtherance of this objective, it will be competent for the Group to bring to the attention of the administering authorities from time to time such matters as they consider pertinent.*

That last term of reference was to give to the Commonwealth, as the Group's final Report discloses, a role beyond Lusaka and Lancaster House into Zimbabwe. More 'interfering', perhaps; but in the best interest of the Commonwealth – which, day by day, it must have been becoming clear to Whitehall, was an asset in Britain's end days in Rhodesia,

The Group's Chairman was the eminent Indian Ambassador Rajeshwar Dayal and his colleagues were ten others of distinction drawn from Australia, Bangladesh, Barbados, Canada, Ghana, Jamaica, Nigeria, Papua New Guinea, Sierra Leone and Sri Lanka.

They were supported by officers of the Secretariat who served in their roles with great credit. As London's *Financial Times* reported on 16 January 1980 under the headline "A FAIR POLL IN RHODESIA":

> *In the course of the Lancaster House conference, the Secretary General, Mr Shridath Ramphal, won – not without difficulty – Britain's agreement to the establishment of a formal Commonwealth observer group which will report to the Heads of Government.*

It was a victory for the Commonwealth; and eventually, for Zimbabwe and one destined to secure Zimbabwe's independence despite the odds ranged against it – at least independence on the basis of 'genuine black majority rule'.

Anthony Verrier's *The Road to Zimbabwe 1890-1980*, published in 1986, provides one of the most insightful accounts of the Lancaster House process, including the eventual elections that brought Robert Mugabe to power. . Of the role of the Commonwealth Observer Group (COG), he had this to say:

> *... in the solid volume entitled Southern Rhodesia Elections: February 1980: The Report of the Commonwealth Observer Group will be found virtually all of the facts which the reader needs to convince him that the culmination of those eighty-eight years saw a British Government as actively engaged in the promotion of the white interests as was its predecessor when the Pioneer Column and five troops of the British South Africa Company's Police marched from Kimberly on 6 May 1891. Maybe there was a certain inevitability in such a culmination...*
>
> *There was no inevitability, however, in the establishment of the Commonwealth Observer Group. Carrington opposed the very idea of such a group, endowed with collective Commonwealth authority, providing, as it were, an imprimatur for the independence election (or issuing a fiat declaring it null and void) even more strongly than he contested the notion*

of a Commonwealth Monitoring Force (CMF)… Carrington was more comprehensively defeated over the establishment of the COG than he was concerning the CMF… Above all, the establishment of the COG ensured that Britain, in Rhodesia, would be watched … by a formidable body of experience, collectively capable of questioning electoral practices, whoever engaged in them.

From the outset of the Lancaster House Conference Carrington, by the manner no less than the substance of his opposition to an election observer group, had thrown down a gage to Shridath Ramphal which the latter was not slow to pick up…

Until 23 November Carrington had successfully resisted all efforts to establish the group. At the Southern Africa Committee's meeting that day, however, Ramphal threw down his gage. In a long well-argued statement made after conducting some backstairs diplomacy of his own, Ramphal insisted that the Lusaka 'Accord' had provided for Commonwealth observation of the election, and that without this process the latter could not be declared valid. Ramphal, in effect, knowing that he spoke for the commonwealth as a whole … asserted that Britain would only have discharged its final responsibility for Rhodesia when forty-one other sovereign states said so….

… on 13 December, just as the well-informed Financial Times was, reluctantly, stating a case for Carrington, that he agreed to the COG on the lines of the Lusaka 'Accord' – as interpreted by Ramphal … The COG was therefore – and finally – established by due process of bargaining. Ramphal had his moment of triumph – after enduring much sour criticism from various quarters favourably disposed to Carrington and white Rhodesia – when on 13 December he gave the COG its terms of reference.

… The COG took its collective self with the utmost seriousness, well aware that any other approach would have rendered it immediately vulnerable to the delays and denials with which any bureaucracy is well equipped … The COG,

> *investigating thoroughly ad reporting much which caused its members disquiet, only overcame difficulties because it was a thoroughly professional show.*

I fully share Verrier's account and his analysis.

* * *

Though these pages of the Zimbabwe episode speak of a Commonwealth struggle with Britain, and therefore with British officials from the Prime Minister down, it was a struggle engaged without personal rancour, and with civility. Hard words were sometimes spoken; like Lord Carrington's answer at a press conference when he said he would swim the Atlantic twice to veto my ever being Secretary-General of the United Nations – a prospect then being canvassed by others. Much more would have been said which I never heard, and vice versa; but at the end of the day there was a subliminal respect for personal integrity, if not always shared conviction. This is specially true of the officers of the British Foreign and Commonwealth Office with whom we interacted in Lusaka, in London and later in Harare. For my part, the Commonwealth's cause was righteous: to end racism in Zimbabwe and all the evils that it spawned, pre-eminently, UDI. Injury in that struggle was like wounds in battle; reminders of proud service.

Zimbabwe's elections were held on 14 February for the 20 seats allocated to the "White Roll" and from 27 to 29 February for the 80 seats assigned to the "Common Roll". On the final day, Peter Carrington telephoned me across St. James's Park and said in effect: 'The battles are over; Zimbabweans will be making their decision; it's all up to them. Would you care to come across the Park and have a chat over a cup of tea'? And so I did, gladly. He had his private staff with him and it was an intimate moment. After a while he said to me: 'Our work is done; at least for the time being; what do you think the people of Zimbabwe will do? I ducked the question saying, 'Come on, Peter, you have had Lord Soames, and British Intelligence and hundreds of your people there, you should tell me what to expect'. 'Fair enough', he said, and through one of his assistants: 'we think the women will vote for the Bishop, and that is a big vote; and we think the emerging African middle-class and the Ndebele will vote for Joshua – enough together to beat Mugabe' – or words to that effect.

I did not have to ponder. I had been receiving reports from the Secretariat's Support Team to the Observer Group which was widely, though thinly, spread throughout the country, I said to Lord Carrington: 'Peter, when in the whole de-colonisation process has a people voted for 'good government' over 'self-government'? It is self-government that Mugabe offers. Secretariat staff in Zimbabwe, small in number as they are, are in no doubt. They have been talking to hotel staff and taxi drivers in the city, and poor people in the countryside; they tell me it will be a 'walk-over' for Mugabe'. Carrington was quiet. We did not argue. He said, simply, 'We shall see'. We finished our tea. I made my way back to Marlborough House.

When the final results were in, at 9 am on Tuesday 4 March, the United African National Council of Bishop Abel Muzorewa had three seats, Joshua Nkomo (the Patriotic Front) had 20 and Robert Mugabe (ZANU-PF) had 57. At the end of the poll, and before the counting was over, the Commonwealth Observer Group had issued an Interim Report indicating that "the election to the end of polling can be considered to have been 'free and fair'." That night, Mugabe spoke to the nation, ending:

> *Let us deepen our sense of belonging, and engender a common interest that knows no race, colour or creed. Let us truly become Zimbabweans with a single loyalty. Long live our freedom.*

That would have been a happy note on which to end this Chapter; but alas there is no happy endnote. I do not intend to follow the history of Zimbabwe over the last thirty-plus year. For one thing, my Commonwealth connection with Zimbabwe ended when I left Marlborough House on a happy note with South Africa's freedom in 1990. What went wrong after the 1979 Lancaster House Conference?

The answer is shrouded in contention. I can offer only my glimpses of tragedy. Two assurances were given and received which appear nowhere in the Report of the Conference laid staidly in the British Parliament but which went to its very core, and if denied in Lancaster House would have led to no Report. The first was the assurance on 'land' by Britain; the second the assurance on 'governance' by Mugabe. Both were renounced, denied, broken.

I have narrated the episode on land which ended with the assurances given to the Patriotic Front on 17 October 1979 and read into the Conference records by Nkomo on the 18 October and given to all the Commonwealth High Commissioners. It was precisely because they were so important that they did so. And the statement – which allowed the Conference to continue – contained these telling words:

> *These assurances go a long way to allaying the great concern we have over the whole land question arising from the great need our people have for land and our commitment to satisfying that need when in government.*

Is it undeniable that the British delegation knew in their minds and hearts what the Patriotic Front understood those 'assurances' to be? Did they themselves know all along that they were not bankable?

In December 2009, thirty years after the Lancaster House Conference, the Africa All Party Parliamentary Group (UK) published a report on land reform in Zimbabwe. They called it – *LAND IN ZIMBABWE: Past Mistakes, Future Prospects.* I was heartened when I saw in its frontispiece a familiar quotation:

> *It was about land in the beginning; it was about land during the struggle; it has remained about land today. The land issue in Rhodesia/Zimbabwe is not ancient history. It is modern history.*
> *Sir Shridath 'Sonny' Ramphal*
> *Secretary-General of the Commonwealth 1975-1990*

Their finding was that,

The narrative that Britain betrayed its promise at Lancaster House has no basis as no agreement was reached on land in 1979. During the course of our inquiry the Africa All Party Parliamentary Group received no evidence from any source that behind the scenes at Lancaster House a deal was reached and a sum of money was agreed upon for land reform that Britain later reneged upon.

In the body of the report is the intriguing statement:

In evidence sessions ... Lord Carrington played down the impasse, stating that land reform was one of many issues that the Patriotic Front and the Smith-Muzorewa camp disagreed on. When asked about the Patriotic Front threatening to walk out of the talks over the land issue, Lord Carrington replied 'they were always threatening to walk out.

And they continued:

Part of this approach may have been influenced by the British view towards the land issue. When talking to the Africa AAPG Lord Carrington made it clear that he saw an agreement on land as a means to an end, rather than a means in itself. 'The only thing that was certainly in my mind was to find a way of getting the land problem settled so we could get an agreement about everything else.

No one seems to have asked 'how was the land problem settled?' The result was, of course, that with the 'assurances' refuted, the Lancaster House Agreement required Robert Mugabe's government to wait ten years before instituting significant land reform'. So the status quo of 1 per cent of the population owning 70 per cent of the usable land (which the Report found) prevailed. The British 'moratorium' was contrived; but at what price to all Zimbabweans?

In her book *House of Stone,* Christina Lamb, has this paragraph:

> *During the Lancaster House negotiations, land reform had been the thorniest issue. But the final agreement had meant that for the time being the white farmers ... were protected from expropriation. The British Government had agreed to help finance land redistribution but stipulated that for the first ten years of independence white farms could only be bought on 'a willing seller – willing buyer' basis.*

That was another way of stating the disguised reality: during the first ten years of 'freedom' there would be no money from Britain for real land redistribution. Ironically, no great white distress in Zimbabwe's first years of independence might have suited South Africa's ANC in their final years of struggle (and negotiation) with Pretoria. Did they welcome the moratorium? Did they urge Mugabe to allow it? There may never be answers to such speculation?

So what became of the' assurances' on land that was the linchpin of the PF's agreement at Lancaster House? In a Postscript to Anthony Verrier's book written in 1986 – six years into independence – he wrote this:

> *In the meantime, Zimbabwe survives. The objective of genuine independence has still not been attained. The landless of 1980 are landless still. A luta continua.*

Whatever the arrangements Mugabe concluded with the British Government post-independence, they clearly trumped the assurances on 'land' that had allowed the Lancaster House Conference to proceed to conclusion. Those arrangements left unanswered the question the PF had asked, through Joshua Nkomo, in their opening statement at the Conference: 'What will be the future of the people's land? We know now the price all Zimbabweans paid for the moratorium on justice.

On 25 October (a week after the 'assurances on land) as the Lancaster House Conference was embattled over 'The Transitional

Period', the Patriotic Front issued a Conference paper entitled 'Essential Requirements for the Transition'. Paragraphs 2 and 3 stated:

> *2. It has always been the corner stone of the policy of the Patriotic Front that the people shall have the right to be governed by a democratically elected government of their choice on the basis of universal adult suffrage. It must therefore be the primary objective of the interim arrangements that the conditions be created and maintained which will enable free and fair elections to be held.*
>
> *3. For the elections to be free and fair and to be seen to be so all parties must be able to participate on equal terms in the whole electoral process.*

Later in the same Paper, the Patriotic Front stated (in paragraphs 6 and 6.1);

> *6. We entirely agree with Lord Carrington's statement that 'it is essential that the parties to the election should feel confident that the overall administration of the country during the election campaign will be fair and impartial as between them.*
>
> *6.1 In a situation of conflict and deep suspicion the Parties cannot be expected to have confidence in an administration of which they form no part.*

The Patriotic Front did not get the interim 'power-sharing' administration for which they were arguing; but they got the democratic governance arrangements for an independent Zimbabwe which was their basic goal. Indeed, those arrangements were the corner stone of the Lancaster House Agreement. They did not become the hallmark of Robert Mugabe's governance of Zimbabwe. In *CATASTROPHE; What Went Wrong in Zimbabwe*. Richard Bourne concludes his Chapter 'Zanu in Power' thus:

Looking back on the 1980s, from a vantage point at the end of the first decade of the twenty-first century, it is clear that there were important shadows over independent Zimbabwe. Reconciliation was superficial. The economy could not match the progress in education and health-care. The land issue festered. Violence and impunity had continued after the end of the war. Democratic values had not transformed a ruling party nurtured in Marxism, a militarist ethic and centralised control. Public expectations in a country which was the envy of its neighbours were not being satisfied. The socio-political situation looked better, and institutions more secure than was really the case. The 1990s led to breakdown.

The breakdown was symbolised by the Commonwealth's refusal to accept the declared result of the 2002 Zimbabwe election and Zimbabwe's suspension from the Commonwealth. When, at the Commonwealth Summit in Abuja, Nigeria in 2003 that suspension was renewed, Mugabe withdrew Zimbabwe from the Commonwealth. More adroit diplomacy may have avoided that extreme result; but in a longer context it was Mugabe's abject refusal to respect those principles of governance that he had espoused at Lancaster House as the corner stone of the policy of the Patriotic Front, that led to the ultimate debacle. One day, Zimbabwe will return to the Commonwealth – when it is recognised on all sides that Zimbabwe did not leave the Commonwealth; Mugabe did.

Helped by the Commonwealth, the Lusaka Accord and the Lancaster House Conference which it generated were great successes. They ended UDI in Rhodesia and brought Zimbabwe to independence. As the Commonwealth prepared for Zimbabwe's Independence, I received a generous letter from President Nyerere in which he wrote:

One day the full history of the struggle will be written. But however far into the future that is done, it will be impossible to assess accurately the effect of individual interventions at crucial points. I can, however, say that we in Tanzania are fully conscious of the great value of the work done by you, and by the Commonwealth generally. Those who in the past have questioned the value of our organisation will have more difficulty in the future. We shall all be able to join in the celebrations on 18th April in the consciousness of something achieved against heavy odds.

It was a message I shared with my staff. It has meaning to this day.

And, after all the hubbub of Lancaster House, it was gracious of Peter Carrington to write me on 12 March 1980 as follows:

Dear Sonny,
... I am very pleased that the Commonwealth was able to play such an important part in these events, beginning with Lusaka and including the report of the Commonwealth observers. The Commonwealth has shown itself, once again, as a force for stability in the world.

I am also grateful for all that you personally have done over these last months to bring us to this present happy situation.

Peter

With Lord Carrington and Her Majesty The Queen in Marlborough House

Had the commitments made at Lancaster House on land and on governance been respected and fulfilled, had the promises, the assurances, the obligations that were at the heart of those commitments been respected on all sides – Zimbabwe today would not be the casualty it is. Britain says it made no promises on land; Mugabe no doubt insists he made none on governance. But today's assertions, defying history, do not alter it; and rewriting history does not change reality.

CHAPTER 21

Apartheid

This book started with slavery's end days in the West Indies and its relevance to my life. This chapter, about *apartheid* in South Africa, speaks to slavery too; for *apartheid* in its many stages and forms was the most cruel legacy of slavery – carrying the stain of race into the end years of the 20th century, and becoming for me, in the 'Thatcher years', a major pre-occupation of my life.

Slavery was more than a system; for slavery to be formalised by law and institutionalised into a system, a measure of bigotry was essential – often gross, sometimes subtle. In this sense, slavery began in the human mind, in the distorted manner in which one man looked on another and made a perverted judgement enabling him to deny that they are equal members of one human race. Slavery rested on an assumption of superiority by the enslaver. And it is always the other, perceived as consciously different and inferior, who is enslaved. In this otherness, lies the beginning of the denial of common humanity.

The basis of 'otherness' is not always race; it may be religion: European Christians and Circassians were for centuries enslaved as 'infidels' by the Islamic Turks and Moors. The difference may be one of class: the West Indian and American plantations were worked in their earliest decades by indentured poor whites and by white criminals. The ruling groups within some African tribes sold their own serf class into the plantation slave trade. The simple distinction between one nation and another, or between one tribe and another, has often been the basis for slavery; which explains why warfare has historically been the most frequent source of slaves.

Race has been a primal reason for 'otherness', with the white race mainly as slave owners and the black race mainly as slaves. But, as we have seen, slavers are nothing if not eclectic; after Emancipation, brown men and yellow, Indians and Chinese, made acceptable substitutes. Academics dispute whether the motivation behind the beginnings of plantation slavery in the New World was purely economic, or whether it was from the start racial, as it certainly became. What is clear is that perceived differences of race and colour allowed awareness of 'otherness' to be placed readily at the service of the economic system of slavery. It was dangerously easy, if appallingly unjust, to proceed from the observed reality that most slaves were black men and women to the irrational belief that black men and women were, and should be, slaves.

The history of our own time affords the most complete example of 'otherness' as a reason for enslavement. Nazi Germany used pseudo-scientific theories based on perverted Darwinism to justify the persecution and enslavement of the Jews. But the concentration camps were not reserved only for the Jews, their most numerous victims; within them were to be found any who had exposed themselves by their otherness to the Nazis: political dissenters, members of religious minorities, gypsies, homosexuals, Slavs, prisoners-of-war, even (another irony in that supremely sick system) the mentally ill. Indeed, the category of 'the other' was on the verge of encompassing anyone who was not an Aryan German Nazi, and in the end the psychosis was becoming self-destructive, with the masters forced to look among themselves for their slaves.

That brings us dangerously close to the present; close enough to put us on notice for our own times. Frantz Fanon recognised the totalitarian impulse as springing from the assumption of superiority when he wrote: *'It is the racist who creates his inferior'*, and asked the question: *'Superiority? Inferiority? Why not the quite simple attempt to touch the other, to feel the other, to explain the other to myself?'* No question is more pertinent amid the anomy and anonymity of our multiracial modern cities where it is all too easy to become alienated from one's fellows, to perceive them as strangers, transforming them into 'others' from whom we can justify withholding what Wilberforce so well described as *'that equitable consideration and that fellow-feeling which are due from man to man'*.

The Martinique poet, Aime Cesaire, correctly perceived that Nazism was the importation into Europe of a system with which black people were all too familiar, the seeds of which had already been sown by the Europeans themselves. *'Before they became its victims'*, he wrote, *'they were its accomplices; that Nazism they tolerated before they succumbed to it, they exonerated it, they closed their eyes to it, they legitimised it because until then it had been employed only against non-European peoples'*. It is one of the least pardonable crimes against contemporary humanity that under the label of *'apartheid'*, false doctrines of racial superiority (even when the epithet was dropped for political reasons) continued to be employed against the non-European peoples of South Africa, and most viciously against its black people. And *apartheid*, as we shall see, *was* not without its accomplices beyond South Africa; those who, for whatever reason, would tolerate, exonerate, close their eyes to, and legitimate it – this most cruel legacy of slavery.

As with slavery, it was the 'otherness' of race that sustained apartheid's creed of separateness. In 1984, 150 years after modern-day slavery was abolished, the reality of South Africa was that 87 per cent of all land was reserved for 4.5 million whites. Nineteen million blacks – almost 80 per cent of the population – were relegated to the remaining 13 per cent of largely scrubland. Here they were denied even the right to belong; legislated out of their own country; deemed to be migrant workers from fantasy 'black homelands'. As with the slavery of the plantation, the laws of *apartheid* discriminated overtly between one group and another; in South Africa, between the whites and all others, with the totally disenfranchised black Africans – the purest 'belongers' – the most oppressed of all. As with slavery, *apartheid* was rooted in 'otherness', the otherness of 'separate development'.

Below is an estimate of disproportionate treatment in South Africa under apartheid around 1978.

Apartheid and the People of South Africa

	Blacks	*Whites*
Population	19 million	4.5 million
Land Allocation	13 per cent	87 per cent
Share of National Income	< 20 per cent	75 per cent
Ratio of average earnings	1	14
Minimum taxable income	360 rands	750 rands
Doctors/population	1/44,000	1/400
Infant mortality rate	20% (urban) 40% (rural)	2.7%
Annual expenditure on education per pupil	$45	$696
Teacher/pupil ratio	1/60	1/22

Apartheid resembled slavery also in its economic rationale. Its basic motive was to provide a permanent subject labour force kept rigidly separate from the ruling class. The Bantustans to which every black South African was by law made to belong, and the townships where the great majority actually lived, were nothing other than segregated pools of cheap labour. The mines and farms of South Africa could not function without that labour. And the means of ensuring control and domination of the labour supply was the rigidly-enforced *'pass laws'*, regulating movement, entrenching insecurity, denying civil liberties, even dividing husbands from wives and children. *Pass laws* had also been a feature of plantation slavery. It was protest against *apartheid's pass laws* which had led to the *Sharpeville Massacre* of 1960 in which 69 unarmed people were killed and 180 injured: shades of the West Indian slave rebellions of the 1820s and the last-ditch intransigence of the West Indian planters.

Apartheid was another slavery; yet, it was possible to descend through the apartheid system, as through the circles of Dante's hell, to a condition of ultimate repression indistinguishable from slavery at its worst. South Africa rejected every expose as propaganda – as did its apologists. Yet, at the time of the 150th anniversary of the end of slavery under English law, the London *Guardian* (on 30 March 1983) reported on the protests of black leaders in Namibia at "the token six-year prison sentence passed on a white farmer found guilty of battering to death a 20 year-old black parole prisoner sent to work on his farm." A photograph produced at the trial showed the farmer holding a chain securing his badly beaten victim. Even the shackles of slavery had been bequeathed to *apartheid.* The manacles in the Wilberforce Museum were not mere relics to remind of past evils; they were grim testimony of *apartheid's* inhumanity of an imprisoned labour force being worked and beaten to death with impunity.

In 1980, Allen Cook, in his contemporary account *'Akin to Slavery: Prison Labour in South Africa'* assessed that the number of black prisoners working for white farmers was at least 90,000, about one-eighth of the total agricultural work force. After arrest for minor pass laws infringements, many of these forced labourers were directed straight to the farms without trial, under the 'parole' scheme. Others who could not find employment accepted placement on farms by the 'aid centres' as an alternative to deportation to the Bantustans. Another mechanism to achieve the same effect, explained Cook, was the 'youth service camp'. The 'aid centres' were administered by the euphemistically-named Department of Co-operation and Development – a new name for the Department of Native Affairs. Even private enterprise mental hospitals provided contract labour under conditions of brutal compulsion for major national and international companies and for the gold mines, with the patients often paid only in sweets or cigarettes; 11,000 are believed to have been thus abused in 1975; then an Act of Parliament prevented the publication of further information.

The true depth of the system, Cook reported, was reached in the farm prisons. These were built at farmers' cost and long-term prisoners allocated to each farmer in proportion to his investment; thereafter the prisoners effectively become the farmers' property. A 1971 advertisement for the sale of grain, wine and sheep mentioned 'winery shed and ten convicts' as among the assets. Here, still, is the dehumanisation of true slavery. *Apartheid* was a monstrous system, with atrocities floggings, torture and extremes of sadism a frequent occurrence.

The London *Times* of 6 June 1983 carried a report from its 'Own Correspondent' in Johannesburg on the *"white man who celebrated his nineteenth birthday by going out and beating a black man to death with karate sticks. He was found guilty of culpable homicide by the Pretoria Regional Court and sentenced to 'serve only 2000 hours 'periodic punishment' at the weekends, of which 800 hours have been suspended conditionally for five years ... He will be free to continue his job on the railways during the week"*. To keep matters in perspective, that was more than three years after Commonwealth efforts at Lusaka had forced action towards Zimbabwe's independence. Commonwealth leaders were not unmindful of their unfinished work across Zimbabwe's borders. It would be work without respite.

The roots of *apartheid* went deep. It did not always have that name but its realities were the same. In 1897 the British statesman Lord Bryce described how a white farmer in South Africa had flogged his African servant to death, was tried and acquitted by a white jury and was escorted triumphantly home by his neighbours 'with a band of music'. Nearly a hundred years later, on 23 March 1989 the London *Times* reported the case of a white South African who beat a black farm worker to death and was fined some £700, with £1,800 to pay to the man's family over a five year period. That was in our time. What had changed in 100 years? The music!

In 1985, Joseph Lelyveld published a book he called *MOVE YOUR SHADOW: South Africa, Black and White.* He was, for the second time, the *New York Times*' correspondent in South Africa. He had been expelled the first time. Lelyveld's expose of the reality of *apartheid* in a South Africa he had come to know well is, for me, the most perceptive and coruscating account of the evil system, even in its guise of reform. In one of many quotable passages, he wrote:

> *It is easy to lampoon official double-talk, but hidden here and there in the acres of verbiage are kernels of real meaning.*

> *Consider the minister of constitutional development. On home ground he once explained in a brief spasm of candor why there could be no place in the parliamentary structure for blacks, even on the segregated basis of the new constitution, which gives coloreds and Indians a subordinated role in the national government. Blacks would outnumber whites, coloreds, and Indians, he said, by a ratio of 36:9:5:2; if only those classified as urban blacks were counted, the ratio would still be 16;9:5:2. "And what would remain of the principle of maintaining civilised standards then?" he asked. On another occasion he went so far as to explain how civilised standards have to be maintained. "It is in the long-term interest of South Africa that the Afrikaner should always have the privilege of the leadership role." Not for just a day, not for just a year, but always.*

It was reminiscent of Ian Smith's peroration that black majority rule in Zimbabwe would come – "*not for a thousand years*".

* * *

On 1 July 1978, a commemorative service was held in Westminster Cathedral, London, in the joint honour of Steve Biko, Chief Luthuli and Martin Luther King. It was in acknowledgement of the unity of ideals to which they held steadfastly despite the evil which confronted, surrounded and tragically took them away just when their cause, and the world, seemed to need them most. I spoke at that service, and said in reference to the immediate challenge of Southern Africa:

> *They themselves would wish our carol of commemoration to be trumpets to action in the cause for which they died. And in Southern Africa today, the challenge to finish the work they began is an urgent challenge. As Biko said, 'the winds of liberation which have been sweeping the face of Africa have reached our very border. There is no more doubt about the inevitability of change – the only questions now remaining are*

> *"how" and "when". In posing those questions he summed up the role of the world beyond those borders: 'We rely', he said, 'not only on our own strength but also on the belief that the rest of the world views the oppression and blatant exploitation of the black majority by a minority as an unforgivable sin that cannot be pardoned by civilised societies.'...*
>
> *Was his belief well founded? Are we ready to commemorate this service of King and Luthuli and Biko to mankind by ending our several accommodations with the evil of apartheid? What do we answer when the questions 'how' and 'when' are asked about the inevitability of change in Southern Africa? Western societies, which have made such immense contributions to the development of human values, cannot allow them to halt at national, still less at ethnic, frontiers. Yet, as another gallant fighter against apartheid, Donald Woods, reminded us recently, 'apartheid could not survive in South Africa today but for the economic succour which its government receives.*

History will record the failure of our human society to show unanimous resolution in *apartheid's* abolition. How can the future judge the power-brokers of that time save in terms of hypocrisy and double-standards when they justified their acquiescence in *apartheid* in terms of solidarity with 'allies' in the East/West contest, or their own national interest in relation to 'trade and investment'? The former was wholly misguided and contradictory and antithetical to the true interests of any who sought the goodwill of Africa. The latter is the modern-day equivalent of what a nineteenth century Parliamentary critic of those who wished to ban slave-grown goods while not attacking the system at source called 'lucrative humanity'. A moral choice was incumbent on all who traded with *apartheid,* and there could be only one decision: that South Africa be made to dismantle *apartheid.* In Hull on the 150th anniversary of slavery's abolition (in a Memorial Lecture called 'Some in Light and Some in Darkness: the Long Shadow of Slavery'), I asked; *"By what quirk of logic, what twist of values can we celebrate emancipation and tolerate apartheid? We tarnish and depreciate the memory of Wilberforce so long as slavery South Africa style flaunts its evil and defies our will to curb it, sensing our resolve to be a fragile thing".* Yet, tolerate *apartheid* is what some did, and with sanctimony. In the *Nelson Mandela Garden* established in Hull (the City of Wilberforce) those words occupy the plaque dedicating the Garden.

One thing is clear. Those who struggled against *apartheid,* who were driven to take up arms against it, were not the ones who ought to have been condemned as 'terrorists', as the *apartheid* regime and their apologists did condemn them. They were the counterparts, 150 years later, of the slaves who in rebellion and uprising throughout the West Indian plantations threw off their chains and made a stand for freedom. Oppression is no less terrorism because it wears an official uniform. Those who fight for freedom do not become 'terrorists' merely because they cannot form themselves into conventional armies. The real terrorists in South Africa were not those who helped the oppressed, but the oppressors themselves who commanded the heights of economic, social, political and military power under the *apartheid* system. They sustained an evil system of racism that was itself the 'alpha' and 'omega' of terrorism against the human personality: a terrorist system that ineluctably bred its own responses of violent retribution.

When Commonwealth Heads of Government considered the question of Rhodesia at their Kingston meeting in 1975 (the one at which I was elected Secretary-General) their communiqué said this:

> *They took note of the determination of the African freedom fighters, supported by African and other States to achieve their objective by peaceful means if possible, and recognise the inevitability of intensified armed struggle should the peaceful means be blocked by the racist and illegal regime. The moral responsibilities in those circumstances would lie with the minority Government and those who had chosen to sustain it.*

The same considerations applied to South Africa. When, in the early 1950s, Herbert Chitepo as a young man, as a fellow 'pupil', talked with me in Dingle Foot's Chambers of the terrible situation in Zimbabwe under the canopy of white rule he never failed to make the link to *apartheid* in South Africa as both providing material support to the Smith regime and underpinning it with the evil ideology of race.

South Africa had been expunged from the Commonwealth as early as 1961 – because of *apartheid.* As with respect to most things South African the regime claimed in 'double-speak' to have 'left' the Commonwealth. The truth was that when in ideological exegesis South Africa under President Vervoed decided to become a Republic, it needed to reapply as such for Commonwealth membership. It signalled its wish to do so – as other Republics before it, like India and Ghana had done. However, the new multiracial Commonwealth, very specially India, Ghana and Canada, made it clear that such an application would not be entertained. There was no place for *apartheid* South Africa in the modern Commonwealth. The application was never pursued. For most of the Commonwealth, (including forthcoming new members like Tanzania) it was a cleansing riddance; but for the entire Commonwealth there remained a duty as part of humanity, and in furtherance of Commonwealth values, to remove the stain of *apartheid* from human society.

The two years following that Cathedral service in London at which I spoke were to see the Commonwealth wholly engaged with ending UDI in Rhodesia and bringing Zimbabwe to independence. Yet we never lost sight of the larger evil in South Africa. In 1979, even as the Commonwealth reached the accord in Lusaka that was to chart the course for Zimbabwe's independence, the Summit's Communiqué looked across the Limpopo stressing *"that the grave problems afflicting the Southern Africa region stemmed from the racist policies of the South African regime embodied in the system of apartheid"*.

But they went further. In order to formally express their abhorrence of all forms of racist policy, wherever and however they might be manifested, they agreed to make a special declaration on the subject. It was issued as the Lusaka Declaration of the Commonwealth on Racism and Racial Prejudice. It re-affirmed *"the Commonwealth's rejection of all policies designed to perpetuate apartheid, racial segregation or other policies based on theories that racial groups are or may be inherently superior or inferior"*. As a testament of the Commonwealth's stand in relation to *apartheid* and South Africa it was pellucid; and the Commonwealth was united – at least in this declaration of intent.

The Lusaka Declaration was a unanimous and comprehensive affirmation by Commonwealth leaders of their stand against racism and racial prejudice, both generally and in the particular context of South Africa, and of their commitments to the eradication of all forms of the evil. The text of the Declaration is in Appendix 6. Below, are some excerpts from it on the specific matter of *apartheid:*

- *We reject as inhuman and intolerable all policies designed to perpetuate apartheid. Racial segregation or other policies based on theories that racial groups are or may be inherently superior or inferior.*
- *We believe that the existence in the world of apartheid and racial discrimination is a matter of concern to all human beings. We recognise that we share an international*

responsibility to work together for the total eradication of apartheid and racial discrimination.

- *We believe that the goal of the eradication of racism stands as a crucial priority for governments of the Commonwealth.*

'We' were all the peoples of the Commonwealth spoken for by all the Heads of all their Governments – without exception, without reservation.

CHAPTER 22

Circling the Wagons

The Commonwealth's triumph at the Lusaka HGM in 1979 in ending white supremacy in Rhodesia sent a signal to South Africa that the days of *apartheid* were numbered. The Commonwealth's Declaration on Racism and Racial Prejudice asserted that those end days were short. What was the response of *apartheid* South Africa? They circled the wagons at home and looked beyond to mobilise those they regarded as friends and protectors – prominently, Britain and the United States; but more specifically, Margaret Thatcher and, from 1981, Ronald Reagan. The personalities are important; for there were many in both Britain and the US who were not friends of *apartheid* South Africa, and who resented their Government's alliance with it, dignified as 'constructive engagement'.

The Anti-Apartheid Movement headquartered in Britain spoke for those many people. Their role should not be forgotten. Quite recently, I encountered some of them and some who remembered their vigils. The occasion was a Commemorative Service in London at St Martin in the Fields on 29 June 2013 to celebrate the life and legacy of Archbishop Trevor Huddleston and mark the centenary of his birth. It was organised by the Trevor Huddleston Memorial Centre in Sophiatown, South Africa and Action for Southern Africa (ACTSA), the successor to the Anti-Apartheid Movement. Nelson Mandela wrote of him: *"No white person has done more for South Africa than Trevor Huddleston"* – words now engraved on his memorial in Bedford, his birthplace in England. *Persona non grata* in South Africa after 13 years of priesthood he was brought back to England ('for his own safety') by the Anglican Community of the Resurrection. He became President of the Anti-Apartheid Movement in London (succeeding the indefatigable Ambrose Reeves), after thirteen years of campaigning priesthood in the townships of South Africa where he displayed the great humanity and courage that were his hallmarks.

Trevor Huddleston and I became close friends during my Commonwealth watch, and we celebrated his 70th birthday in 1983 with a reception in Marlborough House. I passed many an hour in his wise company in the small rooms he occupied behind St James Church in Piccadilly. The Commemorative service in 2013 was a timely reminder of the powerful influence exerted by good people world-wide in what became a global struggle against *apartheid.* I had shared many moments of vigil with Trevor Huddleston outside the South African High Commission on Trafalgar Square in the 1980s. It told a great story of the vanquishing of *apartheid* that after the 2013 Commemorative Service, we all went into the High Commission as guests of the South African High Commissioner.

With Huddleston, Tutu and Nyerere

Ultimately, of course, whether at the United Nations or in the Commonwealth, it was Governments that took decisions. Ahead for the Commonwealth, in the years after the 1979 Lusaka HGM, lay Summit Meetings at Melbourne, New Delhi, Nassau, London, Vancouver and Kuala Lumpur – an eight-year period during which fierce battles to end apartheid would be fought beyond South Africa itself – and at which the Commonwealth's main adversary, often the only one, would be the Prime Minister of Britain – the same Prime Minister who had been so forthright about 'majority rule' at Lusaka, and had made the words of the Lusaka Declaration her own.

The custodians of *apartheid* knew that they could not expect overt support from any quarter on the racism that underpinned *apartheid* – not even from the otherwise active lobby of ideological allies. They knew, too, that the world had changed. As early as 1960, Britain's Prime Minister, Harold Macmillan, had chosen his speech to the South African Parliament in Cape Town (on 3 February) to warn in memorable words:

> *The wind of change is blowing through this continent. Whether we like it or not, the growth of national consciousness is a political fact. We must all accept it as a fact. Our national policies must take account of it.*

And he went on to counsel in words of wisdom:

> *As I see it the great issue in this second half of the twentieth century is whether the uncommitted peoples of Asia and Africa will swing to the East or to the West. Will they be drawn into the communist camp? Or will the great experiments in self-government that are now being made in Asia and Africa, especially in the Commonwealth, prove so successful, and by their example so compelling, that the balance will come down in favour of freedom and order and justice?*

In his scholarly *Survey of Commonwealth Affairs: Problems of Expansion and Attrition, 1953-1969,* Professor J.D.B. Miller made the important point that while to the world at large the main message of Macmillan's 'wind of change' speech was British acceptance of decolonisation, to South Africans its importance lay in those passages in which he stressed that Britain fostered fellowship between the different communities in the colonies which it led to self-government and rejected the idea of any inherent superiority of one race over another. Macmillan had also pointed out that while Commonwealth countries respected each other's sovereignty in matters of internal policy:

> *... in this shrinking world in which we live today, the internal policies of one nation may have effects outside it ... I would myself expand the old saying so that it runs "Mind your own business, of course, but mind how it affects my own business too.*

In effect, concluded Professor Miller, Macmillan *"disengaged Britain from public support for South Africa"*.

Six weeks after Macmillan's speech in the South African Parliament, on 21 March 1960, the world was rocked by the Sharpeville Massacre in which 69 unarmed protesters were shot dead in South Africa, and following it the internationally condemned 'emergency' measures, including banning the African National Congress (ANC) and the Pan-Africanist Congress (PAC) – the two main African nationalist parties – and over 18,000 arrests. Macmillan's wise counsel had been rejected by South Africa; but less predictably it was to be tempered by his own successors at home, notably by Margaret Thatcher. Had his steadying wisdom prevailed within the leadership of Britain's Conservative Party, South Africa might not have been offered the lifeline it was given, and the end of *apartheid* might have come sooner. Nelson Mandela might not have been robbed of a further decade of his freedom; and South Africa of his robust leadership in the decade of the eighties.

* * *

What was the *apartheid* regime's political strategy after Zimbabwe's release from the thraldom of white minority rule? Primarily, it sought to deflect attention from *apartheid* to the fading, but still barely plausible appeal of South Africa as a 'bastion of the West' in the context of the 'cold' war between East and West – a bastion, they urged, that should not be weakened by global action, above all, Western action, directed at *apartheid.* The 'Cold War' was about global domination; but as 'domination' became less and less credible a goal for anyone, it could be no more than a flimsy cloak of abstention from action to end *apartheid.* Still, *apartheid's* despots persisted, driven by the realisation that with racism in Zimbabwe curbed, the world's attention, energised by the Commonwealth, would focus more rigorously on South Africa. The Zimbabwe elections were still pending when South Africa's President, P.W. Botha, played the 'Cold War' card in an offer to the Commonwealth's likeliest 'Cold Warrior' – Margaret Thatcher.

On 5 February 1980, about six weeks after the Lancaster House Conference on Southern Rhodesia ended, P.W. Botha wrote a five page closely typed 'Personal' letter to Britain's Prime Minister. It has lain 'secret' for long; but is now declassified. It is a matter for conjecture how important a part its essential arguments played in strengthening Mrs Thatcher's 'resolve' not to pressure South Africa to end *apartheid.* But it played a part, particularly when Ronald Reagan became President of the United States the following year, bolstering her tendencies with his obsessive anti-Soviet passions. Its significance justifies the lengthy extracts that follow:

> *Dear Prime Minister*
> *... I realise that British and South African interests inevitably diverge. But they also converge. Our interests diverge principally because of the conception which exists of the South African Government's "apartheid" policy ... I consider the survival of freedom and democracy of such vital importance that I respectfully suggest to you that you and I share a heavy responsibility to make the most sincere attempt to bridge our differences in order to cultivate the unity of purpose and strength*

which will be required to resist Russian imperialism. Indeed, your own courageous stand against the extension of Soviet power has played no small part in convincing me that our Governments should proceed immediately to engage in the discussions which I propose. ...

During President Brezhnev's era the Soviet Union has materially increased its power and influence relative to the United States and to the West in general ... He has cleverly used detente as a shield and exploited the American setback in Vietnam and the maiming effect of Watergate to promote subversion and install pro-Soviet governments in the Third World and, at the same time, to impose the Brezhnev doctrine – the right of Russia to intervene in "socialist" countries seeking change. Despite this, he has secured legitimacy through the Helsinki agreements for the boundaries of Eastern and Central Europe, for a quid pro quo which seems to have had little substance. Soviet influence in Europe, in South-East and South-West Asia, in the Middle East, in Southern Arabia, in parts of North, East, West and Southern Africa has grown beyond the point of being ominous. It is real. It has assumed awesome dimensions.

There is no doubt that the Southern African region has now become a prime objective of Soviet ambitions. Control of the vast and valuable reserves of raw materials in our region, in addition to Russia's own resources would enable her to dominate supplies to the industrial West. Control of South Africa's strategic geographical position, the importance of which is significantly enhanced by her technological sophistication, infrastructural development and industrial capacity, would greatly enhance this dominance. It would in fact tip the global strategic balance in favour of the USSR to a degree matched only by control of the total area of the Middle East. ...

An important part of the Soviet strategy in Africa has been to use the United Nations and international bodies which it controls to drive a wedge between South Africa and the major standard-bearers of freedom, on the pretext that South Africa has transgressed the norms of civilisation. Whatever imperfections there may be in South African society, South Africa has a democratic, free-enterprise, Christian society and is spiritually, emotionally and ideologically committed to the democracy of the Greeks, Europeans and Americans. Whatever disabilities may be experienced by segments of our population, successive South African Governments have sincerely worked for their upliftment and progress. We are committed to uphold the human dignity of all persons, irrespective of race or creed. We are committed to the removal of all negative forms of discrimination based on colour. But our problems are complex. Our situation therefore requires understanding and tolerance. ...

The Soviet threat of engulfing South Africa is of immediate concern to all of us. The Soviet Union is already established in Ethiopia, Angola and Mozambique, and its influence in other African countries poses a direct threat to the whole of Africa. But the prime target is Southern Africa. That is why the struggle for Zimbabwe/Rhodesia is so important and why Soviet aims in South West Africa must be frustrated, not only in the interests of southern Africa, but also of the West.

The events in Afghanistan have irrevocably confirmed that the Soviet Union will not hesitate to launch an attack southwards with surrogate forces if it believes that this can be done with impunity. War material has been accumulated in Angola and Mozambique, where, as you know, large tank forces have also been mustered. The build-up is continuing – with inter alia the addition of the technical know-how of the East Germans.

It is clear to me that, if democratic institutions are to survive anywhere in Africa, a common anti-Soviet strategy for Africa as a whole must be worked out by the West and moderate African leaders and quickly. All anti-Soviet governments in Africa from Egypt to South Africa must be supported, their foreign policies co-ordinated and their differences submerged. ...

In view of your clearly stated views on the Soviet threat, I felt it would be constructive to let you have my views on the critical African situation. I would welcome receiving your own views and your ideas as to how we can counter this threat. I hope that your emissary will soon find it possible to visit South Africa for the proposed discussions. South Africa is irrevocably committed to resisting Soviet aggression with all means at its disposal, whatever the consequences. But South Africa could not carry the responsibility in Southern Africa alone.

You will appreciate that if South Africa has to stand alone she must retain the right to act when, where and in whatever manner she deems necessary to promote her own chances of survival, and time is short.

With sincere regards,
P.W. BOTHA

There were other paragraphs of Botha's letter which pleaded for understanding of their *apartheid* policies and hinted at amelioration of them; but the nub of the letter was an invitation that Mrs Thatcher should *"send a personal envoy to meet with me in order that we may discuss not only questions of principle but also – (a) the obstacles in the way of closer cooperation between our Governments; (b) possible ways and means of eliminating those obstacles"*. It was an unveiled proposal to the British Prime Minister to break ranks with her Commonwealth colleagues in their mutual commitments under the Lusaka Declaration of just six months earlier. Mrs Thatcher sent her envoy Lord Hunt of Tanworth to South Africa to see Botha in April 1980 amidst much secrecy, and a dialogue began as between allies facing a mutual threat.

Lord Hunt was a former highly regarded British Cabinet Secretary who after retirement became a non-executive director of Prudential Assurance Company which had considerable interests in South Africa and this was to be the cover for his visit. His report could be summed up in its final paragraph in which he said of Botha:

> *To give him his due he said that he was not asking Britain to act as South Africa's agent: but undeniably he regards our eventual reaction to his proposal as some kind of touchstone. 'If you turn us down we have no hope with anyone else and will have to go it alone'. Yet there was little evidence that he is contemplating the sort of steps domestically that would make it easier to have the closer relations he seeks.*

What Botha sought, of course – mounted on the back of 'the Soviet threat to Africa and the West' – was a special relationship with Britain which would shield South Africa from international and Commonwealth sanctions. Earlier in the report, when describing the sweeteners of future improvement in the conditions of blacks, Lord Hunt had made their limitations clear: *'But he had to say bluntly that majority rule would never be acceptable'.* Yet, for the rest of the decade, Mrs Thatcher was to be South Africa's staunchest ally in the Commonwealth's effort to pressure *apartheid's* keepers by sanctions – which in her own 'double-speak' she always referred to as 'punitive sanctions' – to end the heinous system.

Despite her right-wing ideological convictions and her anti-Soviet instincts, Mrs Thatcher was too intelligent to rely wholly on 'Cold War' considerations in the matter of ending *apartheid* – however much they appealed to her passions. So was there something more? Yes, there was. Something of much more material concern to Britain than any countervailing humanitarian concern for blacks in South Africa.

In September 1980, Britain's Foreign Secretary submitted to the Cabinet's Defence and Overseas Policy Committee a Memorandum (now declassified) drawn up by high-level officials on the extent to which British interests will be at risk if Britain were to either acquiesce in the imposition of sanctions against South Africa or veto sanctions (at the UN) in isolation from 'our American and French partners'. Their conclusion was that in either case the risk would be 'grave': in the first situation, through impairment of exports, imports, employment, investment and banking; the second, through commitments at risk in OAU countries which were over three times those in South Africa itself. They never weighed Britain's larger interest in acting to end apartheid's infamous abuse of human rights. Humanitarianism, morality, internationalism were never in the scales. The report reached the conclusion that:

> *the assessment brings out the importance of doing all in our power to avoid the choice between applying or vetoing sanctions.*

In other words, we must not apply sanctions ourselves and we must encourage other big powers to do likewise at the UN.

And that is the path Mrs Thatcher chose – take 'sanctions' off the road map both in the Commonwealth and at the UN. And that was the path she followed for all of the 1980s with ever increasing conviction. Writing recently of his appointment as British Ambassador to South Africa in 1987 Robin Renwick (later Lord Renwick) affirmed frankly (though without meaning to be critical) just how self-serving were Mrs Thatcher's South Africa policies:

> *I was dispatched by her to be ambassador to South Africa in 1987 because she wanted to play a more activist role than the Embassy had been doing, having been instructed by the Foreign Office to keep a low profile and engage in damage limitation. We had more at stake than any other country – by far the largest investments and, in that and many other respects, the most to lose. Of the 1.5 million English-speaking white South Africans, nearly a million either had or were entitled to British passports. The Home Office had begun to worry what might happen if all or half of them decided to migrate to Britain. Important British interests were at stake; she had no intention of throwing them away.*

He might have added – *by weakening the South African economy through economic sanctions.* Nothing had changed since the 1980 'risk assessment'. 'Vetoing', of course, had relevance only in a UN Security Council context and Britain (under a Labour Prime Minister) had already in 1977 (in the wake of the *Soweto Uprising*) concurred in the Security Council's comprehensive mandatory arms embargo on South Africa. Applying economic sanctions, and internationalising their application, was the route open to the Commonwealth. It was the journey I considered myself duty bound to urge our member states to take. And for all except Britain, it was counsel I hardly needed to give.

* * *

Throughout the decade of the eighties, Mrs Thatcher conducted a campaign in the Commonwealth against the use of sanctions to end *apartheid.* It was not one in which any other Commonwealth country acquiesced; they all remained true to Commonwealth values, opposed Britain's perverse evasion of them, and in the end prevailed in being among the forces that brought *apartheid* to its end – and Nelson Mandela to freedom. It was a proud episode in the life of the Commonwealth – and one in which, like the triumph in bringing Zimbabwe to a negotiated settlement, Britain, so long the abstainer, sought to claim the victory as its own. Besides being unfaithful to history to the point of re-writing it, it is an injustice to those Commonwealth countries who fought her 'no sanctions' policy – very specially the other white members of the Commonwealth, notably Australia and Canada, whose unwavering activism ensured that the Commonwealth did not divide on racial lines over *apartheid.* It is inspiring to recall that they made their stand against *apartheid* on grounds of principle; there were no votes for them at home on what they did on South Africa; there were no material gains for their countries, in fact there were some losses. We shall see how they and other Commonwealth leaders made their stand for principle in 'the Thatcher years'.

For my own part, I did a good deal of talking worldwide in positioning the Commonwealth to help the struggle of non-white South Africans against *apartheid.* The Lusaka Declaration (unanimous as it was) was my 'mission statement' and mobilising opinion to fulfil the mission was my vocation. On 12 November 1980, for example, in delivering the first Kwame Nkrumah Memorial Lecture in Accra, I alluded to South Africa saying, inter alia,

> *The example of Zimbabwe suggests that even in South Africa it is not too late for change; that even there conflict can be averted and the peoples come together for a genuine multiracial union which could offer hope to all.*
>
> *We need to ask ourselves why the world has failed, after all these years of campaigning against apartheid, to extract from the rulers of South Africa, nothing more than gestures, why it has failed, why we have failed, to secure a significant lessening of the rigours of apartheid let alone its total rejection. If we do that honestly and squarely, we will have to admit that we all share in the responsibility for this failure. But a greater blame must lie with those countries that are in a stronger position to influence South Africa and better placed to compel concessions from its rulers.*
>
> *They decline, it is sometimes said, to use their full weight out of concern for South Africa's value to the "free world" or out of solicitude for their trading and investment interests. The first is shameful and contradictory; the second downright shortsighted.*
>
> *Each generation strives to make the world better for its children. In South Africa, we are perhaps already seeing the signs that the next generation is losing faith in our capacity to assure its future. Driven to desperation by their present and denied hope for their future, the children of Soweto have signalled their resolve to make their own future, even if it be only death. Each day the world delays to compel South Africa, Soweto's children will grow in number, and in desperation, and the certainty that their blood will flow will be made greater.*
>
> *Slavery once proved to be too unbearable an affront to man's nobler instincts. We must hope that apartheid, equally barbaric in its denial of dignity, will one day crumble because humanity finds it too repugnant to tolerate. Deliverance may lie in the hands of those who wield power in South Africa, but the world has the*

power to demand that deliverance. To the ultimate use of that power we must dedicate ourselves. And we must not leave it to governments alone, but seek to move governments through their people. Africa cannot do it alone, but must join hands with all those elsewhere in the world who value freedom. All must work to make that day of deliverance dawn, so that the children of all of South Africa's Sowetos may live in the sunshine of a free society.

The following year, in my Introduction to the Secretariat's Biennial Report which I developed as a personal non-bureaucratic message to Commonwealth leaders, I wrote – looking ahead to the Melbourne summit:

For the Commonwealth to remain true to the multiracialism which is part of its credo, and to which it renewed its commitment in the Lusaka Declaration on Racism and Racial Prejudice, its role in the 80s must also encompass the effort to bring apartheid to an end in South Africa. Apartheid has been universally and unequivocally condemned; but it has become abundantly clear that condemnation alone will not bring change in South Africa. Major countries with levers of power which could be used to exert pressure on South Africa continue to plead their preference for persuasion, but to disclaim effective power to persuade. It is not merely that they recoil from international sanctions, but that by the nature and ambience of their relations over a wide field they convey the impression, however unfounded, of sanctioning the status quo in South Africa. This appearance of pardoning apartheid is becoming harder to dispel by mere declamation to the contrary. If South Africa remains un-persuaded, it should not occasion surprise that the call for the world to move beyond condemnation becomes stronger.

In their strategy to secure a withholding of Western pressure, South Africa's rulers flaunt their credentials as a strategic ally of the West. But for the West to be aligned with South Africa – in whatever cause – would be to stand against Africa. It is not possible to be an ally of South Africa and a

> *friend of Africa. What African nationalism seeks is friendship; what South Africa proposes is that the West should withhold it.*

Through the decade of the 1980s I made in all some 480 speeches or statements in whole or in part addressing the issue of *apartheid* and South Africa, most of them dealing with the issue of sanctions. They were made world-wide: in London, of course, but in many of the Commonwealth's then 51 countries; and beyond the Commonwealth, in Europe, the United States and Latin America. They mainly argued the case for effective Commonwealth and international sanctions and exposed the fallacies in Mrs Thatcher's abstentions. They helped to place the Commonwealth in the vanguard of global support of the struggle being waged within South Africa to end *apartheid* and bring genuine democracy to the country.

The main encounters with Mrs Thatcher were at Commonwealth Summit Meetings – in Nassau in 1985, in London in 1986, in Vancouver in 1987 and in Kuala Lumpur in 1989 – though she had begun her opposition to sanctions from the year of her election in 1979. At each of the later Summits the Commonwealth pushed her further than she was willing to go in the matter of sanctions against South Africa; but at each, save the last, she prevented the Commonwealth collectively from going as far as all leaders save her would have gone. Her policy on sanctions provided life support for South Africa; and therefore for *apartheid.* In Melbourne in 1981 world economic issues dominated the agenda, and in New Delhi in 1983 the American invasion of Grenada took centre stage; though at each she effectively blocked a robust Commonwealth sanctions regime. However, by Nassau in 1985 the Commonwealth had had enough of the Thatcher 'veto' and a showdown was inevitable.

Bob Hawke had by then replaced Malcolm Fraser as Prime Minister of Australia, and was as aggressively for sanctions as Fraser, but without Fraser's handicap of Thatcher's Conservative party connections; and Brian Mulroney was Prime Minister of Canada – a Canadian Conservative Party Prime Minister who brought to the issue of *apartheid* all the humanitarian passions of his St. Francis Xavier

University background and his early connections with John Diefenbaker, who as an earlier Conservative Party Prime Minister of Canada had taken enlightened and progressive positions on Commonwealth issues. With David Lange having replaced Robert Muldoon in New Zealand, the white Commonwealth save for Britain was firmly lined up with black Africa. Rajiv Gandhi of India was as militantly supportive as his mother had been, and developed a close personal relationship with Hawke and Mulroney. The Caribbean (with Edward Seaga replacing Michael Manley in Jamaica, but being as resolute on sanctions) was solidly with Africa.

At the Nassau Commonwealth Heads of Government Meeting in 1985, Mrs Thatcher was alone in protecting South Africa against sanctions – as she proudly reported to President Botha within days of the Meeting's end. The truth was that in shielding *apartheid* from Commonwealth sanctions, Mrs Thatcher had drawn closer to President Botha than to any of her 50 Commonwealth colleagues. As the wagons were circled in South Africa, she was within them, at least as far as sanctions were concerned – the world's principal means of pressure. In her isolation in the Commonwealth and much of the world that came with being South Africa's minder, Mrs Thatcher appeared to enjoy the soubriquet of 'the Iron Lady' given to her in 1976 by a Russian military journalist in an uncomplimentary allusion to Otto Von Bismarck known as the "Iron Chancellor" of Imperial Germany.

But there was one voice that would not be at Nassau in 1985 – that of *apartheid's* victims: black South Africans. I tried to make sure their message was heard. Just before leaving London for Nassau, on the evening of Friday, 4 October, Bishop Desmond Tutu and Dr Oliver Tambo dined with me in Marlborough House. Tutu was elected and ordained the first black South African Anglican Archbishop of Cape Town in South Africa and primate of the of the Anglican Church of Southern Africa. He had received the Nobel Peace Prize in 1984 and was a strong voice against *apartheid.* Tambo was the leader in exile of the African National Congress – the physical face that complemented the poster of Nelson Mandela. With us were some leaders of industry, commerce and banking from the City of London, some of the top people of the media, leaders of the Anti-Apartheid Movement in Britain, and key figures of the Commonwealth diplomatic community. It was a rather special night. It was probably only under that Commonwealth roof that such a group could have met in London at that time. Indeed, Tutu and Tambo had themselves not come together ever in the presence of any group of this kind; and, in fact, hadn't seen each other for a while. Their warm embrace as they met was a reminder to us of the oneness of their goal.

The evening was a private affair; not a proclaimed event. No great negotiations were being set in train; no forging of strategies and tactics; just a meeting together of people whose very different lives, pursuits and interests were becoming increasingly entwined, as a result of the crisis in Bishop Tutu's and Oliver Tambo's country, and the way in which it had come to be at the centre of world attention and concern – and would be at the Commonwealth's a week later in The Bahamas.

Desmond Tutu talked with great anguish of the 'killing fields' of South Africa. As we dined, he reminded us (with murals of earlier slaughter of the French by the English looking down on us from the walls of Marlborough House) that young blacks were that moment being killed somewhere in South Africa by its security forces. He abhorred the violence, including the violence of rebellion; but he acknowledged that people had been pushed beyond endurance by the violence of apartheid.

He pleaded with us all to help to end apartheid quickly before his country was consumed not just in flames but in hatred. He could not understand 'technical' reasons for withholding real pressure on South Africa. He asked, it seemed to him, for so little: not for all British trading and financial links with South Africa to be severed, but for some carefully chosen economic measures that would convince white South Africa that Britain was serious in demanding an end to apartheid and political change towards democracy. And he explained how time was running out for peaceful change – and for people like himself who were standing out against violence on all sides. He was genuinely surprised; he told us that he was still being listened to by his own people, particularly young people, when he urged reliance only on peaceful means. He left us in no doubt that the signals Britain sent to South Africa by its position on sanctions mattered a very great deal in terms of how change comes in South Africa, and what its aftermath would be. He said that the black people of South Africa would not forget who helped them in their time of need – and who did not.

Few at that dinner had met or heard of Oliver Tambo. Some 20 years before, with Nelson Mandela and Walter Sisulu, he had helped to vitalise the African National Congress. He had not seen them since the Rivonia treason trial in 1964, which condemned Sisulu, Mandela and others for life to prison cells on Robben Island. Oliver Tambo had continued the struggle against apartheid, accepting with reluctance, as he told us, that the violence of Pretoria left no alternative but a violent struggle to end apartheid. He himself, as the ANC's interim president, had been assigned to keep the struggle alive in exile from his country all those years. He chided the uneven judgement which extolled liberation wars in the Americas and Europe but branded as terrorism the struggle against a system of human degradation which all the world regarded as the most evil form of racism in recent time.

And he too appealed to us, and particularly to our British guests, for help and support. It was not an appeal for arms or even for material help, but for moral support and for international pressure on Pretoria to accept apartheid's end. He told us of his meeting in Zambia with South African businessmen: an occasion of his white compatriots sitting down to talk with him and his colleagues – South Africans talking about their country and its future. It was for him, he said, an occasion of encouragement and hope. It had happened because of the conjuncture of external pressure and internal rebellion.

Oliver Tambo was not young, and that night he seemed frail. His whole life had been distorted by apartheid, yet somehow this was not a man filled with hate, but with hope; not a racist by retaliation, but a black South African looking to a non-racial South Africa in which all races would work together in mutual respect and dignity under a democratic system.

His last plea to us was to make South Africa realise through economic sanctions that apartheid had to go. He said that economic pressure then would save lives in South Africa – black and white alike; far from hurting black Africans, they would help to lift the intolerable burdens of apartheid. And, like Desmond Tutu, he not so much threatened as reminded us that the majority people of South Africa would remember who had helped them. He seemed to leave us with a question each of us had to answer for ourselves, and with responsibility for all the implications of our answer.

I had intended that what Tutu and Tambo said to us over dinner would form the basis of a general discussion; but, as Oliver Tambo ended, I felt that a discussion was out of place and I said so, suggesting instead that we reflect on what they had told us – these two men pursuing a single struggle in very different ways, each respecting the other and the other's role; each conscious that the end of the long struggle could be in sight but that it could also be deferred, depending on how the international community responded to a crisis that was now not theirs alone but ours as well.

And I ventured to express the hope, to the acclamation of all present, that when next these two men come to Marlborough House they would both come from within South Africa, and as citizens of a member country of the Commonwealth; that is, from a South Africa that had seen apartheid's end, and, as an integrated, multi-racial, democratic state that had returned and been welcomed back to the Commonwealth community. That prospect seemed not so distant or impossible but more like the light of a beacon guiding our responses to their pleas.

On the eve of the Summit, I spoke to the annual Meeting of the Commonwealth Press Union in Nassau and told them of that meeting with these great men in London. I said I remained hopeful that when Commonwealth leaders addressed this matter, they would find such mutual reinforcement in their common abhorrence of apartheid as to agree on a collective strategy in the spirit of the Commonwealth's principled stand of the past. In other words, I hoped that, years from then, all of us would be able to look back on the stand the Commonwealth took at Nassau with the same pride we took then in slavery's abolition exactly 150 years earlier.

CHAPTER 23

The Sanctions Filibuster

Lyford Cay in The Bahamas is a Caribbean idyll – a gated enclave of pink bungalows shaded by coconut palms scattered along the blue Caribbean Sea. Prime Minister Lyndon Pindling had persuaded its wealthy expatriate residents to give up occupancy for the 'retreat' weekend to his guest Presidents and Prime Ministers from the Commonwealth. It was no stranger to political celebrities; in 1962, President John F. Kennedy and Prime Minister Harold Macmillan had met there to conclude the *Polaris Agreement.* And beyond the Cay, the larger venue and timing were auspicious. It was in The Bahamas, on the island of San Salvador, nearly 500 years earlier, on 12 October 1492, that Columbus's flagship the *Santa Maria* reached the shores of the 'new world' and changed the course of history for new and old alike. If environments could contribute to political consensus, the choice could not have been better.

On the matter of South Africa, which dominated the Nassau Meeting, Commonwealth leaders needed every help to find a pathway to agreement. I called my Introduction to the Secretary General's Report to the Meeting (my message to Commonwealth leaders) *'A Testing Time'.* And so it was to be – the historicity of the Bahamas and the charms of Lyford Cay notwithstanding.

It was 1985; and in the Report, on *apartheid,* I appealed to our leaders thus:

> *The Commonwealth has an honourable record in the campaign to end apartheid. It was the first international organisation to*

make South Africa unwelcome ... It was a Commonwealth country, India, that first stopped all trade with South Africa, at the cost of losing a significant export market. Commonwealth African countries have stood in the front line against apartheid, also at great cost – with increasing penalties as South Africa began to visit its punitive anger against them. The Security Council's decision to impose an arms embargo in November 1977 came in the wake of a call by Commonwealth leaders in June of that year. It was the Commonwealth's Gleneagles Agreement of 1977 that pioneered world action against apartheid in sport. ...

Many options are open: withdrawal of investments, a freeze on future investments, a ban on bank loans, an end to the import of krugerrands, curbs on South African advertising particularly for tourism and recruitment, withdrawal of route rights to South African Airways and termination of flights to South Africa, bans on imports of agricultural products; the list is a long one....

It is irrefutable that the conjunction of a rising tide of anger within South Africa and a rising demand outside for economic sanctions is making Pretoria pause. Those pressures must be sustained if we are to ensure that it is a pause to recant not to regroup. Collective Commonwealth action at Nassau can help to make it so. It is unthinkable that any Commonwealth country should offer comfort to South Africa at this time. The Commonwealth ... has no option but to be in the vanguard of the final push against apartheid. Neither kinship nor vested interest nor unwarranted acceptance of Pretoria's good faith nor mistaken perceptions of South Africa as an ally must obstruct a worthy Commonwealth response to the challenges and opportunities now at hand.

I was writing to very diverse, but mainly receptive, audiences among our Presidents and Prime Ministers. Prime Minister Dr Mahathir Mohamad of Malaysia was one of the handful of leaders asked to speak at the public Opening Ceremony on 16 October. He was a relative newcomer to Commonwealth deliberations but he spoke with candour about South Africa:

> *There is no government like the regime in South Africa. It is a total pariah. It legalises the morally illegal. Minority is majority. Slavery is freedom. Ghettos are nations. Like Israel, it respects no international norms. Boundaries are not sacred to the racists of South Africa.*
>
> *And this white regime survives in this day and age. And why does it survive? It survives because the people who are fond of criticising alleged racism in developing countries are not prepared to do anything about the most blatantly racist regime in the world.*
>
> *Malaysia does not trade with South Africa. We deprive ourselves of substantial revenue by so doing. But those whose application of sanctions is likely to bring South Africa to its knees, have any number of arguments why they should not apply sanctions. Restrictions on imports from poor countries, restrictions which cause real human suffering in these small states, are all right. But not sanctions against South Africa. The blacks would suffer. That is the excuse.*
>
> *The fact is that the blacks are already suffering. Cures are always painful. As a doctor I should know. But to perpetuate suffering is a poor alternative to the temporary pain of a cure. If sanctions can help destroy a despicable policy like apartheid, then sanctions must be applied by those who can hurt most; by the countries with the biggest economic clout. Failure to do so would mean hypocrisy on the part of these countries. And that will run off on the Commonwealth.*
>
> *If the Commonwealth refuses to do something definite, then the club should cease to pretend. It should admit that it really cannot contribute to solving the problems faced by its members, if not the world. Then we can relax and enjoy our get-together.*

Mrs Thatcher was on the platform; but did not join in the applause. Many who applauded were thoughtful; they knew that the Commonwealth had to deliver at Nassau.

President Kaunda of Zambia opened the plenary discussion on 'South Africa' with a call that was more evocative of the horrors of *apartheid* than any narrative. A young South African, he said, was due to be hanged at 7 o'clock the following day. All the Christian churches in South Africa had taken up the cause because they were convinced of his innocence; so had the UN Security Council; but to no avail. Commonwealth leaders, he urged, must add their voice. I was asked to draft the Statement which they approved, and I was able to report later that day that, through Canadian good offices, it had been delivered to the South African Government in Pretoria: a plea for clemency from the entire Commonwealth's Heads meeting to consider their response to *apartheid.* It made no difference. Benjamin Molosie was hanged the following morning in South Africa – a sobering reminder as Commonwealth leaders began their deliberations that, as the UN General Assembly had declared, *apartheid* continued to be 'a crime against humanity'.

The person who pointed a practical way forward was Prime Minister Bob Hawke of Australia. He broke new ground for the Commonwealth having shared with me in confidence beforehand what he would do. He made it clear that the pressure of sanctions had to be maintained and strengthened. He had himself taken steps in Australia and looked to the retreat of Commonwealth Heads of Government that coming weekend to share his further ideas. But he wanted to complement the pressure of sanctions with the facilitation of dialogue. He proposed that the Commonwealth should appoint a group of truly eminent persons to attempt, on behalf of the Commonwealth, to initiate and encourage the process of dialogue in South Africa. He envisaged that the Group *"should visit South Africa to talk to the black people in that country and help in the process of stimulating genuine and meaningful dialogue with the regime".*

When Mrs Thatcher spoke (just before the coffee break) she indicated agreement with the Australian suggestion but implied that it was presented as an alternative to the application of sanctions. Immediately on the resumption, Bob Hawke asked for the floor to make it clear that he had specifically called for a discussion of sanctions. *"As all would recall he had said that they must address their minds to the question of restrictive measures or sanctions or signals or whatever they might be called".* His idea of an 'Eminent Persons Liaison Group' *"was not to be seen as a substitute for addressing those issues".* Mrs Thatcher knew, of course, that the call for stronger and wider sanctions was inevitable. She had already begun to speak of them as 'measures'; but at Nassau she introduced a new lexicography. Only the UN mandatory arms embargo was a sanction; every other restrictive measure, including those so far imposed by the Commonwealth was a 'signal'. It was this Bob Hawke was debunking. It was clear that the Retreat would deal with both sanctions and what became known as 'the EPG' – the Eminent Persons Group. The Retreat at Lyford Cay would be no picnic.

By accepted Commonwealth practice, the weekend retreat is for Heads of Government and the Secretary-General – and their spouses. No Ministers; no officials. A good deal therefore falls on the Secretary General; and his preparation for it with the aid of Secretariat staff is crucial. I went prepared with outline drafts on both sanctions and the Australian proposal for the EPG. On both I expected contention; on sanctions, from Mrs Thatcher; on the EPG, from a mixed bag including Africans. I had, myself, become converted to the EPG proposal; but for the Commonwealth generally it involved a major strategic change from a policy of Pretoria's isolation to one of dialogue; from talking to black South Africans in exile, to encounters with *apartheid's* victims at home. It was a bold change after two decades of a policy of international isolation of Pretoria; but I felt that Hawke was right; that the time had come, while maintaining the pressure of sanctions, for the Commonwealth to confront *apartheid* in South Africa. No one knew whether Pretoria would cooperate; but the proposal had received Mrs Thatcher's support and for Pretoria to reject it would put in jeopardy Pretoria's goal of her protection of South Africa from further sanctions.

The discussions at Lyford Cay soon took on the character of clusters of discussions on bungalow patios and shuttle diplomacy between them. President Kaunda was the touchstone of African opinion (President Nyerere of Tanzania had not come to Nassau, but his Foreign Minister, my close friend, Salim Salim represented him); but the real activists were Bob Hawke, Brian Mulroney and Rajiv Gandhi. And it was with them that I spent much time hammering out a basic draft – one integrated Accord upon which they insisted. Mrs Thatcher could not have the EPG without sanctions; and on sanctions they wanted to go quite far. I was of course the principal courier; but there were times when tactically we agreed to let Rajiv Gandhi be her persuader; sometimes, Brian Mulroney. In the end, we had a document in which Margaret Thatcher agreed to go further than she had gone before on sanctions while the others spelled out in the same document the eleven additional sanctions they would apply immediately – and what further they would consider if the EPG made no progress. What is more, Mrs Thatcher agreed to a deadline of six months for a review of progress. And there was something else. The Accord allowed for everyone going even further than the sanctions spelled out in the Accord if there continued to be no progress even beyond the six month review, when: *"each of us will pursue the objectives of this Accord in all the ways and through all appropriate fora open to us."* There would be no British veto.

Altogether, it was a very strong message to Pretoria. The several ways in which Mrs Thatcher had tried a filibuster on sanctions had not succeeded. She sought to counteract that failure by miniaturising to the media the concessions she had made. As she triumphantly put it, she was determined to stand out against the *'gadarene rush'* towards sanctions and had succeeded in limiting them to *'a tiny little bit'* – an epithet she illustrated by a thumb and forefinger gesture of smallness. It was an unfortunate performance which angered her Commonwealth colleagues – and some of her own as well. Under the headline: "Anger at the 'tiny sanctions'. London's *Daily Mail's* Political Editor reported on 22 October –

> *Mrs Thatcher's 'they're tiny aren't they' remark about the package agreed in Nassau appears to have united all her political rivals at home.*
>
> *SDP leader Dr David Owen said the new measures were meaningful and necessary but in the Bahamas it had developed into the 'war of Mrs Thatcher's face.'*
>
> *He said: 'It raises serious questions about her diplomacy. I don't know what on earth she is up to. Does she not realise the damage she is doing to Britain?'*
>
> *Labour Front Bencher Peter Shore accused Mrs Thatcher of 'extraordinary damaging antics' at Nassau and demanded some explanation of her 'scornful dismissal' of the package*

"With those four little words", her Foreign and Commonwealth Secretary, Geoffrey Howe (later Lord Howe), complained afterwards in his memoir *Conflict of Loyalty, "she humiliated three dozen other heads of government, devalued the policy which they had just agreed, and demeaned herself"*. But she had done more; she had sent a message of comfort to President Botha in Pretoria that she was still South Africa's protector against sanctions – undermining in the process the prospects of the negotiating facility she had just agreed to establish.

The text of the Nassau Summit's Commonwealth Accord on Southern Africa identifying the sanctions agreed and projected is at Appendix 7.

The most enduring legacy of the Nassau Accord was the Eminent Persons Group. I recognised that many anti-apartheid activists would have misgivings about our shift to 'dialogue with apartheid'. Trevor Huddleston told me that only his confidence in me prevented him from speaking out against the EPG, and that he might yet denounce it if his worst fears were fulfilled. For me, the key lay in the choice of the 'Eminent Persons'. The Accord had looked to the Heads of seven countries *'working out with the Secretary General the modalities of this effort'*. I began that process at Nassau with the seven Heads: the President of Zambia and the Prime Ministers of Australia, the Bahamas, Canada, India, the United Kingdom and Zimbabwe. I secured their support for the Group's independence – they would not be representatives of any Government and need not even be a national of the proposing Government.

I wanted co-Chairmen – one from Africa, one from the white Commonwealth; and I knew who I wanted: General Olusegun Obasanjo of Nigeria (former President) and Malcolm Fraser of Australia (former Prime Minister). Bob Hawke readily agreed to nominate Fraser, if he himself agreed; Kaunda and Mugabe agreed to act jointly in nominating Obasanjo, if he agreed. I was off to a good start. I wanted Pierre Trudeau, and Brian Mulroney agreed – if I could convince Pierre. I went to Montreal directly from Nassau; but Trudeau, while willing, felt his new role of looking after his sons (after his divorce) would not allow it. Instead, Mulroney did the Group a great favour in offering the Rev. Edward Scott, Anglican Archbishop of Ontario. Rajiv Gandhi and I quickly agreed on the sage former Foreign Minister of India, Sardar Swaran Singh; and the Chairman agreed that his nominee would be from the Caribbean, a woman President of the World Council of Churches, Dame Nita Barrow of Barbados. In nominating their other member, Kaunda and Mugabe went outside their countries to Tanzania and the internationally respected former Foreign Minister, John Malacela.

That left Mrs Thatcher who wanted Geoffrey Howe. I explained that a serving government Minister would not meet the agreed test of independence – though I greatly respected Sir Geoffrey. We postponed the discussion to London where the Prime Minister offered to nominate Lord Barber, a former Tory Chancellor of the Exchequer and long standing Chairman of Standard Chartered Bank. As Chairman of Standard Chartered whose presence in South Africa was large, I felt Lord Barber would greatly enlarge the acceptability of the EPG to white South Africans – a necessary factor if the Group was to succeed. I approached Obasanjo and Malcolm Fraser personally and they both agreed, and agreed to work together as Co-Chairmen. I believed we had secured a Group of the highest quality. They turned out to be superlative in fulfilment of their mission.

A pre-requisite of the EPG's mission was the co-operation of the South African Government. On 21 October, before President Botha could be formally approached, he wrote to Mrs Thatcher (who had alerted him from Nassau on 21 October, and written him again from London on the 31st) as follows (declassified):

> *You may be assured that I have much understanding for your position vis-à-vis the Commonwealth. We are moreover gratified by the strong, principled, stand that you ... have taken against economic sanctions and also by your refusal to meet with the ANC for so long as that organisation remains committed to violence.*
>
> *I must, however, tell you – informally and confidentially since we have not been officially approached to date – that my Government will find it impossible to cooperate with the Commonwealth initiative.*

To her credit, Mrs Thatcher replied on 17 November to Botha conveying her 'dismay' at his initial response, and urging that he cooperate with the Commonwealth's EPG mission. *"I am convinced"*, she wrote, *"that it would be infinitely more damaging to South Africa's future interests were you to refuse to have anything to do with the Group"*. And she continued:

> *May I ask you to consider for a moment the full implications if your Government were to reject co-operation with the Group. Your enemies in the Commonwealth would be delighted; they never wanted it anyway. We and others who had hoped for progress through dialogue will be told that we should have known better. The international pressures for sanctions against South Africa will fast gather momentum again. Most of the value of my having held the line at Nassau will be lost. My ability to help preserve the conditions in which an internal dialogue of the sort you are seeking has a chance of success will be critically, perhaps, fatally, weakened.*
>
> *In short I can see no need for you to take a decision about cooperation with the Group now, let alone reject it publicly. If you value my continuing help, I urge you most strongly not to do so. I do not think I could be plainer.*

Protecting the Prime Minister's own flanks had begun to coincide with furthering the Commonwealth's strategy for confronting *apartheid.* President Botha got her 'plain' message, and grudgingly agreed that the EPG could pursue its mission to South Africa.

* * *

This was the most ambitious and delicate undertaking the Commonwealth Secretariat had ever managed. But we had several assets. First in the quality of the Group. General Obasanjo, his military background notwithstanding, was a gifted conciliator and internationalist. Malcolm Fraser, in the Commonwealth's endeavours in Zimbabwe had demonstrated strengths of character and qualities of leadership that made the Co-Chairmen a formidable team. And each of the members brought special, and sometimes unsuspected, qualities to the Group's mission. An example of this was the Group's first encounter with Soweto which at that time was off limits to them. Dame Nita Barrow needed only an African skirt and head-tie to accompany Winnie Mandela undetected into the deprivation of the township.

EPG with Winnie Mandela in South Africa

Another asset was the Secretariat's special support team for the Group (SUGEP – Special Unit for the Group of Eminent Persons) led by Assistant Secretary-General Moni Malhoutra and including other high quality staff members, like Jeremy Pope and Hugh Craft, Directors of the Legal and International Affairs Divisions respectively, and some of our best officers. The Team was dedicated to the Group and answered to the Co-Chairmen. My Deputy, Chief Emeka Anyaoku, accompanied the Group as my link to it. I explained all this to the EPG when I spoke to them at their inaugural meeting in Marlborough House on 12 December 1985. Conscious that the EPG could mark a turning point in the struggle against *apartheid,* the Secretariat spared nothing in its support of the mission. I was hopeful it could be a factor for significant change.

A unique asset was the aircraft of the Canadian Air Force made available to the Group by the Canadian Government – a gesture indicative of Brian Mulroney's unequivocal support of the EPG's Mission.

And so, from 15 February 1986 the Commonwealth Group: from five continents, two former Heads of Government among them, from Australia and Nigeria, former Ministers from Britain, India and Tanzania, an Archbishop from Canada and a woman President of the World Council of Churches from the Caribbean, a rare commingling of integrity, humanity, compassion, understanding and a wide experience – began its mission in South Africa 'to explore the path to peaceful change'.

Over a period of five months, it held 21 meetings with South African Government Ministers including, prominently, South Africa's President P.W. Botha and F.W. de Klerk who succeeded him as well as R.F. 'Pik' Botha, who was Foreign Minister. It also had prolonged discussions with leaders of political and other organisations as well as with prominent academic, political, religious and community figures within South Africa and outside it. It saw and talked with the ANC in Lusaka many times.

Very importantly members of the Group met Nelson Mandela in Pollsmoor prison on three separate occasions. He told the EPG that theirs was the most important visit he had received in 24 years in prison.

As the Group worked assiduously, keeping its own counsel, but building bridges and inspiring confidence, it saw at first hand the growing turmoil in the country, the explosion of anger and unrest, the spiralling cycle of state violence and counter violence, all of which made them keenly aware that South Africa was on a short fuse to disaster. Significantly, while the anti-sanctions enthusiasts in Britain and elsewhere kept urging that sanctions would hurt the black people of South Africa, every black person the Group met said they would happily endure the additional hardship which sanctions might entail if they would bring the hated system of apartheid to an end. These hardships would be as nothing compared to what they had to endure every day.

This was the context in which a possible 'negotiating concept' emerged from the Group; it was a concept' which the EPG believed could provide the path to peaceful change around which consensus was emerging and hope – so long a stranger to South Africa – was beginning to build. The text of the 'Possible Negotiating Concept', as revealed subsequently in the EPG Report, was as follows:

> *The South African Government has declared its commitment to dismantling the system of apartheid, to ending racial discrimination and to broad-based negotiations leading to new constitutional arrangements for power-sharing by all the people of South Africa. In the light of preliminary and as yet incomplete discussions with representatives of various organisations and groups, within and outside South Africa, we believe that in the context of specific and meaningful steps being taken towards ending apartheid, the following additional action might ensure negotiations and a break in the cycle of violence.*
>
> *On the part of the Government:*
>
> *(a) Removal of the military from the townships, providing for freedom of assembly and discussion and suspension of detention without trial. (b) The release of Nelson Mandela and other political prisoners and detainees.*
>
> *(c) The unbanning of the ANC and PAC and the permitting of normal political activity.*

On the part of the ANC and others:
Entering negotiations and suspending violence.

It is our view that simultaneous announcements incorporating these ideas might be negotiated if the Government were to be interested in pursuing this broad approach.

In the light of the Government's indication to us that it:

(i) is not in principle against the release of Nelson Mandela and similar prisoners;
(ii) is not opposed in principle to the unbanning of any organisations;
(iii) is prepared to enter into negotiations with the acknowledged leaders of the people of South Africa;
(iv) is committed to removal of discrimination, not only from the statute books but also from South African society as a whole;
(v) is committed to ending of white domination;
(vi) will not prescribe who may represent black communities in negotiations on a new constitution for South Africa;
(vii) is prepared to negotiate on an open agenda.

The South African Government may wish to give serious consideration to the approach outlined in this note.

On the morning of 19 May, as the Group was leaving for its scheduled meeting with the Government's Cabinet Constitutional Committee at which it expected to receive a considered response on the 'Possible Negotiating Concept', there were unconfirmed reports of South African Government attacks during the night on 'ANC bases' in Harare and Gaborone, and later in Lusaka. The Meeting proceeded inconclusively. When the reports were confirmed later that day it became all too plain to the Group, as it said in its Report, *"that while talking to the Group about negotiations and peaceful solutions, the Government had been planning these armed attacks"*. The ANC saw the attacks as *"the regime's crystal clear response"* to the Commonwealth mission. President Botha had played along with Mrs Thatcher's recommendation for six months; but the EPG's 'Possible Negotiating Concept' was becoming too serious a proposition of change; some of his own Ministers were attracted to it and there was a wave of public support developing around it; it had to be terminated. P.W. Botha knew full well that bombing the three Commonwealth Capitals whose Presidents were parties to the Nassau Accord and sponsors of the EPG would send the appropriate message. And it did: the Government would have nothing to do with the 'possible negotiating concept'. The mission left South Africa that day.

South Africa's Foreign Minister, R.F. 'Pik' Botha, was a prominent interlocutor with the EPG. In his testimony to the Truth and Reconciliation Commission under the Chairmanship of Archbishop Tutu in 1996, against the backdrop of a 39-page submission, he said:

> *The 'possible negotiating concept, Mr Chairman, will in my opinion come to be regarded as one of the most remarkable documents to emerge from the seemingly interminable negotiating processes. ... But, Mr Chairperson in the early morning of 19 May 1986 the South Africa security forces launched attacks on Harare, Lusaka and Gabarone. Each was a Commonwealth capital which the EPG had recently visited in the course of their search for a South Africa solution. Maybe General Obasanjo will tell me it was just one provocation too much. If so, I will understand him. I felt very much the same.*

He then distanced himself from the raids by saying that they were *"not discussed at any meeting at which I was present"* and had they been he *"would have opposed them most strongly"*. But, he pointed out, *"the responsibility for the military implementation of operations vested exclusively in the Chief of Defence Force"*.

The raids and the withdrawal of the EPG led to an upsurge of anger and even more unrest in the townships, which the government sought to control by imposing a state of emergency on 12 June 1986. They also produced a howl of protest around the world and very specially in the Commonwealth. I issued the following Statement immediately:

> *Last night's South African attacks on Botswana, Zimbabwe and Zambia are nothing short of flagrant acts of war. The racist violence which sustains apartheid at home has turned to blatant aggression against black states abroad. The Commonwealth's effort for peace has been doing too well for Pretoria's liking; Pretoria is giving its answer in the most brutally orchestrated manner to our effort to end apartheid through peaceful means. It has declared war against peace in Southern Africa. What more do Western countries need to disengage from South Africa and ostracise it from human society in both economic and political terms? Those who are supine now must never speak again in righteous terms in the name of justice, morality or freedom; especially those whose policies help apartheid. I am inviting the Chairman of the Commonwealth Southern Africa Committee to convene an extraordinary meeting of the Committee in Marlborough House at the earliest possible opportunity.*

The Commonwealth Southern Africa Committee comprised members from every Commonwealth country. The statement it issued when it met on 21 May included the following:

> *The Commonwealth Committee on Southern Africa representing all member countries of the Commonwealth speaks out with one voice in utter and complete condemnation of South Africa's attack on the Front Line States of Botswana, Zambia and Zimbabwe. We reject totally any attempt to justify or claim legitimacy for such acts of wanton aggression which carry the state of terror that characterises and sustains the apartheid system within South Africa and beyond its borders to neighbouring countries.*
>
> *We are conscious of the abhorrence which these raids have generated throughout the international community and we share*

it in full measure but, as members of the Commonwealth, we share a deeper sense of indignation at the grievous damage they have done in a calculated way to the Commonwealth initiative for peaceful change in South Africa. The work of the Commonwealth Group of Eminent Persons offers all the people of South Africa a way out of the wasteland of apartheid. It had lifted the hopes of many within South Africa and outside. The acts of aggression against Botswana, Zambia and Zimbabwe have done incalculable harm to these hopes for peaceful change in South Africa. In thus flaunting its power in the very midst of the process of dialogue with the Commonwealth Group, Pretoria has gravely set back the prospects for peaceful negotiation.

We look now to the processes agreed by Commonwealth Governments under the Nassau Accord and to united action in fulfilment of the Accord's expectations.

Britain conspicuously joined in these condemnations and resolves. Ahead, therefore, lay the Review Meeting of the seven Heads who had nominated the members of the EPG where, as the Accord said: *"if in their opinion adequate progress has not been made within this period, we agree to consider the adoption of further measures"*. But first the EPG had to submit its Report on its Mission; and this they did with the same sense of purpose and the same integrity that had characterised their work in South Africa and beyond. Time was short. They had been allowed six months from 1 January 1986 and were resolved to submit their Report in June. That Report was technically to the seven Heads; but in reality it was to the world which was now involved in the South African tragedy.

That it should reach that world as soon as it was out was, I believed, a duty incumbent on the Secretariat. What followed was something of a publishing miracle. The members of the EPG signed their report, *Mission to South Africa,* on 7 June. On 12 June it was launched by the Co-Chairmen in Marlborough House when, due to the phenomenal efforts of its publishers, *Penguin Books,* and the very special role of Geraldine Cooke, *we* were able that day to put the Report, *Mission to*

South Africa, literally within reach of thousands of people. It was in the bookshops as it was being launched and in bookshops throughout the world within days after that. It was published in several languages and was to become an international paperback best-seller.

With Co-Chairmen presenting the EPG Report

What did *Mission to South Africa* say? Its first words spoke volumes:

> *None of us was prepared for the full reality of apartheid.*
>
> *As a contrivance of social engineering, it is awesome in its cruelty. It is achieved and sustained only through force, creating human misery and deprivation and blighting the lives of millions.*

The message of the Report was clear; apartheid must end. It will end; if necessary through a bloody struggle whose cost in lives may be counted in millions and whose agonies will reverberate in every corner of our multiracial world. However, *apartheid* could end by peaceful means, by a genuine process of negotiation – once white South Africa accepted that the evil system by which it has sustained its dominance must end, and was ready by deeds to bring it about. It showed with unique authenticity how far the Government of South Africa was from that acceptance and that readiness. But it showed too that not all white South Africans stood rooted on the bank of the Rubicon; some were ready and willing to cross. And *Mission to South Africa confirmed* that on the other bank those so long oppressed in South Africa, the victims of *apartheid* were ready even then to join in a peaceful process of building a new South Africa in which all its people, black and white, coloured and Indian, would share in fairness and with dignity

The task of their Group was to advance the process of change in South Africa by bringing all the parties to the negotiating table in peaceful conditions in the country. Their efforts to achieve this by facilitating a process of dialogue among South Africans had been thwarted by the government. It was clear that in the six months of their efforts there had been no progress towards the dismantling of apartheid and the establishment of a non-racial representative government – the essential objectives of the Nassau Accord.

Inevitably, given their findings, the Group had to turn to the question of sanctions. As the Report said: *"against the background in which ever-increasing violence will be a certainty, the question of further measures* (sanctions) *immediately springs to mind".*

"What can be done?" asked the Group. What remaining influence does the international community have? What can major states do to help avert an otherwise inevitable disaster? And it answered *"First of all, the question itself is not whether such measures will compel change; it is already the case that their absence and Pretoria's belief that they need not be feared defers change".* The Group could not be plainer in their conclusion that the absence of sanctions was actually contributing to the maintenance of *apartheid* and the status quo of violence in South Africa. Pretoria's belief that Western countries would not apply sanctions was encouraging it to remain obdurate and intransigent.

So the Commonwealth Group asked: are we *"to stand by and allow the cycle of violence to spiral?" Or will we "take concerted action of an effective kind? Such action may offer the last opportunity to avert what could be the worst bloodbath since the Second World War."* Mrs Thatcher was later to say that *"the Eminent Persons Group did not recommend economic sanctions"* but what else could they be saying in their effort to stimulate meaningful change?

In Southern Rhodesia, in 1965, a British Prime Minister (Harold Wilson) gave Ian Smith an assurance that Britain would not use force against white Rhodesians to counter their seizure of white minority rule. That guarantee led to 15 years of black suffering until in 1980 black Zimbabweans and the Commonwealth forced a change of the status quo. In 1979, from the moment of becoming Britain's Prime Minister, Margaret Thatcher assured white South Africans that she would not impose economic sanctions on them to end *apartheid.* Would that guarantee help to keep black South Africans in servitude for all of the years of her premiership – Commonwealth efforts notwithstanding?

Lord Barber had been a member of the Commonwealth Group of Eminent Persons and I knew how united and how resolute he stood with his colleagues. This did not, of course bind Mrs Thatcher to the Group's recommendations; but would she renounce him in rejecting their call for more pressure on Pretoria? And Britain had been at one with all the Commonwealth in the Committee on Southern Africa in May in its condemnation of Pretoria's aggression against neighbouring states, and its looking ahead *"to the processes agreed by Commonwealth Governments under the Nassau Accord and to united action in fulfilment of the Accord's expectations"* – expectations centred on further sanctions.

* * *

The seven Commonwealth Heads were due to meet in London on 3 August 1986. Three weeks before they met, Mrs Thatcher gave a lengthy interview to the prominent political commentator Hugo Young that was carried extensively in the *Guardian* newspaper of 8 July. It was devoted extensively to 'sanctions'. Centrally, she said, moving away from self-interest (though she had introduced a new argument of giving the Russians a raw material monopoly if the South African economy was damaged by sanctions):

> *There is no case in history that I know of where punitive general economic sanctions have been effective to bring about internal change. That is what I believe. That is what the Labour Party in power believed. That, I believe, is what most of Europe believes. That is what most western countries believe. If that is what they believe, there is no point in trying to follow that route.*

Nothing had changed. The interview was a rehearsal for the forthcoming Commonwealth Meeting which, because of the behaviour of the South African Government and the Report of the Commonwealth Group – and of course the 'expectations' of the Nassau Accord – she could expect to be inflamed by a sense of outrage from the rest of the Commonwealth.

I have earlier mentioned, when writing about the Queen's role in the Commonwealth, the 'working' Dinner she gave on the eve of the Meeting for the Heads attending and myself – and Sir Geoffrey Howe accompanying Mrs Thatcher. It was a Dinner which Her Majesty used with consummate discretion to urge on all, including Mrs Thatcher (who did not at all enjoy the occasion) the absolute necessity for the Commonwealth to be united. There was only one way it could be united, because there was only one member out of line; but it was a much needed touch of healing. By then, however, Mrs Thatcher had developed immunity to compromise.

I was not alone in being troubled by Mrs Thatcher's attitude to the South African issue which I was now sure went beyond reasoned conviction. In his memoir *Conflict of Loyalty*, Geoffrey Howe has described how just before the London Review Meeting he felt constrained to write to his Prime Minister (a private hand-written letter) about how best to handle the meeting in Press terms. He complained that the PM's Press Secretary, *"Bernard Ingham had made it clear that he would welcome a 'break-up' of the Review Meeting with 'emotional outbursts from Kaunda, Mugabe and company'. The*

British press, he argued, would 'crucify' the Prime Minister 'if she was seen to make any concession to blacks. ... When he was reminded of my statement in the House on 16 July (further measures likely to be necessary) he made it very plain that he regarded those words as an albatross of which he was reminded every time he spoke to the lobby." Small wonder that Mrs Thatcher herself was being accused of racism by the anti-apartheid lobby.

Later in the letter, Sir Geoffrey wrote that *'Bernard is said to have made it very plain that as far as he was concerned a bust-up of the meeting would be by no means unwelcome –and would probably add another 5 points to the PM's popularity.'* Sir Geoffrey added in parenthesis *'today's MORI poll suggests a rather different picture'.* In a footnote in the book he explains that *'The MORI poll published in the Times that day (1 August) gave Labour a 9 per cent (41.32) lead over the Conservatives. The percentage who thought government policy was 'not tough enough on the South African Government' had risen from 42 to 56'.* And all this was supposed to be in the interest of ending *apartheid* and its inhumanities in South Africa – a point of which Sir Geoffrey himself never lost sight.

The London Heads of Government Meeting was unique. It was a meeting of seven Heads; but at Nassau the others had empowered this Meeting to take decisions for the Commonwealth and in the Nassau Accord (except for Mrs Thatcher) identified the specific sanctions they were ready to add if there was no progress despite the efforts of the EPG. The others came ready to do that. And they were determined; Bob Hawke, Brian Mulroney and Rajiv Gandhi in particular. They had been forced to pause in Nassau by Mrs Thatcher's filibuster. They were not about to be thwarted again. In any event, the Nassau Accord had contemplated that the Commonwealth could act without Mrs Thatcher, if that became necessary. And, of course, *Mission to South Africa* had said it all for them, including the imperative of imposing effective sanctions and doing so quickly.

That there would be disagreement with Mrs Thatcher was palpable; it was mitigated however in Commonwealth terms by the understanding and support which the visiting leaders believed they found within the British public: from political parties, from the anti-apartheid movement, from each of the four estates of society. And from the viewpoint of African leaders disagreement from Mrs Thatcher was greatly mitigated by the resolute support they had from the white member states of Australia and Canada in particular standing shoulder to shoulder with them. There was a memorable moment during the Meeting when Brian Mulroney said that Canadians well understood the anguish of 25 million blacks oppressed by *apartheid,* because 25 million was all the people of Canada. Commonwealth leaders were of course angry with Margaret Thatcher; but, even more, they were sad.

Richard Wilson in *The Times*

Given all that had happened between Nassau and London – the work of the EPG and its abortion by Pretoria; their conclusions as provided in their Report, the strong views of the Commonwealth Committee on Southern Africa in which Britain joined without reservation, the stirrings of the international community (including the EEC) for sanctions – a coming together of the Commonwealth at London would have been a reasonable expectation. It certainly seemed so to Mrs Thatcher's Foreign and Commonwealth Secretary, Geoffrey Howe. Reflecting on the London Meeting, he wrote in *Conflict of Loyalty:*

> *The Meeting proceeded without any kind of change on Margaret's part. Her own account of the proceedings speaks for itself: 'it was back to more irrationality. ... the formal discussions were every bit as unpleasant as at Lyford Cay'. They need not, of course have been so. Margaret's own statement to the press at the end of the Conference indicates the common ground which could from the outset be identified. 'We have been able', she said, 'to reach agreement on how, in our different ways, we should register our abhorrence of apartheid and the urgent need for further reform in South Africa'. So there was no argument that the EPG mission had achieved any real progress. Further action was still necessary. ...*
>
> *I had been invited to follow them (the Co-Chairmen of the EPG) with my own assessment. As Margaret well knew, I had no alternative but to endorse the EPG's judgment. Even so, she had been concerned to make the most of the changes that had been made in the outer ramparts of apartheid. Yet there was no escaping the conclusion that the Botha government had still not made the quantum leap for which we all looked, Mandela and his colleagues were still in gaol, and the ANC and its parallels were still banned. On these central questions there was no room, or need, for the argument which Margaret insisted on provoking. ... It was a pity that on the way so much effort had been expended and bad blood shed unnecessarily.*

But, though the Thatcher filibuster had continued at London, there was now a significant difference. Its target had become narrowed to a cap on what Britain would do, not on what the Commonwealth would do. And what most of the Commonwealth would do (even without Britain) was becoming the benchmark for international sanctions. Concerted action had begun between the Commonwealth and others. Malcolm Fraser and General Obasanjo, for example, had visited Washington to talk to Congressional players. Two days before the London Meeting the Senate Foreign Relations Committee voted for US sanctions closely following the Nassau list; at London, in adopting their list of sanctions agreed at Nassau, the Commonwealth (without Britain) added three items in synchronisation with the Congressional list, namely:

> *(i) a ban on all new bank loans to South Africa, whether to the public or the private sectors;*
> *(ii) a ban on the import of uranium, coal, iron and steel from South Africa; and*
> *(iii) the withdrawal of all consular facilities in South Africa, except for our own nationals and nationals of third countries to whom we render consular services.*

Commonwealth sanctions were now internationalised – Margaret Thatcher and Ronald Reagan notwithstanding. In fact a groundswell among people was driving a global sanctions programme. The Scandinavian countries with a strong anti-apartheid tradition were prominent in imposing sanctions, and Japan was following. Within a month of the London meeting, 21 American States and 65 American cities had taken disinvestment action, and some US $30 billion of pension fund investments were up for imminent withdrawal. That trend was to grow to proportions that seriously worried Pretoria. The Commonwealth sanctions initiative no longer depended on Mrs Thatcher's support. Her filibuster was running out of steam. That was heartening; but her fractious attitude remained a source of rancour in Commonwealth relations, and a not insignificant boon to apartheid's bosses.

In 1986, that rancour found expression in a partial boycott of the Commonwealth Games in Britain. Led by African Commonwealth countries as an act of reprisal for Mrs Thatcher's obduracy on sanctions, 32 of the 52 participating countries boycotted the Games which are a hallmark of Commonwealth friendship. The misfortune was that the Games were in Edinburgh, and though the African countries and others regarded them as 'British' Games, Mrs Thatcher did not. The Edinburgh folk were staunchly with the Commonwealth and I did everything I could to prevent the boycott. But I did not have from Mrs Thatcher the help I needed. She was more protective of her ideological stand with South Africa than of the interests of the people of Scotland, and particularly of Edinburgh, who politically she counted as against her. I recall one of our conversations when I was appealing to her to join me in trying to save the Games in Britain, when she pulled me up sharply saying: "They're not my Games; they are yours". I did not believe the boycott was justified; and I apologised to the organisers in Edinburgh for not being able to prevent it; but they were forgiving. They knew what we were both up against.

The Commonwealth had two further encounters with Mrs Thatcher in its quest for the end of *apartheid*: at the Commonwealth Heads of Government Meetings at Vancouver in 1987 and at Kuala Lumpur in 1989. They were just as unpleasant; but mattered less, because with Commonwealth sanctions internationalised, Britain's abstentions were not as critical to the outcome in South Africa where *apartheid* was being confronted by the world; but with the Commonwealth still leading the way – and growing in stature in black South Africa and internationally with every encounter with Margaret Thatcher. The filibuster was becoming counter-productive.

CHAPTER 24

Mandela's Freedom

The human spirit survives in South Africa in many ways ... But most of all, its survival is symbolised in the person of Nelson Mandela The walls of South Africa's prisons confine him; but his spirit soars above them: a spirit of freedom, of nationalism rising above 'group'; of courage and resolve that humiliates oppression; a spirit of non-racialism that looks to a democratic South Africa acknowledging black and white as fellow South Africans; a spirit that can release the entire country from bondage.

The human spirit in South Africa is crying out for the world's help, for the world's solidarity. It is proclaiming for all who allow themselves to hear that it is not freedom that white South Africans should fear but freedom's denial.

With those words I had ended my Foreword to *Mission to South Africa.* The EPG itself had quoted Nelson Mandela as saying (on 10 February 1985) a few weeks before they themselves saw him in Pollsmoor Prison – when referring to suggestions for his 'conditional' release:

I cherish my own freedom dearly; but I care even more for your freedom. Too many have died since I went to prison. Too many have suffered for the love of freedom; I owe it to their wives, their orphans, to their mothers and their fathers who have grieved and wept for them. ... Not only have I suffered during those long lonely wasted years. I am no less life-loving than you are. But I cannot sell the birth right of the people to be free. ... Only free men can negotiate. Prisoners cannot enter into contracts. Your freedom and mine cannot be separated.

He had been in prison for 26 years. The EPG called for his unconditional release; as had the ANC. Their *Possible Negotiating Concept* emphasised it. Pretoria's rejection of that formula for peace had to be reversed. Only the pressure of sanctions would achieve that. The whole world was beginning to understand – and to act.

In early September 1986, the Eighth Summit of the Non-Aligned Movement called for comprehensive and mandatory sanctions against South Africa under Chapter VII of the United Nations Charter, seeing this as the only remaining "peaceful option to compel the racist Pretoria regime to abandon apartheid". Pending such action by the Security Council, the meeting endorsed a set of measures, including most of the Commonwealth measures, and commended them to the wider international community for urgent adoption

On 16 September, EEC Foreign Ministers adopted a set of further measures consisting of bans on new investment and on the import of gold coins and some iron and steel products. Although most members were also willing to ban the import of South African coal, a consensus was not achieved.

On 19 September, Japan decided to ban the import of some South African iron and steel products; suspend the issue of tourist visas to South African nationals; apply voluntary restraints on Japanese tourism to South Africa; prohibit the use of South African Airways by its officials; and ban air links with South Africa.

On 2 October, the United States adopted the broadest set of sanctions among South Africa's major trading partners with the enactment by Congress of the 1986 Comprehensive Anti-Apartheid Act. This went beyond the set of measures approved by the United States Senate Foreign Relations Committee and included most of the

Commonwealth measures agreed at the London Meeting: a ban on air links; a ban on new investment including loans; a ban on imports of agricultural commodities and foodstuffs, uranium, coal and iron and steel; termination of double taxation agreements; prohibition of government assistance for investment and subsidies for trade; a ban on government procurement from South African parastatals; and prohibition of the use of government funds to promote tourism to South Africa. The Act also incorporated most of the Commonwealth measures agreed at Nassau. It provided for annual reviews at which the adoption of additional measures would be considered in the absence of significant progress by South Africa to end apartheid and establish a non-racial democracy.

In February 1987, the majority of members of the United States Secretary of State's Advisory Committee on South Africa called for "concerted international pressure" to compel the South African regime to the negotiating table, and urged the President to begin urgent consultations with America's allies (especially Britain, Canada, West Germany, France, Japan and Israel) to enlist their support for a multilateral programme of sanctions drawn from the list included in the Anti-Apartheid Act of 1986.

The Nordic countries, which had already imposed a broad range of sanctions either jointly or individually by mid- 1986, had moved well ahead of other Western industrial countries by embargoing all merchandise trade with South Africa and Namibia. Denmark was the first to do so, in December 1986; trade embargoes by Norway and Finland took effect in July 1987 and Sweden's boycott entered into force in October of that year.

Measures taken by governments had been complemented by action by public authorities and private sector organisations. The pullout of Western transnational corporations had continued. As many as 50 United States companies withdrew in 1986 and another 33 had completed or announced their withdrawal by mid-1987. At that same time, in June 1987, the Reverend Leon Sullivan, author of the *Sullivan Principles*, urged those remaining to leave within nine months. He also called for a comprehensive United States economic and diplomatic boycott of South Africa. Sullivan was on the Board of General Motors, and the Company was the largest American employer in South African. His *Global Principles of Corporate Social Responsibility* became a powerful weapon against *apartheid.*

Meanwhile, the situation inside South Africa had deteriorated sharply since Nassau. Sanctions were beginning to apply pressure for change; but Botha was making a last stand. The regime ruled by a continuing state of emergency under whose cover occurred some of the regime's worst excesses, even by its own record.

In February 1986, a team of experts commissioned by the United Nations Human Rights Commission confirmed allegations of torture, deaths in police custody and other brutalities. Its report stated that the security forces enjoyed "almost total immunity" under the emergency regulations, and described the human rights situation as "the most serious ever in the history of South Africa." By the end of 1986, more than 23,000 people were reported to have been imprisoned under the emergency. Those detained included hundreds of young children, some as young as seven; many had been tortured. On the regime's own admission, the security forces killed as many as 716 people in 1986 alone.

At Nassau, in October 1985, Commonwealth leaders had called on South Africa's rulers to take five specific steps towards ending apartheid and establishing a non-racial democracy, and to do so as a matter of urgency. None of them had been taken. The state of emergency had not been lifted; it had been re-imposed with greater rigour. Black political parties stayed banned and black leaders remained jailed; In July, Nelson Mandela entered his 26th year in prison. No dialogue had been started between Pretoria and the true leaders of the black community; white South Africans spoke with the ANC, but only beyond Pretoria's reach. The apartheid system and its oppressive practices continued in all their inhuman cruelty. And the media had its share of shackles; an autocratic regime decreed what South Africans and the world should know about its tyrannies. Within the wider region of Southern Africa, with Namibia's freedom still blocked, South Africa had opened apartheid's third front through systematic acts of aggression, subversion and destabilisation against its neighbours particularly Angola.

But Pretoria faced ever-growing pressure, internally and abroad. Repression had failed to stifle the yearning for freedom. Since Nassau, some 50,000 blacks, many of them children, had passed through the jails and torture chambers of the apartheid system. But the incarceration and torture of children, in particular, had not so much broken them as hardened their resolve to be free. The extensive rent boycott and the level of trade union activism spoke to the strength of internal opposition in the face of intensified tyranny. Censorship, in the last resort, had failed, as it always must, to suppress the truth.

The world was becoming convinced that sanctions were its only weapon to force Pretoria to negotiation. In the result, many countries had applied economic sanctions; the list of companies, including banks, withdrawing from South Africa had become longer. South Africa's neighbours had strengthened their solidarity in facing up to its economic power and military might, and were drawing increasing support for their efforts to become less vulnerable to apartheid's regional strategy. If Pretoria appeared to remain unmoved, it stood in greater isolation and ignominy.

The Commonwealth could take a fair measure of credit for the international action that had brought this about. Its principled course at the Nassau summit; the work of the Group of Eminent Persons (EPG) in exploring the scope for a dialogue of change and its verdict on Pretoria's intransigence; the decisions taken by the seven Commonwealth leaders who met in London in August 1986; the active international diplomacy of Commonwealth leaders and members of the EPG: these were all major factors. Commonwealth action was not without trauma, and could undoubtedly have been more effective had it been universal; but its role was significant, indeed crucial, in defining the realities and the issues and in stimulating the global response to the challenge of apartheid. Much was expected of and attributed to the Secretary General.

PROFILE: Sonny Ramphal, Commonwealth protector

The Third World's Mr Fixit

In my message to Commonwealth leaders before their Meeting in Vancouver I wrote that, *"the world has no alternative but to keep up the pressure. That is the least it can honourably do to give meaning to its expressed solidarity with those who suffer so greatly under the inhumanities of apartheid"*. It was a message Margaret Thatcher did not hear. Her own account (in *The Downing Street Years)* of her mood at Vancouver is worth recalling:

> *I was less prepared than ever to go along with measures which would weaken the South African economy and thus slow down reform. So as the 1987 CHOGM at Vancouver approached I was still in no mood for compromise. ... But it would not be plain sailing. It seemed to me that the Canadians, our hosts, wanted to be more African than the Africans.*

She was defending Pretoria again – this time against a world trend. Her visceral attitude towards the ANC had not changed (though she called ritually for Mandela's release). As recounted in Anthony Sampson's biography of Mandela – *"at Vancouver in October 1987, the ANC representative Johnny Makatini provoked her with a question and she snapped back that the ANC is 'a typical terrorist organisation'"*. It was reported in the London Guardian of 19 October, and reached the world. As Sampson commented: *"British diplomats were exasperated by her outburst. Geoffrey Howe complained that she had 'once again set back the prospect of dialogue'. And Renwick* (her new Ambassador in Pretoria) *had to remind Downing Street that he was developing private contacts with the ANC"*. And, Sampson added:

> *Thatcher's demonising of the ANC helped Botha's propaganda, while frustrating the moderates of the ANC, including Tambo, who wanted closer contacts with conservatives and business leaders in the West. "If she goes on calling them communists it will be self-fulfilling' the conservative Jamaican Prime Minister Edward Seaga commented after the Vancouver meeting.*

* * *

But other Commonwealth leaders were no longer waiting for Margaret Thatcher to join their thrust for *apartheid's* end. At the public Opening Ceremony, Rajiv Gandhi set the tone when he said:

> *Our task here is to take stock of what has been done, to assess the effects, and to determine what more needs to be done. ... Let Vancouver show that our loyalty to principles and to declared objectives is not fickle. That our resolve to end racism in South Africa is not negotiable.*

Bob Hawke, who had pioneered the EPG proposal at Nassau in 1985, had new ideas about making sanctions more effective and went to work on them vigorously at Vancouver. He had turned his mind to financial sanctions in a context in which South Africa was facing substantial debt rescheduling – major loans from American and European banks that were due to be rolled over in about 18 months.

Hawke was careful in how he proceeded. The night before the Meeting opened he pulled together a small caucus of Rajiv Gandhi, Kenneth Kuanda, Robert Mugabe and me. With the aid of his senior advisor, Mike Codd, he outlined his idea. We were all enthusiastic. He did not include Brian Mulroney in the meeting out of respect for his position as host Chairman of the Meeting; but he was quietly briefed. Mike Codd had done some work on the idea in Australia, but Hawke felt we needed some professional advice on the spot. It was characteristic of him to act vigorously. James Wolfensohn (later to be President of the World Bank) was a respected investment banker in New York and Bob Hawke's close friend. His origins were Australian, though he was now an American citizen. Hawke telephoned him from Vancouver and asked him to come to see him. He was there the next evening by private jet. Hawke had not said too much on the phone; such was their relationship. In her best-selling biography *Hawke: The Prime Minister,* the Australian writer Blanche d'Alpuget (whom Hawke later married), has given a lively account of this episode. On what happened next she wrote:

> *They (the caucus) all sat down together and Jim was so helpful. He did think this would have a major, major impact on the South African economy and he felt it was doable if the right people spoke to the right banks. He offered personally to approach some of the American banks, who were big lenders to South Africa, but asked us to get somebody else to deal with Europe. Then he got on his plane and flew home.*

It was my first encounter with Jim Wolfensohn, and I was greatly impressed. D'Alpuget continued, quoting Mike Codd:

> *Within days we had appointed Tony Cole, who was my deputy on the economic side, a highly competent, respected fellow who went on to become head of the Treasury, to deal with the European banks. He worked especially with the German banks, the biggest lenders to South Africa; and so between Tony and*

> *Jim we actually got the banks on board. We had very secure communications networks set up with the other leaders to keep them informed of progress. And the impact was just what we expected on the business community. None of us was there in South Africa, so we can't say for sure that this was why apartheid came down, or exactly what percentage of the reason it was, but there is no doubt in my mind that it was very, very significant because the business community was saying to the government, 'You've GOT TO move.'*

Mike Codd was being modest. As Blanche d'Alpuget narrated: *"In 1990 the South African Minister of Finance Barend duPlessis admitted that the banks' disinvestment was the 'dagger that finally immobilised apartheid"*. But I suspect that the memory Bob Hawke would most cherish is that memorialised in d'Alpuget's final paragraph:

> *In October (1990) a tall, graceful African stepped into Hawke's office in Canberra, a smile on his face, his arms open to embrace the Prime Minister. Taking a seat he said, 'I want you to know, Bob, that I am here today, at this time, because of you'.*

That tall, graceful African was, of course, Nelson Mandela.

Mrs Thatcher knew nothing of the Wolfensohn encounter or its outcome. Commonwealth leaders who did were content with the Statement in the Meeting's conclusion (in the Okenhagen Statement and Programme of Action on Southern Africa) that *"with the exception of Britain, we will initiate an expert study, drawing on independent sources, to examine ... South Africa's relationship with the international financial system"*. In any event, the Statement's section on sanctions ended;

> *We will continue to take further action individually and collectively as deemed appropriate in response to the situation as it evolves until apartheid is dismantled. In the case of all but Britain that includes sanctions.*

On Canada's initiative, the Vancouver Meeting of 1987 marked the Commonwealth's seriousness of purpose in ending *apartheid* by establishing a Committee of Foreign Ministers *"to provide high level impetus and guidance"*; again, *'with the exception of Britain'.* It comprised the Foreign Ministers of Australia, Canada, Guyana, India, Nigeria, Tanzania, Zambia and Zimbabwe chaired by the Minister of External Affairs of Canada, Joe Clark. The Committee, a rare recourse in Commonwealth practice, did considerable practical work. Importantly, it commissioned a study by independent experts on whether and how sanctions can help to end *apartheid.* Their conclusion after a comprehensive study – *'South Africa: The Sanctions Report',* published worldwide – was: *"We believe that sanctions remain the most effective peaceful path to the ending of apartheid."* Commonwealth action would proceed, and I saw the new Committee of Foreign Ministers under Canada's leadership as an important vehicle for moving forward without impediment from Mrs Thatcher.

Joe Clarke of Canada played a specially vigorous role as Chairman of the Commonwealth Foreign Ministers Committee on Southern Africa. Such a Committee is no substitute for Heads of Government acting together; but as a supplement in specific contexts, (and especially in small number) it can provide valuable continuity between the biennial meetings of Heads. And the Commonwealth's final push on sanctions needed that continuity between Vancouver and Kuala Lumpur. As Joe Clarke has written in his memoir *How we Lead: Canada in a Century of Change,* alluding to the Committee:

> *I became chair and our foreign ministry took a leading role in directing the Commonwealth campaign, along with the Commonwealth Secretariat in London and the government of Australia. Our mandate was to coordinate government actions including sanctions, support the victims of apartheid and importantly, counteract South African censorship and propaganda. Our method was to meet every three months in a different Commonwealth country, consult and publicise anti-*

apartheid leaders, and steadily increase and coordinate sanctions and other measures.

South Africans themselves ended apartheid. But the Commonwealth campaign was widely publicised in South Africa, provided significant financial and moral support to people on the front lines and was much more effective because it was coordinated. Our aggregate impact was greater than if each of us had acted alone, and the fact that we acted as a group encouraged several nations to step up their engagement.

The Commonwealth's Kuala Lumpur Summit of 1989 lay ahead. Before that, however, in mid-August 1989, I had a sad and urgent telephone call from President Kaunda in Lusaka. Oliver Tambo, the acting President of the ANC had suffered a severe stroke on 9 August. With the aid of Roland 'Tiny' Rowland – a British businessman who had lived in Southern Rhodesia and had extensive business interests – he had been flown to the London Clinic and the prognosis was positive. The Government of Zambia had guaranteed to meet the immediate cost in London, but Oliver would need a long period of treatment and recuperation and Zambia could not cover all those costs. Could I think of any way of managing Oliver's recovery? Oliver Tambo had been working tirelessly on what became the Harare Declaration of 21 August 1989; indeed, he had largely drafted the conciliatory document which had received the imprimatur of the OAU and, along with the EPG's 'Possible Negotiating Concept' would become the ANC's 'Negotiating Charter'. Oliver Tambo was never more needed. What could I do? I told Kaunda I would get back to him.

I had a single thought. Sweden. Within minutes I was on the phone to my friend Ingvar Carlsson, Sweden's Prime Minister. I explained the situation to him and he said a remarkable thing: *"Don't ask a favour of me; I will get back to you shortly to see how we can fulfil our duty"*. He did; within the hour: *'Please tell President Kaunda that as soon as Oliver can travel we will arrange for him to come to Sweden where we will do all that is necessary for his recovery'*. It was one of those moments of reassurance that there was goodness in the world. I thanked Ingvar and phoned Kenneth Kaunda.

The end of Nelson Mandela's first visit beyond Africa in 1990 was Sweden where he had an emotional reunion with his old friend Oliver Tambo who had kept the ANC together for him for 27 years and who invited him now to resume the Presidency – which Mandela implacably refused as Tambo, years earlier, had told me he would. The time when he had told me that was on one of my visits to Lusaka when I had asked him a question that had been nagging me, namely, whether when *apartheid* was vanquished would a free South Africa return to the Commonwealth? His answer was unforgettable: *"But, Sonny, black South Africa never left the Commonwealth"* – an assurance he was to repeat later in London at a Lunchtime Meeting at the Royal Commonwealth Society.

Reunion in Sweden

The Committee of Foreign Ministers on Southern Africa duly presented their work, including the Australian study on *'Apartheid and International Finance: A Programme for Change'* to the following Commonwealth Heads of Government Meeting in Kuala Lumpur in October 1989, chaired by Prime Minister Dr Mahathir Mohamad. It was to be Margaret Thatcher's last encounter with her Commonwealth colleagues on South Africa, and though the stage was long past when there was argument about the utility of sanctions in compelling negotiations and peaceful change, she remained truculently opposed to further sanctions. She was particularly angry with the insistence of both Bob Hawke and Brian Mulroney on the necessity for ever-stronger sanctions. She obviously expected them as 'white' and 'western' to see the issues as she did. It had been her problem earlier with Malcolm Fraser.

At the public Opening session in Kuala Lumpur, Brian Mulroney summed up succinctly the achievements of the Commonwealth:

> *The Commonwealth programme of sanctions that we have implemented quietly and effectively, has taken its toll. It was the Commonwealth, not the super-powers, and not the G7, that took the first significant steps to galvanise international concern and transform it into constant and persuasive pressure on the South African Government.*
>
> *The Commonwealth action was followed by the European Community, the United States Congress and others. Suddenly, we were no longer alone, and Pretoria began to hurt. Although neither comprehensive nor perfect, sanctions have clearly worked. South Africans have themselves told us that.*
>
> *The former Governor of the Reserve Bank of South Africa stated in May that South Africa was 'bleeding'. Former South African Minister, Kobus Metring, declared in July, that 'we have to break the isolation to get the money we need for development'. Law and Order Minister Vlok conceded that 'if sanctions are introduced against us we can do nothing ... we do not live alone in this world'. And President de Klerk himself has referred to 'the international stranglehold which ... is presently inflicted on our economic growth potential'.*
>
> *Others see the picture in the same light. United States Secretary of State for African Affairs, Herman Cohen said recently that 'sanctions have played a role in stimulating new thinking within the white power structure'. And Anthony Lewis of the New York Times wrote just a few days ago that 'economic sanctions were a highly significant factor in moving Mr de Klerk.*

Complementing the heightened internal resistance and the new experience of body bags coming home from Angola (particularly after the Cuban led battle of Cuinto Cunivale), sanctions were sounding the death-knell of *apartheid.* Commonwealth leaders, save Mrs Thatcher, had come to Kuala Lumpur to tighten the sanctions knot and bolster international efforts to end *apartheid.* They had not come to battle with Mrs Thatcher – that battle was over as far as they were concerned.

* * *

Mrs Thatcher came to Kuala Lumpur with a new Foreign and Commonwealth Secretary, John Major, who quickly won the respect of his colleagues. When the Heads went on their 'retreat' to Langkawi (where the central issue was *environment)* the Foreign Ministers tackled the separate statement on *apartheid*: *'Southern African: The Way Ahead: The Kuala Lumpur Statement'* in which the Commonwealth's position would be spelled out in a fashion they believed all could 'live with' – including John Major himself. It was a strong statement calling for the intensification of sanctions with special emphasis on new forms of financial pressure. It contained the 'with the exception of Britain' formula where appropriate; but several concessions in language had been made to accommodate the position of Britain. So John Major, with all the other Foreign Ministers commended it to their Heads at Langkawi. There, Mrs Thatcher concurred in it; but then took the quite exceptional course – after the Statement had been issued from the Meeting – of putting out a Statement of her own (via Bernard Ingham) *'Southern Africa: The Way Ahead: Britain's View'*, emphasising her discordant views. I recalled Geoffrey Howe's concerns and complaints before the London Review Meeting: Margaret Thatcher had to demonstrate that she was not in agreement with the 'black' view.

Many Heads were indignant, having made concessions to Britain in the collective statement. Bob Hawke and Brian Mulroney spoke for them in the Plenary. Hawke protested that Margaret Thatcher's

Statement *'was a repudiation of the thrust of what had been agreed at the Retreat'*. Mulroney said that *' he had left Langkawi thinking that perhaps some progress had been made 'by dint of putting some water in the wine', ... so that the South Africans would not get the view that there were two fundamentally opposed positions ... when countries joined a group they paid a price for solidarity – loyalty and fairness to one another'*. Margaret Thatcher fiercely defended her right to act as she did. She said she *'was utterly appalled'* by the objections.

Of course, Mulroney had put his finger on the key issue; Mrs Thatcher's purpose was precisely to send a message to Pretoria that there were in the Commonwealth *'two fundamentally opposed positions'*- hers and the rest, and she could have added, most of the rest of the world. I was myself offended, because, apart from the other issues of principle and procedure, I had already personally presented the collective Statement to the world's press, telling them with some satisfaction that this was the conclusion of Commonwealth Heads.

Kuala Lumpur, and Langkawi, had been wonderful venues; and but for the quite unnecessary contention at the end the Meeting, it provided for me a happy note on which to take leave of Commonwealth Heads of Government, amid heart-warming encomiums. It was a good time. The Commonwealth had emerged with credit and standing from its several encounters with *apartheid.* The tunnel had been dark and the journey long and not over, but the light of apartheid's end was faintly glowing. New challenges lay ahead; the Meeting, for example, had positioned the Commonwealth to play a central role on environment and sustainable development issues; and the Heads had taken up my suggestion that in the years ahead the Commonwealth should be more pro-active in the strengthening of democracy, both within and outside our membership. I would still have another eight months in office; but this was my last Commonwealth Summit. Although none could know as we left Kuala Lumpur, it was Mrs Thatcher's last as well.

* * *

In my final months as Secretary General that faint glow of *apartheid's* end would shine, and never so brightly as on 11 February 1990 as the whole world watched Nelson Mandela, holding hands with Winnie, walk through the gates of Victor Verster Prison to freedom. I watched on television with my family at the official Residence at Hill Street in London – and I choked a little as joy merged into reflection and into joy again. I confess to an immodesty; a momentary reflection that I had helped to make this happen. It was immodest, because so many in so many places had contributed to that moment of freedom. More soberly, I have come to recognise what a great privilege it was to have had the chance in life to play a part at all in this marvellous moment of history.

Five days later, on 16 February, I telephoned Mandela at Archbishop Tutu's Residence in Pretoria, where he was staying. It was a very special moment and I shared it immediately with Secretariat staff as follows:

NELSON MANDELA
I want to share with all Secretariat Staff my telephone conversation with Mr Nelson Mandela early this morning.

I explained to him how much we share in the joy of his release. He said he wanted me to know that the support he had received from the Commonwealth and similar friends around the world was a major factor in easing the pain of imprisonment and sustaining hope. In those difficult years, he said, the Commonwealth's support for the anti-apartheid struggle was a matter of immense satisfaction to him.

I said that in the years ahead I was sure he could look forward to continued solidarity from the Commonwealth, particularly in the difficult period beyond this moment of exaltation. He asked me to convey to everyone in the Commonwealth and in the Secretariat how much value he attached to that support. If freedom and justice are to come to South Africa, he said, that external assistance in crucial.

All members of staff should feel proud at this great moment in our collective work, and I would like to thank everyone for their contribution to our overall effort.

Two months later, on 15 April 1990, Nelson and Winnie Mandela would walk through the doors of that same home in Hill Street where I had viewed his walk to freedom – as our guests. It was the first place they would visit on their first visit to London.

In Anthony Sampson's biography of Mandela, is this sentence relative to that visit to Hill Street:

A few weeks later he went to London. Mrs Thatcher had sent an invitation, but his colleagues dissuaded him from seeing her, and instead he gave priority to loyal friends of the ANC.

Our home was the venue of that reunion: Nelson Mandela, after 27 years in an *apartheid* prison, greeting friends who had been exiled in Britain, friends of the Anti-Apartheid Movement who had crusaded for his freedom, friends world-wide who were prominent in the international campaign for apartheid's end. As he and Winnie signed the Guest Book amid rapturous applause at the threshold of that Commonwealth House I wished I could share the moment with all the Commonwealth Presidents and Prime Ministers who over so many years had been tireless in their efforts to make this moment possible. And I told Mandela so.

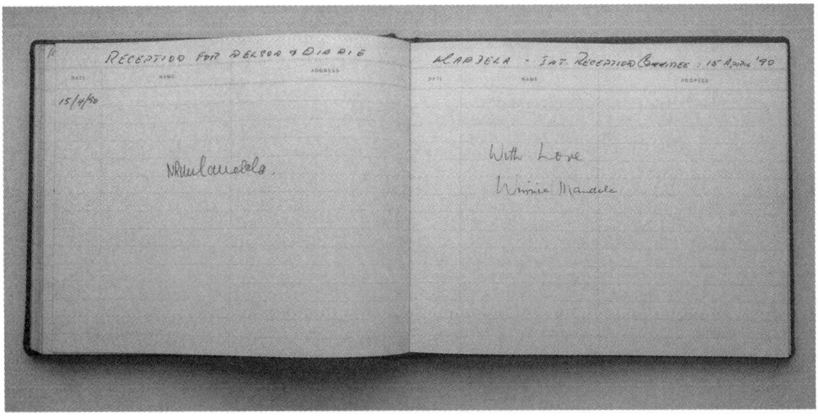

'Hill Street' Guest Book

There were some 200 friends at the reception each of whom wished a word with Mandela and whom he wished to greet. To avoid a scrum, we divided the guests into three groups and assigned each group to one of three rooms in the Residence. Then my wife and I escorted Nelson and Winnie into and around each room in turn so that everyone could greet him personally, and he them. I was impressed with his stamina; he never wilted. Anthony Sampson's description of the event – and he was one of the guests – was:

> *The Commonwealth Secretary Sonny Ramphal gave a reception in Mayfair, at which Mandela and Winnie worked the rooms like monarchs, shaking hands.*

It was an apt description. He carried himself with calm nobility yet had a word for everyone beyond pleasantries. He remembered so much and so many; a memory he attributed to the solitude of prison and the time he had to focus on the past. He exuded leadership, yet insisted at every turn that he was the servant of the people, and particularly the servant of the ANC. But, most of all, Nelson Mandela, after 27 years in prison for his political struggle against the evil of *apartheid* was a man without bitterness – an attribute that was to be vital to the process of nation building that lay ahead.

The day after the Reception at Hill Street, Mandela attended a colossal concert in Wembley Stadium estimated to have been watched by a billion viewers around the world. But, behind the scenes of jubilation, Thatcherism was still at work in support of Pretoria. Anthony Sampson's account is illustrative:

> *The blend of pop music and radical politics was ... televised live by the BBC: the Thatcher government warned them to avoid ANC propaganda or fund-raising, and the BBC's controller Alan Yentob had to exercise 'sensible discretion', anxiously monitoring the pop stars' speeches. ... At the finale, Mandela strode up and down the platform with a clenched fist to thunderous cheers, and paid tribute to Tambo and Father Huddleston, the Chairman of the Anti-Apartheid Movement. 'You elected not to forget', Mandela told the crowd. 'Even through the thickness of the prison walls ... we heard your voice demanding our freedom'.*

Mrs Thatcher notwithstanding, it was a major global platform for Mandela. He did not see her on that visit; but on the next stopover a few weeks later to see Oliver Tambo – now in a 'safe house' in Kent (provided by the British Government), he had a long telephone call to her urging her, without success, to maintain sanctions. She urged him, in turn, to take care of his health.

One of the guests to whom I had introduced Mandela at the Hill Street reception was a Catholic priest, Fr. Michael Campbell-Johnson who was the Jesuit Superior located around the corner from the Hill Street Residence – in Farm Street. Fr. Campbell-Johnson had been known to me in Guyana fifteen years earlier as a 'radical' priest, where against Roman Catholic orthodoxy he had married my daughter and son-in-law though the latter had been divorced. He then spent years in Nicaragua in the time of the 'Sandinistas', before arriving in London as my close neighbour. And we were close in more than street numbers. As I explained to Mandela, there had long been an invisible line of communication between Farm Street and Pollsmoor Prison and Fr.

Campbell-Johnson had helped to maintain it. Mandela was pleased. He said he knew how wide his circle of benefactors was, but seldom met them. Once more in my lifetime I was reminded how interconnected all things were.

I had met Mandela before that wondrous night in our home. His first travel out of South Africa, two weeks after his release, was naturally to Lusaka – to greet the ANC in exile. President Kaunda invited a group of international friends to meet Mandela on this first visit. I was among them, and given a favoured place at the high table of the celebratory meeting we had. Mandela greeted me warmly; and thanked me for all the Commonwealth had done in resisting Mrs Thatcher's opposition to sanctions – which he stressed to me remained essential until negotiations were completed. I was amazed at how much he knew of our battles with Margaret Thatcher, and impressed by his certainty that they must continue. He never confused his freedom with *apartheid's* end and a free South Africa.

I was to meet him again before I left office as Commonwealth Secretary-General. It was May 1990 and his travels had taken him to Nigeria at the time of the Abuja Meeting of the Commonwealth Committee of Foreign Ministers on Southern Africa, chaired by Canada's Joe Clark. Both Mandela and I were invited to address the Committee. It was there, in that environment, that Nelson Mandela spoke the words about me that I have so greatly cherished:

> *Some men have become famous because of the service they have given to their countries, others have become well known because of the manner in which they have taken up issues affecting their regions, and others have become famous because in their fight for human justice they have chosen the entire world as their theatre. Shridath Ramphal is one of those men.*

But there was more. Margaret Thatcher could barely wait for Mandela's release before proclaiming the lifting of such sanctions as she had imposed and calling on the international community to do likewise. This was her deal with de Klerk. Mandela was livid. A few days before the Meeting in Abuja, he had said: *"Only the unserious and people not involved in the South African quest for freedom would call for lifting of sanctions ... If sanctions are reviewed the Government would be encouraged to assert its position"*. In Abuja, he spoke more bluntly:

> *We would like to point out that we are, to put it mildly, amazed at the behaviour of certain countries following the unbanning of the ANC and other organisations on 2 February 1990. I refer to the stand taken by the British Government to lift sanctions against the Government of South Africa and its call to other Governments to do likewise. ... There are no grounds whatsoever for lifting sanctions against the racist regime of South Africa or in ending its diplomatic and cultural isolation ... the call for the lifting of sanctions is a dangerous trend. ... If the trend is not stopped all our gains will be reversed.*

The matter was so serious that before leaving Nigeria I wrote an op-ed piece for the International Herald Tribune (IHT) from Lagos elaborating Mandela's plea and the conclusion of the Commonwealth Committee of Foreign Ministers that the time for the easing of sanctions had not arrived. *"To reduce pressure"*, they said, *"before any changes of substance have occurred would be to run the risk of aborting the process of ending racism"*. It was published in the IHT on 30 May under the headline *South Africans Still Need Sanctions.* It was my last published piece as Secretary-General. At the end of June, I demitted office.

Twenty-four years later, on 3 March 2014, I was reminded of the obtuseness of the British and American Governments in the address given by the then Archbishop Emeritus of Cape Town, Most Rev. Desmond Tutu in Westminster Abbey. It was a most splendid, and unique, 'Service of Thanksgiving for the Life and Work of Nelson Mandela' held, as the Dean of Westminster said, *"in the name of the people of South Africa, of the United Kingdom, and of the Commonwealth."* I was privileged to be there in a place of honour with my grand-daughter, India Hennessy. Desmond Tutu was characteristically gracious; but he specifically recalled, even in that moment of atonement:

> *What would have happened had Mandela died in prison, as was the intended hope of the upholders of apartheid? I suppose most would have regarded him as no better than a terrorist. Persons in high positions in Britain and the US did dismiss him as such. Mercifully for us and God's world, Mandela did not die in prison and this is due very largely to the amazing Anti-Apartheid Movement. I use this great pulpit to say on behalf of our people, Thank you, thank you, thank you. ... I visited 10 Downing Street and the Oval Office in Washington. My pleas for sanctions fell on deaf ears. Without the anti-apartheid movement, Nelson Mandela would so easily have died in prison.*

So much of my Commonwealth life had been spent in the anti-apartheid cause; it was a 'thank you' from an ineffable source I appropriated to the Commonwealth as well. And on that day of thanksgiving for Mandela's life I reflected on how much more we might have achieved in the Commonwealth has Margaret Thatcher carried over to South Africa and *apartheid* the commitment to 'black majority rule' that had made the ending of 'UDI' in Southern Rhodesia possible at Lusaka in 1979. Nelson Mandela, in my view, could have been freed from *apartheid's* prisons as much as five years earlier than he was. What would that have meant for him, for South Africa, for the world?

CHAPTER 25

Leaving Office

I suppose that leaving office after 15 years could be a painful process. It was not for me. The year before, on 12 April 1989, I had called on Mrs Thatcher to brief her on the Kuala Lumpur Summit, then six months away. The question of my successor came up. She mused that this may well be a time of continuing action in many spheres – Pakistan, Namibia, South Africa; then looking searchingly at me she asked: *"Secretary-General, do we have to make a change?"* Answering directly, I said: *"No, Prime Minister"* but I went on to explain that I had always felt, ever since her proposal at New Delhi that I should serve a full third term, that I should not aspire to stay on beyond that. I said, however, that it was not a question of my seeking release. President Kaunda was more forthright. He actually 'scolded' me for not being willing to stay. I knew he was wrong, and told him so. It was time to go when so much had been achieved and so many new challenges lay ahead. The beginning of the end in South Africa was a moment of accomplishment. He admonished me not to give him the same advice.

In Kuala Lumpur, Heads of Government gave a Dinner in my honour. In reply to their compliments I said, inter alia:

> *There is – and who knows that better than political leaders yourselves – there is no perfect time to go; but there is always a time to move over, and I have always been sure that the end of my third term next June was that time ...*

> *You have been extraordinarily kind ... in the generous things that have been said about me. For me, it has been the most enormously privileged of opportunities; because serving you in the Commonwealth has involved so intimate a relationship with the Presidents, Prime Ministers, Ministers and officials, and, increasingly, the publics of Commonwealth countries. A relationship so close that I have felt part of a very real Commonwealth family. ...*
>
> *When Dr Mahathir brought the house down at Langkawi on Saturday night with his rendition of 'My Way', there was more than a hint of nostalgia for me in terms of the last 15 years. Certainly, they were years in which I may have been adventurous in the pursuit of Commonwealth goals as I perceived them; but never, I hope, reckless; persistent, but never perverse.*
>
> *The finest reward of all these years is your present pride in the Commonwealth and your good opinion of me. For all that, I thank you beyond measure.*

The Heads gave me that night a rather special memento – a silver salver with all their signatures engraved on it. It was a gift to treasure all the rest of my life and a constant reminder to me that all that had been achieved in my time had been the doing of these great Presidents and Prime Ministers through whom I had worked. I still look at their signatures with gratitude for the way they supported me.

In Malaysia as the meeting was ending I had an opportunity to say something I had long wanted to at the appropriate time. It was this;

> *I owe a rather special debt of gratitude to successive British Prime Ministers and their colleagues, and to members of the British Foreign Office – in the context of Britain being our host country, and London our host Capital. In all my 15 years I have received nothing but help and kindness and courtesy from them all; and I want to say so with frankness, with sincerity and without equivocation. The Secretariat places great value, as I have done, by the friendship and support we have received from Britain.*

Just before I left for Malaysia the London *Financial Times* (on 9 October 1989) carried a long interview I had done with Robert Mauthner under the headline: *Concern for the Health of Nations*. In it I said this:

> *Yes, we've had disagreements. But they were not so much personal disagreements as occasions on which I had to say to the British Government that the substantial weight of Commonwealth opinion is against this.*
>
> *Given Britain's centrality in some of the events, it was almost inevitable that there would be times when the Commonwealth and the Secretary General would be nudging Britain to go the further mile. I think on every occasion we did it and Britain went the further mile, it did itself credit.*
>
> *So, I don't look back on that somewhat bruising experience as something undesirable or harmful. I think it was an occupational hazard. What I am pleased about is that there was never rancour. I had a lot of fights with Lord Carrington in particular. But we remain friends.*

Nothing was closer to my heart at the time of leaving than the Secretariat itself. There was much I said about my gratitude to the staff that had worked with me to make all we did happen. But the most touching recollection is of what they said to me. Moni Malhoutra, the Assistant Secretary-General, spoke at a Dinner the staff gave for me; and in his moving tribute he said this:

> *If I were asked to single out the most distinguishing characteristics of your Secretary-Generalship I would pick three things above all else – not just faith, but implacable faith; not just a sense of purpose, but a most concentrated purpose; and linked to them both, an enduring vision. These have been the hallmarks of your work ...*
>
> *Nineteenth century missionaries proselytised with the Bible in one hand, the sword in the other. You did so for the*

> *Commonwealth empty-handed on the sheer strength of your convictions and your capacity to inspire confidence. You are entirely right in giving the Commonwealth's leadership the credit for the political investment which they have made in the Commonwealth during the last 15 years, for without that investment nothing else would have been possible. But I am equally sure that without you that investment would not have been made in anywhere near the same measure. It was a case of your faith, purpose and vision involving them, moving them and carrying them along – because they believed in you and because they trusted you ...*
>
> *In you, the Commonwealth has had its Hammarskjold. I could, on behalf of all of my colleagues in the Secretariat, pay no higher tribute to you.*

I hope I was even a little worthy of all he said.

Before that staff occasion in Marlborough House, the Queen and Prince Philip, on 22 May, had a farewell lunch for Lois and me at the Palace. It was more intimate than formal, with a small number of Commonwealth High Commissioners, and senior Secretariat colleagues and Palace Officials – in the Music Room. It was like a family send-off following immediately on my private but formal leave-taking audience when she had honoured me with the GCMG. It remains a very special memory.

And there was another very special occasion. On 14 June 1990, Mrs Thatcher gave a farewell Dinner for me at 10 Downing Street. It was a splendid occasion; and she was both gracious and generous, lyrical and serious. After calling up the line from *Midsummer's Night Dream: 'Sweet moon, I thank thee for thy sunny beams'* to support her claim that *'one thing you can be sure of with Sonny: however difficult things are, Sonny beams'* – she went on more seriously:

> *So, Sonny, our main purpose in coming together tonight is to say thank you. Your fifteen years as Secretary-General have been remarkable ones for the Commonwealth: – It has grown*

from thirty-four members to fifty. – It has seen Rhodesia come through to independence as Zimbabwe. – It has seen Namibia come through to independence and join the Commonwealth. – It has seen Pakistan restored to the Commonwealth and the Maldives joining it. – It has seen Malaysia move from being highly critical of the Commonwealth to chairing a Commonwealth Prime Ministers' meeting. – It has seen the practical side of the Commonwealth's work, which is what matters most to the smaller states, continually strengthened and made more effective. ...

You and I have not always agreed, in particular over the best way to deal with the very real problems of South Africa – although we always shared the aim of wanting to see the end of apartheid. And that is now in sight.

But where we have disagreed at Commonwealth heads of government meetings, you have always tried to find a constructive way to accommodate differences, and that has made it possible to avoid damage to the Commonwealth itself.

It is a remarkable institution. No one could ever have invented or designed it. It depends very much on the genuine enthusiasm of its members – above all the Commonwealth heads of government – for maintaining the historic links and traditions. It depends on the easy way we communicate – there is no need for any interpretation – the informality, the deep and genuine personal friendships. They are what make the Commonwealth and give it a unique influence. We don't try to duplicate the work of other international organisations. We consult. We help each other. We cherish our professional, sporting, legal links. We have in common our parliamentary traditions and style – a style which allows room for controversy, indeed encourages it, but always on the basis of respect and friendship. Many is the time I have taken part in quite heated debates at Commonwealth Prime Ministers' meetings and then we have gone out for a cup of coffee and been the best of friends. We don't tell each other what to do: we listen and we make up our own minds.

In all this the personality and the energy of the Secretary-General are very important indeed: and, Sonny, you have had both. With it goes one of the most silver tongues of all time. You will be a very hard act to follow. And may I say how delighted we all were when Her Majesty the Queen recently appointed you an honorary G.C.M.G.

I am very pleased that some of your family are here with us tonight to celebrate and say thank you. We know you will continue to live here with us for much of the time, and that is a great delight.

My wife sat on Mrs Thatcher's left and when I rose to reply the Prime Minister reached out for Lois' hand and held it throughout my speech, whispering to her: "Family is so important" – the other Margaret Thatcher!

* * *

My 'Thatcher years' had not all been adversarial. I encouraged the Commonwealth to stand by her in the difficult days of the Falklands conflict. International opinion was not automatically with Britain – as the Argentines tried to present the issue in 'anti-colonialist' terms. It was, of course, no such thing; it was blatant aggression. I needed no conversion to that view: Venezuela's claim on Guyana's territory, and Guatemala's on Belize – both in violation of international law – were living examples of how territorial aggrandisement can wear a mask of virtue.

I did not linger. On Friday 2 April 1982, when the Argentine aggression began, I was preparing to leave for Trinidad. I immediately spoke with Lord Carrington at the Foreign Office, and dispatched personal messages that afternoon to all Commonwealth Presidents and Prime Ministers – mobilising support for Britain, and copying it to all Commonwealth Ambassadors in New York where action at the UN had become intense. A part of that message was:

It is deeply disquieting that, despite a personal appeal for restraint by both the UN Secretary-General and the President of Security Council, Argentina rejected every attempt to seek a diplomatic solution to its dispute with Britain.

I am sure you will agree that, in the face of such unprovoked aggression, there is need for Commonwealth countries to stand by Britain in this matter, consistent with your support for the principles of territorial integrity, the right of self-determination and the rejection of the use of force to unsettle long established boundaries – principles for which the Commonwealth has consistently stood. I hope you will find it possible in whatever way you consider appropriate to make clear your condemnation of this Argentine action and to use all your influence to ensure a de-escalation of the matter.

On the following Monday (5 April) I wrote Mrs Thatcher from Port of Spain saying that *"I want to let you know directly how much I share your condemnation of Argentina's reprehensible conduct in this matter"*, and telling her what action I had already taken. I added:

We have already had in our time too many acts of aggression by those who calculate on getting away with it in a world devoid of any real measure of collective security. Argentina's aggression requires from the international community a stand for the maintenance of law and order world-wide. I am sure that this is how your Commonwealth colleagues will see it. I shall certainly do all in my power to so encourage them, so that their friendship and support might be a strength to you at this time,

In the days ahead, please be aware of my own resolve to do whatever I can to help.

I used my presence in Trinidad to specially secure Caribbean support for Britain within the Latin American Group, which Argentina was trying to portray as being in solidarity with her. Speaking in Port of Spain on 6 April, I described Argentina's invasion of the Falkland

Islands as: "Gross, unprovoked and utterly unwarranted". Calling for Argentina's withdrawal in accordance with the UN Security Council's resolution, I stressed the importance of not being diverted from what was really at stake:

> *the seizure of territory by force, the attempt to change long established boundaries otherwise than by peaceful means, and the repudiation of the principle of self-determination.*

Many Commonwealth Heads wrote directly to Mrs Thatcher, and of course, Britain had handsome Commonwealth support at the United Nations. Later that month, on 27 April, speaking about *'International Collective Security'* in Central Hall, Westminster, at the Parliamentary Mass Lobby *'Disarm for Development'* I summed up the 'Falklands' issue in this way:

> *It illustrates all too poignantly the urgency and the relevance of the concept of 'national security' evolving into one of 'common security'. It is a need which underlines the inadequately recognised fact that in making a firm and unambiguous response to Argentina's aggression Britain is rendering a service to the international community as a whole. In confirming – by negotiation if possible – but in confirming that naked unprovoked aggression is a crime against the international community ... the British Government deserves your positive support – not only as patriots, but as internationalists. It is one of the reasons why Commonwealth countries in Latin America have stood full-square behind Britain in this matter.*

No one could have wished for the 'Falklands war'; but it was satisfying to have an occasion when the Commonwealth could be on Margaret Thatcher's side.

PART VII

THE GLOBAL NEIGHBOURHOOD

CHAPTER 26

Grenada and Small States

A. THE 'PRE-EMPTIVE' STRIKE

Large states have problems deriving from their size, and their large size presents problems to the global neighbourhood. So too have and do small states, and the scale from large to small is bewildering. The United States, the most powerful country in the world, is over 9 million square kilometres and has a population of over 300 million. Grenada is just less than 350 square kilometres, and has a population of just over 100 thousand; it is among the smallest and weakest countries in the world. It is at the southern end of the Caribbean archipelago, with a high level of literacy, and the principal producer of nutmeg in the world; hence its pseudonym *The Spice Isle.* A Grenadian politician of the 1930s, T.A. Marryshow, was a pioneer of regionalism among the English-speaking countries of the Caribbean, and Grenada has traditionally been a strongly regionalist member of the Caribbean Community (CARICOM).

In 1983, the United States invaded Grenada militarily on variously stated grounds: that it posed a threat to the security of the United States; that it was invited to do so by neighbouring islands in the Caribbean; that it was asked to do so by Grenada's Governor-General; that it did so to rescue United States students at a US off-shore University, that Cuba was building a military base on the Island. None was wholly true; none provided a valid basis for the invasion in international law.

Grenada is a member country of the Caribbean Community to which so much of my life was devoted. It is also a member of the Commonwealth and the Queen is its Head of State. Throughout the period of Grenada's turmoil from 1979 to 1983 and immediately afterwards, I was Secretary-General of the Commonwealth. My involvement in this bizarre, even grotesque, situation with the Caribbean, Commonwealth and international implications was ineluctable. For me, it was also poignant, for it was my region of the world. I knew most of the regional players personally; they were my friends, and I knew intuitively that I would have to stand against most of them. Above all, I had a deep sense of shame.

Before its independence in 1974, Grenada was first an Associated State of Britain – a 'dependency'. As such, it became a member of the West Indies Associated States Council of Ministers (WISA). In 1979, the membership of WISA comprised seven states: Grenada, Dominica and St Lucia which were by then fully independent countries; Antigua and Barbuda and St Kitts-Nevis which were still Associated States of Britain; and Montserrat, a British colony. It is this same group that formed the Organisation of Eastern Caribbean States (OECS) in 1981. Together, they are a chain of the smallest countries in the world. In 1979, they were – as they are now – informally, a sub-group of the Caribbean Community which at the time included Barbados, Belize, Guyana, Jamaica, the Bahamas and Trinidad and Tobago – all, however, small themselves.

The Caribbean generally had a long record of free elections and acceptable democratic governance; but from time to time it threw up unorthodox Prime Ministers and none more bizarre than Eric Gairy, first elected Premier in Grenada in 1967 – then becoming Prime Minister on independence in 1974. He was essentially fascist by disposition, given to cult and occult activities and repressive governance. He was an ardent believer in 'UFOs' – on which he once addressed the UN General Assembly. At his first Commonwealth Heads of Government Meeting (in 1977 in London) he embarrassed everyone (save himself) by rising before the Chairman (Britain's Prime Minister James Callaghan) could start the Plenary Session saying,

'Let us pray', and in the stunned silence that followed proceeding to do just that. It was his first Meeting and I suppose it was his gauche way of announcing himself. Many leaders from politics, the private sector, trade unions and other facets of Caribbean society despised, but tolerated, him.

Not surprisingly a left-wing movement of largely younger people emerged in Grenada under the name of 'the New Jewel Movement' (NJM) led by a young, charismatic attorney, Maurice Bishop, and his more austere deputy, Bernard Coard. Bishop's father had been killed during an anti-Gairy demonstration that both of them had helped to organise. In March 1979, when Gairy was out of the island (addressing the United Nations), Bishop and the NJM staged a bloodless coup. The NJM suspended the Constitution, declared Bishop Prime Minister, and banned all political parties except itself. The NJM was then converted into the People's Revolutionary Government (PRG) and ruled Grenada by decree. The PRG later formed the People's Revolutionary Army whose recruits were required to take an oath of loyalty to the NJM.

Maurice Bishop

However, the PRG did not sever its links with WISA, CARICOM or the Commonwealth, and although it had suspended the Constitution it left Sir Paul Scoon the Governor General and the Queen's representative, in place. The coup was popular in the sense of getting rid of Gairy. But many had misgivings about the method. Contributing to both popularity and misgiving was the proclamation of the NJM as a 'Marxist Socialist' Party and its development of specially close ties with Cuba. Nonetheless, when the member governments of WISA decided to replace the loose grouping with a formal treaty organisation, the OECS in 1981, none of the governments objected to the membership of Grenada and, indeed, one of the signatories to the Treaty was Maurice Bishop as Prime Minister.

The coup was on 13 March 1979. I contacted Bishop immediately and within days flew to Grenada with a small delegation from the Secretariat. What do you do in the face of a popular coup? My instinct was to get Bishop to regularise the situation as quickly as possible by announcing his intention to call early general elections (which he would have won at a canter) and restore the constitutionality of governance and a return to the rule of law.

I met Bishop on the balcony of a small house. He had not yet occupied Government Headquarters. He had Bernard Coard with him. And they were heavily and obviously body-guarded; though there was no general air of militarisation. They were glad to see me; it was a mark of recognition. But their pleasure was more material; they wished help from the Commonwealth: project funding from the Caribbean Development Bank; technical assistance from the Secretariat, and general support from Commonwealth countries. Maurice Bishop was clearly the political leader; Bernard Coard, more the technocrat, but with heavy socialist overtones.

I came quickly to the point. Caribbean countries and Commonwealth countries generally, could not be comfortable with a coup as a basis for recognition, however unworthy the Government it replaced, without some promise or indication of regularisation of the situation on democratic lines. There was a general air of relief that Gairy was gone; but they must not expect congratulation for bringing it about by force. I said that obviously the NJM was riding a wave of popularity. An early general election would confirm their legitimacy and make assistance of all kinds available. It soon became clear that I was talking to the deaf. There was no issue of legitimacy, I was told.

The revolution was their election; it needed no confirmation. Their power derived directly from the people; all the world's great revolutions were like that. To talk of elections was to question the legitimacy of the revolution. In all this Coard was the more ideological and uncompromising of the two. I argued that however strongly they felt about their domestic situation, other countries with whom they have to deal, would not share their passion and therefore their conclusion; this was the *realpolitik;* they needed to acknowledge it as a practical reality, and make it possible for others to not merely recognise them, but to help. I believed that my appeal to pragmatism may have made a small dent in Bishop's revolutionary armour; I was sure it bounced off of Coard's without a mark.

In the end, Coard's resistance prevailed with the PRG, including Bishop, who as late as two years later asserted (to an American interviewer):

> *... the revolution came on 13th March 1979; that is just two years ago. Under the system we inherited, elections were held once in five years. After you had your revolution in America, it took you thirteen years to call your elections. After the British had their revolution in the 17th century, it took them over 150 years to call their elections. So what is the problem? What is the reason for the pressure? We are going to call our elections. But we will do it at the appropriate time. Meanwhile we are going to get down to some serious business of building the country and dealing with the priorities that our people have set for Grenada.*

Meanwhile, in our discussion in Grenada, I persisted, aiming to continue the effort at another level. I proposed that a Group of eminent persons from the Region might be constituted by the Commonwealth as a Caribbean Advisory Group to assist the Government in the process of transition ahead. Bishop agreed with this, and Coard concurred without enthusiasm. The Group was duly set up and it was chaired by an eminent Dominican, Justice Telford Georges (later the first Chief Justice of Zimbabwe) and included William Demas, (Chairman of the Caribbean Development Bank) and former Secretary-General of the Caribbean Community. It was serviced by the CARICOM Secretariat.

The Group held meetings with Bishop and his colleagues and advised them strongly that the holding of elections was the *sine qua non* of progress. This was just as strongly resisted by the PRG. In the face of this obduracy, the Group concluded that they could make no progress and disbanded. With Caribbean advice spurned, the Bishop Government turned to Cuba which was an ideological soul mate in any event; but it did not turn its back on the Caribbean Community. In the Community, however, it lived an uneasy life, as it sought to inject its Marxist philosophies into regional policy. Its closest friend was Guyana, whose socialism was more pragmatic; but who defended Grenada's right to pursue its chosen path. So too, with less intensity, did Trinidad and Tobago, Belize and The Bahamas. Hence the emergence of the notion of 'ideological pluralism' within the Community – and its grudging acceptance by more rightist pro-American Governments.

The political flag-bearer of this latter faction was Edward Seaga in Jamaica, who had in a recent general election ousted Michael Manley, an avowed social democrat – whose socialism, however, was more rhetorical than practical. Seaga, by comparison, was a 'Cold War' ideologue with close personal links to the new right wing of the Republican Party in Washington. President Reagan was elected only three weeks after Seaga's own victory in Jamaica – with his doctrinaire right wing in the ascendancy. Seaga was the first official visitor that Reagan met in Washington. This political conjuncture was to provide a propitious environment for the invasion of Grenada nine months later.

Seaga despised 'ideological pluralism' in the Caribbean Community, and soon began to float the idea of 'CARICOM 11' – effectively expelling Grenada and Guyana. He was at best a luke-warm regionalist; his Party (the Jamaica Labour Party) was responsible for taking Jamaica out of the West Indian Federation in the 1960s. If Jamaica was to be in a Caribbean Community in the 1980s it could not be one, he argued, that included a Marxist Grenada and a Socialist Guyana. But, in this, he had gone a mile too far; such a break-up of regionalism for those who had struggled so long to achieve it was too much. Despite sympathy in some quarters with his political extremism, 'CARICOM 11' found insufficient support. But Seaga remained 'the voice of Washington' in the Caribbean.

Hostility to Grenada continued from within the Caribbean, essentially from Jamaica, Barbados, Dominica and St Lucia. At successive CARICOM Summits, at Jamaica in November 1982 (led by Barbados) and at Trinidad in July 1983 (led by Jamaica), attempts were made to amend the CARICOM Treaty – the Treaty of Chaguaramas – to facilitate the expulsion of Grenada. Both foundered on the Treaty's 'unanimity' rule. Guyana's Prime Minister, Forbes Burnham was prominent in baulking these efforts as was Vere Cornwall Bird of Antigua and Barbuda; but Leaders of the Opposition in Jamaica (Michael Manley) and in Barbados (Errol Barrow) voiced resistance too: the latter expressing concern at what he saw *"as a trend of intolerance within the Caribbean Community of the idea of philosophical and ideological pluralism"*.

Meanwhile, all was not well with Bishop's government in Grenada. In recently declassified documents is a note of 6 December 1983 from the Foreign and Commonwealth Office in London to 10 Downing Street summarising secret papers of the PRG found after the invasion. The somewhat patronising, but probably not inaccurate, assessment of the years the PRG ruled Grenada was:

> *(1) The initial impression is of parish pump politics larded with Communist jargon which is barely understood by the participants. Before seeing these documents however we knew of the existence, but not the depth, of the personal and ideological clash between on the one hand Bishop and his supporters who were regarded as soft left or, in the jargon, 'right opportunists' and petty bourgeois and, on the other, the small hard-line group of power- hungry ideologues led by Coard. The inescapable build-up of*

pressure on Bishop to relinquish hold on real power or to see it wrested from him is striking.

(2) The claims of Bishop and Coard to be operating an advanced democracy were clearly a sham. All the decisions were made by a small caucus of people. No democratic control was evident or intended for the future.

(3) The papers illustrate the vulnerability of small states to a determined and unscrupulous group, especially when the previous regime has been discredited through its corruption.

(4) The influence of Cuba and the USSR does not appear to have been very direct in the Party deliberations. The Cubans apparently were not conscious of what was going on. At one point, Bishop expressed reluctance to tell them of trouble. There are some critical references to Cuba.

The last conclusion may not have been the whole story. Cuba did not meddle; but seems to have suspected Coard's disloyalty, and may even have warned Bishop of their misgivings.

* * *

Mohammed Shahabudeen was my successor as Attorney-General of Guyana – as I have earlier recounted – and went on to become a particularly eminent Judge of the International Court of Justice (ICJ). His book, *The Conquest of Grenada: Sovereignty in the Periphery* is one of many scholarly works on what happened in Grenada; but the only one, I believe, which described it as a 'conquest'. In the Preface he explained why:

I have decided to call the outcome 'The Conquest of Grenada' because this, it seems to me, rightly describes what happened. And to appreciate what happened it is necessary to call it by the name which it properly bears. 'Invasion' and 'intervention' come near to the truth, but do not quite bring out its enormity, 'rescue' is transparently inaccurate. Acceptance of this and other euphemisms would serve not only to cloud the reality of the event but to induce a mood submissive to suspension of the meaning of sovereignty in favour of the assertion of superpower predominance.

It is this last thought which has in turn led to the subtitle Sovereignty in the Periphery. Does what happened in Grenada, and more particularly if we accept it, imply the existence of some kind of differential concept of sovereignty? Is the sovereignty, which we in the region would like to think we have, qualitatively different from that of other nations, and, if so, is the qualitative difference so large as to imply a difference of kind?

He was writing about 'smallness'. It is well to bear these musings in mind as the story unravels.

From an early stage in the Grenada saga, even before the Reagan regime, 'Cold War' considerations had occupied American political and military minds; but the Carter administration was not hawkish. With Reagan's election in 1981, however, there was open intensification of belligerence. It was almost as if Grenada presented a ready-made model on which to demonstrate American 'Cold War' intolerance, intransigence and unilateralism – all part of the mantra of the new right: a model enhanced by the new Jamaica/US 'alliance' forged by Seaga.

The posture of the Reagan administration was that the Bishop regime was part of the Cuban/Soviet axis, and an enemy of the United States. Among the reasons they cited for this high-blown assessment were as insubstantial, and in some respects less than accurate, as:

In the United Nations, Grenada voted with the Soviets and their allies in over 92 per cent of the votes of the 1982 General Assembly – a Pro-Soviet record exceeding even that of Nicaragua.

> *The bulk of the financing for the new airport in Grenada came from Cuba, which was providing services valued at $40 million, supplemented by $2 million each from Syria, Iraq and Algeria and $6 million from Libya. Construction was in the hands of Cuban workers with arms and the training to use them.*

Seven months before the US invasion, before any question of Bishop's demise or threats to the safety of American students, Ronald Reagan, had already set the stage for military action. In a speech at the Washington Hilton to the National Association of Manufacturers on 10 March 1983, he said:

> *That tiny little island is building now, or having built for it, on its soil and shores, a naval base, a superior air base, storage bases and facilities for the storage of munitions, barracks, and training grounds for the military. I'm sure all of that is not simply to encourage the export of nutmeg ... It isn't nutmeg that's at stake in the Caribbean and Central America; it is the United States national security. Soviet military theorists want to destroy our capacity to re- supply Western Europe in case of an emergency. We've been slow to understand that the defence of the Caribbean and Central America against Marxist-Leninist takeover is vital to our national security in ways we're not accustomed to thinking about.*

On the first anniversary of the invasion, the *New York Times* (of 25 October 1984) was to say that the United States *"now concedes that its own forces could use the airport for military purposes. But it says that the airport is intended mainly to aid the development of tourism and other aspects of the Grenada economy, which is what the Cubans said"*. The British firm Plessy PLC was involved in the construction, and two US firms were sub-contractors.

In his own election campaign in 1981, Seaga had pledged to break diplomatic relations with Cuba and to draw Jamaica close to the United

States – direct reversals of the policies pursued by Michael Manley who had been in charge of the country's affairs for the previous decade. True to his word, Seaga broke diplomatic relations with Cuba and established close relations with insiders in the Reagan camp who were later to become key players not only in the Reagan government, but later in the administration of George W Bush. Prominent among them were Richard Perle (*The Prince of Darkness*) and Paul Wolfowitz, antecedents of Bush's *Vulcans* and of *The Project for the New American Century* – early architects of American unilateralism and the doctrine of 'pre-emption'.

Seaga had come to office at a time when the Caribbean's relations with the United States and Cuba were far from uniform. Prior to his becoming Prime Minister, Jamaica (under Manley) and Guyana (under Burnham), were friends of Cuba – though in a 'Non-Aligned', not a 'Cold War', context. The OECS countries (other than Grenada) and Barbados continued to be strongly linked to the US while Trinidad and Tobago, under the Prime Ministership of George Chambers, stood aloof from ties to either side though both Barbados (under Barrow) and Trinidad and Tobago (under Chamber's predecessor Dr Eric Williams) had joined Guyana and Jamaica in 1972 in breaking the US diplomatic embargo of Cuba, by joint recognition. The Bahamas, led by Sir Lynden Pindling, was literally on America's doorstep and while Pindling would do nothing to offend the US, he was anxious not to encourage its undue influence. Belize – the other member of the Caribbean Community and Common Market (CARICOM) at the time – was under threat from Guatemala, which claimed all of Belizean territory. Never certain about whom the US would support in the Belize-Guatemala dispute, the Belizean leader, George Price, was also wary of the Americans.

In 1982, with the death of Dr Williams of Trinidad and Tobago an opportunity arose to heal differences in the Community, and Seaga eagerly hosted a Summit Meeting; but its conclusions did not please him in two important respects. First, in the Ocho Rios Declaration, the Heads asserted that:

> *While recognising that the emergence of ideological pluralism in the Community responds to internal processes and is an irreversible trend within the international system, we are committed to ensuring that it will not inhibit the processes of integration.*

Second, the Conference:

> *considered that the international system was increasingly characterised by the use of force ... and by the assertion by the great powers of spheres of interest, and it affirmed the inadmissibility of interference in the internal affairs of States.*

As the subsequent invasion of Grenada by the US with the active participation of Jamaica, Barbados and the OECS countries would demonstrate, the affirmation of *the inadmissibility of interference in the internal affairs of States* exercised no constraint on the CARICOM member states who violated it.

There is little doubt that the US government wanted to invade Grenada. What they needed was a plausible cover. An invitation from neighbouring countries would help; but was probably not enough for international law. Certainly, it would be easy enough to get such an invitation from the members of the OECS, some of whom were genuinely fearful of the example that Grenada set in their own countries among radical groups with external links. Many of them had such groups (financed, they believed, by the Cuban and Libyan regimes) which were active thorns in the sides of their governments. Leaders of these groups, including Maurice Bishop, had met on Union Island in the Grenadines prior to the March 1979 coup d'etat in Grenada, and had declared their intention to remove their governments from office by whatever means necessary – a threat which these governments of small states did not take lightly.

From the outset, my own influence in London was deployed in support of continued Commonwealth engagement with Grenada. In 1979 WISA leaders hoped that the British Government would intervene or at least sever relationships with the Bishop regime; but the British government argued that Britain recognised states not governments, and since Sir Paul Scoon had been retained as the Governor-General and the representative of the Queen, diplomatic links would continue. Bishop himself attended both the 1979 and 1981 Commonwealth Summits in Lusaka and Melbourne respectively, and became something of a spokesman for the cause of small and disadvantaged states. He was articulate and persuasive, and was well liked by the majority of his Commonwealth peers. Over time, even the WISA/OECS countries were beginning to recognise that he was a moderating influence in the regime in Grenada. But the fact that he was, was his undoing.

In 2013, thirty years later, *The Round Table: The Commonwealth Journal of International Affairs* published a special issue on *'The Invasion of Grenada: 30 Years on: A Retrospective'*. In providing the context of the several analyses that followed, the Editor summarised the events in Grenada that precipitated the invasion, thus:

> *By its fourth year the revolution appeared to be running out of steam as the economic situation deteriorated and the government had become increasingly detached from the people. As the PRG Central Committee turned in on itself in the summer of 1983, Bishop was the focus of their attention – the quality of his leadership and failure to place the party on a firm Marxist-Leninist footing were criticised. The proposed solution was joint leadership between Bishop and his Deputy Prime Minister Bernard Coard...*
>
> *Bishop initially agreed to the joint leadership proposal, but subsequently changed his mind. There was no going back though and the Coard faction denounced Bishop, placed him under house arrest, and expelled him from the party. The crisis might have ended there, but for ordinary Grenadians this had come as a complete shock. Bishop was the charismatic leader and epitomised the revolution. Coard was the unpopular hard core ideologue to whom the public had never warmed. Hence, when*

crowds of Bishop's supporters freed him from house arrest and he led them to Fort Rupert, the Coard faction felt that they had to respond and sent armoured personnel carriers to retake the Fort. In the ensuing melee between 30 and 40 Bishop supporters were killed and Bishop and seven colleagues were executed by firing squad.

The Caribbean image, as an idyll of tranquillity, was shattered overnight. Matters worsened the following day when Hudson Austin, the commanding General of Grenada's 'People's Revolutionary Army', announced the formation of a Revolutionary Military Council (RMC) headed by him and identified with Coard to run the country; and imposed 'a four day round-the-clock shoot-to-kill curfew'. The Governor-General, Sir Paul Scoon, was still in Government House and he recalled that General Austin visited him on the morning of 21 October to outline the RMC's plans for a mixed civilian-military government with Scoon continuing as Governor-General.

In London, I followed these events with horror and alarm. On 20 October, the day after Bishop's death, I issued the following statement from Marlborough House:

I share the deep sense of horror which is widespread throughout the Commonwealth at the tragic loss of life in Grenada, including that of the Prime Minister and Ministers of the Government. I feel sure that Commonwealth Caribbean Governments, in particular, will wish to use every influence through co-ordinated responses to ensure that the will and the interests of the people of Grenada are respected and the integrity of the island state preserved.

I had begun to learn what was unfolding among Caribbean countries, and was both shocked and troubled. There seemed to be three lines of action: one led by Dominica (only a little bigger than Grenada) whose President, Dame Eugenia Charles, was Chairperson of the OECS, acting prominently with the Prime Ministers of St Lucia (which housed the Secretariat of the OECS) John Compton (later, Sir John), and of Barbados (which was not a member of the OECS) J.M.G. "Tom" Adams. Another was led by the Prime Minister of Trinidad and Tobago (George Chambers), who was the Chairman-in-office of the Caribbean Community. The third, more clandestine, was the Jamaica-United States cabal which had been long established. The first and the third were to merge and the second, perhaps the most legitimate actor, was to be discarded.

The first move in this direction came when on 21 October, representatives of the OECS governments met at the Dover Convention Centre in Barbados with 'Tom' Adams and Edward Seaga. An uneasy relationship had persisted between Grenada and the rest of the OECS. But, once Bishop was killed and the military government established, the leaders of the rest of the OECS were resolved that unconstitutional government should not succeed – as an example to ambitious groups within their own countries. If they had had the means to enter Grenada and topple the regime they would have done so unhesitatingly. In the face of their own lack of capacity, the option eagerly put to them by Seaga, with Adams' support, namely, that of inviting the US to invade, became very attractive to these small, relatively helpless, islands of the OECS.

And the US was on hand. Seaga and Adams had seen to that. Present at the meeting were representatives of the US government led by Milan Bish, the US Ambassador to Barbados and the Eastern Caribbean. Supported by Seaga and Adams he explained (wrongly) how an invasion could be undertaken 'jointly' using Article 8 of the OECS Treaty (which provided for collective defence against 'external' attack) and 'inviting' the US to mount an invasion of Grenada with them. The stage was quickly set. As early as 30 October the New York Times was reporting that *"the wording of the formal request was drafted in Washington and conveyed to the Caribbean leaders by special American emissaries"*. The OECS countries signed the letter of invitation that night – addressed to Barbados, Jamaica and the United States – to mount an invasion of Grenada with them. Of course, motivations were different among the agreeing parties. The US, in particular, had long wanted just such a show of force in a 'Cold War' context, and Seaga was a 'warrior' with them. 'Tom' Adams was thoughtfully mindful of the insecurities of smallness. Most of the governments of the OECS were acting out of fear.

Six months before all this, on 21 April 1983, Maurice Bishop had written to me formally as Secretary-General asking me to forward his letter to all Commonwealth Governments. I did so, to all 49 countries. It was a global *cri de coeur*:

> *As has often been stated by the Government of Grenada, the United States began a policy of economic, political and military aggression against our country since the triumph of our Revolution on March 13, 1979.*
>
> *The US is continuing its acts of economic aggression against our small country. Attempts have been made to prevent us from receiving assistance from regional and international financial institutions ... [examples].*
>
> *We are now increasingly concerned because these attacks on our economy have also been given political impetus in the form of adverse pronouncements by top United States personnel... [examples of hostile statements, ending with President Reagan's 'nutmeg' speech "it is not nutmeg that is at stake in the Caribbean, it is the United States National Security"].*
>
> *Given the historic record of US military interventionism, it is our opinion that the pronouncement of the President of the United States that Grenada constitutes a threat to the national security of the United States of America is an indication of hostile designs. This is for us cause for grave concern.*
>
> *Our interests lie in seeking economic advancement for the 110,000 people of our small country.... Our position is and has always been that we seek better relations with the United States Government, and remain willing to work towards the establishment of normal relations based on mutual respect for each other's sovereignty and national aspirations.*

In our concern, we draw these matters to your attention for your information and close consideration and for whatever assistance you can provide to prevent this ominous threat of aggression against our country from materialising.

It is intriguing that when Mrs Thatcher received her copy she scribbled in the margin: "I really don't think we can ignore it. Why did Mr Ramphal circulate it? We really must ask". She had overlooked that Bishop had asked for general circulation. But was she being more protective of Reagan's image than Grenada's security? In any event, Britain did ignore the warning, and the plea. It is ironic that when the *"ominous threat of aggression"* did materialise, Bishop's own death would provide the pretext for it.

On the day following the Barbados 'invitation' meeting, on the evening of Saturday 22 October and the morning of Sunday 23 October, a 'special meeting' of CARICOM Heads was held in Port of Spain under the Chairmanship of Trinidad and Tobago's Prime Minister, George Chambers to consider the situation. Chambers later reported fully to his Parliament on the discussions which commenced with 'agreement in principle' on four proposals, namely:

1. *No involvement of any external elements in the resolution of the Grenada situation.*
2. *The resolution of the Grenada situation should be wholly regional, that is to say, CARICOM in nature.*
3. *The regional situation pursued should not violate international law and the United Nations Charter.*
4. *Any proposed solution should have as its primary purpose the restoration of normalcy in Grenada.*

On the basis of this 'agreement in principle' the meeting considered Chambers' further concrete proposals for:

1. *The immediate establishment of a broad based civilian Government of National Reconciliation acceptable to the Governor-General.*

2. *Acceptance of a fact-finding mission comprising eminent nationals of CARICOM states*
3. *The putting into place of arrangements to ensure the safety of nationals of other countries in Grenada and/or their evacuation where desired.*
4. *The acceptance of deployment in Grenada of a peacekeeping force comprising contingents contributed by CARICOM countries.*

Chambers had had his Governor-General, Sir Ellis Clarke, consult with Sir Paul Scoon in Grenada and he had also spoken to me by telephone. I encouraged him to proceed on the lines of these proposals and discussed the ways in which the Commonwealth would be able to assist in their implementation. He later reported to his Parliament:

> *As Chairman, I intimated to the meeting that I had reason to believe that the persons exercising authority in Grenada would be willing to treat on the basis of these proposals and objectives.*

And he added:

> *By 3.05 am on Sunday when the adjournment was taken it was apparent that consensus had emerged in support of the proposal and objectives, so much that Heads of delegations including some of the OECS had suggested names of eminent persons who would comprise the fact-finding mission to Grenada. It had also been agreed that I as chairman of the Meeting would be entrusted with pursuing the initiatives.*

When the CARICOM Meeting resumed later than planned on Sunday 23rd, it was clear that there had been a caucus of the OECS countries, Barbados and Jamaica. They asserted that there was no consensus on the previous discussion and that they did not want to resume it. Instead they wanted discussion of a Jamaica Paper and an OECS Paper earlier submitted. The Jamaica Paper dealt with amendments to the Treaty of Chaguaramas directed at the 'unanimity rule'; while the OECS paper proposed 'sanctions' against Grenada. It was clearly a filibuster. The meeting never returned to the Chambers' injunction against military intervention and his proposals for Caribbean fact-finding and peacekeeping missions.

Nothing was said by anyone at the Trinidad Meeting – a Summit Meeting of the Community – of the decision taken in Barbados the previous Friday to invade Grenada in the footsteps of the Americans. The *Wall Street Journal* of 28 October reported Chambers as saying he was deceived by Jamaica, Barbados and the OECS countries. Others dubbed the Meeting 'an exercise in duplicity'. And so it was. While Chambers and his colleagues from Belize, Guyana and The Bahamas were pursuing non-military responses to Grenada, troops from Jamaica and some OECS countries were flying into Barbados to join Barbadian forces and await details from Washington of "Operation Urgent Fury", as the US named the Grenada invasion.

* * *

In the early morning of 25 October, without notice, Dame Eugenia Charles, the Dominica Prime Minister and Chairperson of the OECS, was awakened and flown by the US to Washington to appear on television at President Reagan's side as he announced that the Grenada invasion was launched that morning. The announcement was the first inkling the OECS and other CARICOM countries had that the invasion was on. CARICOM was notified by the US Ambassador in Trinidad and Tobago calling the Foreign Ministry. Not even Margaret Thatcher, the British Prime Minister, and close friend of Ronald Reagan, had been told that the invasion would take place.

Mrs Thatcher's reactions form a story all of its own. On 24 October, as CARICOM leaders were leaving Trinidad at the end of a meeting that left them deeply divided, Reagan wrote to Thatcher saying that: "the nations of the OECS have unanimously decided to pursue a collective security effort to restore peace and order in Grenada and have formally requested United States support and participation". He told her that he was: "giving serious consideration to the OECS 'request', and advised that "they have already assembled forces in Barbados from the various island nations". He concluded by saying that he knew she "would want to be kept informed of any role the United States may decide to play in support of the island nations of the Caribbean" and undertook to inform her "in advance should our forces take part in the proposed collective security force".

Later that same day, Reagan wrote to Thatcher again to say:

> *I have decided to respond positively to this request (from the OECS to intervene in Grenada). I understand that Barbados and Jamaica have also responded favourably.*

But, he did not tell her when the operation would take place.

At 12.30 am on 25 October, Thatcher sent Reagan the following message:

> *This action will be seen as intervention by a Western country in the internal affairs of a small independent nation, however unattractive its regime. I ask you to consider this in the context of our wider East/West relations and of the fact that we will be having in the next few days to present to our Parliament and people the siting of Cruise missiles in this country. I must ask you to think most carefully about these points. I cannot conceal that I am deeply disturbed by your latest communication. You asked for my advice. I have set it out and hope that even at this late stage you will take it into account before events are irrevocable.*

By then, *Operation Urgent Fury* had been launched, and it went ahead without the knowledge of the British government.

Greanadians at gunpoint

The next day, 26 October, Reagan called Thatcher to explain that he did not tell her that the invasion was on because there was a security leak on his end; it was a security leak about which he said he was so concerned that *"we did not even give a firm answer to the Caribbean States. We told them we were planning, but we were so afraid of this source and what it would do; it could almost abort the mission, with the lives that could have been endangered."*

On the day of the invasion and in subsequent media statements, Thatcher and her Ministers did not conceal aggravation that the US had invaded a Commonwealth country and one of which the Queen was still Head of State. Mrs Thatcher was genuinely annoyed on at least three grounds: she believed the invasion was wrong in principle; it made problems for her in the *cruise missile* debate in Britain, and she was irritated that her 'close and special friend' Ron should have gone ahead with the invasion without telling her he was and despite her advice that he should not. On a phone-in programme on the BBC World Service on the morning of 30 October she said:

> *If you are going to pronounce a new law that wherever communism reigns against the will of the people, even though it has happened internally there, the United States shall enter, then we are going to have really terrible wars in the world.*

And she was right; but her public hostility abated in private conversations with Reagan; the 'special relationship' had to come first. The record of Thatcher's telephone conversation four days earlier with Reagan indicated little more than formal affront at being blindsided – and her advice ignored. Perhaps her basic attitude to the invasion was reflected in her own words to him: *"I just hope Ron, that it (the restoration of constitutional government in Grenada) will be very soon and that they will manage to put together a government which can get back to democracy."* Thereafter, it was pleasantries between two good friends as follows:

Reagan:	*As I say, I'm sorry for any embarrassment that we caused you, but please understand that it was just our fear of our own weakness over here with regard to secrecy.*
Thatcher:	*It was very kind of you to have rung, Ron.*
Reagan:	*Well, my pleasure.*
Thatcher:	*I appreciate it. How is Nancy?*
Reagan:	*Just fine.*
Thatcher:	*Good. Give her my love.*
Reagan:	*I shall.*
Thatcher:	*I must return to this debate in the House. It is a bit tricky.*
Reagan:	*All right. Go get 'em. Eat 'em alive.*
Thatcher:	*Good-bye.*

On the morning of this conversation between Reagan and Thatcher, I was interviewed by the BBC's 'Today' programme about the invasion. I was in far more sombre mood than the Prime Minister. Questioned about whether I was asked for advice prior to the invasion, I said:

> *No I was not. I wish indeed I was. I would not have had any difficulty in saying that there were other ways that must be pursued ... that we don't in fact help Grenada or help the*

Caribbean by taking the law into our own hands, or worse still inviting external powers to take the law into their hands on behalf of the region.

I went on to make it clear that I was against the US invasion, declaring:

In the wake of what obviously was a divided region, a divided Caribbean on the question of intervention of any kind, I would have thought that the United States, in this situation, as a friend of the region – and it has been a friend of the region in many respects – would have been counselling calm and wisdom, would have been counselling negotiation, would have been helping the region to put great pressure on the quite grotesque regime that killed Maurice Bishop and seized power, before resorting to this kind of armed intervention.

I issued a separate statement from Marlborough House which went to all Commonwealth Governments and to the CARICOM and OECS Secretariats to this effect:

I have already condemned unreservedly the killing of Prime Minister Bishop and some of his colleagues. Now the tragedy is deepening. Today's external intervention will occasion further disquiet within the Commonwealth.

If there is a lesson in these events, it must surely be in the chain of tragedy that begins with the overthrow of constitutional government, and the deep passions and anxieties that are aroused when the contests of super powers are brought within regions of small developing countries.

But nothing must obscure the urgent need to provide the people of Grenada with the earliest possible opportunity to determine their own future free of pressures or constraints of any kind. And I offered the thought that: There may be a role for the Commonwealth to play in contributing to the restoration of constitutional government in Grenada.

The OECS meanwhile had formally notified me of their decision to *"take appropriate action"* and that *"bearing in mind the relative lack of military resources in the possession of the OECS countries, the member governments have sought assistance for this purpose from friendly countries within the region and subsequently from outside"*. Then followed the important words:

> *Three Governments have responded to the OECS member governments' request to form a multi-national force for the purpose of undertaking a pre-emptive defensive strike in order to remove this dangerous threat to peace and security to their sub-region and to establish a situation of normality in Grenada. These Governments are Barbados, Jamaica and the United States"*

"A pre-emptive defensive strike" – the language of Washington's hard right that was to resonate world-wide in conflicts beyond Grenada from Iraq to Afghanistan over years to come. Late that first night of the invasion, as the world was beginning to react to the news, I received a message from the Director-General of the OECS, Dr Vaughan Lewis, to the following effect:

> *Member States of the Organisation are of the view that the necessity now is for the Caribbean and Commonwealth countries to put themselves in a position to speedily arrange for peacekeeping forces to be put in place to create a situation that will allow the non-CARICOM personnel to withdraw from Grenada.*

But, of course, by now, matters were out of the hands of the small OECS countries for whom the Director-General spoke.

B. INTERNATIONAL REACTION

The international response was so immediate that late the same day of the invasion the United Nations Security Council took up the situation in Grenada as an emergency matter and met for 10 hours into the night in debate on a draft resolution *calling "for an immediate cessation of the armed intervention in Grenada and for the immediate withdrawal of the foreign forces from that country*". Under other provisions of the text, the Council would have deeply deplored "*the armed intervention in Grenada" as "a flagrant violation of international law and of the independence, sovereignty and territorial integrity of that State"*. The vote on the draft Resolution was 11 in favour to one against (United States) with three abstentions (Britain, Togo and Zaire). Of the five Permanent Members, three were in favour, including France; and Britain was not against. The single American vote against was a veto, and so the Resolution failed.

On 2 November the General Assembly, whose decisions are not enforceable, debated a similar resolution which was adopted by 108 votes to 9. The nine countries voting against were Barbados, Jamaica, four OECS countries, Israel, El Salvador and the United States. Britain did not vote against; it abstained – as in the Security Council.

These were resounding condemnations by the international community of the invasion of Grenada, and unambiguous demands for the withdrawal of the American and Caribbean military. The voting was not on East-West lines; nor on North-South. It was not the 'non-aligned' against the West. It was a global rejection of the notion of a 'pre-emptive defensive strike'. It was an unusual coming together of an outraged international community. I felt humiliated that some Caribbean Commonwealth countries, whose international standing as a Region was so high, stood indicted. I took comfort in the fact that it was only some.

A factor in all this was the situation of the Governor-General, Sir Paul Scoon, which was not widely understood. In Commonwealth countries that have retained the Queen as Head of State (and as I write there are 15 of them along with the United Kingdom), she is represented in those countries by a Governor-General who is normally a citizen of the country concerned. This was the case with Sir Paul Scoon, a Grenadian former senior civil servant. His authority did not derive from the British Government but directly from The Queen. In normal circumstances his position was purely formal and any powers only came into play at a time of crisis as defined by the country's Constitution.

A primary US objective had been to get Sir Paul Scoon off the island to the carrier USS *Guam* lying offshore. This was accomplished the next day before flying him back to Grenada's Point Salines Great House where a draft letter of 'invitation to intervene', back dated to 24 October (the day before the invasion) was delivered to him for signature. The signed letter reached the US Ambassador in Barbados the next day, 27 October – too late to be of use to US Ambassador Jeanne Kirkpatrick in the Security Council but in time to become the new 'justification' for the invasion.

While I always harboured suspicions that the Scoon 'invitation letter' had been backdated at the insistence of the US government, I had conformation of the details only after US government documents were declassified years later. An article by Robert J. Beck in the *Round Table 30-year Retrospective* which he entitled *"The Grenada Invasion, International Law and the Scoon Invitation"* gives an authoritative account. His conclusion is:

> *Sir Paul did not initiate his informal, oral invitation or author his formal written one, and that even though he genuinely supported 'Operation Urgent Fury' the Governor-General's invitation did not legally justify the operation.*

As I said I was sceptical about the 'Scoon invitation' from the outset. So were many others. As early as 1984, *The Economist* had judged the 'invitation' *"almost certainly a fabrication concocted between the OECS and Washington to calm the post-invasion diplomatic storm. As concoctions go, it was flimsy"*.

That only made my task harder: to get US troops out of Grenada and to place authority in Grenada back into Grenadian hands. The OECS Secretariat had said in their formal announcement of the invasion:

> *It is the intention of the member governments of the OECS that once the threat has been removed, they will invite the Governor-General of Grenada to assume executive authority of the country under the provisions of the Grenada constitution of 1973 and to appoint a broad-based interim government to administer the country pending the holding of general elections.*

I recognised that this was conditioned on "once the threat has been removed"; but I would assume it had been. Seized with the notions of constitutionality and an interim administration, I immediately began to work on assembling such a team. Concurrently, I sought out constitutional lawyers known to the Caribbean, who could advise the Governor-General. I needed to talk to Scoon; but there was no normal service. Fortunately, facilitated by an American satellite link, he rang me on 28 October.

Sir Paul confirmed that he was in authority and would make a radio broadcast that night principally to confirm that he was in authority. He volunteered that he would not touch on the withdrawal of the forces in Grenada, but would thank them for their assistance. I asked whether he wished to discuss the question of a Commonwealth security presence in the light of indications I had had from OECS countries, including Dame Eugenia Charles. He said it was too early for that but he would talk to me later. I told him I had begun to think of it but that I wanted him to know that the Commonwealth would only move in response to a request from Grenada, and only in the context of the withdrawal of foreign forces.

He referred to 'a caretaker administration' and asked if I could contact Alister McIntyre and enquire whether he would head it. Alister was an excellent choice – an eminent Grenadian, at the time Assistant Secretary General of the UN at UNCTAD in Geneva. I assured him I would do so immediately. I offered Tony Rushford of the UK (who had drafted the Grenada Constitution and whom he knew) as a legal adviser. He was wholly positive. He also asked for Nicholas Braithwaite who was a senior Grenadian at the time working for the Commonwealth Secretariat heading the Caribbean Youth Programme in Guyana. He said he would call me the next day; and did.

I was able to confirm that McIntyre was agreeable to head an Interim Administration subject to talking with Scoon about 'satisfactory arrangements being in place regarding the replacement of the external forces presently in Grenada', as well as the Administration being wholly technocratic in nature. I was also able to confirm that the UN Secretary-General had agreed in principle to McIntyre's release. With regard to McIntyre's condition that American forces would be withdrawn to be replaced by Commonwealth security, Scoon confirmed that "this was his thinking also and he would want to discuss the question fully with Alister, principally in terms of timing which was inevitably responsive to the existing situation".

That was the beginning of a series of telephone communications between us over these logistical matters. In them I had the impression that Scoon either could not or did not wish to discuss the issue of troop withdrawal. As it turned out, Scoon eventually rejected the idea of withdrawal of US troops, and Alister McIntyre could not take up the task for reasons of ill-health. But, I had laid the foundation with Scoon – and, behind the scenes, with Seaga and the leaders of the OECS through 'Tom' Adams – for an interim administration whose priority task would be the holding of general elections.

We were now into November and looming (on the 23rd) was the Commonwealth Summit in New Delhi under Indira Gandhi's Chairmanship.

I had a two-fold task. The first was to ensure that the Commonwealth stood resolutely by its principles of internationalism, by the rule of international law; the second, to contrive that Caribbean participation with the US in the invasion of Grenada did not fracture the Commonwealth. And I had a third goal deriving mainly from my origins – to rebuild a relationship among the Heads of Commonwealth Caribbean governments who had not met since their stormy encounter in Trinidad on the days before the invasion, and who remained bitterly divided on all that transpired since.

Grenada was not on the agenda of the Commonwealth Meeting as representatives of 41 countries came together in New Delhi under the chairmanship of India's Prime Minister, Indira Gandhi; but there were agenda items that would accommodate the inevitable discussion – like '*World Political Scene*'. The first day of the meeting went by with no reference to Grenada except for a brief but biting comment by Indira Gandhi in her statement at the opening ceremony. It was a comment directed as much to the Caribbean countries that had participated in the invasion as it was to the US. She said:

> *In the wider interest of peace, all powers should accept and strictly observe the principles of peaceful coexistence, non-intervention and non-interference. We cannot acquiesce in the reasons being advanced to justify the use of force by one state against another, to install regimes of particular persuasion or to destabilise regimes deemed to be inconvenient. Recent unfortunate events in Grenada have caused profound disquiet.*

The first day and the morning of the second were taken up by a lengthy discussion on East-West relations and the question of disarmament. Then, close to mid-day on the second day, the seething anger of the African countries was unleashed over what they considered to be the cover that Caribbean countries had given to the US to invade Grenada.

First, Zambia's Kenneth Kaunda, and then Robert Mugabe of Zimbabwe spoke to the issue. They both claimed that a precedent had been set for powerful neighbours such as South Africa (still then under the apartheid regime) to invade them. Kaunda declared that *"those of his colleagues in the Caribbean who had acted with the United States had created a real nightmare for him personally and for his country."* Mugabe was even more direct. He stated:

> *If their colleagues in the Commonwealth could sanction this kind of thinking by sanctioning the invasion of Grenada, the*

African member states were entitled to regard them as acting against African interests...
Powerful states, which wanted to promote their own ideological systems throughout the world, were trying to use their might to manipulate small states, even by way of invasion if this was considered necessary, and to seek to establish within such states regimes which they could manipulate as puppets.

Later in the debate, Tanzania's President, Julius Nyerere, practically accused the leaders of the Caribbean countries that participated in the invasion of lying. He said:

It was in the nature of man to try to justify and find good reasons for what he had done. Those in the Eastern Caribbean had given their good reasons for joining the Americans in the invasion. Frankly, he thought they were overdoing it... The Americans had invaded a small Caribbean country. It was not possible for the Commonwealth to keep quiet about it, and he hoped the Commonwealth would find some appropriate way of expressing its anger.

Edward Seaga, the Jamaican Prime Minister and architect of the Grenada invasion had chosen not to attend the Commonwealth Meeting. Therefore, it was left to 'Tom' Adams, the Barbados Prime Minister and the leaders of the OECS countries to justify their position. They did so with reasonable success, garnering sympathy from the leaders of other small island states and Australia's Prime Minister Bob Hawke. Their defence, wisely, was not avowal of a new doctrine of 'pre-emption'; but an assertion of their sense of helplessness – of their smallness.

I had so orchestrated the debate, with Mrs Gandhi's help, that the OECS and Barbados leaders were given free rein by the Chair to speak while encouraging the Caribbean leaders who had opposed the invasion not to speak. Thus, Belize and the Bahamas remained silent and the only brief interventions by Chambers (Trinidad and Tobago) and Burnham (Guyana) were to draw attention to a Statement circulated by Chambers of his remarks to his Parliament in which he described the CARICOM meeting he had chaired prior to the invasion. My purpose, of course, was to ensure that the Caribbean countries did not set upon each other in the councils of the Commonwealth.

Apart from the Africans, there was no overwhelming mood in the meeting to condemn the Caribbean countries that had participated in the invasion. Lee Kuan Yew, the Prime Minister of Singapore, seemed to speak for many when he said:

> *Leaders were presented with a paradox: each knew in his heart that the Eastern Caribbean states response was right ... it would have been much more convenient if Barbados and Jamaica between them had had the resources to have taken on the Cubans (presumably in Grenada). The matter would then not have been raised at the meeting, nor would their action have caused great objection in the United Nations, which would have seen it as an example of the Third World resolving its own problems.*

In summing up the session, I made no mention of the differences between the African leaders and the leaders of the Caribbean countries that had participated in the invasion. Instead I focused on what I called *"a forward looking approach, particularly one concerned with the recuperation of Grenada and a return to constitutional government."* I informed the meeting that I had been "endeavouring to make the Secretariat ready to respond to any requests that might emerge from Grenada, and had been assisting in the establishment of an Advisory Council, the initial step towards a return to constitutional government. The discussion ended on a uniquely Commonwealth note: an invitation to Heads to attend the pending India-West Indies cricket Test in Bombay.

The Heads of Government went off to a 'retreat' weekend on 26 and 27 November in Goa. Unlike other 'retreats' I have described, my plan was that there should be no more debate on Grenada. Instead, I drafted and circulated three paragraphs for the Communiqué reflecting the nuances of the plenary debate. I ensured that all the Caribbean countries were content with it; and then persuaded the leading African countries not to object to it. This process was so successful that when the entire draft Communiqué of the Meeting came before the Heads of Government (who had insisted on seeing it and amending it as they saw fit) the three paragraphs on Grenada were accepted without comment. This acceptance of my judgement by leaders who had differed amongst themselves so greatly was, I liked to think, a measure of the confidence they reposed in me. It was at this New Delhi Meeting that I was re-elected as Commonwealth Secretary-General for a third term – on a proposal of Mrs Thatcher.

The section of the Communiqué on Grenada did four important things:

1. *It agreed that the emphasis should be on reconstruction not recrimination, and affirmed the Commonwealth's readiness to help;*
2. *In welcoming an interim administration, it did so with the expectation that it would function free of external interference, pressure, or the presence of foreign military forces;*
3. *It emphasised that the Commonwealth leaders attached great importance to the early return by Commonwealth Caribbean countries to the spirit of fraternity and co-operation that had been characteristic of the region; and*
4. *It required the Secretary-General to undertake a study of the special needs of small states consonant with the right to sovereignty and territorial integrity.*

Immediately after the Commonwealth conference, I resumed contact with Scoon and the interim administration that had been appointed in December 1983 with Nicholas Braithwaite as its Chairman and arranged for a two-man Commonwealth Secretariat team to visit Grenada from 6 December to explain the Commonwealth position as stated in the Communiqué and to explore ways in which the Commonwealth's assistance could be mobilised. They met a stone wall on the withdrawal of US troops and formed the clear impression that *"the views of the OECS, Jamaica and Barbados at present dominate the thinking of the interim administration on security. Any change in the security arrangements would therefore require the prior acceptance of these countries."*

The deeper truth (as they reported to me privately) was that the interim administration itself and the Governor-General were content to keep the US troops in occupation since the presence of the troops consolidated their own positions and their authority. What they wanted from the Commonwealth was assistance in reconstruction but if such assistance *"is conditional on acceptance of the New Delhi Communiqué, Grenada could get on well without it"*.

I felt I had to talk directly to the Americans and arranged through the Embassy in London to visit the State Department on 20 December. I had no inside track with the Reagan Administration and had no idea who I would see; but it turned out to be Richard Perle. The essence of what Perle told me was a critique of the New Delhi Communiqué (which Reagan had already conveyed to Mrs Thatcher) ending with the discomfiting statement that *"those who invited us to Grenada, wish us to stay somewhat longer than the Commonwealth does. We will listen to them"*.

So, I knew well what to expect from the Grenada administration when I accepted an invitation shortly afterwards from Scoon to visit Grenada on 4 January 1984. I decided to combine it with visits to the key players in the Caribbean – leaders of the OECS, Jamaica and Barbados. I added the Bahamas, Trinidad and Tobago and Guyana, whose governments had opposed the invasion.

Throughout the visits I stressed the importance of the withdrawal of US troops and their replacement by policemen drawn from the Caribbean. By now I had a preliminary plan for a Commonwealth Police Support Unit worked out by the Secretariat with expert advice. And, everywhere, I emphasised the importance of this in the context of the holding of credible elections.

The OECS leaders that I saw – V.C. Bird Snr (Antigua and Barbuda), Eugenia Charles (Dominica), John Compton (St Lucia) – had no problem with the withdrawal of US troops and their replacement by Caribbean policemen. They were pleased that the Bahamas had agreed to provide policemen for the Caribbean contingent and they particularly welcomed Trinidad and Tobago's agreement to contribute. 'Tom' Adams of Barbados was also content to go along with this. All were agreed that Guyana should not participate in the provision of Caribbean troops since its leader Forbes Burnham had been the most hostile and critical of the invasion and of those Caribbean governments that had been part of it. They were all also very keen that the interim administration should hold early elections, or, in the words of 'Tom' Adams he would "pull out Barbados personnel and allow the operation to mash-up".

The most important meeting was with Jamaica's Prime Minister, Edward Seaga, who was clearly in regular contact with the US administration and who was guiding the thinking of the Interim Administration through the Jamaican public servant, Alan Kirton, the Deputy Chairman. Seaga was obviously not in favour of the withdrawal of US troops. He told me unashamedly that *"the emphasis should be on building up a major military presence in Grenada as a tangible manifestation of the resolve of governments of the region to defend themselves"*. It was his view that the US troops *"might have to remain for about a year – in any case until after the elections"*.

My view of all this was summarised in my office note at the end of the meeting with Seaga. It was:

> *SSR and party left Jamaica feeling uneasy about the outcome of the mission ... Certainly there was little to encourage belief that Jamaica would be helpful. Rather the contrary. Seaga seems to be directing policy for Grenada ... As the mission left Jamaica, it felt it had now heard the definitive reaction: American forces, however small, would remain in Grenada. The Commonwealth should keep out of the law and order situation and limit its role to providing some money to help Grenada ... That was the same*

line that SSR had been given in Washington when he called on the State Department on 20 December, 1983. Both heard from SSR that this was not on.

I left the region disappointed with the result of my visit to Grenada and Jamaica in particular. I knew then that the Commonwealth could play no role in Grenada at that time. The sad reality was that the OECS countries and Barbados who had been so manipulated by the United States and Seaga were not in control of their creation. Their smallness left them no alternative but to be silent followers. For my own part, the Commonwealth had remained true to itself at New Delhi and I had averted a Commonwealth crisis – and Caribbean leaders were talking with each other again; but American troops were still in the Commonwealth Caribbean.

When the Interim Administration, together with the Caribbean governments that had invaded Grenada, formally announced that US troops would remain in the country, I issued a terse press release stating that the decision *was "a setback to the 'healing process' in relations between Caribbean countries that the Commonwealth sought at New Delhi"*. It said Commonwealth leaders had looked forward in a spirit of *'reconstruction'* to the Interim Administration in Grenada *'functioning free of external interference, pressure or the presence of foreign military forces'*. The Secretariat had tried to help in the phasing out of foreign forces and their replacement by a Commonwealth Police Support Unit. And I ended by saying: *"The Secretary-General will now report on his efforts to Commonwealth governments generally; but will not propose any further initiatives."*

Nine months later, in September 1984, I received a request from the Interim Administration in Grenada for the Commonwealth to witness general elections set down for 3 December. American forces were still in Grenada. I duly circulated the request to Commonwealth governments and received negative replies from all who chose to respond. The communication from Kenneth Kaunda, the President of Zambia, summed up the Commonwealth response. In a letter to me, he said:

> *As long as foreign military forces continue to be deployed in Grenada up to the election time and after, Zambia cannot support the presence of a Commonwealth Observer Team, because to support such a suggestion would be contrary to the Commonwealth Summit decision of last year in New Delhi on the matter".*

I informed the Grenada administration of the Commonwealth's position.

Elections were held while US troops were in occupation and with "state trials" in process in relation to the events of October 1983. These factors would have influenced both the decisions of persons to form themselves into parties to contest the elections and the participation by the electorate in the vote.

Thirty years later as I write this, I continue to believe that Caribbean governments let themselves down through the majority who sided with an American invasion of their region – and those among them who participated actively in engineering it. The vote in the UN General Assembly negated credits that the Caribbean had worked hard to build up in the years since Jamaica's and Trinidad and Tobago's independence in 1962. It was especially harrowing for me as a Caribbean man; but I took comfort in the robustness with which the Commonwealth stood on the side of principle.

But the Grenada episode was not all a dark spot for the Caribbean and the Commonwealth. Aware that small countries would continue to be susceptible to the internal conditions that caused the coup d'etat in Grenada in 1979 and again in 1983, and to the risk of invasion by larger powers intent upon procuring their own interests, I was able to proceed from the fact that I had received a mandate from the New Delhi Summit for a study of the special needs of small states, including their security needs.

In 1984, I appointed a distinguished group drawn from small and large states of the Commonwealth to produce the study. It was chaired by Telford Georges, the same jurist from Dominica whose Caribbean Advisory Group had tried to persuade Maurice Bishop five years earlier to hold elections. The Study was ready by August 1985. It was entitled, "Vulnerability: Small States in the Global Society." It became a seminal document on the problems of small states, informing the work not only of the Commonwealth, but also of the United Nations, the World Bank and the International Monetary Fund. It led to the Commonwealth Secretariat being today the lead institution on 'Small States'.

Small states are not scaled-down models of larger states; they are unique; and so are their needs and the challenges they pose for themselves, their regions and the world community. Twice on my Commonwealth watch – in the Falklands and in Grenada – smallness was a factor in a major threat to world order. After the Falklands, I had warned the Commonwealth: *"Tomorrow it could be another small country – this time with no capacity to provide or invoke a response – that is the victim of aggression"*. It was to be Grenada. Global society has to make the world a safer place for small states; and to make them safe for the world.

CHAPTER 27

Our Country, the Planet

The 1980s were not good years for international negotiations. In the UN system on which multilateral negotiations were centred the record was one of dismal failure. Nations were divided between rich and poor, and those material divisions were mirrored by ideological divisions of free market thinking and that of justice and equity; between the power contours of the status quo and the compulsions of change. The Cold War era was passing, but was not being replaced by the kind of world promised in the loftier passages of the UN Charter. The Bretton Woods Institutions, which were the economic handmaids of the Charter, were prey to the same divisions and disappointments. The nation state system was not proving equal to the task of preparing for the 21st Century on a basis of equity, fairness and democratic principles.

Everyone knew it was not the best of times; many feared humanity might be heading to the worst of times; and the many who knew that we had to do better, were on all sides. Spontaneously, the world looked for new ways; and the decade of the 1980s and into the 1990s became times when the world turned to people from all estates acting independently of Governments, but acting together, to provide counsel on those ways forward – on development, on disarmament, on environment, on humanitarian issues, on deadly conflict and, inevitably, on global governance. Independent, international Commissions became the order of the day – offering the world not only road maps for practical action but also philosophies of survival which made following them a human imperative.

I must say a word about them; for, without seeking to, I became involved with them all. But I shall limit my recall to the ones in which I played an especially prominent part – and whose analysis and recommendations have a continuing relevance for our times. In an earlier Chapter, in the context of the world's economic challenges I have dealt with the work of the Brandt Commission and my particular role in it. In this Chapter and the next I will address my engagement with the Brundtland Commission on Environment and Development and the Carlsson-Ramphal Commission on Global Governance, and the global issues whose resolution they tried to advance.

The *World Commission on Environment and Development* was set up under a UN General Assembly Resolution in 1983 *"to propose long-term environmental strategies for achieving sustainable development by the year 2000 and beyond"* and related purposes. 'A global agenda for change' was what the Commission was asked to formulate. The Prime Minister of Norway, Mrs Gro Harlem Brundtland, was its Chairman, and in 1984 she insisted on my being a member. I say 'insisted', because having been a member of both the Brandt and Palme International Commissions on 'development' and 'disarmament' respectively, I was reluctant to commit to a third. But Mrs Brundtland had been a member with me of the Palme Commission, and was most insistent. She seemed to think that I was a reliable interlocutor for the developing world within global realities. We had become close friends through the life of the Palme Commission; I respected her character and her competences; but I still declined. Eventually, she sent her official aircraft from Oslo to bring me to Geneva for the Inaugural Meeting of the Commission on 1 October 1984. 'Gro' was hard to deny.

Besides, she had assembled an impressive list of Commissioners with some of whom I had worked before, like her Vice-Chairman Mansour Khalid of Sudan, Susannah Agnelli of Italy, Bernard Chidzero of Zimbabwe, Saburo Okita of Japan, Mohammed Sahnoun of Algeria, Emil Salim of Indonesia, Janez Stanovnik of Yugoslavia and Maurice Strong of Canada. The Secretary-General was the respected environment professional Jim MacNeill. Over a period of two years, with Commission meetings, site visits and public hearings worldwide, and highly expert Advisory Panels on Energy, Industry and Food Security the Commission produced, in 1987, its widely acclaimed report *Our Common Future.*

Brundtland Commission in Oslo

For my own part, I was greatly helped in my contributions to the Commission by the Commonwealth Secretariat's Economic Division under Dr Bisnhodat Persaud and the specialised assistance of Dr Vincent Cable (now, as I write in January 2014 Minister for Business in the Conservative-Liberal Democrat coalition government in Britain) who worked particularly closely with the Commission's Geneva Secretariat. Together, our contribution was substantial. We earned a good name for the Commonwealth in this global milestone effort.

The Commission's most memorable contribution was its refinement of the concept of 'sustainable development' on the one hand, and on the other, its functional elaboration of it in the context of the opening words of its first chapter: *"The Earth is one; but the world is not"*. The refinement was in the now famous words: *"Sustainable development is development that meets the needs of the present without compromising the ability of future generations to meet their own needs"*. For me this always was the essential ethic of human survival. I shall return to it, for its infusion was, perhaps, my most important contribution.

In 1992, the United Nations Conference on Environment and Development was held in Rio de Janeiro. The Brundtland Report – *Our Common Future* – had laid the groundwork for the Conference – the *Earth Summit.* Its insistent call for sustainable development had galvanised world opinion and led five years later to Rio. That 1992 Conference is the nearest gathering I have witnessed of the world's people – 172 countries participated, 108 at the level of Heads of State or Government, and some 2,400 representatives of non-governmental organisations attended. Seventeen thousand people were involved in the parallel Global Forum. Something was stirring in the world.

The message of *Our Common Future* was confirmed for me with poignancy in the year we submitted our Report. In October 1987 in Vancouver, at a Commonwealth Heads of Government meeting, as Commonwealth leaders were debating world political and economic issues which were high on the current global agenda – including the end of *apartheid* – they were startled by a voice from the Indian Ocean raising new alarms. What President Maumoon Abdul Gayoom of the Maldives said was this:

> *There was growing scientific evidence that the seas of the world were rising and that they would continue to rise, probably by about one and a half to six feet in the next 100 years. What would be the global effect of such a rise in sea level? A two metre, or six feet, rise would, in the United States, inundate major portions of Louisiana and Florida, as well as beach resorts along the coasts. In the Netherlands, it would reduce by 10 per cent the safety of the vast coastal infrastructure presently protecting the country. In Egypt, it would erode up to 20 per cent of the nation's arable land unsettling up to 21 percent of the country's population or over 10 million people. In Bangladesh, such a rise would swamp up to 27 per cent of the total land area, displacing up to 25 million people. For Maldives, it was not necessary even to imagine a six feet rise because that would be quite sufficient to submerge the entire country. It would be the death of a nation.*

There was a thoughtful quiet before the Chairman called the next speaker. No great debate followed; but the concern this voice from the Maldives had generated found expression in the Communiqué:

> *Heads of Government specifically asked the Secretary-General to convene a group of experts to examine the implications for Commonwealth countries of rises in the sea-level and other natural disasters resulting from possible climatic change.*

The 'death of a nation' from climate change – the extinction of a multitude of barely habitable islands 400 miles south -west of India, but with a history of settlement going back to the 5th Century BC – was too much to ignore.

It was not ignored; the Group of Experts for which Commonwealth leaders called was duly assembled under the Chairmanship of Dr (later, Sir) Martin Holdgate the eminent Director-General of the International Union for the Conservation of Nature (IUCN) in Switzerland. The nine other members were all respected professionals whose collective Report: *Climate Change: Meeting the Challenge* commanded attention and respect throughout the environmental community leading eventually to Commonwealth inter-action with the Intergovernmental Panel on Climate Change (IPCC) that was later, in 2007 (jointly with former US Vice President Al Gore), to win the Nobel Peace Prize *"for their efforts to build up and disseminate greater knowledge about man made climate change, and to lay the foundations for the measures that are needed to counteract such change"*. The Commonwealth Report had produced a scientific consensus on predicted global warming and sea-level rise that was to be of service to the wider international community. The small voice from the Indian Ocean had not been alarmist.

In 1992, came the *Earth Summit* in Rio. It was in many respects the successor to the first *UN Conference on the Human Environment* held at Stockholm in 1972. Barbara Ward and Rene Dubois had jointly written the 'official' book for that Conference: *'Only One Earth'*. It was the first book I had read on 'the environment'; and it captivated me. Barbara Ward (Baroness Jackson), who among her many other pursuits was writing for *The Economist* became one of my 'most admired' persons – so much so that when I published my first book in 1979, *One World To Share,* I asked if she would do me the honour of writing the Introduction. She read the manuscript, and agreed. I can never forget the final paragraph of her Introduction:

> *And if we shrug and say, 'What can one man do?' Mr Ramphal has a single startling historical anecdote. The Leeward Islands in his own Caribbean in the eighteenth century attempted and failed to achieve a system of federal jurisdiction. But among those who tried to learn from the experiment was one American born in the Caribbean who later took his knowledge and his thought to the North American colonies. His name was Alexander Hamilton. His 'Federalist' papers inspired and moulded the constitution of the largest free federalism created by man. We must never under-estimate the influence of the eloquent, reflective and disinterested mind. We should not under-estimate Mr Ramphal.*

I remained in touch with Barbara Ward. She was one of the few 'world citizens' we invited to have a special conversation with the Brandt Commission.

Barbara Ward died not long after. At the Memorial Service for her in Westminster Cathedral in London I said in my eulogy:

> *Visionary but always practical, passionate but never strident, Barbara Ward wove together some of the noblest strands of human ideas and ideals into the tapestry of a planetary credo. She would have shunned the label of philosopher/teacher; but that she was ... her work is a continuing heritage. It will live in her teaching, in the vision of only one earth that she gave to us, and in her message that we must learn to care, and to share, our planet better than we now do.*

Ten years later, in early 1991, Maurice Strong had lunch with me at *The Athenaeum* in London. I was no longer Secretary-General of the Commonwealth; and he was now Secretary-General of the *Earth Summit*, leading with great dynamism a global preparatory process for the World Conference on Environment and Development at Rio in 1992. As I said earlier Maurice and I had worked together on the Brundtland Commission. He had previously served as Executive Director of the United Nations Environment Programme and Secretary-General of the United Nations Conference on the Human Environment. We talked about his monumental preparations for the 1992 *Earth Summit*; and then he said: *"but there is one piece, Sonny, that is not in place. Barbara Ward and Rene Dubois had written 'Only One Earth' as the official book of the Stockholm Meeting 20 years ago – the intellectual underpinning of the global effort. I want you to do the same for Rio.* And he continued: *I want a presentation of the issues on the agenda of the Earth Summit that would be both a personal statement out of your varied experience and a worldview that took account of the perceptions of developing countries.* I knew Maurice well; I knew this was serious; I was absolutely stunned. My first reaction was that I was not equal to the task; to follow in the footsteps of Barbara Ward and Rene Dubois was altogether beyond my capacity. I pleaded as much to Maurice Strong; but he would not have it. "Of course, you can do it", he said, "and, in fact, only you". It was flattering, but was it true? In the end, like Gro Brundtland, Maurice Strong was hard to deny.

It was a new time for me; after 15 years of institutional support, I was on my own. There would be technical help, of course; so with *Only One Earth* before me as a beacon, I set to trying to provide a worthy sequel for Rio. I called it in the end: *Our Country, the Planet* and it was formally launched at the United Nations in March 1992, before the *Earth Summit*. It was eventually published in several languages. It is not for me to say whether *Our Country, the Planet* fulfilled the high expectations of that lunchtime in London with Maurice Strong. I hope it did. But on the back cover of the book are two comments that I specially value. The first is by Elliott Richardson, former US Attorney-General and Chairman of the UN Association of the United States:

> *This book is impressive in its sweep, its depth, and the universal embrace of its compassion. It was written, moreover, with real eloquence. The reader who is not stirred to seek action must be one of those whom not even Mark Antony could have moved.*

The other comment is by Gro Harlem Brundtland:

> *Sir Shridath Ramphal's book sums it all up. Unless industrialised and developing countries join forces in a new more equitable international co-operation to save our endangered planet, we will all be in grave peril.*

On the front cover of the book is the painting by the celebrated artist Robert Rauschenberg *"Last Turn – Your Turn"* donated as the official painting of the *Earth Summit* and, uniquely, as the cover of *Our Country, the Planet.* Incorporated in the work is part of the world-wide pledge adopted by the *Earth Summit:*

> *I pledge to make the Earth a secure and hospitable home for present and future generations.*

A few years after the Earth Summit, I found myself in Patagonia, in Southern Argentina, after a meeting in Buenos Aires. Wandering in that strange and desolate land, I came upon a craft shop and small bookstore in which to my amazement was a copy of *Nuestro Hogar el Planeta* – the Spanish translation in their collection Biblioteca de Ecologia. I had not seen it before. I bought a copy and inscribed it: *'In Patagonia'.*

Our Country, the Planet had a sub-title*: Forging a Partnership for Survival* and it is to that matter of 'survival' that I turn – to the ethical compulsions that must drive humanity if survival is to be secured. The ethics of survival, which lay at the heart of *Our Common Future,* are as compelling now as they were in 1987 and at Rio in 1992. But they were to be as prominently absent at Rio's successor Summits: Rio + 10 (in Johannesburg) in 2002 and Rio + 20 (in Rio) in 2012 as they were at Rio itself in 1992 – though Rio+20 does offer some hope of "building a bridge to sustainable development".

Why was that so? It is surely beyond debate, as *Our Common Future* argued, that the human species has been unwittingly, unevenly, and with quickening intensity unravelling the fabric of Earth's surface, its biosphere, and its enveloping atmosphere. In the process we have not only imperilled existence everywhere but committed generations to come to an increasingly problematic and uncertain future. Our generation (and at 85 I am speaking of the generation into which I have encroached), as custodians of the present and trustees of the future, must take responsibility for these acts and their impact on the planet. Aware of the magnitude of our wrongdoing and its consequences, we surely must change the ways we encounter nature.

"Not till we are lost, in other words not till we have lost the world, do we begin to find ourselves and realise where we are and the infinite extent of our relations", wrote the great naturalist of the 19th century, Henry David Thoreau. Some factors are unchanging. We have only one Earth. Our science may increase its bounty and our husbandry make its resources go further, but its capacity to support life cannot be indefinitely extended. On the eve of India's independence Mahatma Gandhi was asked if, after independence, India would attain British

standards of living. His reply was prescient: *"It took Britain half the resources of this planet to achieve its prosperity. How many planets will a country like India require?"* If life on Earth is to be sustained, as I recalled in Barbara Ward's Memorial, we shall have to care for the planet, and share it, better than we have done. That is the essence of an enlightened response. But it will not come merely by our wishing it. We are as we are; and it is being as we are that has brought us to this pass.

* * *

Enlightenment precedes change. That should give us hope, since it is our cerebral gift most of all that sets us apart from other species. The same capacities that have borne the human race to great peaks of achievement have allowed it to adapt in the face of threats. Change must be driven by reason, but it has to be guided by ethics as well. There is an ethical dimension to our predicament; there must be an ethical dimension to our response to it. Unless there is, the response will not be worthy of our highest potential as a species. We will not be true to ourselves, and we will be false to the generations that follow us.

> *The desire for an ethical dimension to human conduct is of course not new; nor is it the preserve of minds not tuned to political realities. Over the centuries scores of great men have laid down a mosaic of ethical concepts treating with almost every aspect of human life. Yet, strangely enough ... millions of persons the world over appear to be groping for new ethical guidelines as if they had never before been traced, or as if the old ones were no longer relevant ... Men everywhere are now living under a new shadow of fear ... It is no wonder that this is the anxious age and that we want an ethic for survival.*

Those were the words of another American, born a few generations later than Thoreau, the great statesman of the post-war period, Adlai Stevenson. He spoke them at the inauguration of a foundation in his name in New York in May 1961, when he was US ambassador to the UN. The fear of which he was speaking was the great fear of his time – *"the horrendous and universal implications of nuclear holocaust"*. Today, the new shadow of fear is cast far less by the possibility of a nuclear holocaust than by the prospect of environmental disaster; but the shadow is as menacing in the 21st century as it was in the 20th. How much has changed, how much remains the same! For many, the age is just as anxious, the need for an ethic for survival just as desperate.

As Adlai Stevenson acknowledged, the search for ethical guidelines for human endeavour is age-old. But it is my premise that never before in human history has the need for these guidelines been as great as it is now. The all-encompassing nature of the danger that faces us is beginning to be widely acknowledged; and in a strange reversal of the human predicament, the threat comes not from hostile forces of nature ranged against the human race, but from the power human genius has vouchsafed us over nature itself. The threat to human survival comes now from ourselves. When we speak of survival today, we no longer mean – as in past ages – survival of family, of tribe, of race, of culture, or even of civilisation. We mean, comprehensively, saving the human race from itself.

The ethical dimension of this predicament is inescapable. It was given poignant expression on 21 February 1990 in Washington by Vaclav Havel, just released from imprisonment for upholding freedom in then communist Czechoslovakia, in a moving address to the US Congress. Among the many important things he said was the following:

> *Without a global revolution in the sphere of human consciousness, nothing will change for the better in our being as humans, and the catastrophe toward which our world is headed ... will be unavoidable ... We are still incapable of understanding that the only genuine backbone of all our actions – if they are to be moral – is responsibility: responsibility to something higher than my family, my country, my firm, my success, responsibility to the order of being where all our actions are indelibly recorded and where, and only where, they will be properly judged.*

As we think of our responsibility to the planet, including our responsibility to ourselves, we must admit that it is only such a revolution in human consciousness that will provide the ethical impetus for change, and only change that will set right our relationship with nature and secure our common future.

There are many sources of resistance to a revolution through which we would acknowledge responsibility to something higher than ourselves or our country. At each stage in our evolution, the impulse to mark out and possess turf has been as irresistible to us as to several other species. It was perhaps inevitable, therefore, that we evolved into a world of states separated by frontiers, and perhaps equally inevitable that the virtuous attributes we developed in the process of our evolution, like loyalty and solidarity, came to be expressed mainly in relation to our separate national communities. The great Cuban nationalist of the nineteenth century, Jose Marti, proclaimed *"para nosotros la patria es America Latina"* ("our country is Latin America"), and many Europeans today have a vision of a single European home; but regionalism of that kind is about as far as our allegiance reaches.

In responding to the crisis of the environment, nothing would be more calamitous than for us to be influenced by considerations of otherness – the very opposite of the values necessary to create a global alliance for sustainable living. Without those values, without a sense of human identity transcending national loyalties, without an acknowledgment of others on the planet as fellow countrymen and women, without a conception of the world as one human community, we are unlikely to summon up the will to act together to save ourselves. Without the ethics of survival to guide us, we are likely, when faced with disaster too close to be ignored, to try to save ourselves and leave others to their fate. In so doing, we would be overlooking the fact that their fate is ours too. We are bound together by a common destiny. We would be missing the crucial truth that we cannot save ourselves alone. An ethic of solidarity – moral underpinnings for joint action to save our endangered human family – cannot develop or subsist within a culture that allows otherness its head.

Yet, *Our Common Future* recognised that there are limits to our philosophy. As we reach toward new concepts of belonging we must temper our vision with realism, lest our reach too far exceeds our grasp. Bankers and businessmen may have reached the limits of geography in daily transactions that skirt the world, but the nation-state continues as the essential unit for the organisation of human society and the conduct of its affairs and seems destined long to remain so. Recognising the planet as our country does not call for an end to nation-states; it is not premised on the replacement of national by global government; it does not mean we have to abandon human variety any more than national identity means smothering cultural heritages. That is why *Only One Earth* spoke of each of us having two countries, "our own and Planet Earth."

In recent times science has undermined dogma and revelation, which had been the traditional trappings of active minds seeking answers to inexplicable mysteries. Science now provides for many the basis for a sort of faith, the humanism Rene Dubois exemplified that could perhaps meet the need for an articulated code of ethical conduct. But our scientists and philosophers and humanists have not yet succeeded in explaining ethical humanism in a way that reaches any significant number of people. When someone does finally emerge to provide us with a rationale for universal ethical conduct, it must, as Albert Schweitzer insisted, go beyond the realm of conduct between humans and deal with human conduct toward nature.

The image of the noble savage was never a wholly valid one. Early humans were as ignoble in some respects as we are; we are as savage in some respects as they were. Yet the world's indigenous peoples have much to teach us, particularly in their evolved respect for nature, their caring for Earth, and their intuitive understanding of the value of sustainable living. From such respect, caring, and understanding have come knowledge, skills, and virtues that in our arrogance we either ignore or disparage. We would do well to be more humble and learn from our fellow humans who have lived in greater harmony with nature.

Problems and possibilities in the changing global neighbourhood were among the themes of another Commission on which I served in the 1980s – The Commission on Humanitarian Issues, chaired by Crown Prince Hassan of Jordan and Sadruddin Aga Khan, was one of five international commissions in the 1980s. Each was an effort to find a new worldwide vision and a new way in an area crucial to human survival. Each functioned as a kind of international think tank, independently of governments and burdened neither by orthodoxy nor by short-term national interests. As a member of them all, I know that, together, they brought home the reality that we are all one people facing common crises, needing common security, sharing a common future.

What the overall experience of the Commissions' search for responses to pressing world problems confirmed for me is the interconnectedness of those problems. Development, security, environment, humanitarian issues – these cannot be treated effectively in isolation. Our response to them must be unified by ethics. Ethics alone can provide the essential foundation on which to build responsive programmes and structures. Without ethics we build in vain: or we do not build at all. The work of all the Commissions recognised the importance of that foundation.

Future generations must be at the forefront of our attention as we consider the challenge to human survival. The concept of sustainable development crystallises our obligations when it speaks of meeting the needs of the present without compromising the ability of future generations to meet their own needs. In a very real sense, we do borrow the present from the future. Perhaps earlier civilisations understood this concept better. When the leaders of the Iroquois nation in North America met in their Council to take important decisions, they began with this commitment: *"In our every deliberation we must consider the impact of our decisions on the next seven generations"*. In the second decade of the third millennium, is there a national Cabinet, anywhere in the world, that is guided essentially by the impact of its decisions on even the next generation?

In the book *Sustaining Earth,* to which both Professor Ghillean Prance and I contributed, he recounts a personal experience involving the "bush Negroes" of Suriname – my Guyana neighbours. They are the descendants of escaped African slaves who resumed tribal life in the forests of Suriname and have maintained many of their ancient traditions. During an expedition a scientist asked one of these Surinamers to cut down a large tree for botanical specimens. He demurred, and eventually did so only after chanting a prayer that made it plain that he was not cutting the tree willingly and that the white man who had ordered it should take the blame for its destruction. Professor Prance commented in *Sustaining Earth: "The trees of the forest have a spiritual value to the people and are not their own property to destroy. This attitude leads to better protection and a more prudent use of resources than in our society."* Those were values from African culture, not so different from the Amerindian values that assert that the sky is held up by the trees and that man and nature will perish if this roof of the world disappears. Chico Mendes, the Brazilian rubber tapper who was murdered for his militancy in protecting Amazonia's "trees of life," was a part of both these cultures. With the perspective of belonging, I know we need to live in harmony with the forests of Amazonia as we draw on their great resources in a sustainable way.

In 1990, an internationally prominent Guyanese writer, Wilson Harris, born in my home town of New Amsterdam, in what was then British Guiana, wrote a mystical novel entitled *The Four Banks of the River of Space.* In it he envisions himself in a dream world revisiting the rain forest of Amazonian Guyana in the 1950s:

> *I came upon a Macusi woodman with an axe on his shoulder. He was – in the circumstances of my invisibility – unable to see me but I possessed the outrageous liberty of scanning his features and inspecting him from top to toe. There was a faint sweat in his eyes like a spider's web or the distilled breath of the river upon glass. He was sturdy as rock. His employment was to fell several acres of rainforest timber. A mere drop these were on my canvas of space that invoked the mid-20th century into which I had come. But one wondered how it would spread in the future. The rainforests were the lungs of the globe. Trees needed to be felled, yes, but the breath of the rivers and the*

forests was a vital ingredient in space. It was an issue of living contrasts interwoven by the soul of the dance through every monstrous desert that lay hidden in the coarse soil of place – deserts that had not yet happened in South America but which we could inflict on ourselves if we were not watchful and capable of attending to the voices of the dead in our midst.

Those monstrous deserts lie in wait for us if the forests of Amazonia are not given the security of sustainable development. In the sustainable development of the rain forest lies its health and the vitality of the people in it and around it – health and vitality that in turn will guarantee sustainability for the world. That will call for much imagination; for new concepts of paying for preserving the planet's life. An imaginative and enlightened programme between Norway and Guyana – *the Low Carbon Development Strategy* – which aims to use Guyana's Amazonian forest conservation to mitigate international climate change, is pointing the way forward.

* * *

When the Report of the Commission on Environment and Development was launched on 27 April 1987, Mrs Brundtland did not hand it over to the UN Secretary-General – as she might have, since it was mandated by a UN resolution – or to world leaders. She had a public ceremony in London where she handed the first copies of *Our Common Future* to a sample of young people from around the world. One of those invited to receive it from Mrs Brundtland was Jenny Damayanti of Indonesia. She made this plea in receiving it:

Please, Presidents, Prime Ministers and Generals, listen to the poor, to the voice of the hungry people who are forced to destroy the environment. Listen to the silent death of dying forests, lakes, rivers, and the seas, the dying soil of the earth, poisoned and trampled by human greed, poverty and inequality. We, the young, hear them loud and clear!

I was there; I recall how her statement moved me. And the symbolism of entrusting *Our Common Future* to the future generation was powerful. But Gro Brundtland wanted more than symbols. She wanted to develop from the next generation leaders who would be worthy of the challenges ahead. Out of that desire and determination arose LEAD International – the Leadership in Environment and Development Programme – and my involvement in it.

* * *

At an early stage after the launch of *Our Common Future in 1987,* Gro Brundtland engaged the Rockefeller Foundation in a discussion of this need: the *Earth Summit* would come and go; but where was the generation of leaders to carry forward its ethos and ensure that the world fulfilled its ambitions for our common future? The Rockefeller Foundation is one of the oldest and largest charitable organisations in the world – and among the most globally enlightened. Out of those early discussions came an identified need to develop and support a new generation of leaders who, equipped with a fresh combination of perspectives and skills, would be linked through their experience and careers in a global network focussed on environmentally sound development. As the world was preparing for the 1992 *Earth Summit* in Rio, LEAD was born.

In 1993, with the Earth Summit behind me, I was invited by Peter Goldmark, the President of the Rockefeller Foundation, to become Chairman of the International Steering Committee that would guide the LEAD Programme. The Director of the Environment Division of the Foundation was Al Binger, an able, young Jamaican scientist who headed the Programme with great flair. From the beginning, LEAD had been recruiting talented individuals from key sectors and professions all over the world to be part of a growing network of young leaders committed to changing the world. These young leaders would become graduates of LEAD's Fellows Training Programme – an intensive and demanding programme designed to enhance leadership ability, strengthen sustainable development knowledge and foster relationships that would continue to support Fellows in their work.

The LEAD Programme's First International Session was held in Chiang Mai, Thailand. In my closing words to the participants I tried to place the work of LEAD in the context of our human effort to respond to the challenge of sustainable development. My final words were these:

> *In his 'Historia de la Eternidad', the Latin American writer Jorge Luis Borges captured succinctly the need for an ethic of human survival when he wrote:*
>
> > *"The Universe requires an eternity... Thus they say that the conservation of this world is a perpetual creation and that the verbs 'conserve' and 'create' so much at odds here, are synonymous in Heaven".*
>
> *To make them synonymous on Earth as well is the central challenge of sustainable development – and the central challenge for homo sapiens.*

CHAPTER 28

Global Governance

I was not quite seventeen when the United Nations Charter was signed in 1945 at San Francisco in my name and those of every other human being with whom I shared the planet. "We, the peoples" it began. Over the years that immediately followed a sense of ownership did not develop but as the years went by and my sense of internationalism enlarged, I endowed the Charter with superior virtue and authority; yet not for all time and in all respects. In 1995, on the 50th Anniversary of the signing, I was in San Francisco, both to pay homage to the Charter and to urge the need for change with the changes of 50 years.

The first years of the decade of the 1990s were heady days of change. The Berlin Wall had fallen in 1989; 'glasnost' and 'perestroika' had signalled transformation of the USSR – that was eventually to turn to cataclysm in the break-up of the Soviet Union and the revival of old nationalisms often leading to new conflicts. The 'Cold War' was over. In its wake came a new fervour for democracy and market oriented economic policies. Released from the tensions of East-West conflict there was talk of 'a peace dividend' – a new increment of resources for development and collective security. It seemed a time of opportunity for international co-operation; and I shared with caring internationalists world-wide the sense that it was a moment of possibility – a moment that might not come again soon.

During the end years of the 1980s another Commission had been formed: the South Commission – Chaired by the former President of Tanzania, Julius Nyerere. It dealt with the situation of developing nations and in particular with the possibilities and needs of strengthening South-South co-operation. It presented its report, *The Challenge to the South,* in 1990. I had been a member of the Commission along with such 'third world leaders' as Abdlatif Al-Hamad (Kuwait), Gamaini Corea (Sri Lanka), Celso Furtado (Brazil), Enrique Iglesias (Uruguay), Michael Manley (Jamaica), Carlos Andres Perez (Venezuela), Qian Jaidong (China), Marie-Angelique-Savane (Senegal), Abdus Salam (Pakistan), Nitisastro Widjojo (Indonesia) and others. The Secretary-General of the Commission was Manmohan Singh, later to be India's widely respected Prime Minister.

While recognising the importance of an international environment conducive to development, and calling for efforts to revive the North-South dialogue, *Challenge to the South* stressed the responsibility of developing countries to ensure a better future for themselves. It devoted much attention to economic and political reform in developing countries, and the importance of improving domestic economic management. It advocated a people-oriented strategy and came out strongly for strengthening democracy and for curbing authoritarianism, corruption and militarisation. The last paragraph of the South Commission's report expressed this clearly:

> *In the final analysis, the South's plea for justice, equity, and democracy in the global society cannot be dissociated from its pursuit of these goals within its own societies. Commitment to democratic values, respect for fundamental rights – particularly the right to dissent – fair treatment for minorities, concern for the poor and underprivileged, probity in public life, willingness to settle disputes without recourse to war – all these cannot but influence world opinion and increase the South's chances of securing a new world order.*

The Report's prescriptions are as valid now as they were then.

Nyerere's Commission joined Brandt, Palme, Brundtland as the primary global Commissions of the 1980s. There was one basic common denominator in the thinking of all four: that no nation can resolve its own problems without relying on others. The Commissions spelled out human interdependence. They emphasised that people must work together to be able to live in one world, to reach a common security, to have a common future. Some of the world's best-regarded minds were agreed on these global fundamentals. From East and West, from North and South; *'how can humanity move forward?'* was their common quest.

Moved by this same question in early 1990, after the momentous changes of 1989, Willy Brandt used his unique convening power to assemble members of his own Commission, together with several representatives of the other Commissions. I was among them. We met at Königswinter, outside Bonn in a Germany soon to be re-unified following the fall of the Berlin Wall in 1989. We reviewed the 1980s and outlined new prospects for the 1990s. There was solid agreement that the major challenges of the 1990s could be mastered only by coordinated multilateral action.

As a result of the Königswinter meeting, Prime Minister Ingvar Carlsson of Sweden, Minister Jan Pronk of the Netherlands and I were asked to be a Working Group, tasked to make an assessment of the new opportunities, and to suggest major areas for multilateral action. One year after the Königswinter meeting, at the invitation of Prime Minister Carlsson, a unique group of world leaders assembled in Stockholm to carry the Königswinter vision forward. They included world figures like Willy Brandt, Benazir Bhutto, Gro Brundtland, Ingvar Carlsson, Jimmy Carter (by proxy), Vaclav Havel, Edward Heath. Enrique Iglesias, Michael Manley, Thabo Mbeki, Robert McNamara, Julius Nyerere, Jan Pronk, Edward Shevernadze, Maurice Strong and Brian Urquhart. And there were others, including myself. At the end, we signed the Stockholm Initiative. Inspired by the themes of the earlier independent Commissions – and on the basis of a memorandum presented by our Königswinter Working Group – we tried at Stockholm to outline some elements of special relevance for the 1990s and to humanity's future.

In what we called the Stockholm Initiative, we put forward (on 22 April 1991) a number of proposals which we believed required urgent comprehensive action. We were all convinced that the moment was a uniquely propitious one for an initiative to be taken – one that responded with imagination and boldness to the manifest needs of the present and the future. We called the Initiative *Common Responsibility in the 1990s*. There were 28 specific proposals under six heads:

Peace and Security – including 'improved United Nations capabilities for anticipating and preventing conflicts, in particular the establishment of a global emergency system';

Development – including 'the goal to eradicate extreme poverty within the coming 25 years, through a committed effort to achieve sustainable development';

Environment – including 'fees... levied on the emission of pollutants affecting the global environment';

Population – including 'that national and cultural leaders mobilise the political commitment and the technical means for making a breakthrough in limiting population growth';

Democracy and Human Rights – including the strengthening of the United Nations role in monitoring how countries live up to their commitments to conventions and declarations concerning human rights and democracy; recognising that democracy can develop only through popular internal will.

Global Governance – including 'that the United Nations takes on a broadened mandate at the Security Council level, following the wider understanding of security which has developed, and that its composition and use of the veto be reviewed'.

The last two proposals were procedural – and crucial:

- *that a World Summit on Global Governance be called, similar to the meetings in San Francisco and at Bretton Woods in the 1940s; and*
- *as a matter of priority, the establishment of an independent International Commission on Global Governance.*

The idea was to secure dispassionate and enlightened examination of the issues before they reached the stage of inter-governmental dialogue. Once that initial work was done the Commission's report could become the basis for a World Summit on Global Governance. It had all begun with Willy Brandt at Königswinter and he was determined to see it through. After consulting the surviving chairpersons of the other International Commissions besides his own – Gro Brundtland and Julius Nyerere (Olof Palme having fallen to an assassin's bullet in the streets of Stockholm) – he invited Ingvar Carlsson, now Prime Minister of Sweden, and me to be co-chairmen of the new Commission, and to constitute it. For myself, I had none of the doubts that I had harboured before joining the Brundtland Commission. This seemed to be the due culmination of all those earlier efforts – the apotheosis of internationalist striving.

Sweden's Prime Minister Ingvar Carlsson

Boutros Boutros-Ghali, then Foreign Minister of Egypt, had participated in the Stockholm Initiative; but by April 1992 he was the UN's new Secretary-General whom Ingvar Carlsson and I consulted before going forward. He commended the effort and assured us of his support. By September we had constituted the Commission. It included some participants in the Stockholm Initiative but also others, like Oscar Arias (Costa Rica), Kurt Biedenkopf (Germany), Allan Boesak (South Africa), Manuel Comacho Solis (Mexico), Barber Conable (USA), Jacques Delors (France), Frank Judd (UK), Wangari Matthai (Kenya), Olara Otunnu (Uganda), I.G. Patel (India), Celina Peixoto

(Brazil), Adele Simmons (USA), Yuli Vorontsov (Russia). As with previous Commissions, all members served in their personal capacities and not under instruction from any government or organisation.

Ingvar and I believed that we had assembled a Commission of outstanding quality. But there was one member we missed for interesting reasons. We both wanted to have on the Commission Al Gore of the United States. It was June 1992 and I was attending the Earth Summit in Rio as author of *Our Country, the Planet.* We made contact with Al Gore and he agreed that he would meet me in Rio to talk about the Commission. The same was true for Wangari Matthai, the Kenyan environmentalist. As it turned out, I met them together at the Rio Conference Centre – and both were enthused about membership. Al Gore cautioned me, however, that he could not give a final answer for a few weeks because of discussions he was currently engaged in at home. It turned out to be discussions over being Bill Clinton's running mate – which he did become, and later Vice-President. Both he and Wangari went on to be Nobel Peace Prize winners.

The Commission worked tirelessly throughout 1993 and 1994. It was less adversarial, more cerebral, than the others. As a group of internationalists with a common vision of one world, we worked at redesigning global governance for the new time already at hand. The Commission was notable for the breadth of its consultations – with scholars, with international practitioners and with people through civil society organisations world-wide. We had a small but excellent Secretariat under the Swedish diplomat Hans Dahlgren working from the Commission's offices in Geneva.

The Commission on Global Governance (as we called it) published its Report *Our Global Neighbourhood* in January 1995 – at the start of the year that would mark the 50th anniversary of the establishment of the United Nations in 1945. Our beginnings at Königswinter and Stockholm had not been seized of this conjuncture; nor had the Commission until our work began. But the conjuncture could not have been more apposite. In the Introduction to the Report by the Co-Chairmen, we wrote:

The development of global governance is part of the evolution of human efforts to organise life on the planet, and that process will always be going on. Our work is no more than a transit stop on that journey. We do not presume to offer a blueprint for all time. But we are convinced that it is a time for the world to move on from the designs evolved over the centuries and given new form in the establishment of the United Nations nearly fifty years ago. We are in a time that demands freshness and innovation in global governance.

As this Report makes clear, global governance is not global government. No misunderstanding should arise from the similarity of the terms... This is not to say that the goal should be a world without systems or rules. Far from it. A chaotic world would pose equal or even greater danger. The challenge is to strike the balance in such a way that the management of global affairs is responsive to the interests of all people in a sustainable future, that is guided by basic human values, and that it makes global organisation conform to the reality of global diversity...

We conclude by urging the international community to mark the fiftieth anniversary of the United Nations by beginning a determined process of rethinking and reform... this is a time for the international community to be bold, to explore new ideas, to develop new visions, and to demonstrate commitment to values in devising new governance arrangements...

Removed from the sway of empires and a world of victors and vanquished, released from the constraints of the Cold War that so cramped the potential of an evolving global system throughout the post-war era, seized of the risk of unsustainable human impacts on nature, mindful of the global implications of human deprivation – the world has no real option but to rise to the challenge of change in an enlightened and constructive fashion. We call on our neighbours, in all their diversity, to act together to ensure this – and to act now.

Two decades after the Charter of the United Nations was adopted at San Francisco in the name of 'We, the peoples', Jean Paul Sartre had given wise and felicitous expression to our human dilemma when he wrote:

> *And when one day our human kind becomes full grown, it will not define itself as the sum total of the whole world's inhabitants, but as the infinite unity of their mutual needs.*

The question the Commission asked was whether we had become full-grown over the years of the Charter? How much have we matured? Do we still define ourselves as the sum total of the whole world's inhabitants with emphasis on the several parts of that sum? Or are we beginning to see ourselves in terms of the unity of mutual needs with emphasis on our oneness – our inseparable humanity?

* * *

San Francisco 1945 was a watershed in the evolution of a world of separate nation states. In 1995, in the 50 years that had passed since the UN was established, those separate parts remained the central feature of our world order. Certainly, nation states were not about to disappear, or the nation state system to lose its centrality. Yet something had happened on the way to the 21st. century. Several of the elements of the nation-state system had become less creedal, less assertive, less defining, even less hallowed. Sovereignty, self-determination, even non-intervention had yielded some of their innocence. We still spoke of them in the language of orthodoxy, but we knew that global realities had curbed their claims; that they no longer reflected universal truths or represented undiluted norms. We were in transition from a world still of states to one more of people. It was a transition to a new order and, as in all transitions, there was contention between old habits and perceptions and new realities and needs. All that the Commission said about our global neighbourhood was conditioned by this awareness.

Commissions before ours had addressed specific areas of global affairs: 'development', 'security', 'environment', 'the South', even 'humanitarian issues'. All had a bearing on the quality of 'survival' and their recommendations in substantive policy areas still command attention. What the end of the post-war era both allowed and required was work on 'how' we were going to manage human affairs so that in these and other fields of global endeavour we could answer the challenges of the future. Our central task was to suggest how world governance could be developed and improved to enlarge the probabilities of success.

We published our report in January – at the start of the UN's 50th anniversary year – calling it *Our Global Neighbourhood:* a signal we thought, of the kind of world that globalisation and technological change were creating. We saw the title as a fair description of global reality. We were under no illusion that it was a wholly benign neighbourhood or that it was cohesive, integrated or secure. What it reflected was the reality of a human community. But we saw the title also as embodying an aspiration for a neighbourhood evolving in worthier ways – a fulfilment to which global governance had much to contribute.

The Commission was not unique in its perceptions of a new world – one in which our human citizenry simply must live as good neighbours if we are to fulfil our hopes for civilisation. Nor was the global neighbourhood a novel perception. In his first Inaugural Address on 4 March 1933 – another time of uncertainty, in some ways like the 1990s – President Roosevelt counselled his fellow Americans: *'In the field of world policy, I would dedicate this nation to the policy of the good neighbour'* – a vow President Clinton reaffirmed at the impressive Charter Ceremony in San Francisco marking the UN's anniversary. But for no one was it more than imagery.

The framework of global governance in the 1990s was essentially what was put in place around the end of World War II at Dumbarton Oaks, at Bretton Woods and finally at San Francisco. It still is. Though a few changes have been made, and many new institutions created, the basic structure is much the same as that laid down then. The architecture of the institutionalised global system is that of the mid-

1940s; it mirrors the state of the world and of international relations at that time.

Consistent with the world of embattled states that shaped their ends at San Francisco, the UN's founders saw future dangers to peace and security arising essentially from conflict between nation states. It was the scourge of war between countries against which the United Nations would stand guard. Wars between states are not becoming extinct. But, the Commission asked, can it any longer be just the security of states and the integrity of frontiers that concern us, when the higher probability today is that threats to the security of people will arise instead from situations within countries? Liberia, Rwanda, Somalia, Sri Lanka, the former Yugoslavia were all contemporary examples; and there were others in the making. This was the very crux of the transition from a world still of states to a world more of people, and we urged, the central challenge of adjustment the UN system faced.

If global security was to be given the breadth of meaning such realities demand, global governance must take account of these insecurities, certainly those that so grievously afflict people that they compel the concerned attention – not just the meddling – of human society worldwide. The Commission concluded that the time had come to establish arrangements that respond to such threats to the security of people. We suggested that 'a global consensus exists today for a UN response on humanitarian grounds in cases of gross abuse of the security of people'.

But we knew that there were countervailing factors. Article 2.7 of the UN Charter expressly forbids the United Nations from intervening in matters 'essentially within the domestic jurisdiction of any state'. How do we square the Charter with a duty of intervention on humanitarian grounds in these cases of gross human insecurity arising out of the 'domestic affairs' of countries? Is there any way to do so without qualifying Article 2.7 – by amendment, by interpretation, by practice – but qualifying it?

There could be another course, and some did argue for it. That is to leave the Charter intact as a permanent bar to UN intervention in domestic situations, and to rely on responses outside the Charter. A case may exist, it was argued, not for UN intervention but for a general right or duty of humanitarian intervention to be exercised by any state or states in a position to do so. This is the case for what one of our Members called intervention by the 'sheriff's posse' – vigilante action, unilateral intervention, action outside the United Nations altogether. The Commission urged most strongly that this was not the way to go. We must insist that, save only for self-defence, the use of force against countries and people is permissible only under the authority and control of the United Nations acting for our global community. That must be, said the Commission, the basic norm of global security. But the norm was being blurred and its defiance was to continue to the present time.

In this context, the Commission advanced the proposal for a permanent rapid deployment force – a 10,000 strong international Volunteer Force – under the exclusive authority of the Security Council and, like peacekeeping forces, under the day-to-day direction of the Secretary-General. It would not take the place of preventive action, of traditional peacekeeping forces, or of large-scale enforcement action under Chapter VII of the UN Charter. Rather, it would fill a gap by giving the Security Council the ability to back up preventive diplomacy with a measure of immediate and convincing deployment on the ground. It would provide the immediate spearhead and reconnaissance element for a later, much larger, operation, should that prove necessary.

As the UN marked its 50th birthday, a window for ensuring global security through genuinely global effort seemed open; but, maybe, not for long. Would the UN be a central player in international humanitarian intervention, or would it be marginalised? A world in which the UN is marginalised will not be safe for many countries – where 'security' could be made the pretext for intervention by the strong. One in which the UN is central could ultimately be safer even for the strong.

We proposed an amendment to the Charter to allow the UN to intervene in domestic crises on humanitarian grounds in appropriate cases; but to avoid filibusters by Governments while people were slaughtered, we also saw the need for machinery to virtually require the Security Council to consider whether or not it should act. That is why the Commission called for international civil society to be invested with 'a right of petition' – a right to bring to the UN cases where the security of people is or could be grievously endangered. In doing so we were encouraged by the way a similar right provided by the Committee of 24 in the early days of decolonisation allowed petitioners like the Rev Michael Scott and Chief Albert Luthuli to bring Southern African issues to the UN. We proposed a small independent Council for Petitions to entertain such complaints. A decision of the Council that a petition is a valid one would effectively place the issue before the Security Council which would then decide whether or not it should intervene under Chapter VI or even Chapter VII which allow intervention in certain circumstances. A reference by the Council for Petitions would be no guarantee of Security Council action, but we believed that even the possibility of it would have a deterrent effect and enhance the security of people.

These very different approaches to global security were the new wine of internationalism. It would not do to pour it into the old wineskins of an unreformed Security Council. The Commission attached critical importance to the reform of the Security Council. We proposed a two-stage reform process designed ultimately to do away with the veto, to replace permanent membership with a new class of standing members who would serve for several years but not be permanent, and to enlarge the Council in respect of both long and short-term (or rotating) members to make it more representative of UN membership without making it unwieldy. We also called for the Council's composition to be subject to regular review. It should not be left to a small body of privileged permanent members to decide whether or when a review should take place.

We were not for curbing the Council or braking its new activism; in fact, we were strongly in favour of strengthening the UN's peace-keeping and peace-making role and of enabling the UN to respond more promptly in emergency situations through the UN Volunteer Force. Such enlarged powers made it all the more necessary that the Council's representativeness should be genuine.

This was how the Commission developed its ideas and proposals on global security to reflect the transition from a world of states to a world of people, from the conventional security of countries to the security of people worldwide. And the security of people is jeopardised on many fronts. The insecurities that afflict the hungry, the homeless, the destitute, the unemployed, those who are ill without healthcare, those who are cold without heating, those who are old without social support, are real. For them security is a meal, a roof, a job, medicines, warmth and relief from poverty in general. Their insecurities may be more chronic than the physical insecurities of war or repression. But they are as pressing.

For the most part, the Commission acknowledged, the world avoids thinking of these calamities; it can no longer. We used to think of them as occurring in faraway places; but no place on the planet is any longer distant. Their crises are not theirs alone. The global neighbourhood is not a mirage. Like all other neighbourhoods, it has to be good for all its people if in the longer term it is to be good for any. Nor is this a wholly new understanding of security; it reflects, after all, the kinship between 'freedom from fear' and 'freedom from want' that the Atlantic Charter, and later the San Francisco Conference itself, underlined.

The time had come, the Commission believed, to establish an Economic Security Council as an apex global economic body within the UN system but reaching beyond governments in its functioning. The world needed a global forum that could provide leadership in economic and social fields. It should be more representative than the Group of Seven or the Bretton Woods institutions, and more effective than the present UN system. Such an Economic Security Council would meet at high political level. It would have deliberative functions only; but real influence would derive from the relevance and quality of its work and the significance of its membership.

Finally, we asserted, there can be no global security in any of its dimensions without the ascendancy of the rule of law worldwide. The rule of law has been a critical civilising force in every free society. It is what distinguishes an authoritarian from a democratic society, what secures liberty and justice against oppression, what elevates equality above dominion. Respect for the rule of law is as essential to the global neighbourhood as to the national one.

Global security without law would be a contradiction in terms. But a large shadow had indeed fallen between acknowledgement and performance. When the founders of the United Nations drew up the Charter they genuflected at the altar of the rule of law. They established the International Court of Justice as the cathedral of law in the global system, but no one was obliged to worship there. The rule of law world-wide was an optional extra. States could take it or leave it; each could decide, in effect, if it was going to be above the law of nations. And, several did.

The International Court of Justice was marginalised. The development of international law could have been a major chapter of the post-war era; it was to be a mere footnote. The era was characterised instead by the rule of military power and economic strength exercised often in denial, and sometimes even in defiance, of international legal norms. For the Commission, the global neighbourhood of the future had to be characterised by law not lawlessness; by rules which all must respect; by the reality that all, even the weakest, are equal under the law; that none, even the most powerful, is above the law. It made proposals to that end.

* * *

But reforming the global order was only partly a matter of institutional reform; more fundamentally, it involved learning to live by neighbourhood values – not just changing structures of governance but changing ourselves. The UN is not a thing apart; it is 'us'. It is a complex collectivity, it is true; but in essence it is made and maintained by its members. The UN is 'us' because its systems, its policies, its practices are those that member-states have ordained. Its decisions are decisions taken or declined by its members. Some aspects of management are in the Secretary-General's keeping, and the Report spoke candidly about reform in this area and made several recommendations. But the greatest failings of the UN have not been structural or administrative; they have been collective failings of the member states. The UN is its members. When they denigrate it, they are often weaving alibis for their own derelictions. When they disown it, they repudiate themselves.

This has vital implications for the future of global governance. It means that when governments or people speak of reform of the United Nations, and indeed of improvement in the management of global affairs more generally, they are really addressing a process of change that has to begin in national behaviour – on the banks of the Potomac, for example, not just on the banks of the East River in New York. It is on the threshold of national values that strengthening the UN must begin.

There was a great and noble task, the Commission believed, in strengthening the United Nations – in fulfilling the larger vision that inspired the founders at San Francisco, in preparing the United Nations through renewal and reform for the next 50 years. Our global neighbourhood, we believed, needed the UN as never before; but needed the UN not as it was before, serving the world of its first 50 years, but as it must be thereafter serving the new world of its next 50 years and beyond.

At the Charter Ceremony that marked the 50th anniversary commemoration Maya Angelou recited a moving poem she had specially written for the occasion. It could have been an anthem to *Our Global Neighbourhood.* We could put off, she wrote, for far too long, the time when we come to 'the brave and startling truth' that:

We, this people, on this wayward, floating body
Created on this earth, of this earth
Have the power to fashion for this earth
A climate where every man and every woman
Can live freely without sanctimonious piety,
Without crippling fear.

That was the real challenge to the UN at 50 and it is a challenge that continues to this day; for the world has deferred too long that time of truth – the time 'when we come to it'.

On the day after the Charter Ceremony I spoke in San Francisco to the XXII Congress of the World Federalists Movement on the Commission's recommendations. And the next day I addressed the 35th Assembly of the World Federation of United Nations Associations (WFUNA) to the same effect. Ingvar Carlsson, with special opportunities as Sweden's Prime Minister, shared this function of spreading the message of *Our Global Neighbourhood* – as did other members of the Commission in their several domains.

Clearly, all the proposals coming forward in the UN's anniversary year could not be considered and taken to a conclusion in 1995. Besides the proposals of our Commission, there were those in the Secretary-General's Agenda for Peace and its Supplement and in his Agenda for Development, those in the Volcker/Ogata Report and others from the Ford/Yale Group and from the Carnegie Commission Against Deadly Conflict into which I had been inducted. Much later were to be Secretary-General Kofi Annan's ideas on *'humanitarian intervention', and* the endorsement by 192 world leaders at the 2005 World Summit of the concept of *Responsibility to Protect (R2P)* developed by the International Commission on Intervention and State Sovereignty. It was the culmination of a process to the evolution of which *Our Global Neighbourhood* had made an important contribution.

At a personal level, I feel a special sense of fellowship with my Co-Chairman, Ingvar Carlsson, and the dedicated internationalists who were the Commission's members. One of these was Adele Simmons, at the time President of the MacArthur Foundation of the United States. When our Report was ready, as part of our promotional work, she accompanied me to present a copy to Mrs Hillary Clinton who had been sent an advance copy. Adele knew her well in a Democratic Party context. She explained that she had read enough to recognise that *"you have been doing God's work"*. That was more encouraging than the World Federalists who after close consideration concluded that in eschewing 'world government' we had failed to go far enough; or the 'black helicopter' far eight critics who believed we had gone much too far. I like to think that the 'first lady' was nearer the mark.

PART VIII

ENDINGS

CHAPTER 29

Honours and Intrigue

When I was eighty (in 2008), my former Commonwealth colleagues and friends in London generously marked the moment with publication of a book of essays: *Shridath Ramphal: The Commonwealth and the World.* I was deeply touched by the act of friendship it represented. I was specially indebted to Richard Bourne who edited the book, and to all who contributed to it – and particularly to Patsy Robertson who organised the launch occasion.

In truth, throughout my years of active work, many have been generous to me in their honours and awards: governments, academic institutions, non-governmental bodies. In the book of essays above they are all listed in an annexed *curriculum vitae.* But to omit all reference to them here would be ungenerous to those who by their actions had been supportive of what I tried to do. Each honour was both an acknowledgement of my efforts and a statement of support for them; each an encouragement (where appropriate) to the Commonwealth to hold its course. It was not just a personal matter.

Chronologically, Commonwealth states which bonded me to them in this way were Guyana, Britain, Australia, the Maldives, New Zealand, Nigeria, Zambia, Pakistan, Jamaica, the Caribbean Community, India, Belize and South Africa. The photographs below speak for them all. The first is of the Queen conferring the *Order of Australia* in the State Room of the Royal Yacht *Britannia* in Melbourne Harbour on the occasion of the 1981 Commonwealth Summit. The other is of President Thabo Mbeki in South Africa conferring the *Order of the Supreme Companions of Oliver Tambo (Gold)* in 2007, after Oliver had died – a rather special memento of a great man with whom my life had been entwined.

From the Queen on 'Britannia'; from Thabo Mbeki in Pretoria

But honours take other forms than national insignia, and the most familiar is the conferment of degrees by Universities. During the time I was Secretary-General of the Commonwealth I was specially favoured and I have always acknowledged that the honorary degrees I received in this way are ones I share with the Commonwealth and the Commonwealth Secretariat. They were massive statements of support for the Commonwealth's principled stand on contemporary issues, and on none more so than the anti-apartheid cause – as the public orators on these occasions frequently testified. In all there were honorary degrees from 28 Universities world-wide, and 4 honorary Fellowships – the first of these being from my alma mater, King's College, London, in 1975 – the year of my assumption of office as Commonwealth Secretary-General.

Then there were the unforgettable moments of notable awards like the 2002 Indira Gandhi Prize for Peace, Development and Disarmament. I recall this occasion here particularly, since it seemed like a completion of the circle of destiny that began with my great grandmother's flight from India via the indenture system over a century before. The Indira Gandhi Prize is the Indian 'Nobel peace prize'. It is held in high esteem; and higher still for me in that it commemorates the highest values to which Indira Gandhi's own life was dedicated. It was a grand occasion presided over by the then President of India, Dr Abdul Kalam, in the Ashoka Hall of the Rashtrapati Bhavan in the presence of Sonia Gandhi and beneath the Michael Werboff portrait of Indiraji. The citation of the Prize was as follows:

> *Awarded to Sir Shridath Ramphal in recognition of the great services rendered by him for Peace, Disarmament and Development for the last three decades.*

In her welcome speech as Chairperson of the Indira Gandhi Memorial Trust, Sonia Gandhi, the Italian born widow of Rajiv, referred to the qualities of her mother-in-law, who a BBC global poll two years before had found to be the 'Woman of the Millennium', and continued:

> *Sir Shridath Ramphal mirrors some of these qualities. Indian by blood, Guyanese by birth, West Indian by loyalty and internationalist by conviction, Sonny Ramphal, as he is popularly known, is a world citizen and a man of many parts. He, too, has devoted his life to bridging divides, both within his own Caribbean region as well as beyond it.*
>
> *I do not know which comes first, Caribbean "oratory" or Caribbean "cricket". But Sonny's oratory has captivated many*

all over the world. When he was Foreign Minister of Guyana and later Secretary-General of the Commonwealth, he was referred to not as 'His Excellency' but 'His Eloquence'. His has been a powerful and insistent voice raised in the cause of our common humanity, our planetary interdependence and our common future.

As the only individual who served in each of the successive World Commissions on international poverty, disarmament, environment and global governance, he has helped to shape opinion and choices on these key issues. As Commonwealth Secretary-General, Sonny Ramphal lifted the Commonwealth out of its groove, converting it into a purposeful international player. He put the Commonwealth in the vanguard of the international campaign against racism, articulating and leading the Commonwealth's struggle to end apartheid in South Africa, with a passion and determination rare among the heads of international organisations. For this, he is remembered with gratitude by all South Africa and by us here.

And he has worked tirelessly to bridge the divides, not just between North and South, but within the South itself, calling for greater unity and institutionalised co-operation between developing countries, in order to enhance their negotiating power with the industrialised world. He was a pioneer in doing so.

Today, the values of enlightened internationalism for which Indiraji stood, and which Sonny Ramphal has helped to advance, are under threat. The choice facing the world is a stark one: a choice between global order based on a system of international law binding on all, or global disorder based on the rule of the strong. More than two millennia ago, the Greek historian Thucydides said that "large nations do what they wish, while small nations accept what they must". His words uncannily describe how far into the past the world has regressed. We need more voices like Sonny Ramphal's in arousing world opinion to this unprecedented threat to our common future.

In my acceptance speech, and in response to these compliments, I said what follows – in acknowledgement of my ancestral links which made the ceremony in India's Capital, and in commemoration of Indira Gandhi, so much more special:

> *A hundred and twenty three years ago, in 1880, a brave widow, still in her twenties, escaped from the stigma of widowhood in India at that time and, seeking survival, left the shores of India in desperation with her young son of nine bound for the sugar plantations of British Guiana. They were venturing far across the kala pani – two more offerings to the new system of slavery which went by the name of indenture, with all the wretchedness and dreadful loss of life which it entailed.*
>
> *That widow was my great grandmother. She did not live long in Guiana; but her son, my grandfather did, overcoming the degradations of the system. Her courage and faith were rewarded in the life she gave him and the generations that followed.*
>
> *As I accept the 2002 Indira Gandhi Prize from the hands of the President of India in the grandeur of the Rashtrapati Bhavan, my thoughts go back to that brave woman and linger on her ancestral share in the honour done to me today.*

Accepting the Indira Gandhi Prize

Early the next year, on 9 January 2003, the anniversary of the day Mahatma Gandhi returned to India from South Africa, I was the recipient of a quite different honour from the Government of India – the *Pravasi Bharatiya Samman Award* – inaugurated by the VJP Government under Prime Minister A.B. Vajpayee – specifically to honour members of India's vast diaspora. I was among the 10 first recipients of the Award at the Inaugural Ceremony that year. As I received the handsome insignia from the Prime Minister, I said to him:

> *I accept this, Prime Minister, in humility, in the name of my ancestors who endured the indenture system to emerge into a new time*

It was, indeed, like a closing of the circle that began with my great-grandmother's departure from India on the *Ellora* over a century earlier.

* * *

If glimpses of these moments of honour seem somewhat vaunting, it is a good place to mention what did not happen; what I did not accomplish. I refer to the matter of election to the office of Secretary-General of the United Nations. I was twice a candidate, and twice failed to be elected. As with other positions which touched my life, I did not aspire with great ambition to this highest of international offices; although I was pleased to have been thought, by some at least, to have been worthy of it. On both occasions, my obvious internationalism coupled to my being from the developing world led others to believe that I might be right for the post.

The first person to convey this to me was Sean MacBride, then – in 1971 – having just ceased to be Secretary-General of the International Commission of Jurists (ICJ). As a lawyer, I had long valued the ICJ as a watch-dog of the rule of law world-wide. I got to know Sean MacBride professionally when shortly after becoming Attorney-

General of British Guiana in 1965 I persuaded the Premier (Forbes Burnham) to invite the ICJ to mount a Commission of Inquiry into 'discrimination' in the country. It was the first time a Government had taken such an initiative, and the ICJ was pleased. Over the period of the Inquiry, I came to know Sean well and to hold him in esteem.

Sean's father, an Irish nationalist, had been executed by the British for his part in the 'Easter rising' of 1916. His mother, Maude Gonne, immortalised by Irish Nobel Laureate W.B. Yeats in his love poems, was also a leading revolutionary and one of the founders of Sinn Fein. Sean sustained this revolutionary lineage and was one of the founders of the Irish Republican Army (IRA). Eventually, he became the first Foreign Minister of the independent Ireland and thereafter pursued an internationalist career He was a founder of Amnesty International and Secretary-General of the ICJ from 1963 to 1970. I say all this to explain why his opinions mattered so much to me. Later, in 1974, he was to be the winner of the Nobel Peace Prize.

At the end of 1971 the United Nations needed to elect a new Secretary-General. U Thant, the Burmese diplomat who had succeeded the Secretary General I most admired – Dag Hammarskjold – would be stepping down. Kurt Waldheim, the Austrian diplomat, was an early candidate – from the start of the year. As the year progressed his campaign gained momentum; and it troubled many – Sean MacBride among them. He wrote to me in Georgetown from Geneva urging me to advance my candidature and pledging his readiness to campaign for me. I had not even thought of the position and it was still early days in my international career. But Sean had not written to me alone; he wrote to the same effect to the Prime Minister, Forbes Burnham, with whom he had developed a close acquaintanceship since the days of the ICJ Inquiry in 1965. Burnham was quite separately troubled by the prospect of Waldheim as the UN's Secretary-General believing the then only rumoured allegations of Waldheim's past connections with the German 'SS'. It was, I believe, this factor as much as any other that led him to support MacBride's proposal.

I was flattered, of course, but not enthused; and my 'campaign' was conducted in the corridors of the UN by our Ambassador, Rev

George Talbot and, perhaps even more vigorously, by his able and respected young deputy Dr Anne Jardim, herself a political aspirant within Guyana, in whom I was content to repose the campaigning. There were nine candidates and the Security Council system was to reduce the field by successive rounds of voting; with the veto in the hands of the five 'Permanent Members' – Britain, China, France, the USA and the USSR – a basic tool of elimination. I made it to the second round of voting, then fell out, though without any vetoes. Waldheim went on to win – to Burnham's chagrin. I was left to take comfort in having been considered for this highest of international offices.

Ten years later, Waldheim was seeking a third term; but the situation was different. Russia and the United States were content with him (it was said, because they knew that the rumours of 1971 were true and could be used to bend him to their will), and Britain and France would follow the US. China, however, was adamant that the next Secretary-General should be from 'the Third World'. And the Third World had produced a candidate in Ambassador Salim Ahmed Salim of Tanzania who had once been Ambassador to China and then Permanent Representative to the UN where he had been prominent in the campaign in 1971 for Beijing (the PRC) to occupy the China seat in the UN – which it did.

China made it clear that it would support Salim as the 'third world's' candidate; but the Americans did not disguise their displeasure with Salim – it was said because of his 'dancing in the aisles' when the PRC won the China seat 10 years earlier – to the deep hurt of the US. The international community did not forget that the US Ambassador to the UN in 1971, George H.W. Bush – who bore that humiliation personally – was now, in 1981, President Reagan's Vice-President, with special superintendence from Washington of US/UN affairs. In the result, in 16 rounds of voting, the Americans vetoed Salim 16 times; and China vetoed Waldheim a like number.

At that point, it became clear to both that the vetoes blocking their success were unlikely to be dropped. They each agreed to step aside from the ballot – without withdrawing their candidatures. That changed everything. I had been urged by many on the international scene to make myself available; and for a long time. On 25 July, 1979, for example, Alexander MacLeod, the experienced Diplomatic Correspondent of *The Scotsman,* ended a 'profile' of me in this way:

> *He has been mentioned as a possible successor to Waldheim at the UN, and says: I make it a rule not to want that sort of thing. If you set out to get a post like that, in a sense you demonstrate your lack of fitness for it. The main thing is to serve the international community, and you don't have to be UN Secretary-General to do that.'*
>
> *That is a polished diplomatic answer. Ramphal proffers it with the air of a man who would not be embarrassed if, in the way such things happen, he one day receives a summons from New York to serve a constituency somewhat larger than the quarter of mankind the Commonwealth represents.*

A year later, that is much the way it happened; and my response was positive – but not while Salim was in contention. We were, first of all, close friends. He had been accredited to Guyana while I was in charge of foreign affairs many years earlier. He and his wife Amne had become family friends. But, beyond that, I thought he was a good choice for Secretary-General, and he was the 'third world's' candidate. I declined to allow my name to go forward while he was on the ballot, though it was well known that I could become available if that changed. Again, I did not campaign or seek national or Commonwealth endorsement. I did, however, call on the Ambassadors of each of the Permanent Members whose veto would be fatal were I ever to be on the ballot. I made it clear to each of them that Salim had my personal support and that I hoped they would elect him. My name would not go forward so long as there was a chance of that happening.

When Salim and Waldheim came off the ballot, my name emerged in the reckoning. A good example of support for me was an editorial in the much respected Christian Science Monitor of 10 December 1981 which said, *inter alia*:

Now that both Mr Waldheim and Mr Salim have withdrawn their candidacies (but not their availability), the way is clear for consideration of a number of other aspirants from the third world. It remains problematic that any of the five new candidates in the contest will win approval of the Security Council. But there is no question that someone like Shridath Ramphal of Guyana, secretary general of the Commonwealth nations, would be a superb choice. Certainly one can sympathise with the majority view at the UN that it is time for someone from among the developing nations to head up the Secretariat again. The industrialised 'North' has no corner on capable diplomats and administrators and it is only fair that the office be rotated geographically.

The week before, Anthony Sampson had reviewed the scene in a special Commentary in the London '*Observer*' of 29 May under the headline *'UN cynics favour Sonny the idealist'*. After surveying the probabilities, he concluded:

Last, but not least, is the most obviously qualified candidate of all, the Secretary General of the Commonwealth, Shridath ('Sonny') Ramphal who runs his own miniature UN from Marlborough House. Ramphal is obviously well placed as a bridge between North and South and between East and West...

Ramphal himself, though he became a barrister of Gray's Inn and was knighted by the Queen, could never be regarded as a pawn of the West. He has often infuriated the Foreign Office by supporting Third World causes particularly during the Zimbabwe negotiations when he predicted that Mugabe would win the election. He was the chief spokesman for the Third World on the Brandt Commission and played a key role in negotiating the final report with Ted Heath.

As a candidate for the UN he would have the support of nearly all, if not all, of the 45 members of the Commonwealth: Mrs Thatcher may have her misgivings, but she could hardly be seen to veto a candidate favoured by all the rest of the Commonwealth. The Americans and French could have no serious objections. The Chinese would probably support a candidate with strong black support. The Russians would have no grounds of veto.

Perhaps the most serious worry about Ramphal is that he might be tempted actually to do something with the UN – to run it efficiently, and to bring back some of its old sense of purpose and idealism, as a community of nations.

Olara Otunnu, the Ambassador of Uganda, became President of the Security Council (by rotation) for December 1981. It was his role to manage the election process; but he also had a role as a member of the Council. In that role, he supported me as an alternative 'third world' candidate to Salim whom, like me, he had supported. It was he who proposed my name in the new round of voting. The Security Council, by this time anxious to avoid the protracted voting that characterised the Salim/Waldheim contest, accepted the procedural process proposed by its President of a 'straw' ballot in which the five Permanent members would indicate those candidates they would 'discourage' (i.e. veto) while the other 10 members would indicate which candidates they would 'encourage' (i.e. vote for). In this way, the Council would have some idea of the chance of the real ballot producing a result. In the straw ballot I received one discouragement. Most other candidates received one or more 'discouragements', save for Perez de Cuellar of Peru (described by Anthony Sampson in his Commentary as "a kind of Latin American Waldheim") who received no 'discouragement'. The voting followed the straw ballot, and Perez de Cuellar, was elected with only one round of voting.

Who vetoed my candidature? I am still not certain. My conversations with the Ambassadors of the five Permanent Members offered some clues. The Chinese Ambassador was encouraging, accepting me in the absence of Salim as a viable 'third world' candidate. The British and American Ambassadors were non-committal, but with Jeanne Kirkpatrick decidedly less encouraging than the British Ambassador, Sir Anthony Parsons; a calmer Lord Carrington was still at the Foreign Office but unlikely 'to swim the Atlantic' as he said he would during the heat of the struggle within the Commonwealth for a Zimbabwe under majority rule. The French Ambassador was not negative generally, but left me in no doubt that they placed much importance on the Secretary-General being French speaking – which I was not.

But my most memorable encounter was with the Russian Ambassador, Oleg Troyanovsky. The Ambassador was a suave, experienced diplomat. He made me feel welcome as a candidate and said that he wanted to be frank and open with me: Russia knew and admired me and the work I had done most recently in relation to the independence of Zimbabwe. They also admired Guyana and its positions at the UN. *"However"*, he continued, *"your candidature presents us with a problem; you remind us too much of Hammarskjold, and as you know he was a major problem for Russia; we even at one stage suggested a 'troika' in place of a single Secretary General"*. I said in reply: *"Ambassador, thank you for being so candid with me, I did admire Dag Hammarskjold as a great internationalist and servant of the UN. I can live without being Secretary-General for the reason you have given me"*. He quickly added that he was not saying that they would veto me; but I could not count on their support. I understood that to mean that they would not use the veto against me – unless it became necessary to prevent my election. So the 'discouragement' and the ultimate veto could have been Russian; or it could have been French. It was, on my best information, American; though I harbour doubts to this day. I was, of course, disappointed; but my conversations with the five Ambassadors had prepared me for the result; and the Russian explanation was a compliment I have lived with; for if it was an American veto, the explanation was probably the same. When it was all over the Ambassador of Ireland, Noel Dorr, said to me ruefully that the 'right' Secretary-General had to be elected 'by stealth' – as Hammarskjold had been – his qualities relatively unknown. I was comforted.

CHAPTER 30

Journey's End

I left the service of the Commonwealth in mid-1990; but the cares and commitments with which that service had endowed me never left. My life was transformed, of course, but the continuities were astonishing.

A handful of colleagues came with me from the Secretariat – Charles Gunawardena, Elsa Mansell, Janet Singh and Bernie Lee-Dare – to man the small office I set up in London to undertake immediate tasks. The most urgent of these was my assignment as Chairman of the West Indian Commission whose work I have already described. Later my pursuit of democracy in a global context would continue from that Office with the development and initial Chairmanship of the International Institute for Democracy and Electoral Assistance (IDEA). This pioneering effort had been inspired by Bengt Save-Sodeberg of Sweden and from a humble start has grown into one of the world's leading institutions in the field of 'democracy and electoral assistance'.

I retained my keen interest in environmental matters since the first signal of the issue of 'climate change' at the Commonwealth Summit at Vancouver in 1987, and the much praised Holdgate 'expert group' report *Climate Change: Meeting the Challenge* while still at the Secretariat. Between 1990 and 1994 it was from that new Office that I fulfilled my role as Chairman of the International Union for the Conservation of Nature (IUCN), and of the LEAD Programme which I have already mentioned. IUCN is the world's oldest conservation institution, and the Commonwealth's work on environment issues and my membership of the Brundtland Commission had given me credentials for this high non-governmental office to which I was invited. But perhaps most special of all my undertakings at this time was co-chairing the Commission on Global Governance with the Prime Minister of Sweden, Ingvar Carlsson – as described in the preceding Chapter. My global plate was full.

In between these international roles was my new Caribbean responsibility as Chief Negotiator of the Regional Negotiating Machinery (RNM) that Caribbean Heads had set up to help the Region prepare for the plethora of trade and related negotiations which engulfed them as the new century approached. I undertook this with some reluctance, because of its magnitude; but was persuaded to accept leadership of the RNM once P.J. Patterson, then Prime Minister of Jamaica, assumed Chairmanship of the Prime Ministerial sub-Committee to which I reported, and Sir Alister McIntyre accepted the role of my Deputy.

For four years, from 1997 to 2001, working between the Caribbean and London with some of the best technical talent of the Region, led initially by Dr Bishnodat Persaud (who had earlier headed the Economic Division of the Commonwealth Secretariat) we took regional preparations for international negotiations to a new level. They were years of immense satisfaction, intellectually as well as in terms of team-work, both in the RNM and with Caribbean Heads of Government. Working with P.J. Patterson and Alister McIntyre once again in this intensive manner, dedicated to excellence, was for me a fitting way to end my formal service to the Caribbean – which in one way or another (from Federation to the RNM) had occupied over 50 years of my life.

At that formal end, it was gratifying to hear from the Prime Minister of Belize, Said Musa, speaking as Chairman of CARICOM, these generous sentiments:

> *It is some 9 months since Sir Shridath Ramphal – Sonny Ramphal to all of us – intimated his wish to pass the baton of*

leadership of the RNM to other, younger hands. We asked him to stay on – at least until the WTO Ministerial in Doha. And he did – and to what good effect, for at Doha his was a vital voice, not only for the Caribbean but also for the larger developing world ...

The RNM, under Sir Shridath's leadership, has helped us to learn the lesson that for us there is no other way as we pursue our cause in the harshly globalised, much less caring, much more demanding world of the present.

And it helped us to recognise too the role of rigorous intellectual work in the evolution of regional strategy. In the Cotonou negotiations with Europe, in the FTAA negotiations with the Americas, in the WTO negotiations with the world – that essential intellectual foundation of our policymaking is now an RNM hallmark. It has helped us to find our way through the negotiations maze; and it has won us respect. We are grateful, Sir Shridath.

The following year, 2002, the same Prime Minister invited me to be Belize's facilitator in the Mediation Process for the Belize-Guatemala Border Dispute undertaken by the Organisation of American States. The Guatemala-appointed facilitator was the eminent American lawyer, Paul Reichler, of the firm of Foley Hoag LLP. In the mediation process we worked to bring the mediated dispute to resolution – which we did; only to have Guatemala renege on the agreed process. For me, it was another experience of the David and Goliath syndrome I had encountered in Guyana's dealings with Venezuela – another experience of greed and expansionism trumping justice and integrity across borders separating countries of unequal strength. I developed a close fellow feeling for Belize. Later, Paul Reichler and I would be happily and successfully associated in the international arbitration (to which I have earlier alluded) that settled the Guyana-Suriname maritime boundary in accordance with international law."

* * *

I could not end these remembrances without offering a glimpse of my overlapping years as Chancellor of three very different Universities – the University of the West Indies (UWI), Warwick University and the University of Guyana. Primary education has been a prominent part of the legacy of colonialism; but not tertiary education. It was a British Prime Minister, Benjamin Disraeli, who on 11 March 1871 said in the House of Commons: *"A University should be a place of light, of liberty and of learning"*; not surprisingly, Universities were not part of the colonial project. But, as the winds of change began to blow in the early post-war world of Empire, colonial policy, stoked by regional demand, began to acknowledge tertiary education as an instrument of change.

As I was journeying to London in 1947 to study law, the final plans were being made for the establishment, at Mona in Jamaica, of the University College of the West Indies, affiliated to the University of London and admitting in its first year undergraduates in Medicine only. Atlee's Labour Government in Britain (with Creech Jones as Colonial Secretary) was supportive; and London University integrally so. UCWI was established in 1948 and achieved independent University status in 1962. It served all the English-speaking countries of the West Indies and the few remaining British dependent territories – who were together the 'contributing territories', except Guyana – whose government had opted out of the University, as it had opted out of the Federation of The West Indies – decisions which I had publicly deplored.

In 1963, Guyana established its own 'University'; but despite some distinguished Chancellors, like E.M. Duke, Sir Arthur Lewis and William Demas, by the time of its 25th anniversary in 1988, it fell far short of its goals as a University. Political leadership, however, had changed, and President Desmond Hoyte, less of a political dogmatist than each of his predecessors, was determined to bring it closer to the 'Disraeli' ideal. Besides, he was more of a functional regionalist having been a teacher at the Grenada Boys Secondary School, one of the best in the region, in his early days. In that anniversary year, he invited me to be Chancellor of the University of Guyana. I was extremely diffident.

Hoyte knew all my reservations about UG and shared many himself. He urged me to help him inaugurate change. I agreed to try – for three years. But they were not easy years; a culture of mediocrity had taken tenacious hold, and the resources to enable change were non-existent.

In my first graduation address the next year, I spoke from experience – and plainly:

> *In my installation address (last year) I talked about 'compulsions for excellence'. This University can accept nothing less in terms of its duty to the society which sustains it materially... And it can also accept no less in relation to the young people of Guyana who come here for tertiary education – for University education that equips them to serve Guyana, and to serve in the wider world... If what our young people get is something less; if they leave Turkeyne (the location of the University) less well equipped in knowledge, in skills, in learning, in what I call 'tertiary literacy', then we at the University have cheated them, robbed them of the gift of University education in its full sense; deceived them into believing that they are graduating from a place of learning and can take their place in the world confident of their abilities to perform as graduates and to go further.*

For these reasons I had proposed to the Council a Chancellor's Commission *"to examine the present condition and the future prospects of the University"*. It was an eminent Commission headed by an old friend of the University, Professor (now Sir) Roy Augier of the UWI. At the 1982 Graduation I commended the Report *'To Reshape and Renew'* to the University, the Government and the people of Guyana, and added:

> *So far as the University is concerned we are at 'a defining moment'. We must not opt for the old terms; we are at the cross-roads; we must not take the wrong turning. The Commission's proposals can be a guide to those choices... I think of the*

Commission's over-arching vision of the University of Guyana as part of a single University system serving CARICOM countries at a level of sustained relevance and excellence ... This being the last Graduation Ceremony in my term of office as Chancellor, there is no higher cause that I can urge in valediction.

So ended my three years as Chancellor of the University of Guyana. My legacy, I believe, was to have pointed the way forward 'to reshape and renew'. But by then, there was a new Government; one that looked back to the beginnings of the University – and made looking forward harder. But to have pointed the way was a matter of satisfaction to me.

* * *

In 1950, in a still colonial setting, Princess Alice, Countess of Athlone, became UCWI's first Chancellor, then UWI's in 1962. Three Chancellors later, in a time of robust independence in the West Indies, after Sir Hugh Wooding of Trinidad and Tobago and Sir Allen Lewis of St Lucia, the Vice-Chancellor Sir Alister McIntyre – with whom I had worked closely over so many years and in so many regional endeavours – came to see me in London at the Commonwealth Secretariat. It was in mid-1989. He said he was conveying an invitation to me from the University's Council to be UWI's next Chancellor. I was flattered, but cautious. I was already Chancellor of the University of Guyana. I reminded Sir Alister of this and of my Guyanese origins and asked whether he was sure that the latter in particular would not be an impediment. Alister, in turn, looked surprised; he said the Council's wish was unanimous; *"Of course everyone knows where you were born; but they regard you as a West Indian regionalist; they know that you do so yourself; in fact, for us, you are a role model, and UWI would be honoured to have you as its Chancellor."* I was deeply touched. It was a special moment in my life. I felt honoured; and very happy.

Over a decade earlier, in 1978, when I was Commonwealth Secretary-General, UWI had conferred on me an honorary degree at its St Augustine Campus in Trinidad. In the course of my response, I said this:

> *In that sense of being that derives from within and is assured and unchanging, I have been a West Indian from the first moments of my rational awakening. The land of my birth, my country that I was privileged to help bring to sovereign statehood, commands my devotion and my loyalty; but in a further dimension of belonging, the West Indies is, also, my native land. I trust that I am not, in this regard, a member of a vanishing tribe.*

I was to remain Chancellor of UWI for fourteen years – two terms of seven years each, the maximum allowable by the Statutes of the University. They were wonderful years. For most of them I was in London; but there were pluses. First of all, no University Vice-Chancellor, who really runs the University, wants his Chancellor hovering over him. The Chancellor's best function is to be there when he needs to be, or can be of special use, and, in these times of rapid communication, to be within reach. That will vary from University to University, as it did with me.

Empathy with the Vice-Chancellor is crucial; and I was fortunate to have as my Vice-Chancellors two of the best: Sir Alister McIntyre and Professor Hon. Rex Nettleford. The Vice-Chancellery was on the Mona Campus in Jamaica; but the Vice-Chancellors were widely respected throughout the region making up for the archipelagic nature of the University. But compensating most was the development of Campuses beyond the centre – at St Augustine in Trinidad and Tobago and at Cave Hill in Barbados. Just as I had received my honorary degree at the St Augustine Campus, so I was installed there as Chancellor. And, of course, graduation ceremonies were held on each Campus which meant that I had annual opportunities to be close to the major centres of the region.

I never overlooked the fact of the special meaning of Graduation Ceremonies for West Indian families. It was their occasion at least as much as that of their graduating offspring. For most, it was a time of fulfilment of family ambition and sacrifice, and I took special care to ensure a welcoming environment for them. So, whatever the vicissitudes of weather, the occasion as theirs had to be preserved. And for the graduands, too, I tried to make it a special personal moment. So that it was handshakes and congratulations and eye contact with each. All over the region today, I meet graduates who greet me with happy recollection of that moment.

Graduations everywhere are grand affairs: all academics are robed; the Chancellor, most grandly. My gown at UWI was of a special vintage. It was the original gown of Princess Alice, the first Chancellor. And in those early days it had a train which was carried by an undergraduate. When Sir Hugh Wooding succeeded her in 1971 both the times and the man required that the train had to go; and so it did. But the gown in all its splendour of black and gold remained through my time. It has now been consigned to the UWI Museum in the new Regional Headquarters of the University at Mona – where I have gazed on it with remembrance of the years I wore it.

But my Chancellorship had its quota of substantive work. UWI had routine periodic reviews of its systems; but in the early 90's the Vice-Chancellor, Sir Alister McIntyre felt the need for a full scale review of our structures – streamlining the University for 21st Century – with help from beyond ourselves. Out of my conversations with him and the Council emerged a Chancellor's Commission. Among its members was Michael Shattock, Registrar of Warwick University (my other University), who brought unique experience of the development of a successful new University acclaimed for its relevance to society – one of the mandates of the Chancellor's Commission. What emerged was a major Report on *'A New Structure: The Regional University in the 1990's and Beyond'*. Its recommendations were substantially adopted and implemented. In a related contribution, I headed a Legal Committee which revised the Statutes of the University to reflect the adopted changes.

On 26 September 2003, I presided over my last meeting of the Council of the University in the Senate Building. The Council is composed of representatives of the 'contributing countries', usually Ministers of Education, and members of staff and students. Afterwards, we retired to lunch in the Assembly Hall – my farewell lunch as Chancellor. After generous words of tribute from the Vice-Chancellor, Professor Nettleford, I responded with some sentiments about the University, ending:

> *This is a special place; it is so because it is a West Indian place. It must remain so, if the University is to remain specially great. There will be change in the character of tertiary education in our region. It is right and natural that there should be. But there must always be a place – and a place of primacy – within our Caribbean Community for UWI; for UWI as the hub of a system of tertiary education serving the region as a whole, while others serve only a part of it.*

In that same Assembly Hall, I had conferred on Nelson Mandela, at a Special Convocation, an Honorary LL.D on his first visit of 'thanks' to the West Indies. On leaving the Chancellorship, I was overwhelmed to be made *Chancellor Emeritus* of the UWI. So I have not left the University.

Mandela's UWI Degree

* * *

It is not often that one knows the route by which honour comes to be bestowed; but at the end of 12 years of service as Chancellor of the University of Warwick in England, (now known more informally as 'Warwick University'), at a farewell Dinner in London on 27th May 2002, the Pro-Chancellor and Chairman of Council, Mr Rhys Williams, explained it all in these words:

> *So, where can one start a tribute to someone who has done so much? I have chosen what I believe to be your first direct contact with Warwick. In late 1983 you, then Secretary-General of the Commonwealth, opened the Centre for Caribbean Studies. Your speech on that occasion was to trigger the thought in the minds of some of those present, that you might be a fitting successor to our then Chancellor, Lord Scarman.*
>
> *Anyone who hears you speak is inevitably enthralled and after this taster, it was probably inevitable that you would be invited to give the Radcliffe Lectures and so you were in 1987. Your theme then was "The Ethics of Human Survival", arguing that peace should mean much more that the mere absence of war upon which we are wont to congratulate ourselves. You also eloquently highlighted the environmental threat to our planet and the need to search for more co-operative forms of internationalism.*
>
> *This virtuoso performance prompted in its turn, the award to you of an Honorary LL.D from Warwick in 1988 – at that time your 21st such honour! And shortly after this you accepted the invitation to become our Chancellor in the summer of 1989.*

That explained in retrospect how in that summer Sir Arthur Vick, the then Chairman of Council of Warwick University called on me at the Commonwealth Secretariat to convey this wholly unexpected invitation By then, of course, I knew a little of Warwick and admired much about it. It was, first of all, a modern University, founded only in 1965. Under the dynamic leadership of its first Vice-Chancellor, Jack (later Lord) Butterworth, it rapidly rose to the highest ranks. Butterworth was Vice-Chancellor for 22 years. In his obituary of him in London's *Guardian* newspaper of 24 June 2003, Michael Shattock (Warwick's widely admired Registrar who had been helpful to me as Chancellor of both UWI and Warwick) described him as having created in Warwick *"the most original, forward looking and quoted exemplar internationally of a University relevant to the needs of modern society"*. And so Warwick continued to be – along with the Universities of Oxford and Cambridge, the only multi-faculty institution never to have been ranked outside the top ten of British universities. To be the Chancellor of Warwick was a great honour.

Sir Arthur Vick did not need to persuade me; but I wondered if the Council knew of my Chancellorship of the University of the West Indies. Of course they did – and saw no problem. I explained that my term of office as Commonwealth Secretary-General would be ending the following year. The Council had assumed that. I was aware that as Chancellor I would be succeeding two eminent lawyers: Cyril Radciffe (later Viscount Radcliffe) and Leslie Scarman (later, Baron Scarman). The latter had won my particular admiration for his Report on the Brixton riots of 1981, highlighting racial disadvantage and inner city decline, and calling for urgent remedial action. To be succeeding him at Warwick was no small distinction.

With Lord Scarman at Warwick

In my first years as Chancellor the Ceremonies, by courtesy of the Chaplain, were held in the magnificence of Coventry Cathedral – the architectural wonder that had risen on the ruins of its bombed predecessor, while preserving reverential reminders of it. Later, for the convenience of Graduates and their guests as the University grew, those Ceremonies were held on the University's Campus in the quite grand Butterworth Hall; but nothing could replicate the grandeur and solemnity of those early Graduation Ceremonies.

One of the occasions I particularly recall in Coventry Cathedral was a Special Convocation, on 24 October 1990, at which the University honoured Germany's Willy Brandt and I conferred on my old friend the honorary degree of Doctor of Laws. He gave a moving and quite unforgettable address on peace and war in that place of reminders. In declaring the congregation open, I had said, *inter alia:*

> *As we listen to Herr Brandt, I invite you to consider how we face again the age old truth that has so often challenged our humanity that while undoing wrong is a vital thing, undoing it for the right reason and in the right way is no less important ... To have Willy Brandt with us such a moment is precious in itself, to have him speak to us here in this reverential place that is so much a symbol of the regeneration of the human spirit is doubly treasured: for the message of his life has been one of human solidarity, a message of peace and of love; a message of hope and of faith. It is as such a messenger that I welcome this great citizen of the world to our University. And it is in the prospect of his message that I welcome you all to this Special Convocation by which he joins our company of scholars.*

It was the year of the 50th anniversary of the 'Coventry blitz'.

That was at the start of my Chancellorship; and we were to welcome many other eminent persons to Warwick over the ensuing years. Towards the end, however, we welcomed another very special guest to Warwick – in very special circumstances. In November 2000, Bill Clinton at the end of his two terms as President of the United States came to Britain to make his last major foreign policy speech as President. On the recommendation of Britain's Prime Minister, Tony Blair, Clinton chose Warwick University as the venue for that valedictory. At the press briefing in Washington on 7 December his spokesman explained: *"Warwick is one of Britain's newest and finest research universities, singled out by Prime Minister Blair as a model both of academic excellence and independence from the government."* It was not a University occasion; but Warwick was the chosen venue for his farewell to the world as President. That was a notable gesture to our University. As Chancellor, I was host to our honoured guests and sat next to Mrs Clinton as the Vice-Chancellor. Sir Brian Follet, introduced the Prime Minister, who in turn introduced President Clinton. The whole world was tuned in to Warwick, and the President gave a speech truly worthy of the occasion; as if, shed of the political inhibitions of the Presidency and a proximate home audience he could be the internationalist he intuitively was – and has been post his Presidency. I told Hillary Clinton how much I liked what he had said, and how well it would be received in the developing world. She was visibly pleased.

There is a political vignette I should share. Though both the President and the Prime Minister arrived on the Campus in helicopters; the Blairs got to Warwick first – about half an hour earlier. Normally, as Chancellor, I would share the Vice-Chancellor's Office. But today we both had to leave it free for the Prime Minister to make 'an important telephone call', before the President arrived. It was a call to the President-elect to personally congratulate him and promise continuation of the special relationship – before he showered encomiums on Bill Clinton in introducing him. In that introduction of the out-going President, he pointedly said that he had just talked with the in-coming President – as if he knew that Washington was listening in.

Welcoming President Clinton to Warwick

* * *

In 1996, Nelson Mandela, now President of South Africa, made a State Visit to Britain as guest of the Queen. John Major was Prime Minister. President Mandela stayed at Buckingham Palace; and the Queen's Private Office was in control of his programme of engagements. By then, eight British Universities had already invited President Mandela to accept honorary degrees from them. Warwick was one of them. With a State visit looming each University conveyed their wish for space for their special Convocation. When the Palace received notice of them all it convened a meeting of representatives of the Universities and made it clear that there was no possibility of multiple convocations. The Private Office said that the Queen had been consulted and had proposed a single Degree Ceremony on the lawns of Buckingham palace where all eight Universities could confer their honorary degrees simultaneously on President Mandela.

Oxford was one of the eight, and Lord Jenkins was its Chancellor. His representative had instructions to oppose any arrangement which involved the conferment of an honorary degree by Oxford outside the precincts of Oxford. It had never happened in Oxford's long history, it was explained; Oxford would have problems with the arrangement proposed. All others agreed with the single ceremony. The Private Office undertook to convey Oxford's 'problem' to the Queen. The answer came back that Oxford's problem was understood, but 'Her Majesty considered it a problem for Oxford'. The Ceremony would proceed with those Universities that could participate. That, of course, was an end of the matter. Oxford found out that there had in fact been a precedent and they would join the other Universities.

On 10 July 1996, a once-ever dais rose from the steps of the Palace leading to the lawns around which were arranged in a huge semi-circle seating for representatives, including students, of all eight Universities, whose Chancellors, Vice-Chancellors and Public Orators were arrayed in a counterpart semi-circle on the dais. It was a magnificent spectacle; a galaxy of academic robes in this majestic constellation – and on a day of summer sunshine. Very few, if any, of those on the dais knew personally the great man about to be honoured – save me. As the proceedings started, Prince Philip, as Chancellor of Cambridge, led President Mandela out of the open doors of the Palace to join us already on the dais.

As each University was called, the appropriate Orator addressed the President (for no more than 5 minutes) and ended by inviting their Chancellor to confer their honorary degree. The Oxford oration was read to the President in peerless Latin, and so was the oration by Cambridge. When Warwick's turn came, I started by explaining to our guest that given our relationship I would address him myself – and in a language he would understand. When I finished by conferring Warwick's honorary doctorate, I offered my hand in congratulation; but received from him a spontaneous familial embrace. A photograph of that moment, which Warwick cherishes as much as I do, is below. To make matters worse for the others, I took a wrong turning in going back to my place and had to occupy more time in retracing my steps – amid cheers from the Warwick 'benches'. University rivalries being what they are, Warwick considered we had stolen the show. That had not been my intent; but like so much else recorded here, it happened with the flow of events.

I began this book with lines from a favourite author. I end it with verse from a favourite poet. In *A Passing Glimpse,* Robert Frost wrote reflectively:

I often see flowers from a passing car
That are gone before I can tell what they are.

I want to get out of the train and go back
To see what they were beside the track.

Heaven gives its glimpses only to those
Not in a position to look too close.

In the preceding pages, I have gone back to offer close-up glimpses of the global life I feel privileged to have lived, and of the many people and conditions whose sharing of that life made it happen.

APPENDICES

APPENDIX 1

SELECT BIBLIOGRAPHY

PART I: Beginnings, Chapters 1-4

Anstey, Roger T. (1975), *The Atlantic Slave Trade and British Abolition 1760-1810,* Macmillan, London.

Bryant, Joshua (1824), *Account of an Insurrection of the Negro Slaves in the Colony of Demerara*, Chronicle, Georgetown.

Burn, W.L. (1937), *Emancipation and Apprenticeship in the British West Indies,* London.

Checkland, S.G (1971), *The Gladstones: A Family Biography 1761 – 1831,* Cambridge.

Draper, Nicholas, (2013), *The Price of Emancipation: Slave Ownership, Compensation and British Society at the end of Slavery,* Cambridge University Press.

Furneaux, Robin (1974), *William Wilberforce,* Hamish Hamilton, London.

Gibson, Carrie (2014), *Empire's Crossroads: A History of the Caribbean from Columbus to the Present Day*, Macmillan, London.

Mittelholzer, Edgar (1952), *Children of Kaywana,* Peter Nevill, London.

Ramphal, Shridath (2008), *Triumph for UNCLOS: The Guyana-Surinam Maritime Arbitration,* Hansib Publications, London.

Rodney, Walter (ed.) (1979), *Guyanese Sugar Plantations in the Late Nineteenth Century: a Contemporary Description from the Argosy,* Release, Guyana.

Rodney, Walter (1981), A History of the Guyanese Working People, 1881-1905, The Johns Hopkins University Press.

Rodway, James, (1891-1894), *History of British Guiana,* Vol. I, 1668-1781; Vol. II, 1782-1833; Vol. III, 1833-1839, Thomson, Georgetown.

Seecharan, Clem (2011), *Mother India's Shadow over El Dorado: Indo-Guyanese Politics and Identity 1890s – 1930s*, Ian Randal Publishers, Kingston.

Shannon, Richard (1992), *Gladstone,* Vol. 1, 1809-1865, Hamish Hamilton, London

Shepherd, Verene (2002), *Maharani's Misery,* University of the West Indies Press.

Thompson, Alvin O. (ed.) (2002), In the Shadow of the Plantation; Caribbean History and Legacy, Ian Randal Publishers, Kingston.

Tinker, Hugh (1974), *A New System of Slavery: The Export of Indian Labour Overseas 1830 – 1920,* OUP, Oxford.

Voltaire, tr. John Butt (1987), *Candide,* Penguin Books, Harmondsworth, England.
Webber, A.R.F., (1931), *Centenary History and Handbook of British Guiana*, Argosy, Georgetown
Williams, Denis (1995), *Ancient Guyana,* Department of Culture, Guyana.
Williams, Eric (1981), *Capitalism and Slavery,* Andre Deutsch.

PART II: Beckoning Worlds, Chapters 5-7

Benn, Dennis (2003), *Multilateral Diplomacy and the Economics of Change,* Ian Randle Publishers, Kingston.
Jackson, Rashleigh (2003), *Guyana's Diplomacy, free press,* Georgetown.
Insanally, Rudy (2012), *Multilateral Diplomacy for Small States,* Georgetown, Guyana.
Mordecai, John (1968), *The West Indies: The Federal Negotiations,* George Allen and Unwin Ltd, London
Searwar, Lloyd ed. (1973), *The Guyana Journal*, Vol. 1 No. 6, Ministry of Foreign Affairs, Guyana.

PART III: Caribbean Odyssey, Chapters 8-11

Hall, Kenneth & Chuck-A-Sang, Myrtle ed. (2007), *CARICOM Single Market and Economy: Genesis and Prognosis*, Ian Randle Publishers, Kingston
Kissinger, Henry (2012), *Years of Renewal,* Simon & Schuster UK Ltd
Lewis, Gordon K. (1968), *The Growth of the Modern West Indies.* MacKibbon & Kee, London.
Payne, Anthony (2008), *The Political History of CARICOM,* Ian Randle Publishers.
Ramphal, Shridath, (2000), *No Island is an Island*, Macmillan Education, London.
Ramphal, Shridath, (2012), *Caribbean Challenges*, Hansib Publications, London.
Report by a Group of Caribbean Experts (Ch. William Demas) 1981, The Caribbean Community in the 1980s, CARICOM Secretariat, Georgetown.
Sanders, Ronald (ed.) (2002), *Antigua Vision, Caribbean Reality – Perspectives of Prime Minister Lester Bird*, Hansib Publications, London
The West Indian Commission's Report (1992), *Time For Action,* University of the West Indies Press
Williams, Eric (1962), *The History of the People of Trinidad & Tobago,*
Williams, Eric (1970), *From Columbus to Castro: The History of the Caribbean 1492 – 1969,* Andre Deutsch, London.

PART IV: The Commonwealth, Chapter 12

Chadwick, John (1982), *The Unofficial Commonwealth: The Story of the Commonwealth foundation 1965-1980*, George Allen & Unwin (Publishers) Ltd., London.
Dale, Sir William (1983), *The Modern Commonwealth*, Butterworth & Co Ltd., London.
de Smith, S.A. (1964) *The New Commonwealth and its Constitutions,* Stevens, London.
Judd, Dennis & Slinn, Peter (1982), *The Evolution of the Modern Commonwealth, 1902-80*, The Macmillan Press Ltd., London.
Miller. J.D.B. (1974), *Survey of Commonwealth Affairs: Problems of Expansion and Attrition, 1953-1969*, R.I.I.A. Oxford.

Ramphal, Shridath (1950), *The Second Commonwealth of Nations,* in King's Counsel 1950.
Roberts-Wray, Sir Kenneth (1966), *Commonwealth and Colonial Law*. Stevens& Sons, London.
The Commonwealth at the Summit (1987). Commonwealth Secretariat

PART V: The Economic Challenge, Chapters 15-17

Brandt Report (1980) *North-South: A Programme for Survival,* (1983) *Common Crisis, North-South: Co-operation for World Recovery,* Pan Books, London
Commonwealth Report (1976): *Towards a New International Economic Order*
International Economic Issues: Contributions by the Commonwealth 1975 – 1990 (1990) Commonwealth Secretariat
Manley, Michael (1982), *JAMAICA: Struggle in the Periphery, Third World Media.*
North-South Roundtable (1982), *Cancun: a Candid Evaluation,* Roundtable Paper 8
Quilligan. James (2002), *The Brandt Equation: 21st Century Blueprint for the New Global Economy,* Brandt 21 Forum, PA. USA
Quilligan, James (2010), *How the Brandt Report Foresaw Today's Global Economic Crisis,* Integral Review. Vol. 6 No. 1, USA

PART VI: The 'Thatcher' Years, Chapters 18-24

Anyaoku, Emeka (2004), *The Inside Story of the Modern Commonwealth*, Evans Brothers, London
Bourne, Richard (2011), *Catastrophe: What went Wrong in Zimbabwe,* Zed Books, London.
Carrington, Peter (1988), *Reflect on Times Past,* Harper Collins Publishers Ltd. London
Chan, Stephen (2011), *Southern Africa: Old* Treacheries *and New Deceits,* Yale University Press, New Haven.
Cook, Allen (1982), *Akin to Slavery: Prison Labour in South Africa,* International Defence and Aid Fund for Southern Africa.
Commonwealth Committee of Foreign Ministers on Southern Africa (1989), *South Africa: The Sanctions Report,* Penguin Books, London
Dowden, Richard (2008), *Africa: Altered States, Ordinary Miracles*, Portobello Books, London.
Lamb, Christina (2007), *House of Stone,* Harper Perennial, London
Lelyveld, Joseph (1985), *Move Your Shadow: South Africa, Black and White*, Times Books, New York.
Mandaza, Ibbo (1997), *Race, Colour and Class in Southern Africa*, Sapes Books, Harare.
Martin, David and Phyllis Johnson (1981) *The Struggle for Zimbabwe,* Monthly Review Press, New York.
McKinnon, Don (2013), *In the Ring: A Commonwealth Memoir*, Elliott and Thompson, London.
Olusegun Obasanjo (1987), *African Perspective: Myths and Realities,* Council of Foreign Relations, New York

Renwick, Robin (2013) *A Journey with Margaret Thatcher: Foreign policy Under the Iron Lady*, Biteback Publishing, London.

Sampson, Anthony (1999), *Mandela – The Authorised Biography,* Harper Collins Publishers, London.

Smith, Arnold (1981) *Stitches In Time: The Commonwealth in World Politics*, Andre Deutsch, London.

Thatcher, Margaret (2011), *The Downing Street Years,* Harper Press, London.

The Commonwealth Group of Eminent Persons (1986), *Mission to South Africa: The Commonwealth Report, Penguin* Books, Harmondsworth, England.

Verrier, Anthony (1986) *The Road to Zimbabwe 1890-1980*, Jonathan Cape, London

PART VII: The Global Neighbourhood, Chapters 25-28

Brundtland Report (1987), *Our Common Future* – The World Commission on Environment and Development, OUP, Oxford.

Carlsson/Ramphal Report (1995), *Our Global Neighbourhood* – Commission on Global Governance, *OUP*, Oxford.

Harris, Wilson (1990) *Four Banks of the River of Space,* Faber and Faber. London.

International Humanitarian Issues, Report of the Independent Commission (1988), Winning the Human Race? Zed Books Ltd., London

Knight, Andy & Egerton, Frazer (ed.) (2012), *The Routledge Handbook of the Responsibility to Protect,* Routledge, New York

Maumoon, Abdul Gayoom (1998), The Maldives: A Nation in Peril, Ministry of Planning, Human Resources and Environment, Maldives

Nyerere Report (1990), *The Challenge to the South* – The South Commission, OUP, Oxford.

Ramphal, Shridath (1992), *Our Country, The Planet: Forging a Partnership for Survival,* Island Press, Washington. D.C.

Royal Society of Canada, Constance Mungall & Digby J. McLaren ed., Planet Under Stress: The Challenge of Global Change, OUP, Toronto

Sanders, Ronald (2005), *Crumbled Small: the Commonwealth Caribbean in World Politics,* Hansib, London.

Shahabudeen, Mohammed (1983), *The Conquest of Grenada: Sovereignty in the Periphery,* Guyana.

Strong, Maurice (2001), Where on Earth are We Going, Texere Ltd., New York

The Round Table, the Commonwealth Journal of International Affairs (2013), *The Invasion of Grenada: Thirty Years on: A Retrospective,* Vol. 10, Special Issue.

Urquhart, Brian and Childers, Erskine (1990*), A World in Need of Leadership: Tomorrow's United Nations,* Dag Hammarskjold Foundation, Uppsala, Sweden

Ward, Barbara and Dubos, Rene, (1972), *Only One Earth: The Care and Maintenance of a Small Planet,* Andre Deutsch Ltd.

PART VIII: Endings, Chapters 29-30

Bourne, Richard (Ed), (2008), *Shridath Ramphal, The Commonwealth and the World: Essays in Honour of His 80th Birthday*, Hansib Publications, London and Hertfordshire.

APPENDIX 2

AUTHOR'S OTHER PUBLICATIONS

Books

One World to Share: Selected Speeches of the Commonwealth Secretary-General, 1975 – 79 (Hutchinson Benham, London) 1979

Inseparable Humanity: An Anthology of Reflections of Shridath Ramphal, edited by Ron Sanders (Hansib Publications, London), 1988

An End to Otherness: Commemorative Addresses by the Commonwealth Secretary-General (Commonwealth Secretariat, London), 1990

Our Country, The Planet: Forging a Partnership for Survival. (Lime Tree, London, and Island Press, Washington DC) 1992

No Island is an Island (Warwick University, Caribbean Studies, Macmillan), 2000

Triumph for UNCLOS: The Guyana-Suriname Maritime Arbitration, Hansib Publications, London, 2008

Caribbean Challenges: Shridath Ramphal's Collective Counsel, (Hansib Publications, London), 2012

Monographs

Safeguarding Human Rights: The Guyana Contribution (UN Seminar on Human Rights, Jamaica – Guyana Ministry of External Affairs) 1967

Building the Foundations (Carnegie Seminar on Diplomacy. UWI IIA, Trinidad – Guyana Ministry of External Affairs) 1967

Development or Defence: The Small State Threatened with Aggression (Address to the 23rd Session of the General Assembly) 1968

Friendship with Integrity: Guyana – Suriname Relations (Address during 'Guyana Week' – Guyana Ministry of External Affairs) 1969

A Time for Peace-Keeping: International Security and the Small State (Address to the 24th Session of UN General Assembly) 1969

Decade of Decision: The Caribbean in the 70s (Address to the National Press Club of Trinidad & Tobago, Guyana Ministry of External Affairs

A Search for Understanding: Patterns of Conflict Resolution (Guyana Ministry of External Affairs) 1970

Peace – Justice – Progress: The International Imperatives (Address to the 25th Anniversary Session of the UN General Assembly) 1970

West Indian Nationhood: Myth, Mirage or Mandate? (Opening address at Colloquium on 'Caribbean Perspectives', UWI IIR, Trinidad) 1971

The Charter's Mandate: Fulfilment Through Internationalism (Address to the 26th Session of the UN General Assembly

Dialogue of Unity: A Search for West Indian Identity (Address to the Caribbean Ecumenical Consultation for Development, Trinidad) 1971

A Peaceful, Just and Habitable Planet: New Dimensions of Environment (Address to the 27th Session of the UN General Assembly) 1972

The Prospect of Community in the Caribbean (Address at the Royal Commonwealth Society, London) 1973

New Dimensions of Preventive Diplomacy (Address to the Security Council in Panama City – Guyana Ministry of Foreign Affairs) 1973

Just, Enlightened and Effective Arrangements: New Approaches to Relations with the EEC (Statement on behalf of the Caribbean Countries at the Opening of the 'Lome Negotiations', Brussels – Guyana Ministry of Foreign Affairs) 1973

The Energy Catalyst: Toward a New International Economic Order (Address to the Sixth Special Session of the UN General Assembly on Materials and Development) 1974

An Ideology of Change: Toward an Egalitarian World Community (Address to the 29th Session of the UN General Assembly) 1974

To Care for CARICOM (Farewell address to Caribbean leaders, Montego Bay, Jamaica –Guyana Ministry of Foreign Affairs) 1975

The Other World in This One: The Promise of the New International Economic Order (Opening address at the 44th Couchichng Conference, Canada, the Round Table, No. 261) 1975

The Commonwealth in World Affairs (Address to the New Zealand Institute of International Affairs, Wellington, NZ) 1975

Nkrumah and the Eighties (Kwame Nkrumah Memorial Lectures, Accra/Cape Coast, Third World Foundation Monograph 9) 1980

Sovereignty or Solidarity (Thomas Callander Memorial Lectures; University of Aberdeen), 1981

Challenges for the Lawyer in our Interdependent World (The Cambridge Lectures, Butterworths), 1983

Words are as Water (Opening address to the International Conference on Sanctions Against Apartheid Sport, London, Commonwealth Secretariat) 1983

'Some in Light and Some in Darkness': the Long Shadow of Slavery (Hull Lecture commemorating the 150th Anniversary of the Abolition of Slavery Act) – Third World Foundation Monograph 12 London), 1983

The Trampling of the Grass (Inaugural Silver Jubilee Lecture of the Economic Commission for Africa, Addis Ababa – UNECA 085 -245, 1985

Peace: an Ambition Beyond Armistice (The Bertrand Russell Peace Lectures, McMaster University, Ontario, Commonwealth Secretariat) 1985

Rekindling Nehru's Internationalism (The Jawaharlal Nehru Memorial Lecture – London, Commonwealth Secretariat) 1985

A World Turned Upside Down (Address to the Annual Conference of the Geographical Association. – London) 1985

The End of the Beginning: Apartheid in Crisis (Address to the International Defence and Aid Fund for Southern Africa, London – Commonwealth Secretariat) 1985

Towards a Global 2000 (The Inaugural New Sarum Lecture, Salisbury Cathedral, Wiltshire) 1985

Roots and Reminders (Address to the Royal Commonwealth Society of India, New Delhi); 1986

For the South: A Time to Think (Paper for 'South-South II', Kuala Lumpur): 1986

Making Human Society A Civilised State (11th Corbishley Memorial Lecture, Royal Society of Arts, London) 1987

The Ethics of Human Survival (The Radcliffe Lectures, Warwick University) 1987

'Life is One and the World is One': Reflections on Peace (1987 Indira Gandhi Memorial Lecture, the Association of Indian Diplomats, New Delhi), 1987

The South African Crisis: Why the Bell of Apartheid Tolls for Everyone (Third ISIS World Affairs Lecture, Kuala Lumpur); 1988)

One World to Share (The 'One People's' Oration, Westminster Abbey, London) 1988

Compulsions of Excellence: Shadows and Reality (Address on Installation as Chancellor of the University of Guyana, Turkeyne): 1988

The Black must be Discharged (Kapila Fellowship Lecture, Gray's Inn, London) 1988

A Heritage of Oneness (Inaugural Lecture in The Genesis of a Nation Series, Guyana, Commonwealth Secretariat) 1988

Endangered Earth. Inaugural Address of the Cambridge Lectures on Environment and Development, 1989.

Vivat, Floreat, Crescat (Address at the 40th Anniversary Convocation of the University of the West Indies, Jamaica), 1989

Keeping the Faith: From Kingston to Kuala Lumpur and Beyond (a Valedictory Address, London): 1990

Global Governance in the Global Neighbourhood (Address in the Waging Peace Series of the Nuclear Age Peace Foundation, Washington DC) 1994

Global Governance and New Dimensions of Human Security (Sir John Crawford Memorial Lecture, Washington DC), 1995

Global Governance (The Second Global Security Lecture, Oxford) 1995

West Indian Space in the 21st Century (Address in the West Indian Lectures Series, Kingston, Jamaica) 1998

Governance and the New Imperium (Address to the Mona Academic Conference, 'Governance in the age of Globalisation, UWI, Kingston): 2002

Can the Rule of Law in the Commonwealth be Secure in a Lawless World (Address to the 50th Anniversary Commonwealth Law Conference, London); 2005

An End to Otherness (Rotary Centenary Lecture, Guyana) 2006

'Rough handling' Federation (Federation's 50 Anniversary Lecture, UWI, Barbados) 2008

Caribbean Diplomacy (Address inaugurating the CARICOM Diplomatic Training Programme, Guyana) 2009

The Paradox of Heritage and Hesitancy (Address inaugurating the Caribbean Association of Judicial Officers, Trinidad) 2009

Is the West Indies West Indian? (Sir Archibald Nedd Memorial Lecture, Bar Association of Grenada) 2011

Vision and Leadership: The Infinite Unity of Caribbean Needs (Inaugural G. Arthur Brown Memorial Lecture, Central Bank of Jamaica) 2011
Creating a Regional Jurisprudence (Inaugural Distinguished Jurist Lecture, Trinidad & Tobago Judicial Education Institute), 2011
A Joyous Race Just Begun (The Rex Nettleford Memorial Lecture, Rhodes House, Oxford) 2011
Labouring in the Vineyard (The 2012 Dr Eric Williams Memorial Lecture, Central Bank of Trinidad and Tobago) 2012

APPENDIX 3

MEMBERS OF THE WEST INDIAN COMMISSION

Shridath Ramphal (Chairman), Chancellor, the University of the West Indies
Alister McIntryre (Vice-Chairman), Vice-Chancellor, the University of the West Indies;
Leonard Archer, Secretary-General of the Bahamas Trade union Congress;
William Demas, Former President of the Caribbean Development Bank;
Howard Fergus, Speaker of the Legislative Council of Montserrat;
Marshall Hall, Managing Director of the Jamaica Banana Producers Association;
Alan Kirton, Former General Secretary, Caribbean Conference of Churches;
Vaughn Lewis, Director-General, Organisation of Eastern Caribbean States;
Sandra Mason, Senior Magistrate, and Deputy Chair Barbados Child Care Board;
Gillian Nanton, Senior Economist, St Vincent and the Grenadines;
Phillip Nassief, Chairman and CEO, Dominica Coconut Products;
Rex Nettleford, Professor and Pro Vice Chancellor, UWI;
Roderick Rainford, Secretary-General, CARICOM Secretariat;
Frank Rampersad, Co-ordinator, University Centre Project, Trinidad & Tobago;
Neville Trotz, Secretary, Commonwealth Science Council.

To them must be added **Ian McDonald,** Editorial Consultant in relation to the Commission's Report and the Commission's Director-General, **Donald Brice.**

APPENDIX 4

COMMONWEALTH EXPERT GROUPS 1975 – 1990

1975 – ***Towards a New International Order;*** Chairman: Sir Alister McIntyre (Grenada)

1977 – ***The Common Fund;*** Chairman: Lord Campbell of Eskan (Britain)

1978 – ***Accelerating Industrialisation;*** Chairman: Gov. L.K. Jha (India)

1980 – ***The World Economic Crisis;*** Prof. H.W. Arndt (Australia)

1982 – ***Protectionism: Threat to International Order;*** Chairman: Sir Alec Cairncross (Britain)

1982 – ***The North-South Dialogue: Making it Work;*** Chairman: B. Akporode Clarke (Nigeria)

1983 – ***Towards a New Bretton Woods;*** Chairman: Prof. Gerald K. Helleiner (Canada)

1984 – ***The Debt Crisis and the World Economy;*** Chairman: Lord Lever of Manchester (Britain)

1985 – ***Technological Change;*** Chairman: Prof M.G.K. Menon (India)

1985 – ***Vulnerability: Small States in the Global Society;*** Chairman: Justice P.T. Georges (the Bahamas)

1986 – ***Jobs for Young People: a Way to a Better Future;*** Chairman: Peter Kirby (Australia)

1988 – ***Engendering Adjustment for the 1990s;*** Chairperson: Mary Chinery-Hesse (Ghana)

1989 – ***Climate Change: Meeting the Challenge:*** Chairman: Sir Martin Holdgate (Britain)

APPENDIX 5

MEMBERS OF THE INDEPENDENT COMMISSION
ON INTERNATIONAL DEVELOPMENT ISSUES

Willy Brandt, (Chairman), Federal Republic of Germany; Federal Chancellor 1969-74, Chairman of the Social Democratic Party, Nobel Peace Prize 1971.

Abdlatif Y. Al-Hamad, Kuwait. Director-General of Kuwait Fund for Arabic Economic Development,

Rodrigo Botero Montoya, Colombia. Minister of Finance 1974-6, Editor and Publisher of *Estrategia Economica y Financiera.*

Antoine Kipsa Dakoure, Upper Volta. Coordinating Minister for Drought Control in the Sahel 1973-5, Minister of Planning 1970-76,

Eduardo Frei Montalva, Chile. President of Chile 1964-70. Former Chairman of the Christian Democratic Party,

Katharine Graham, USA. Chairman of the Board, Washington Post Co, since 1963, Publisher, *Washington Post 1969-79.*

Edward Heath, United Kingdom. Prime Minister 1970-74, Leader of the Conservative Party 1965-75,

Amir H. Jamal, Tanzania, Minister of Finance, Cabinet Minister since 1962.

Lakshmi Kant Jha, India. Governor of Jammu and Kashmir, Governor of Reserve Bank of India 1967-70, Ambassador to the USA 1970-73,

Khatijah Ahmad, Malaysia, economist and banker, Managing Director of KAF Discounts Ltd since 1974.

Adam Malik, Indonesia. Vice-President, President of National Assembly 1977-8, Minister of Foreign Affairs 1966-77, President of UN General Assembly 1971-2.

Haruki Mori, Japan. Ambassador to the United Kingdom 1972-5, Vice-Minister in the Ministry of Foreign Affairs 1970-72, Ambassador to the OECD 1964-7.

Joe Morris, Canada. President-Emeritus of Canadian Labour Congress, Chairman of International Labour Organisation's Governing Body 1977-78, Chairman, ILO Governing Body 1977-8, Vice-President ICFTU 1976-8.

Olof Palme, Sweden. Prime Minister 1969-76, Chairman of the Social Democratic Party,

Peter G. Peterson, USA. Chairman of the Board of Lehman Bros. Kuhn Loeb, Secretary of Commerce 1972-3,

Edgard Pisani, France. Senator, Member of the European Parliament, Minister of National Equipment 1966-7, Minister of Agriculture 1961-5*Mr Pisani replaced Mr Pierre Mendes-France, former Prime Minister of France, had to resign for personal reasons in summer 1978.

Shridath Ramphal, Guyana. Commonwealth Secretary-General, Minister of Foreign Affairs and Justice 1972-5, Attorney-General and Minister of Stale for External Affairs 1966-72.

Layachi Yaker, Algeria. Ambassador to the USSR, Member of the Central Committee of the Party of the National Liberation Front, Member of Parliament and Vice-President, National People's Assembly 1977-9, Minister of Commerce 1969-77

Jan P. Pronk, (*Honorary Treasurer),* Netherlands. Minister for Development Cooperation 1973-7, Research Assistant to Professor Jan Tinbergen 1965-71.

Goran Ohlin, *(Executive Secretary)*, Sweden, Professor of Economics at Uppsala University since 1969, Staff Member of the Pearson Commission 1968-9,

Dragoslav Avramovic *(Director of the Secretariat),* Yugoslavia, Senior economic staff positions in the World Bank 1965-77, Director, Economics Department, Industrialisation Studies, Commodity Studies, Debt Studies, Special Adviser to UNCTAD on Commodity Stabilisation 1974-5,

Goran Ohlin, Jan Pronk and Dragoslav Avramovic became *ex-officio* members of the Commission.

APPENDIX 6

THE LUSAKA DECLARATION OF THE COMMONWEALTH ON RACISM AND RACIAL PREJUDICE (1979)

We, the Commonwealth Heads of Government, recalling the Declaration of Commonwealth Principles made at Singapore on 22 January 1971 and the statement on Apartheid in Sport, issued in London on 15 June 1977, have decided to proclaim our desire to work jointly as well as severally for the eradication of all forms of racism and racial prejudice.

The Commonwealth is an institution devoted to the promotion of international understanding and world peace, and to the achievement of equal rights for all citizens regardless of race, colour, sex, creed or political belief, and is committed to the eradication of the dangerous evils of racism and racial prejudice.

We now, therefore, proclaim this Lusaka Declaration of the Commonwealth on Racism and Racial Prejudice.

United in our desire to rid the world of the evils of racism and racial prejudice, we proclaim our faith in the inherent dignity and worth of the human person and declare that:

(i) the peoples of the Commonwealth have the right to live freely in dignity and equality, without any distinction or exclusion based on race, colour, sex, descent, or national or ethnic origin;

(ii) while everyone is free to retain diversity in his or her culture and lifestyle, this diversity does not justify the perpetuation of racial prejudice or racially discriminatory practices;

(iii) everyone has the right to equality before the law and equal justice under the law;

(iv) everyone has the right to effective remedies and protection against any form of discrimination based on the grounds of race, colour, sex, descent, or national or ethnic origin.

We reject as inhuman and intolerable all policies designed to perpetuate apartheid, racial segregation or other policies based on theories that racial groups are or may be inherently superior or inferior.

We reaffirm that it is the duty of all the peoples of the Commonwealth to work together for the total eradication of the infamous policy of apartheid which is internationally recognised as a crime against the conscience and dignity of mankind and the very existence of which is an affront to humanity.

We agree that everyone has the right to protection against acts of incitement to racial hatred and discrimination, whether committed by individuals, groups or other organisations.

We affirm that there should be no discrimination based on race, colour, sex, descent or national or ethnic origin in the acquisition or exercise of the right to vote; in the field of civil rights or access to citizenship; or in the economic, social or cultural fields, particularly education, health, employment, occupation, housing, social security and cultural life.

We attach particular importance to ensuring that children shall be protected from practices which may foster racism or racial prejudice. Children have the right to be brought up and educated in a spirit of tolerance and understanding so as to be able to contribute fully to the building of future societies based on justice and friendship.

We believe that those groups in societies who may be especially disadvantaged because of residual racist attitudes are entitled to the fullest protection of the law. We recognise that the history of the Commonwealth and its diversity require that special attention should be paid to the problems of indigenous minorities. We recognise that the same special attention should be paid to the problems of immigrants, immigrant workers and refugees.

We agree that special measures may in particular circumstances be required to advance the development of disadvantaged groups in society. We recognise that the effects of colonialism or racism in the past may make desirable special provisions for the social and economic enhancement of indigenous populations.

Inspired by the principles of freedom and equality which characterise our association, we accept the solemn duty of working together to eliminate racism and racial prejudice. This duty involves the acceptance of the principle that positive measures may be required to advance the elimination of racism, including assistance to those struggling to rid themselves and their environment of the practice.

Being aware that legislation alone cannot eliminate racism and racial prejudice, we endorse the need to initiate public information and education policies designed to promote understanding, tolerance, respect and friendship among peoples and racial groups.

We are particularly conscious of the importance of the contribution the media can make to human rights and the eradication of racism and racial prejudice by helping to eliminate ignorance and misunderstanding between people and by drawing attention to the evils which afflict humanity. We affirm the importance of truthful presentation of facts in order to ensure that the public are fully informed of the dangers presented by racism and racial prejudice.

In accordance with established principles of International Law and, in particular, the provisions of the International Convention on the Elimination of all Forms of Racial Discrimination, we affirm that everyone is, at all times and in all places, entitled to be protected in the enjoyment of the right to be free of racism and racial prejudice.

We believe that the existence in the world of apartheid and racial discrimination is a matter of concern to all human beings. We recognise that we share an international responsibility to work together for the total eradication of apartheid and racial discrimination.

We note that racism and racial prejudice, wherever they occur, are significant factors contributing to tension between nations and thus inhibit peaceful progress and development. We believe that the goal of the eradication of racism stands as a critical priority for governments of the Commonwealth, committed as they are to the promotion of the ideals of peaceful and happy lives for their people.

We intend that the Commonwealth, as an international organisation with a fundamental and deep-rooted attachment to principles of freedom and equality, should co-operate with other organisations in the fulfilment of these principles. In particular the Commonwealth should seek to enhance the coordination of its activities with those of other organisations similarly committed to the promotion and protection of human rights and fundamental freedoms.

APPENDIX 7

THE COMMONWEALTH ACCORD ON SOUTHERN AFRICA (1985)

1. We consider that South Africa's continuing refusal to dismantle apartheid, its illegal occupation of Namibia, and its aggression against its neighbours constitute a serious challenge to the values and principles of the Commonwealth, a challenge which Commonwealth countries cannot ignore. At New Delhi we expressed the view that "only the eradication of apartheid and the establishment of majority rule on the basis of free and fair exercise of universal adult suffrage by all the people in a united and non-fragmented South Africa can lead to a just and lasting solution of the explosive situation prevailing in Southern Africa." We are united in the belief that reliance on the range of pressures adopted so far has not resulted in the fundamental changes we have sought over many years. The growing crisis and intensified repression in South Africa mean that apartheid must be dismantled now if a greater tragedy is to be averted and that concerted pressure must be brought to bear to achieve that end. We consider that the situation calls for urgent practical steps.

2. We, therefore, call on the authorities in Pretoria for the following steps to be taken in a genuine manner and as a matter of urgency:

(a) Declare that the system of apartheid will be dismantled and specific and meaningful action taken in fulfilment of that intent.

b) Terminate the existing state of emergency.

c) Release immediately and unconditionally Nelson Mandela and all others imprisoned and detained for their opposition to apartheid.

(d) Establish political freedom and specifically lift the existing ban on the African National Congress and other political parties.

(e) Initiate, in the context of a suspension of violence on all sides, a process of dialogue across lines of colour, politics and religion, with a view to establishing a non-racial and representative government.

3. We have agreed on a number of measures which have as their rationale impressing on the authorities in Pretoria the compelling urgency of dismantling apartheid and erecting the structures of democracy in South Africa. The latter, in particular, demands a process of dialogue involving the true representatives of the majority black population of South Africa. We believe that we must do all we can to assist that process, while recognising that the forms of political settlement in South Africa are for the people of that country – all the people – to determine.

4. To this end, we have decided to establish a small group of eminent Commonwealth persons to encourage through all practicable ways the evolution of that necessary process of political dialogue. We are not unmindful of the difficulties such an effort will encounter, including the possibility of initial rejection by the South African authorities, but we believe it to be our duty to leave nothing undone that might contribute to peaceful change in South Africa and avoid the dreadful prospect of violent conflict that looms over South Africa, threatening people of all races in the country, and the peace and stability of the entire Southern Africa region.

5. We are asking the President of Zambia and the Prime Ministers of Australia, the Bahamas, Canada, India, the United Kingdom and Zimbabwe to develop with the Secretary-General the modalities of this effort to assist the process of political dialogue in South Africa. We would look to the group of eminent persons to seek to facilitate the processes of dialogue referred to in paragraph 2(e) above and by all practicable means to advance the fulfilment of the objectives of this Accord.

6. For our part, we have as an earnest of our opposition to apartheid, reached accord on a programme of common action as follows:

(i) We declare the Commonwealth's support for the strictest enforcement of the mandatory arms embargo against South Africa, in accordance with United Nations Security Council Resolutions 418 and 558, and commit ourselves to prosecute violators to the fullest extent of the law.

(ii) We reaffirm the Gleneagles Declaration of 1977, which called upon Commonwealth members to take every practical step to discourage sporting contacts with South Africa.

(iii) We agree upon, and commend to other governments, the adoption of the following further economic measures against South Africa, which have already been adopted by a number of member countries:

- (a) a ban on all new government loans to the Government of South Africa and its agencies;
- (b) a readiness to take unilaterally action may be possible to preclude import of Krugerrands;
- (c) no Government funding for trade missions to South Africa or for participation, in exhibitions and trade fairs in South Africa;
- (d) a ban on the sale and export of computer equipment capable of use by South African military forces, police or security forces;
- (e) a ban on new contracts for the sale and export of nuclear goods, materials and technology to South Africa
- (f) a ban on the sale and export of oil to South Africa;
- (g) a strict and rigorously controlled embargo on imports of arms, ammunition, military vehicles and paramilitary equipment from South Africa;

(h) an embargo on all military co-operation with South Africa; and
(i) discouragement of all cultural and scientific events except where these contribute towards the ending of apartheid or have no possible role in promoting it.

7. It is our hope that the process and measures we have agreed upon will help to bring about concrete progress towards the objectives stated above in six months. The Heads of Government mentioned in paragraph 5 above, or their representatives, will then meet to review the situation. If in their opinion adequate progress has not been made within this period, we agree to consider the adoption of further measures. Some of us would, in that event, consider the following steps among others:
(a) a ban on air links with South Africa;
(b) a ban on new investment or reinvestment of profits earned in South Africa;
(c) a ban on the import of agricultural products from South Africa;
(d) the termination of double taxation agreements with South Africa;
(e) the termination of all government assistance to investment in, and trade with, South Africa;
(f) a ban on all government procurement in South Africa;
(h) a ban on the promotion of tourism to South Africa;
(g) a ban on government contracts with majority-owned South African companies.

8. Finally, we agree that should all of the above measures fail to produce the desired results within a reasonable period, further effective measures will have to be considered. Many of us have either taken or are prepared to take measures which go beyond those listed above, and each of us will pursue the objectives of this Accord in all the ways and through all appropriate fora open to us. We believe, however, that in pursuing this programme jointly, we enlarge the prospects of an orderly transition to social, economic and political justice in South Africa and peace and stability in the Southern Africa region as a whole.

Lyford Cay
20 October 1985

INDEX

The Robert Batchelor 1987 painting of
Marlborough House from Carlton Gardens